The Empire and the Glory
Napoleon Bonaparte: 1800–1806

Books by
FLETCHER PRATT

THE HEROIC YEARS

ORDEAL BY FIRE

HAIL, CAESAR!

THE NAVY: A HISTORY

THE NAVY'S WAR

SHORT HISTORY OF THE ARMY AND NAVY

THE MARINES' WAR

ROAD TO EMPIRE

EMPIRE AND THE SEA

THE EMPIRE AND THE GLORY

THE EMPIRE AND THE GLORY

Napoleon Bonaparte: 1800-1806

FLETCHER PRATT

Illustrated by Inga

WILLIAM SLOANE ASSOCIATES, INC.
Publishers   New York

First Printing

Printed in the United States of America
by H. Wolff Book Mfg. Co., New York
Published simultaneously in Canada by
George J. McLeod Ltd., Toronto

LETTER IN DEDICATION

Dear Ted: In the days when noble dukes handed out rolls of guineas in exchange for a dedication, there was doubtless a good deal of sense behind the practice, at least on the author's part. All anyone can get out of it today is an amount of satisfaction so small that I do not remember anyone's boasting of having a book dedicated to him. But you do bear a certain amount of responsibility for this book, which I wish to acknowledge in this way; and so I make this dedication to Dr. Theodore Morrison, who taught me how to think.

ACKNOWLEDGMENTS

Several people have helped materially in preparing this work. The author wishes to express his gratitude to Dr. Norbert Lederer and Mr. Laurence Manning for a great deal of assistance on musical matters, to Lt.-Col. Don A. Hittle, who has contributed some valuable data on the army reorganization and staff work, and to the indefatigable labors of Mr. George E. Mayo.

CONTENTS

PREFACE   xi

1. THE CAPTAIN IS IN CONFERENCE
(Paris: 18 brumaire, An VIII)   1

2. RENAISSANCE
(Paris: 19 brumaire–22 frimaire, An VIII)   9

WRONG END OF THE TELESCOPE—I   34

THE WORM'S-EYE VIEW—I—*Return of the Emigrés*   37

THE WORM'S-EYE VIEW—II—*A Scandalous Case*   37

3. ORGANIZATION
(Paris: frimaire–pluviôse, An VIII)   39

THE WORM'S-EYE VIEW—III—*A Visit to the General*   51

4. ARMY OF PHANTOMS
(Paris, Genoa, Geneva: pluviôse–floréal, An VIII)   52

WRONG END OF THE TELESCOPE—II   67

5. SCENES OF YOUTH REVISITED
(Genoa, The Lombard Plain: 25 floréal–23 prairial, An VIII)   69

6. SURPRISE
(The Plain of San Giuliano: 25 prairial, An VIII)   87

WRONG END OF THE TELESCOPE—III   96

7. FAMILY MATTERS
     (Paris: messidor, An VIII–frimaire, An
     IX)   99

8. SAUL SLAYS HIS THOUSANDS
     (Paris, The Valley of the Danube: 5
     floréal, An VIII–12 frimaire, An IX)   110
   WRONG END OF THE TELESCOPE—IV   139
   THE WORM'S-EYE VIEW—IV—*A Little
     Child Lost*   143
   THE WORM'S-EYE VIEW—V—*Home to My
     Mountains*   143

9. DETECTIVE STORY
     (Paris: floréal, An VIII–28 nivôse, An
     IX)   145
   THE WORM'S-EYE VIEW—VI—*Diplomatic
     Correspondence*   161

10. SWEET PEACE
     (Paris, Lunéville, Amiens: ventôse, An
     IX–vendémaire, An X)   163
   WRONG END OF THE TELESCOPE—V   176

11. THE LAW AND THE PROPHETS
     (Paris: 11 nivôse, An IX–An XIV)   178
   WRONG END OF THE TELESCOPE—VI   200

12. THE SUBTLETIES OF BROTHER JOSEPH
     (Paris: 28 germinal, An X–9 frimaire,
     An XI)   204

13. LOUISIANA
     (Madrid, Paris: 1801–May 22, 1803)   220
   WRONG END OF THE TELESCOPE—VII   240

CONTENTS

14. PREPARATION FOR AN EVENT
    (Paris: to 30 ventôse, An XII) — 244
    WRONG END OF THE TELESCOPE—VIII — 266

15. DRUMS FAINTLY HEARD
    (Berlin, Vienna, St. Petersburg: March
    21, 1804–August 10, 1804) — 268
    THE WORM'S-EYE VIEW—VII—*The Jealousy
    of Zaïre* — 277
    THE WORM'S-EYE VIEW—VIII—*Dispute
    over an Island* — 279
    THE WORM'S-EYE VIEW—IX—*Back from
    Siberia* — 280

16. EVENT, BE BORN!
    (Paris: 10 frimaire, An XIII) — 281
    WRONG END OF THE TELESCOPE—IX — 305

17. DISCORDANT
    (Vienna, The Coasts of the Ocean: sum-
    mer 1804–August 1805) — 308
    WRONG END OF THE TELESCOPE—X — 326
    THE WORM'S-EYE VIEW—X—*At the Camp
    of Boulogne* — 328

18. THE ARMY OF THE COASTS OF THE OCEAN
    (The English Channel, Bavaria: mid-
    September–October 21, 1805) — 331
    WRONG END OF THE TELESCOPE—XI — 355
    THE WORM'S-EYE VIEW—XI—*A Neat Leg* — 356

19. END OF AN ERA
    (Berlin, The Valley of the Danube:
    October 21, 1805–November 13, 1805) — 359
    WRONG END OF THE TELESCOPE—XII — 375

20. END OF AN ARMY
    (North Italy, Moravia: October 28–
        December 3, 1805)   .   377
    WRONG END OF THE TELESCOPE—XIII   406

21. THE GOLD OF THE AMERICAS
    (Paris: summer An XIII–January 27,
        1806)   409
    THE WORM'S-EYE VIEW—XII—*Chain-gang
    to the Galleys*   427

22. CHARLEMAGNE
    (Western Europe: summer 1806)   429
    THE WORM'S-EYE VIEW—XIII—*The Happy
    Pair*   445

23. AT LAST, NOT'UNG!
    (Berlin, Erfurt: to October 4, 1806)   447
    WRONG END OF THE TELESCOPE—XIV   466

24. PRUSSIA: MIDNIGHT
    (Saxony: October 3–14, 1806)   469
    THE WORM'S-EYE VIEW—XIV—*A Lady
    Looks at Battle*   495

25. REJECTED
    (Central Europe: Forever)   497

    BRIEF TIMETABLE   507

    INDEX   509

PREFACE

LIGHT BEATS SO FIERCELY round the central figure of this book that not only is the supporting cast frequently invisible, but even that master figure tends to be seen as static, as though everything true at the end of his career were true throughout. We think of the lonely man at Longwood or the arrogant Emperor who preferred the invasion of France to a peace which would leave her with the outlines of 1805; and among the biographies a common pattern is formed by those which, either to praise or to blame, treat all Napoléon's actions as the product of a single-minded drive toward dominion.

This is both a literary and a historical error. It is a literary error of the first magnitude because it makes an assumption about character in history that would never be permitted in any other kind of writing: allows the man a fairly clear view of the goal toward which he is actually progressing, not that far different one toward which he thinks he is moving. It omits the most important fact about any historical decision: the atmosphere in which it was made, the fact that the decision itself helped warp that atmosphere in the direction of a result we know. The French liberals, for example, conducted their struggle against tyranny in the case of the Concordat on grounds that brought them into conflict with their own ideals and gave liberal thought a bad name for mere obstructionism from which it could not free itself for a generation; but they failed to perceive their own inconsistency because they were operating in the atmosphere generated by the Revolution.

It seemed to me very important to take into account not only the information on which people acted—the most striking example of that is the Austrian and the Russian general staffs' discussing a plan of campaign for weeks without realizing they were speaking in terms of two different systems of dating—but also the emotional background against which the actions were undertaken. History is altogether too frequently written as though its characters were, or should have been, free intellects, inhabitants of a passionless world. Or if not completely passionless, a world in which passion and sex are coterminous expressions.

The effort has been made to give this book another plan; to indicate that although Friedrich Gentz found good rational reasons for his opinions by 1812, those opinions were formed in an atmosphere of unreasoning passion. It is to serve this purpose of reporting the past as the past saw itself that the extracts from contemporary documents are intercalated between chapters.

The "Worm's-Eye View" sections are narratives of incidents by minor actors who took part in them, the "Wrong End of the Telescope" sections being accounts of events by people who saw them from a distance.

For the same purpose—to give the contemporary atmosphere—the French Revolutionary calendar has been used for the period during which it was employed in France. It is a confounded nuisance, but it is almost impossible to understand the French cast of thought in the period, to realize how completely that collective mind had walled itself off from the rest of the world through the Revolution, without using the strange calendar. The note on calendar concordance (p. xv) may help.

In only one case, the extract from Casanova's memoirs, does one of the documents fail to be strictly contemporary with the material beside it. The adventurer was in St. Petersburg some years before the time of Alexander I; but life in the neighborhood of a Tsarist court had not changed in the least by the latter date, and the quotation gives so vivid and accurate a picture of that life that it was worth including.

With regard to Napoléon and the men surrounding him, the historical question is perhaps even more important than the literary method of treating it. He is the dominating figure of the period because he either controlled or only narrowly missed controlling all its successive crises. But there were crises, he had to make an effort to control them, and in that effort his own ideas were often profoundly modified. It is impossible to form judgments on economic, political, or even ethical grounds without recognizing the continual process of alteration, both in the central character and in the medium in which he moved. This continual change of background took place at a speed unprecedented in history and prevented Napoléon himself from entertaining, at least for the period covered by this book, any fixed theories whatever.

He was, in fact, chiefly interested in making things work —in constructing a machine that would work. All the old machinery in France had been wrecked by the Revolution, not only the political machinery, but every device that makes human relations possible. He had to discover everything, beat everything out as he went along. He has since been accused of insincerity and at the time was frequently accused of irresolution, but the real significance of both charges is that he could see no clear line. He often changed techniques while the game was in progress. Nothing about the background of this book is so important to grasp as the fact that from 1800 to 1806 the political and administrative institutions of France floated on a shifting sea, and so did her relations with the exterior world. Even that most stable institution, the Army, underwent radical alterations, as can be perceived by comparing the army of Jena with that of Marengo.

After the conquest of Prussia there were changes, but the pace slowed down. It became a different world and one in which the issues were considerably different. The center of gravity shifts at that point. The French Revolution has

reached its apogee, it is no longer adequate to keep the spot-
light on Paris and to examine events in terms of the French
frame of reference. This is the reason both for giving the
book the form it has and for ending it at this precise point.

Bernard De Voto has remarked that history is not history
at all unless it is *written;* that is, the author cannot escape
his literary responsibilities because his raw material happens
to be actual instead of imagined event and emotion. The
view meets hearty approval from this corner. There has
been too much talk, especially from academic circles, about
the austere regimen of history, meaning such matters as
reverence for objective fact and the preservation of an impartial viewpoint. I do not mean to deny the importance of
these things (provided there is any such thing as objective
fact in the case of human reactions), but they have been so
much insisted upon that it is fair to charge historians as a
class with dealing in them to the exclusion of characteriza-
tion, climax, dramatic unity, and the interest of the reader.

That these latter have been neglected is one of the reasons
why people read fiction instead of history; it was not so in
Titus Livy's day. If it be replied that Livy was not careful
about his facts, why the answer is that there is no inescapable
law of nature that prevents history from having the qualities
usually sought in fiction, while still remaining accurate. Those
qualities are certainly obtained by the manner of presentation
to some extent, but basically they lie in the selection of the
material; the historian choosing, as the novelist does, a story
that has a beginning point and works to a recognizable
termination.

The tale of the high period of the French Empire, before
the darker, fiercer elements came in in 1807, is of interest
not only in itself, but also for the effects which it has not
ceased to produce. I remember being in a French movie house
before World War II or the emergence of Hitler, when
French thought was as far as it possibly could be from mili-
tancy or imperialism. The audience was composed of average, middle-class French workingmen and their families,

Jean Leblancs. One scene in the film being shown, which had nothing to do with Napoléon, required that the silhouette of the Corsican be thrown for a moment against a background of rolling smoke. The audience burst into furious handclapping, and not a few stood up to cheer the apparition.

Those ordinary Frenchmen were not shouting for military renown, but for a lost golden age, of which glory was only a part. The Empire in fact represented a great and even joyous outpouring of the human spirit. The men who made it were a set of the most uninhibited individualists ever assembled outside a lunatic asylum. There is about them something of the same fascination that attends the knights of the Table Round (Malory's, not Tennyson's), the paladins of the Charlemagne epics, or the vikings of the Saga of Burnt Njal. There was never anything in the least mean or petty about them, and seldom anything cruel. They did things on a truly imperial scale, and usually accompanied their doings with a warm human sympathy that is not often encountered in historical occasions. When Ouvrard engaged in a swindle, his objective was nothing less than the whole currency of France; the hard Ney often outwatched the stars, writing some of the tenderest love-letters in the world to his wife; and when the Princess Hatzfeldt visited Napoléon in the matter of her husband's espionage, he handed her the fatal letter that proved the man's guilt—"You have it in your hand; throw it in the fire, it is the only evidence on which he can be convicted."

That Calendar

The French Revolutionary calendar was the device of a mathematician named Romme, who later had his head cut off—not for the trouble he caused, but for lack of civism. It is impossible to understand the era without reference to the calendar, since not only this book, but every other history, speaks of "the day of vendémaire," "the coup d'état of brumaire," and so on. The calendar, inaugurated in 1793, placed the An I of the new era in 1792, and its structure was quite logical, but the French could never persuade anyone else to use it.

New Year's Day, which was 1 vendémaire, normally fell on September 23. The months had 30 days apiece, and all had names indicating the seasons in which they fell. At the end of the year five complementary days, *journées complémentaires,* were inserted, with a sixth in leap years, which caused the relation of the Revolutionary calendar to the Gregorian to fall slightly askew in those years, between February 29 and the sixth complementary day, September 22. Normally the concordance was:

Vendémaire	ran from	September 23	to	October 22
Brumaire	" "	October 23	"	November 21
Frimaire	" "	November 22	"	December 21
Nivôse	" "	December 22	"	January 20
Pluviôse	" "	January 21	"	February 19
Ventôse	" "	February 20	"	March 21
Germinal	" "	March 22	"	April 20
Floréal	" "	April 21	"	May 20
Prairial	" "	May 21	"	June 19
Messidor	" "	June 20	"	July 19
Thermidor	" "	July 20	"	August 18
Fructidor	" "	August 19	"	September 17

and on September 18 the complementary days began.

The calendar was abolished by decree as of January 1, 1806. As early as 1804 it began to fall out of use, and by the end of 1805 had disappeared from all but the most pedantic official correspondence.

The Empire and the Glory
Napoleon Bonaparte: 1800–1806

NOTE

French surnames carrying a *de* always create a certain amount of trouble. The rule that the particle is omitted when the surname only is used—that, for instance, one speaks of "Louis de Bourmont" but of "the reply of Bourmont"—has not been followed in this book because during its period the men bearing such names habitually used the particle (especially in official documents) even when omitting the prename, in order to show their aristocratic status. It was a subtle way of demonstrating their disapproval of the Revolution.

THE CAPTAIN IS IN
CONFERENCE

Paris: 18 brumaire, An VIII
(November 9, 1799)

BONAPARTE came in with the expression of a satisfied cat, dropped his hat on a chair and went over to kiss Joséphine, who had clutched the covers round her when she saw he was not alone. "Good morning, madame," he said, and without waiting for a reply turned to Bourrienne:

"So I talked a lot of nonsense, did I?"

"A certain amount, mon général."

"I'd rather speak to soldiers than to lawyers. Those bastards make me nervous. I'm not accustomed to assemblies, but I'll doubtless get better at it."

The thing had evidently gone off all right. Joséphine at once began to ask about M. Gohier, with whose wife she exchanged visits, and was told that he was a respectable old muttonhead who would probably have to be banished to Cayenne for the part he had played in trying to keep the moribund constitution from being overthrown.

Bourrienne remarked that Gohier's very respect for the system of government had killed it—as in the case of that King of Castille who allowed himself to be burned to death because there was no one in the room with rank sufficient to touch the royal person when his clothes caught fire. The or-

ganic law forbade fewer than three of the five Directors of
the Republic to deliberate or to take action on any subject;
when old Sourface found there was only one besides himself
unresigned, he refused to do anything but contemplate his
navel, whereas with the help of Bernadotte——

"By the way, have you seen him, Bourrienne?" asked
Bonaparte, and when the secretary shook his head: "No
more have I. That Bernadotte! He has been mixed up in
every intrigue in Paris. He wished nothing less than to be
my colleague in authority. For that matter, I am told he
said that if it were necessary to outlaw me, he would find
soldiers for the government to execute its decree. I repent
the advances I have made to him. It's that wife of his; she
has the most complete ascendancy over him. I'll have to get
him out of Paris, away from her and her coteries. It's the
only revenge I can take, with brother Joseph married to
that sister of hers. Ah, bah, these family considerations are
idiotic."

The others knew, but neither of them mentioned, that
Jean-Baptiste-Jules Bernadotte never let women influence
him toward any course but getting into bed and not even
that if political advantage could be found elsewhere. Still,
some excuse had to be found for the Minister of War in the
government just overthrown by Bonaparte's *coup d'état;* it
would never do to lock up a family connection. There was a
little silence, in which the secretary stood up.

"Good night, Bourrienne. Don't forget we are sleeping at
the Luxembourg tomorrow."

II

The next day was a *décadi* but there were no crowds; only
little groups that gathered round the walls where Police
Minister Fouché's men were putting up bulletins, wet with
fresh paste. "Citizens! The Republic was menaced with
early dissolution. The legislative body has rescued liberty at
the brink of the precipice and placed it on indestructible

foundations. . . ." Spies who mingled with the groups reported that the comment was generally favorable to the change of government; in the faubourgs, no comment, the workmen were sitting at home over their soup; and of the Jacobin generals who might have led an opposition, Jourdan was hiding somewhere, Bernadotte had been seen leaving the city with his wife in boy's clothes, and Augereau was strutting around in the most perfect good humor, telling everyone how he had been forced to pretend Jacobinism to conceal his real sentiments in favor of Bonaparte.

The afternoon meeting of the three provisional consuls at the Luxembourg was chiefly to prepare a slate of temporary ministers and to establish agenda for the more serious work that would begin the following day. Roger-Ducos struck the keynote of the occasion when he came into the conference room to find Bonaparte and Sieyès standing a trifle uncomfortably just inside the door, each unwilling to claim the fauteuil of presidency for himself, or to see the other take it. "Let's sit down and get started," said the third consul, and striding across the room, took an ordinary chair. Sieyès, as the man of first eminence, imitated him, and the fauteuil was left for the little General.

No protocol. They fell at once to discussing what was to be done. There was a military emergency with the Austrians on the Rhine and holding nearly all Italy, but they could hardly campaign again before spring, and General Bonaparte would make himself answerable for things in that department. There was a constitutional emergency, but Sieyès had in his head that plan of a perfect governmental instrument on which he had been meditating since '89, and it could be discussed in detail as it was reduced to paper. There was an administrative emergency, which all three agreed must receive an out-of-hand, if temporary, settlement on the basis of talent and experience rather than of connection. But the financial emergency was too grave to permit either postponement or offhand solution. At the very moment of sitting down, the new rulers of France discovered that their treasury

did not hold the twelve hundred francs necessary to send a
courier to the Army of Italy with the news of their accession
to power.

General Bonaparte said his brother Joseph knew a banker
who would lend the nation enough to meet running expenses

They fell at once to discussing what must be done

for a few days, but that an immediate and fundamental reorganization of the whole system of finance with the help of
an expert was clearly the first task before the three. At this
point Sieyès spoke up: he knew just the expert they wanted,
one Martin Gaudin, long connected with the tax and postal
services and perfectly familiar with their detail, said to be so
modest that he turned the mirrors to the wall in the evening
so he would not blush at seeing himself undressed. He, Sieyès,

had tried to persuade this paragon of self-effacement to take over the finance ministry in the closing days of the Directory, but Gaudin had replied that only radical measures could effect a cure, and the Directorial executive lacked the force to push such measures past the opposition of the legislative councils. He might feel differently about an administration supported by the Army.

Bonaparte, whose taste was always in favor of these quiet specialists, agreed that this Gaudin should be offered the Ministry, and they proceeded to nominate the remainder of the cabinet. There was no objection to replacing the dubious Bernadotte at the War Office by General Berthier, Bonaparte's personal chief of staff, or of leaving Justice in the hands of Cambacérès, almost the only man in the defunct government who had distinguished himself in any capacity. Sieyès offered the happy suggestion that Navy & Colonies should be given to Forfait, the noted marine inventor, but as he was not in town at the moment, a man named Bourdin should keep the seat warm for him; it would show that the new administration could count on services as great as those chemist Monge had rendered to the Revolution. Bonaparte instantly capped this with the name of Laplace the astronomer for the Interior Department, and the others, ignorant that Laplace had just dedicated his new book on celestial mechanics to the General, accepted with delight.

The other two places—Foreign Affairs and Police—provoked some discussion. There was no question (said Sieyès) of Citizen Talleyrand's perfect acquaintance with the courts of Europe; of his fine intelligence, persuasiveness, breadth in handling large affairs. He could conciliate the King of Dahomey to the man who was about to be his dinner. But the great diplomat's conduct during the recent *coup d'état* had been more than a little equivocal, and this was due to the objects for which he employed his enormous talents. "The bad example of making money out of what ought to be dearest to all men, honor, has apparently gained him also," said Sieyès, and added that corruption having been the en-

demic fatal to the late Directory, the government which replaced it could not afford a minister whose reputation was
dying of the same disease.

The General was probably unconvinced by this line of
argument, but he had his personal reasons for wishing to see
Talleyrand have a stripe—felt that the diplomat had played
him false in the matter of the Egyptian expedition—and it
was besides very important that the new administration
should have no aspect of reaction that would rally against it
the old Jacobins, with their knowledge of the technique of
revolution and their wide following in the Army. It was
covenanted that Talleyrand should give place to his undis-
tinguished German secretary, Reinhart, and the meeting
passed on to the Police Ministry, now held by Fouché.

Sieyès wanted the place for Alquier, Secretary of the
Council of 500, who had been a police magistrate before the
Revolution and presumably knew something about the business. It was true that Fouché had been, in some sense, the
mechanic of the *coup d'état*—with his meetings between
Sieyès, Bonaparte, and the men they wished to win over, his
careful reports on the possible leaders of opposition, the disposition of his own men on the great day itself. But this was
only time-service. The man was unsure and his record, both
back in the days of the Convention and as a creature of the
late Director Barras, lent a note of immorality to the government more disgraceful than that Talleyrand himself
would impart.

General Bonaparte observed to himself that the Abbé, like
other liberal ideologers, regarded as moral anything that
helped him to attain power, and as immoral anything that
might eject him from it; and aloud that moral tone was less
important to the new government than force and the appearance of solidity. The former was a nice metaphysical desid-
eratum, a proper consideration for the government of Louis
XIV, with twenty generations of royalty behind him; but
how could the adhesion of valuable men to a still-unstable
revolutionary government be secured if those who showed

themselves most energetic were dismissed as the reward of their services?

Moreover, to the old revolutionists of the An II Fouché's presence in the Ministry would be even more of a guarantee than Talleyrand's absence from it that this government, which declared the Revolution at an end, was not itself counterrevolutionary. The General did not labor the point, but both the others knew what he meant. Fouché was a *votant*—voter for execution on the key question of the late Citizen Capet—and had been Robespierre's personal emissary for the mass shootings at Lyon, an act still regarded with approval in the more puristical Jacobin circles.

Roger-Ducos began to look thoughtful at this point. Sieyès, a poor debater, could think of no effective reply, so they let Bonaparte have his way about this one office.

It was decided to dispose of the now unemployed members of the legislative councils by sending them at government expense to explain in the provinces what was going on in the capital. While a tentative list was being drawn up by a secretary, a knock on the door announced that M. Gaudin, to whom Sieyès had dispatched a note, was waiting. The Abbé brought him in to introduce him, a tallish, stoop-shouldered man, with a friz of gray hair over each ear, wall-eyed with much looking at books of account, so that he wore an expression of perpetual astonishment. The lips were firm.

"You have been a long time in the finance department?" asked Bonaparte.

"Twenty years, General."

"We need your help and I think you can do a job for us. Come, take the oath; we are in a hurry."

Gaudin extended his hand and repeated the words after Sieyès without appearing in the least surprised by this precipitancy. When he had finished: "Go to the Ministry," said Bonaparte, "and take possession. We want a report by tomorrow, covering our situation and what is needed to restore the financial service, which is everywhere in disorder. In any case come and see me this evening, and we will talk things over."

All four rose, Gaudin to go to the Ministry, Roger-Ducos to a salon where he stood around vacuously waiting for people to admire him, Sieyès to his apartments to meditate on the constitution, but Bonaparte to have a long conference with Fouché about the men of the new ministry before a quick supper and his talk with Gaudin.

2

RENAISSANCE

Paris: 19 brumaire–22 frimaire, An VIII
(November 10–December 13, 1799)

IT IS said that the Abbé Sieyès emerged from that conference to remark that "We have a master—*qui tout sait, tout veut, et tout peut.*" The story is probably inaccurate; to whom did he say it? We know what Sieyès was up to during most of that evening, and he was not discussing his colleagues with outsiders.

Not that he considered them as sharing that pinnacle above criticism on which he placed himself. To his neat, precise, abstract mind Roger-Ducos was not an intellect at all, only a series of impulses, a kind of quintessence of the average mind, valuable less for anything he said than because one could obtain an idea of general popular reaction by watching him. Bonaparte was merely an executive, brought into the combination (where any one of several others would have done) mainly to give the new government the support of the true patriotism, the civic virtue, of the Army that had saved the Revolution.

What archons held office in the time of Solon? On that brumaire afternoon the General had displayed extraordinary powers; but they were the powers one might expect from a soldier—quick analysis and the ability to make snap decisions when rightly directed, no depth to him. He had even

9

failed at part of his business of making the *coup d'état*—for it had never been Sieyès' plan to clean out the old government by force of arms; the thing should have come about, and was planned, as a spontaneous demand on the part of the whole people.

But to whom could these ideas be communicated? The Abbé did not like to talk, and did it badly; when ideas were on the table and quick thinking was required, he was mute. Alone among the great figures of the Revolution he was neither an orator nor a man of action. As a *votant* he had pronounced for the death of Louis XVI with *"La mort sans phrase"*—death and no talking about it. He lived the meditative life, and meditation had led him to the conclusion that men of action were without ideas and men of the word without character. "I detest society," he had written. "If you talk about some cheap intrigue, they almost kiss the floor trying to act worthy of having taken part in it; they look on your infamy as an honor. It shocks me; if I ever get into government affairs I'll say, 'Bah! you miserable rats, do you think I am like you? I hate you, one and all.' "

The date of the entry was the late period of the Directory and its content is not exactly surprising, since the "society" Sieyès knew consisted of the Directors and the few members of the legislative councils who formed their party. They fell out neatly into two divisions. One contained the morose old wheel horses of the Revolution like Roger-Ducos and Gohier, who never had an idea in their lives nor a word to say for themselves, who had survived the fever-era of the guillotine through insignificance. The other division, which maintained all the salons and did most of the talking, consisted of the entourage of Barras, leader of the Directory since its foundation. They were clever, shallow, witty, corrupt, and licentious, the camp-followers of the Revolution who had become its heirs when the great, gloomy Terrorists went down in the avalanche they themselves had started—maintained a kind of court without the politeness of the ancien régime.

Beyond them lay the neo-Jacobins, meeting in cellars amid

an indescribable odor mingled of garlic, human sweat, and stale wine to cry that "All merchants are essentially anti-revolutionary, especially dealers in wine, bakers, and butchers; nearly all farmers are aristocrats"—therefore the Terror should be renewed. Beyond them again, the genuine aristocrats, the Royalists, gathering in garrets by candlelight to plot how information could be conveyed to London or Vienna, or help to the revolt in La Vendée.

No place in a society thus compounded for those ardent conversations under the plane trees which the young seminarist Emmanuel-Joseph Sieyès had held with older ecclesiastics, when he exposed his skepticism and his "knowledge of man, which is so different from the knowledge of men" while they listened with an indulgence hardly concealing the fact that they were forced to admit all his observations as just—the clerical world, secure and ordered, where homage was rendered only to thought. No place in all this for the little groups that used to gather in the Bishop's palace at Tréguier to discourse gently of an evening on the philosophy of John Locke and Condillac or the metaphysics of Bossuet. There would be music after, with the charming young Emmanuel Sieyès, canon in the chapel of the King's aunt, taking the tenor part; or when they tired of that, describing his latest meditations on political economy and the constitutions of peoples, a subject he had so thoroughly mastered that the Duc d'Orléans invited him up to Paris to hear his ideas. The Abbé Sieyès was proud that those ideas owed nothing to the manner in which they were expressed; for he had studied languages, too, and had decided that the fatal defect in most human thinking lay in the false relation between ideas and the words used to express them. Eloquence (where it existed) served only to falsify that relationship still further. It directed attention to the means of expression, covered defects in unity and the harmony among parts in a system of thought. Eloquence was unnecessary and even dangerous in an intelligent society . . .

An intelligent society. At this point the Abbé Sieyès

(whether delivering his meditations aloud or to the privacy of that diary in which he recorded his dislike of his contemporaries) would shake himself into the realization that the society in which he lived had possessed, for putting things right, only enough intelligence to admit its own intellectual bankruptcy and to call in a man who had exhausted political economy. The disease of the state manifested itself in various forms, as some organic human illness might appear to be chills and fever or merely labored breathing. The facts that government funds stood at 19 on the hundred, and that Martin Gaudin refused to be Finance Minister on the ground that the Directory had no finances nor any means of getting them, were such symptoms. The fact that the armies were beaten on every front and Italy in the hands of the Austrians was another.

The Abbé Sieyès normally lived in too rarefied an atmosphere to pay much attention to what went on among peasants or artisans, but he had his own private police force or statistical service, and on a recent mission to Berlin had observed with his own eyes other expressions of the disease that was eating up France—in Alsace the fields lying fallow that were once so carefully tilled by the most industrious farmers of Europe, at St. Quentin and Lille the great factories that normally employed 10,000 men working with only a sixth of that number and those on part time. Add the nightly brawls between bands of those gilded youths, *jeunesse dorée,* and the hairy old Revolutionists—those brawls that had ceased by magic when the late *coup d'état* threw out the Directory and called to the regulation of the state the Abbé Sieyès.

For a man thoroughly versed in political economy it was not difficult to perceive the common thread. France was simply in the grip of the bad political system imposed when the constitution of the An III had been botched together with insufficient meditation, in order to get some kind of permanent government in and the National Convention out before the swelling rightist reaction should turn the country back to the Bourbons. Sieyès had recognized the defects of the old constitution at the time and had been so exercised over them that he refused election as one of the five original Directors. The legislative authority was at once so powerful that it could paralyze the executive and so responsive to the currents of popular opinion, as expressed through minority groups like the Jacobin Club, that it was irresponsible. There was no local administrative authority whatever, the constitution-makers of the Year III in their hurry having forgotten to provide one.

In the early days of the Directory a factitious appearance of efficiency had been produced because the executive consisted of Barras, Rewbell, Carnot, La Revellière, and Letourneur—three extraordinarily able men and two uncommon for their honesty. They did not have to concern themselves with administrative problems since they had inherited in the communes the old comités installed when Robespierre and the Terrorists were still dominant in the Convention. These comités served very well in holding down the rightist reaction; but by now they had fallen out of joint with the times. Part of them resigned when it became apparent that the Directorial government was anything but Jacobin, and within those communes there had been no government to speak of since.

Part of the comités continued the old Jacobin practice of pulling down everything that was on top. During his return from the Berlin trip the Abbé Sieyès had seen with his own eyes how this worked out at Heiligerbourg in Alsace. The high Terror had decreed the arrest of rich men under suspicion of incivism—good. But in this town, where they had long since exhausted the real rich, they were throwing into prison (as Sieyès passed through) four small farmers and a day laborer. A similar mechanical persistence of policy had led the Jacobin commune of Troyes to levy a fine of 500 livres against a shop in that place—without investigating enough to discover that it had just been opened by a poor shopgirl who set it up on borrowed money.

Who would work when this was the reward of work? One did not have to be Emmanuel Sieyès and a master of political economy to perceive that a reform of the administrative authority was called for. The Directory itself had made a report to this effect, but it got no further because the Jacobins in the legislative were still so strong they could hamstring any measure they regarded as counterrevolutionary. If the five original Directors had still been in office—Rewbell with his industry, and the terrible Carnot, whom Jacobinism recognized as its own—they might have carried the project through. But by the time the defects of the administrative authority became evident the great Directors had been replaced by average political-minded citizens, deutero-Jacobins themselves, therefore only half willing to disturb the arrangements of communes and comités, but more importantly, men without talent for either administration or persuasion.

Emmanuel-Joseph Sieyès was strongly in favor of those men without talent, average citizens. He believed in them; they applauded the depth of his remarks on general subjects, while brilliant people like Talleyrand were apt to laugh or to make an epigram merely for the sake of hearing themselves talk. (The Abbé had never forgotten the diplomat's reply to someone who remarked that Sieyès was profound—"Yes, like a hole in the ground.")

A good governmental instrument was a device in political mechanics which should function as well through mediocrities as through men of genius; better perhaps, since the latter were by definition ambitious.

Sieyès would have vehemently denied that this system of ideas or the aphorisms which he made the foundation of his constitution ("Confidence must come from below and authority from above") bore any resemblance to the arrangements of the Roman Catholic Church. In fact he attributed the principle to Baruch Spinoza, which would have very much surprised that philosopher. But the fact is that whenever Sieyès pictured the ideal society he invariably adumbrated an extension of that in the Bishop's palace at Tréguier or that at St. Sulpice, where he had been a seminarist. Society celibate, clerical, secure, its problems compressed into the narrow frame between dogma and ethics, society where authority came down in indubitable succession from Peter the fisher, society in which was debated at pleasant length every question that had no relation to daily life. That society operated smoothly in the hands of the most ordinary men. It made use of talent without being subjugated by it, never had any financial difficulties, preserved a nice balance among the legislative, governing, executive, and administrative authorities, the result of a constitution well thought out by meditative men.

If Sieyès had added history to his studies he might have realized that the constitution under which the Church was able to function so admirably as a political entity had been the product of centuries of trial and error, in which the individual contribution was limited to a grain of mustard seed. But he despised history as the relict of dead political systems, as Egyptian and Hebrew are the detritus of dead languages. "To judge what is passing by what has passed," he set down, "is to judge the known by the unknown. It would be more accurate to examine the past in the light from the present and to agree that the pretended truths of history have no more reality than the supposititious truths of religion."

John Locke and Condillac had not erected their monumental philosophies on this frozen and inaccurately reported news from the past; they used their senses to penetrate the more deeply the world about them. The use of the historical method involved the sort of *a posteriori* reasoning that was unworthy of a metaphysician. It led straight to Montesquieu. Montesquieu was another political economist; or, as the Abbé put it, the last one before the era of Sieyès.

II

M. le Consul Sieyès naturally found conferences on executive matters boresome, and, for himself, unnecessary. They took him from his proper function of meditating a constitution that would not be (his word) concisionary. It was at his instance that the executive sessions sat at five o'clock, when everyone was anxious to get away to dinner and proceedings could be held down to a snap vote that would render legal the projects already prepared.

When the wall-eyed Gaudin appeared on the afternoon of the 23rd brumaire and began to strain his myopic vision over an armful of papers in the candlelight, Sieyès folded his hands and, assuming that expression of benevolent interest with which churchmen conceal their absence from the scene, settled down into a waking dream. He knew perfectly well that the Finance Minister's proposals would amount to nothing more than another battle in a campaign against shadows. The true difficulty lay at a level no executive could reach. It was double: down in the communes, where administrative authority was still Jacobin, or nonexistent, where no lists of taxables had been compiled or assessments made. The direct taxation of Jacobinism was confiscation. Up at the top the too-powerful legislative had abolished all indirect taxes and had refused to allow any other financial resources than levies on capital in the form of progressive forced loans. Both obstacles would disappear as soon as the new constitution came into force, and Gaudin's palliatives would be unnecessary. Indeed, government funds had risen to 21 on the Bourse that very day, over the mere news that an advisory commission of fifty from the old Legislative would sit with Sieyès to write a new constitution.

Happily for the Abbé, he did not hear from Gaudin any of that eloquence he found so distasteful. In a squeaky monotone the financier remarked that nothing had so contributed to ruin the finances of the government as the progressive forced loan. It was assessed by communal taxing juries against the supposed portable wealth of the subject, a system itself intolerable, since there was no appeal or supervising authority to prevent the personal preferences of the jurors from determining whether their neighbors should pay a great deal or nothing at all. The system also hung like a collar of lead around the neck of commerce and industry, for anyone who did a considerable amount of business *ipso facto* became heavily liable; thus drying up the springs of revenue and——

General Bonaparte interrupted to propose the abolition of the progressive forced loan. *"D'accord,"* said Roger-Ducos, Sieyès nodded, and it was written down.

The main sources of revenue (continued Gaudin without appearing to regret the omission of his further remarks) were from the direct taxes, which accounted for 300 millions of the 500 million normal budget, and the sale of properties escheated to the nation by the Revolutionary laws. The latter stream had practically dried up during the rightist reaction of recent date, with its promise of a restored monarchy and all lands reverting to their former owners. The late government had been so incompetent that it made no collections on many of the lands actually sold. Public confidence in the stability of the government needed to be restored for this source of revenue to open again. The Finance Minister found himself unable to offer anything specific, but he believed that the presence of General Bonaparte, as guarantee of the Army's support, would do much.

The nationalized properties were, however, a temporary, exhaustible resource which the Directory had abused by treating it as a normal source of income while neglecting the true foundations of national prosperity. Back in the An II the National Convention had placed both the compilation of tax rolls and the collection of taxes in the hands of the 48,000 communes of France, where the Directory had simply left them, satisfied with its less permanent revenue. But the communal administrations had in part ceased to function (Sieyès yawned) and, where they did function, were so far behind in their duties that although the An VIII had begun, not a single roll for the year had been received. In some jurisdictions the arrears ran back to the An V. If these were now brought up to date the proprietors in these districts would simply be ruined without benefit to the treasury.

M. Gaudin would not pronounce on the value of an act of oblivion for these taxes; thought it might be a matter for consideration in the individual case. Unfortunately the only officers at present authorized to consider such cases were 5,000 commissioners sent out by the National Convention more than seven years before. Their primary duty was to inquire into the politics of the communes. In tax matters their authority was advisory only, and in practice they confined themselves to seeing that enough taxes were taken in to pay their own salaries. These commissioners should be destituted of their functions.

Sieyès woke up enough to observe that the chances of improvement were small unless authority to tax issued from the central seat in Paris. Local bodies never tax themselves except for local purposes.

Gaudin agreed. He would destitute the commissioners only in favor of another and better set of functionaries. There should be a supervisor from Paris for each of the ninety-nine départements, each with a staff of ten permanent assessors. To prevent abuses and to furnish a means of appeal there should also be a staff of ninety-nine inspectors, rotating among the départements. Collections should be a matter of accountancy. As soon as the rolls were received in Paris from the supervisors, the collectors (who were also the assessors) should be debited with one-twelfth of the amount due from their districts for the year, with a similar debit each month. Drafts for the debited amount would be made monthly by the central authority on the collectors. But it should be assumed that it would take three or four months to collect the taxes, and the debits arranged accordingly— January's taxes not debited till April—so that the collectors would be encouraged to get the taxes in early and enjoy for themselves the use of the interest. This system would replace the 5,000 irregular commissioners by 1,000 regular employees and make it possible to pay them so much more that good men would be secured, while the total cost of collection would be reduced from five millions to three.

The financier produced a paper with the supporting figures and Bonaparte, to whom they were already familiar, offered a motion to put his proposals into effect. Voted; and Gaudin returned to the charge.

A great deal of bad government paper (he said) had been placed in circulation as a result of the Directory's inability to meet its obligations. Government employees, who had received no pay in six months, had been given a series of Bonds of Arrearage, whose sole value was that the Legislative had decreed that they could be received in payment of taxes. The armies cantoned on French soil, having no money through the failure of the Treasury to pay them, had taken upon themselves to issue "Requisition Bonds" in exchange for goods and foods seized locally, a system of gross abuses, since there was no control on the amounts issued, often fantastically above the level of the goods.

Roger-Ducos wished to know how far this practice had gone, what quantity of the paper was in circulation.

M. Gaudin replied that neither he nor anyone else could say, since the total had not been reported to Paris, and he looked at General Bonaparte, who instantly seized his cue.

—The soldiers (he said, fully aware that Maret the secretary was writing this down and it would be in the *Moniteur* in the morning) are starving. It is to the deficiency of victual exactly that we owe the troubles of the Army of Italy, which has supported even military disasters with the most exemplary fortitude. Certain formations have now deserted almost completely, dissolving into those bands of brigands which now infest the southern part of the country. I know of an entire division which has left its station in defiance of orders, to move to another district where it imagined more food might be had. The matters of commissariat and discipline are the business of the Minister of War, General Berthier, who has them in train; we are at present concerned only with the business of bad government paper.—

There are two other classes of bad paper (Gaudin continued). One is a series of "Delegations" issued by the

Treasury direct to army contractors in exchange for such items as food and weapons; the other the "Rescription" series of bonds, secured by nationalized properties and receivable in payment for them, which have been sold by the Directory at considerable discounts to bring in a little ready cash. All four types of paper—Arrearages, Requisitions, Delegations, Rescriptions—have floated to Paris, where they form the basis of the orgy of speculation which has practically driven real money out of circulation and reduced the country to a basis of barter.

Repudiation, even of the Requisitions and Delegations which had been issued under circumstances that practically guaranteed corrupt bargaining, could not be considered. It would sacrifice the honor of the nation. (Not a hint in the Minister's manner of the long argument he had had with Bonaparte on the subject, the General wishing to repudiate and be damned to all speculators.) The remedy Gaudin proposed was to extinguish the two more suspicious classes of paper at once, but not in cash or at full value. The holders should receive title to nationalized properties to the extent of fifty per cent of the face value of their bonds, a measure which would at once increase the amount of taxable property and place it in the hands of those best able to pay—the persons who had surplus cash for speculative purposes. The Arrearages and Rescriptions should be perfectly acceptable either for national property or for taxes, but with a strict time limit, which would result in the early extinction of these obligations also.

Voted without debate, M. Sieyès being anxious to get to his food. As they rose the expression of kindly interest faded from his face and he drew the General aside to say that his private police had turned up a royalist plot to murder all three consuls in their beds. He was anxious.

"Have they corrupted our guard?"

"No."

"Then go have your dinner. In war as in love, my dear sir, one must come to close quarters to conclude matters."

The next day government bonds went up five points to 26.

III

What of Paris, what of France? While Sieyès is translating his ripened meditations into projects of law and Bonaparte rushes through the streets like a comet, now to the Temple to strike with a chisel held in his own delicate hands the fetters from men held prisoner because they were no more than related by blood to emigrated nobles; or hurries from a meeting with Berthier at the War Office, to come singing up the steps of the Luxembourg ("God and His angels alone know with what a wretched voice he sang"). It is for a meeting with individuals who come wrapped in cloaks and are ushered in by way of the back stairs. Paris would be in a tumult if it could see their faces, for they are Hyde de Neuville and D'Andigné, under whose orders the royalists of La Vendée stand in arms at this very moment—come to remind the General who had inherited the Revolution of another general who sold a similar legacy for a dukedom and lived out an honored life as *victor sine sanguine*. George Monk, Duke of Albemarle; Napoléon Bonaparte, Duke of—shall the title be Corsica, or even Languedoc or Lorraine?

What then of Paris? There is the war, but its drumtaps sound faint and distant along the corridors of the Palais Royale. There is even a rumor of early peace, born of the purely fortuitous circumstance that thrust the new government into power just as the Rhine began to carry ice down from the mountains past where France faces Austria across the dark stream, which caused the leaders of both sides to make an armistice till spring. The rumor is false; but it adds to the general allegresse of a city beginning once more to believe in tomorrow.

The police records have nothing to mention, *rien à signaler;* the nightly riots between Sansculottes and Incroyables have ceased as though they never were anything but a ceremonial observance. Sansculotte and Incroyable still moved through the streets to their bals, the latter in wonderful waistcoat and mountainous hat, pomander ball in one hand

and cudgel in the other, lisping through lips so delicately held it was impossible for them to pronounce the letter R; the former with shirt open, red cap and phrases about tyranny—each accompanied by the female of the species.

But in two weeks Sansculotte and Incroyable have already become slightly old-fashioned. The police have nothing to signify in their regard, the newspapers mention them no more, in the salons and cafés the talk is all constitution, constitution, General Bonaparte and his ministers, General Bonaparte and his savants. The Republic had no need of Lavoisier and sent him to the guillotine; but the new government has called the author of the *Mécanique céleste* to operate the terrestrial mechanics of the nation, and for the first time since Pythagoras it is polite to discuss pure mathematics at the dinner table. M. Laplace has already found the wonderful young Cauchy (who thinks, alas in error, that he has discovered a proof of Fermat's Theorem), son of his old friend, and has promised him an education in the new scientific school he proposes to set up. Old Lagrange is out of retirement with his manners of a bygone age; epigrams on analytic functions flash among the candles of 7 rue de Mont Blanc, where banker Récamier exhibits to the world the most beautiful woman in France—his wife.

7 rue de Mont Blanc. It is the new world within four walls. Fatherly old Récamier himself is there, with his aureole of white hair, twenty-seven years senior to his Juliette, perfectly happy in a platonic marriage which decorates his salon with an exceptionally fine piece of living furniture and enables him to entertain with credit any company whatever. He is usually in a corner whispering bonds, deals, and whether they should make the prices rise on 'change tomorrow with two or three others of the financial oligarchy, perhaps Ouvrard, Armand, or one of the Michel brothers. Now and then one will detach himself from the group to move over toward Madame on the chaise longue, kiss her hand and assure her of his undying love. It is the fashion of this salon to present such avowals in public and to hear them

criticized for style and sensibility—when the topic is not the infinitesimal calculus, Providence, or what order of thoughts is most truly noble.

The last was the type of subject likely to be brought up by Camille Jordan who, like all the rest of the men, more than half meant what he said when he periodically laid his heart at Juliette's feet. As an old friend of the family he was privileged, but it puzzled him no little that she could be the mistress of a salon and show her breast as she sat for Gérard the painter without being the mistress of any of the men who frequented the place. So different from the salons of the Directory, where the fair Cabarrus had been queen, passing lightheartedly from bed to bed; so different from that of Germaine de Staël, where Jordan had acquired the taste for those politico-philosophical speculations that offered opportunity for neat remarks.

Jordan saw from the beginning that his own case with the beauty was hopeless and fell readily enough into that attitude of an indulgent father toward a charming and talented child which was adopted by the lady's own husband. So did the elder of the two Montmorencies, who had come back from exile, now that the accession of the new government had made it clear that the danger of another Terror was really ended. The old Montmorency had come to 7 rue de Mont Blanc because Récamier was his banker, and continued to come because he found it the only place in Paris where the taste of the old régime met the intelligence of the new. The two old men did much to set the tone of the gatherings on a pitch of perfect good humor and good sense, so that sooner or later they were joined by many others—Comte de Narbonne, who had been Louis XVI's minister, and Barrère, the once-Jacobin orator; the Duchesse de Fitzjames of the royal Stuarts of England, and Madame de Staël herself; General Moreau, Fouché of the police, and Bernadotte the Jacobin general. Only Sieyès was too busy with his meditations to come; but Lucien Bonaparte did, the stormy brother of the Consul, and created something of a situation by making love to Juliette, not in public, but through a series of passionate letters signed "Romeo" and delivered in private. She showed them to her husband, who said the Bonapartes were too powerful to antagonize, with the very form of the new government unsettled. At the next evening's reception Madame Récamier handed all his letters back to the would-be lover, remarking with a delightful and ingenuous smile that he ought not to give up politics for literature—the bold and free style which made him so good an orator was little suited to the expression of tender sentiments, as in the first chapters of the little romance he had let her read.

Jean-Louis David was there when she did it; burst into immoderate laughter and began next day a portrait of Madame, seated on that chaise longue which was part of the set Barante had designed for her, and which was to be the foundation of an entire new style. J.-L. David could afford to laugh; he did not fear the minor Bonapartes or anyone else, was riding the crest as absolute arbiter of taste, a long way now from the days when he had sworn to drink poison if Robespierre fell. He had designed the costumes for all the new officials—on lines that made Miot de Melito, returning from Holland, wonder whether he was not watching a national masquerade.

Big, flabby-fat, assertive, his dress untidy but gorgeous, David was just the man to be arbiter of elegance in a republic uncertain of its own aesthetic validity. People were paying thirty-six sous merely to look at his new masterpiece of the Sabine women; he even found time to obtain from General Bonaparte an order for a picture from poor old Greuze, who at sixty-nine was living on a piece of bread and a little thin soup every day, no longer popular. The commission did not much help the old man, who died within the year, cold and miserable, begging everyone to buy another picture. But the benefit to J.-L. David was not small; it permitted him to hear the most flattering remarks about his generosity when for an evening he deserted Madame Récamier's classic halls (where, after all, one had to stand) for one of the new type of public houses called *restaurants*. They came about, says legend, perhaps accurately, through the enterprise of a certain baker named Lamy who, when his bread was out of the oven, replaced it with an enormous pot-au-feu from which he served visitors. "Come, let us *restore* ourselves with some of the baker's pot-au-feu."

The caterers thought these establishments a menace and sent a delegation to beg that they be forbidden by the new constitution. They might have spared themselves the trouble; Grimod de La Reynière had already declared that good eating could only be done in a large place, with conversation for the sauce—Grimod, whom Talleyrand, legist Cambacérès, and not a few others employed to spy round the new restaurants and discover all that was best. They found Leblanc's, where a hundred hams hung from the ceiling; Cauchois', which specialized in stuffed calves' heads; Lambert's, where the cream cheese was an ecstasy. For Paris, after the wolf-age of the Revolution, had suddenly discovered its stomach—no more of those melancholy repasts of the old régime, brought from the caterer's and consumed from cold gold plates amid stale and stately courtesies, no more either of the inglutition of joints held in the fingers and fingers wiped on the trousers. The Jacobins are down, we are polite in our eating, and Anthelme Brillat-Savarin can write:

"The ortolan should be taken by the beak, sprinkled with a little salt and adroitly introduced into the mouth, bitten off close to the fingers and chewed vigorously, so that a sense of deliciousness invades the whole system and the eater becomes aware of pleasures unknown to the vulgar."

While Brillat-Savarin was at Leblanc's munching ortolans, the vulgar had their restaurants, too, places where huge platters of beef, pork cutlets, or roast geese stood on a counter, every minute renewed from the open fire before which spits perpetually turned, every minute disappearing under the ministrations of scores of waiters who bore them away to tables through an incessant brouhaha of conversation, clacking forks, and savory odors.

After the dinner—for restaurants had brought with them the custom of the early dinner instead of the late supper—one is off to the amusements. Perhaps the opera to hear the paradisical new melodies of Cherubini; or the Divan, where M. Deschapelles will entertain with a dozen simultaneous games of chess and whist; or the café for a little flutter of gambling. (M. Sieyès, to whom écarté and ombre are the most natural things in the world, entertains a curious prejudice against lotto, and has persuaded Fouché to issue an order against it.) For the vulgar there are the spectacles.

The spectacles, to which the police devote more attention as organs of public opinion than they do to the press. Sufficiently singular entertainments, written in the afternoon and produced the same evening by actors who read from script except when it comes to the fine speeches. It is a remarkable spectacle that runs as much as a week. The characters are personified qualities, like those in a medieval mystery:

27 brumaire: Report on the theaters.

Reaction is trying to accomplish something by means of the theaters as is clear from the pieces they have submitted.

In one the authorities are ridiculed under the style of M. Direct, Sr. and Jr., a pair of idiots; in another there has been introduced an imbecile of the last order who, costumed as a legislator, debauches the leading character of the piece and excuses his evil intentions only by his stupidity. At another place there was a piece which showed the common man groaning under the bureaucrats who even put a stamp on his back to indicate that he is being taxed on the basis of one door for his mouth and two windows for his eyes; in a third there are Jacobins named Brigand, Dagger, and Headbuster. It is worth remarking that though villainous Jacobins appear in many, there is a royalist villain in none.

For the Central Bureau
Du Bois, Piis, DuBos

IV

Thus public Paris, where the drumtaps of the war sound faint and it is noted that street singers are again making the rounds; Paris feeling its way toward a new society, it is not quite sure of what nature, though it suspects a return of the monarchy and is willing to prepare for it by making Jacobins comic villains of a spectacle. For even though General Bonaparte's midnight visitors remain hidden beneath their cloaks, these things are obvious—that the brumaire *coup d'état* has wrenched from the Jacobins their power to paralyze the executive; that thirty-eight of them, including old General Jourdan, the hero of Fleurus, are listed for deportation to Cayenne; that many of the émigrés have openly returned; that in La Vendée General Hédouville no longer fights the Chouans but negotiates with them.

This would be on orders from Paris. A few minutes after Hyde de Neuville and D'Andigné there came into the room "an unhealthy-looking little man in an olive frock coat, with stringy hair and an air of extraordinary negligence." A secretary? The royalist ambassadors gave him a glance and were about to go on with their conversation when Talleyrand, who had accompanied them, nudged D'Andigné and had the honor to present them to Monsieur the Consul of the Republic. They already knew that a pacification in La Vendée was an indispensable preliminary to any restoration; D'Andigné bowed low and presented a letter, draft of a preliminary armistice for closing out the civil war, down which Bonaparte rapidly ran his eye.

"It is too long by half," said he, "and contains nothing final. We can settle this whole business in five minutes."

The pair, not a little taken aback (for they were only to feel out this General Monk and get a preliminary armistice, could sign nothing definitive), replied that they asked nothing better. What the Chouans wanted was a general amnesty, act of oblivion, property to be restored to all Vendéans now borne on the list of émigrés, conscription laws not to be enforced for the time being—"accorded, accorded, accorded." At "Catholic religion to be restored" the General paused:

"Religion? I'll re-establish it all right, but not for you; for me." He smiled, charmingly. "Not that we nobles have much religion; but the people must have it."

There was a little more babbling back and forth at the moment and a great deal down in Vendéan headquarters at Angers later, when the men who had been sent up to get a basis of discussion came back with a definitive treaty. But the terms were too broad to be refused, and in another month the seven-year revolt flickered down into mere hopes for a restoration. Hopes how strong? D'Andigné came from the conference less confident than he had entered it that this was General Monk; but Georges Cadoudal, the military leader, was still sanguine and persuaded the Comte d'Artois (who called himself Monsieur de France) to write a somewhat naïve letter asking the Consul for his crown.

No answer. The Consul was friendly enough to these ex-rebels, delighted to see them always. When the Comte de Bourmont called, he was offered a post in the administration and pressed to accept it. "Look here," said Bonaparte, "you want to re-establish the Bourbons, no? You'll never make it while I'm head of the government; though after I'm dead you can do as you please—I won't care. But you'll get nowhere unless you are somebody important, and if you people refuse to come into the government, I'll have to pardon the Jacobins—and they'll take off your heads."

The argument did not prove convincing to de Bourmont, who must whirl down his own parabolic orbit toward a strange destiny and a maculate baton. Perhaps he had heard too much Paris gossip before calling. Forgive the Jacobins, indeed! As though it were something in the future—had not the Consul permitted General Bernadotte to strut the salons? had he not stricken General Jourdan from the list of those destined for the dry guillotine of Guiane? Even Talleyrand could not get his ministry of foreign affairs back till he had made a personal and public appeal in favor of another on the exiles' list, one Jorry, insignificant even as a Jacobin, who possessed only the advantage for publicity purposes of having once won a libel suit against Talleyrand.

That fact was the key. An administration of acts of oblivion, in which public and private wrongs alike are forgiven, not to rebuild an old world, but to set up a new one. At some reception or other Bonaparte pinched the ear of Legist Cambacérès and remarked amiably, "They'll string you up when the Bourbons come back." But at the same time had written a permit for old Chateaubriand to return from beyond the seas or the tomb—who found the great chateaux in ruins with trees and parks cut down for firewood, roads empty, people staring in hungry apathy. On the few carriages were ropes instead of harness; occasional ragged women dug in the fields. When he reached a town it was a *décadi;* the local magistrate read the official *Moniteur* aloud in the public square, after which everyone put on a red cap and shambled spiritlessly through the carmagnole, with denunciations for incivism following. The road to the east was not safe; a band of Companions of the Sun was about and would toast the feet of anyone who looked prosperous.

v

From such a soil, what institutions would grow? Emmanuel-Joseph Sieyès, considering the matter in an atmosphere of pure intellection, uninhibited by any reference to the past, answered himself, "Naked democracy is absurd." Contact with the world he had both through his own eyes and through his private police; where Chateaubriand saw a bankrupt civilization sliding down into a future when some young Atala would barbarously love among the ruins, the last of the political economists perceived a nation merely waiting to be told what to do. It continued the attitudes of the Revolution because it had received no further orders. The people, left to themselves, produced such institutions as the companies of Jesus or the Sun, Chouans, or Chauffeurs— brigand associations, whose development should be regarded not as a proof of the evil inherent in mankind, but as the natural man's attempt to achieve political institutions without the benefit of political philosophy.

"No one should exercise any public function without the

confidence of those over whom it is exercised," pronounced
the Abbé. This fundamental was the legacy of the Revolution. But its continuance had left another: "No officer should
be elected by those he must govern"—or you get perpetual
Revolution and the Directory.

These were the principles. It was now necessary only to
translate them into a written document, a work of some
difficulty for a profoundly meditative man, who despised
eloquent phrases. Happily Sieyès had a friend, Boulay-de-la-
Meurthe, who could draw him out and would take notes. In
the evening, after a day of meditation, Sieyès would drift
around to Bonaparte's apartment. There would be wine on
the table and most of the men present from the constitutional
commission of the old Legislative, including Daunou who, as
a professor of moral history, represented a point of view
diametrically opposite the Abbé's own and made an admirable foil for the exposition of the latter's ideas. Sieyès would
listen till he caught the thread of whatever provision of the
new constitution was being discussed, then give birth to an
aphorism which opened the gates of conversation, and the
whole evening would pass in the most fascinating argument
on a high philosophical plane.

Next morning the commission in official session would
draw up the constitutional section in accordance with Sieyès'
developed thoughts, a task at which Daunou's experience in
phraseology made him particularly valuable. Boulay-de-la-
Meurthe was usually present to warn from his notes when
the words tended to slip away from the master's ideas. In
fact, he not infrequently represented Sieyès at the following
night's discussion, when the written constitutional article
would be compared with the principle on which it had been
formed. Sieyès himself liked to avoid these occasions, when
smooth Daunou and waspish Bonaparte were apt to find
quibbling flaws in his grand plan.

Yet the plan was his in all essentials. It was he who had
detected that Montesquieu's classic division of the powers
of government into legislative, executive, and judicial had

been an oversimplification. There were in reality five such authorities in any operative government, those overlooked by political economists before Sieyès being the Administrative (which has charge of local government and the collection of taxes) and the Governing (whose function is to assure stability and to preserve the whole). By an ingenious system of election the Administrative could be chosen so that it furnished both a training school for Legislators and a method of selecting those most worthy in its restricted field to take on higher responsibilities.

Each of the départements of France should be divided into four communes for electoral and administrative purposes. The primary electors, who are the whole people, should choose one-tenth of their number as "communal notables." From these the executive of the central government would select the communal administrative authorities (including Gaudin's assessors); from themselves these communal notables would elect one tenth again, "the départemental notables." The executive would choose a départemental administrator, or prefect, from this list, and in turn the départemental notables would elect one-tenth of their number, "notables of the nation."

From this list the legislative authority would be chosen. It consisted of three chambers with sharply defined duties— a Council of State, men who also held executive posts within the government ministries, charged in their legislative function with preparing new laws when necessary; a body of one hundred Tribunes, whose function would be to debate proposals for the law; and a Legislative Jury, which would hear in silence the arguments of Councilors and Tribunes, voting aye or no on the projected law in secret session.

The Council of State was to be responsible to the Ministers, and the Ministers in turn to the supreme executive authority—two Consuls, one of whom was to have the direction of internal affairs, with the ministries of Justice, Police, Finance, Treasury, Administration, Public Works, and Commerce; the other, of external affairs, controlling the departments of War, Marine, Foreign Relations, Colonies, and Conquered Territories. No act of the Executive was valid without a ministerial signature, and ministers might be prosecuted by the Tribunes before the Legislative Jury for misfeasance or malfeasance.

Thus far the constitution was all Sieyès and evoked nothing but squeals of admiration for the manner in which he had met the capital difficulty of every government since 1789— instability, one more revolution through the forms of election, the thing that had three times forced the Directory either to violate the fundamental document under which it existed or to be eaten alive by a Royalist from the right or a Jacobin from the left. At last here was a government which would react slowly enough to currents of popular opinion to insure that its own actions were not extreme.

But when the articles relating to the Governing Authority were reached, there was a check. Sieyès conceived of it as containing two elements: a College of Conservators and a Great Elector, the official head of the state. The College was to hold office for life, the elder statesmen of France. It would confirm laws, or annul them as unconstitutional; choose members of the Tribunate and the Legislative Jury from the notables of the nation; and finally choose the Great Elector; have the power of "absorbing" into its own number that head of the state or any other functionary "who became dangerous to the liberties of the public."

The Great Elector should have no function but that of selecting the two Consuls and the members of the Council of State, but would receive a salary of five million francs a year for these light duties, with a palace and a guard and the right to preside at all public functions.

The first clash came over the question of absorption when it was proposed on the evening of 11 frimaire. Bonaparte, who had insensibly taken more and more part in the discussions, was sharply opposed to it, and with a mordant sarcasm that set most of those present laughing but put Sieyès' teeth on edge. The Abbé cried angrily that they were dealing here with no loose assemblage of provisions, but with a carefully integrated plan, to remove any feature of which would destroy the integrity of the whole.

That set Daunou ablaze, who had written the defunct constitution and had been waiting to thrust a knife into this new one. He inquired whether the new document was inalterably inscribed on twelve tables of stone?—and soon the whole pack were crying. The discussion lasted for six hours and ended without a decision. On the following night Sieyès did not come, Bonaparte took the lead, and some fifteen articles were turned out with a speed and logic that surprised everyone. When the article on absorption came up on the evening succeeding this, it was put to a vote as though at a formal meeting. There was a complete silence in which everyone looked at Sieyès, but not a single voice in favor of the proposal, not even that of Boulay-of-the-Meurthe. No absorption.

The stage was now set for the consideration of the other Governing Authority, the Great Elector, whose position was considered a couple of nights later. Daunou, Talleyrand, dared to express doubts about having such a decorative phantom as the chief person in the state. Sieyès had foreseen difficulties on that point and, trying to rally support, had told the General it would be easy to make him Great Elector. But now in the whole committee Bonaparte threw in two or three objections in his most incisive and vulgar style, and Sieyès was stung into explaining that it was necessary to have an honored but powerless head of the state in order to prevent monarchy. "Bah!" cried the General. "Your Great Elector will be a shadow, a colorless shadow of a *roi fainéant*. How can you imagine that a man of any talent or activity would consent to settle down like a pig and fatten on his millions?"

It was Rœderer the constitutional lawyer who replied; for Sieyès' face had altered, he fell silent, and next day told Boulay-de-la-Meurthe that he had really intended the Great Elector's post to be occupied by no mere executive, but by a man of profoundly meditative temperament, immune to petty passions. He continued to argue, or Boulay for him, as the commission transformed the Great Elector into a Premier Consul, chosen for ten years by the Senate, to whom the other consuls should be merely advisory assistants, and who could appoint and dismiss other state functionaries at his pleasure. To all the objections of the Abbé there was the answer that he himself had pointed out the necessity for a strong Executive in a nation reorganizing itself from the bottom while maintaining a war against more than half of Europe.

On the night of 22 frimaire Sieyès again did not come to the meeting. The discussion turned on certain details of the judicial organization, and Bonaparte remarked that they were now settling business which belonged in the sphere of the Legislative, which ought to fill in curtain walls around the solid structure already achieved. Why not sign the document at once, give France the benefit of a regular administration instead of this provisional consulate, under which nothing done could have any aspect of permanence? There was some discussion, but before dawn caught the spires of Montmartre they had all set their names to the new constitution and to the attribution of General Napoléon Bonaparte as First Consul, with Jean-Joseph-Régis de Cambacérès as Second Consul and Charles-François Lebrun as Third. The new government was formally to take office on 4 nivôse; and by the old calendar that was Christmas Day.

WRONG END OF THE TELESCOPE—I

Newport Mercury:

FEB. 4

FROM the inftallation of the firft Directory to the Abrogations of their Power on the 10th November laft, *Thirteen* Perfons have fuftained the office of Director, and of thefe only *three* have been allowed to complete their conftitutional Term—the other *ten* have been driven from the Seat of Power by the Violence of contending, and alternately fucceſsful, Factions.

Paris police reports:

12 nivôse An VIII [JANUARY 2, 1800]

PUBLIC SPIRIT—The decree of the first consul in favor of the liberty of worship has made the greatest sensation in Paris. There have been considerable gatherings at the doors of the churches. A considerable number of those previously closed have now re-opened, to the satisfaction of a crowd of persons of every sex, who demonstrate their pleasure in the liveliest manner.

SPECTACLES—The public continues to applaud all the passages which contain any allusion to the results of the revolution of 18 brumaire.

9 pluviôse, An VIII [JANUARY 29, 1800]

PARIS is calm. A few malcontents are unhappy; but no general spirit of faction. Opinion is forming in favor of the government with great speed, and appears to be becoming very strong.—The death of Toustain has crushed the traitors.—The arrest of Ouvrard has terrified crooks; the good citizens, who always rally round justice, congratulate the government on the firmness and generosity of its principles.

Mémoires of A.C. Thibaudeau:

BEING opposed to compliments and solemn receptions, I had not announced my forthcoming arrival at Bordeaux. Some people of the town living in Paris did it for me. I was awaited with confidence by everyone but a few exaggerated revolutionists and partisans of the Bourbons who remained enemies of the consular government. On the banks of the Dordogne, I saw some horsemen on picket who, when I appeared, turned rein and galloped toward Bordeaux. When I reached the Garonne, what a spectacle! The magnificent quai was filled with the National Guard in arms and by people who came to welcome the new prefect with acclamations; the lovely river was covered with ships and boats, filled with people of both sexes and every rank of society; there were sounds of music, the boom of cannon, cries of *"Vive la République! Vive le Premier Consul! Vive le Préfet!"* A great movement of curiosity, of interest and of joy. . . .

Newport Mercury:

PARIS, Nov. 21 VICE-ADM. BRUIX is denominated Chief of the Council of the French Admiralty.—It appears to be the intention of this Council, to demand the abolition of the trial by jury; to which privilege, the infubordination of the French feamen is attributed.—"On land," fays the Counful Buonaparte, "an undifciplined bravery may fometimes be the means of victory—but never by fea."

Fr. Gentz—Historisches Journal:

FOR the first time since the Republic came into existence, the desire for peace promises to be more than a trick of war or a cloak for extortion.

Commercial Advertiser, New York:

THE Consuls were installed in their new residence at the Thulleries on the 19th, with great pomp. On the 21st Buonaparte receiv- all the Foreign Ambassadors, and afterwards entertained them at dinner.

The Chief Consul continues to make it the great object of his policy to conciliate men of all opinions, and to banish all distinctions of party. Almost all the victims of the 18th Fructidor, who were recalled, have been restored to the full rights of citizens. Even Camille Jordan, who was generally considered as a Royalist, is permitted to return to France and is placed under the superintendance of the police at Grenoble.

Mr. Canning to Granville Leveson-Gower:

I SAY nothing to you about Buonaparte's Revolution because I have so much to say that I know not when I would end. I am in raptures at it. The destroyer of the National Representation of the French Republick is a public benefactor to Europe. I care not whether he restores the King or becomes himself a Despot, so that he be bloody and tyrannical enough. Heaven prosper all his projects against French Liberty and Republican principles, whatever they may be! But as to peace —peace with a Government six weeks old! No-no-no! If the old form of things had endured and the rest of Europe had been dastardly we might have found some difficulty in carrying on the war. But now it is our own fault if we do not take a new lease of it.

THE WORM'S-EYE VIEW—I

. . . M. de la Tour du Pin and I had never been inscribed on the list of émigrés. It was nevertheless necessary for us to have a certificate of residence in France, signed by nine witnesses, a formality which deceived no one. To get it I went round to the municipality of the quarter with my squad of witnesses. When the certificate had been signed and filled out with the necessary falsehoods, the Maire handed it to me very politely, remarking in a low tone, "This won't prevent you getting your trunks from London," and laughed.

During this period the best company in Paris was found under the dome of a building in the Place Vendôme where the Commission des Émigrés sat, a tribunal easy enough to conciliate when one did not come with empty hands. Among the crowd one encountered the greatest names of France mingled with agents of every species. Two phrases dominated every conversation—"Have you been struck off the list?" "Are you going to be?" Thus they talked, surrounded by witnesses to their continued residence in France and carrying certificates saying how unjust it was to have inscribed their names on the fatal list— people who spoke with the accents and gestures fashionable in Coblenz, London, and Hamburg.

Mme. de la Tour du Pin—Journal d'une Femme de Cinquante Ans

THE WORM'S-EYE VIEW—II

. . . I had an opportunity of seeing the First Consul's demeanor in an affair of interest. On the night cf the 20th of April of the An IV, the Chateau de Vitry, at that time the property of M. du Petitval, was entered by a troop of assassins, who murdered M. du Petitval, his mother-in-law, his sister-in-law, and three servants. Nothing was stolen; plates, diamonds, watches remained in their places, the papers only were missing. The relatives of the victims made an effort to obtain justice; the preliminary steps were taken by the local authorities, but suddenly these symptoms of activity relaxed.

I was one day in the apartment of Mme. Bonaparte when the First Consul was present; she was persuading him to admit a person who had been promised the favor of an introduction.

"I have already said," replied the First Consul, "that I would not give audience in this affair; accusations without proof have no other effect than to increase scandal. However," he added after walking to and fro for some time without speaking, "let your protégé come in." M. de Bois-Préau was admitted, coming to solicit the First Consul's interference to obtain justice against the murderers of his relative, du Petitval. The stranger presented a memoir of several pages in close writing. The First Consul took it and glanced through it.

"This, Monsieur," he said, "is a delicate affair. Your accusations are founded only on moral proof; this is not sufficient before a legal tribunal." The First Consul as he spoke continued to walk about the room with his hands behind his back. What M. de Bois-Préau said I did not hear, but he replied, "I know it, I know it, but proofs, the proofs are indispensable."

"Proof is no doubt necessary," said the petitioner. "Nevertheless, General, I think that if you as chief of state would take vengeance into your hands, it would be secured."

The First Consul smiled. "You give me credit," said he, "for more than I possess; a power which, if it were accorded me, I should certainly not use. Justice is open to you; why do you not use it? For myself I regret that it is not within my power to assist you." He then saluted M. de Bois-Préau, who retired with an air of melancholy.

When the petitioner had departed, the First Consul resumed the memoir and read with great attention. Words escaped him at intervals which showed the profound indignation it inspired. "It is infamous," he exclaimed at length. "It is incredible; a police inert if not guilty. Let Citizen Cambacérès be informed that I wish to speak to him."

Duchesse d'Abrantès—Memoires

3
ORGANIZATION

Paris: frimaire—pluviôse, An VIII
(December 1799—February 1800)

I WENT to Malmaison one morning. Madame Bonaparte
received me with wonderful graciousness, and after
lunch took me into the gallery. We were alone; it gave
her the opportunity to chatter in a way to put one to sleep
about the objects of art and vertu in the place. This little
picture by Albane, the Pope had constrained her to accept
it; that danseuse and the Hebe were the gift of Canova; the
city of Milan had offered her another and another. I didn't
even bother trying to analyze her little lies. With the admiration I possessed for the General, she would have made more
impression upon me by simply saying he had conquered all
these treasures at the point of the sword."

The reaction was not singular. To France, a country at
war both along the frontiers and within its own structure,
the General in the Luxembourg offered not only the recap-
ture of those ecstatic hours when the standards of imperial
Austria were borne through the streets while all the bells of
Paris caroled for joy. The émigrés returned, Vendée laying
down its arms, no proscriptions or rolling heads, the churches
open, and it does not matter what a man's background be, if
he have the three administrative graces—honesty, industry,
ability. It is a new and better world.

Look at the roll of this Council of State. In the military section, Brune, son of a poor pettifogging lawyer, who had given up the pamphleteer's trade to follow a drum to the wars; no politics, but a capacity for administrative detail that was far from small; with Marmont, of noble birth, no politics either, Bonaparte's old personal friend, who had done so much to organize artillery in the campaigns; Lacuée, an enlisted private from the old army, who became lawyer and legislator under the Revolution and had to flee for his life when the Girondins went down.

The Navy section has Champagny, noble, but a noble who had joined the Tiers État, sat in prison, and nearly lost his head when Robespierre came to power, too moderate for the sea-green man; Ganteaume, seaman without politics or many ideas, yet had brought some order into the tangled affairs of Brest arsenal; and Fleurieu, noble, who went to prison for royalism when the Directory broke the back of the rightist reaction.

In the section of finance there were Defermon, once a fierce Jacobin, but he turned against them, had been outlawed for it and lived in hiding till Bonaparte threw out the Directory; his probity was proverbial and he was to pay off the public debt of France; Duchâtel, noble and receiver of taxes under the late King; and Du Fresne, one of those old work-horse civil servants the Revolution had not even bothered to displace.

Justice had Boulay-of-the-Meurthe, Sieyès' friend; with Berlier, a *votant* and hot Jacobin gone cold enough to become one of the most judicial minds of France; and Réal, public accuser during the days of the Terror, spy for Robespierre and then for Fouché, "a man sold to power" whose virtue was that he honestly delivered a considerable degree of talent to the power that purchased him.

Next to them in the section of the Interior sat Rœderer, philosopher and publicist of almost terrifying erudition, disciple of Sieyès and deadly in debate; with Cretet, a new man come up during the Revolution along obscure byways of finance; Regnault de St. Jean d'Angély, who had been up to his neck in plots of a quasi-royalist aspect five years before, but a powerful orator in a gay, gasconading style, and had done well under Bonaparte's lead as Governor of Malta; Fourcroy, the most brilliant scientist of France, and presently in charge of public education, no politics neither; Chaptal, another man of science, whose one excursion into politics had been on the side of the Girondins.

Right, left, and center, with a certain balance toward those who had been in the Revolution but moderate in it, or had grown out of violence to responsibility, an administration of confidence with all pasts forgiven. "The Revolution is over," pronounced the public placards; when the new prefect enters Bordeaux the people turn out to receive him with vivats and an escort of cavalry, whereas from the missionaries of the Terror they ran to hide. The Revolution is over, the roads become safe, justice no longer stumbles on a leaden foot. *Liberté, égalité, fraternité,* but the second is the first in importance; égalité is what France thought she had gained from the Revolution, and found there had been substituted, as a key to privilege, the test of a man's political opinions for the test of his armorial bearings. But now—now there have been named to sit side by side in the Senate (this is what has become of Sieyès' College of Conservators), now there have been named to the Senate that Monge who was Minister of Marine under the Terror, Garat the liberal, De Tracy who was once a Royalist, Perregaux the financial oligarch; and if a man has committed a crime, it does not matter how highly placed he be or by what standards high—the First Consul is appealed to and the accused must face the just and terrible Cambacérès.

Bonaparte is appealed to. This is the key of the new administration. The delight with which that régime was hailed, the universal readiness to co-operate, was in no small part an expression of the universal desire for security and order that follows on the heels of any great upheaval. Any government which offered as much would doubtless have been similarly approved, whatever its professions of principle. The question of how this security was achieved became purely academic beside the triumphant fact that the ship was in harbor at last; and to this extent Bonaparte was a beneficiary.

Of the seventeen Councilors of State, the legislative and administrative mechanicians of the government, no fewer than nine had been either in prison or in hiding during the better part of seven years. In the main it escaped attention that the new structure under which they were living was the somewhat arbitrary creation of a single mind, for it was seen as Sieyès' constitution, and Sieyès, with Roger-Ducos, Cambacérès, and Lebrun, drew up the list of twenty-nine Senators, who were to co-opt the necessary colleagues to get the instrument running without having to go through the complex process of an election for which no machinery had yet been set up. General Bonaparte was merely the man to see when the police had been supine about an unsolved murder, and it would hardly have mattered if he had appeared in quite another guise. Like the lady who called at Malmaison, they were quite ready to allow him to write executive decrees with the point of the sword.

Like Bonaparte himself, the majority of Frenchmen had been so long concerned with form and idea in government as to be convinced that form and idea were illusions. Defermon and Gaudin, for instance, otherwise the perfect antithesis, the one who had been forced to change his residence daily because his thoughts as to the form of society happened to conflict with those officially held, the other almost immune to thoughts outside his business. Both were pure technicians, withheld from the application to the common good of undoubted talents by opposite means, but for the same reason —that while problems of political economy are being worked out in the laboratory of the nation, mere executives need not apply. "The Republic has no use for chemical experiments," said the Revolution and sent Lavoisier to the scaffold.

The Consulate has use for a chemical experimenter at the

head of its educational system; it has use for an ex-Foreign Minister of the Directory, Delacroix—make him prefect of Marseille; an ex-Director, Letourneur—prefect of Nantes; and his ex-Finance Minister, Faypoult—prefect of Ghent. Time was lacking to elect the lists of notables according to the elaborate and ingenious system of Sieyès, with Austrian armies hammering at the border and local government in ruins. Let the lists be made, by all means. It is the duty and privilege of Frenchmen to see the task well done, but in the meanwhile the central executive authority must appoint men to get the machine running.

What men? The central executive authority had no lists of notables and could only seek out those who in one way or another displayed a certain amount of ability as mere executives. Not quite so difficult a task as might be imagined, for each of the successive revolutions that made up the Revolution dismissed the executives of the previous dispensation and brought forward a certain number of new men. In this administration where all pasts are forgiven there is no reason why they should be forgotten. It is forgiven to M. Français de Nantes that he once made fiery speeches in favor of rendering the practice of any religion a crime, but not forgotten that he was one of the ablest tax-lawyers of France, and he is made prefect of Lyon; forgiven to Beugnot of Bar that he spent two years in jail for being involved in royalist plots, but not forgotten that he administered the affairs of the district courts with the utmost skill—make him prefect of Rouen. . . . Forty years later some of those prefects were still in office, the single-minded, quiet, dutiful executives who remade France.

Bonaparte was thus a beneficiary. But it is important to recognize that he was the beneficiary chiefly of his own system; because his public proclamations could say the Revolution was over and mean it, because when de Bourmont or D'Andigné came to persuade him to restore the Bourbons, he could persuade them instead to join the new France. It seemed clear to every Frenchman how this had come about.

It was because the Chief of State was himself a scientist-technician-executive, in however different a field. No science, no business, is conducted on so honestly empirical a basis as that of war. When the guns begin to shoot, all forms, all ideas, lose importance in the face of the practical question of who shall hold the field at the close of action, and no favoritism can reinstate a regiment in a position that the enemy has taken at the point of the bayonet.

"I would not hesitate to order the arrest of the Minister of the Interior himself!" cried Fouché one day, after Laplace had been succeeded in office by Bonaparte's brother Lucien. It is possible that the remark was made with malice prepense, for the great policeman's most impulsive action was thought out at least a week in advance. But he knew his man; the First Consul smiled and approved.

II

This devotion to specialized efficiency produced its own series of drawbacks. The tribunate was one of them. The constitution made it a kind of authorized Opposition headquarters, a place where the stormy, argumentative spirits could exercise their lungs without too much hampering the operations of the government. In accordance with this idea the committee of selection (Sieyès, Cambacérès, Roger-Ducos, Lebrun) had placed on the list as tribunes men like Chénier the poet, Andrieux the orator, Sieyès' argumentative friend Daunou, and above all, Benjamin Constant.

Benjamin Constant. He was living with Germaine de Staël at the time, drinking deep the heady mixture of sensibility, idealism, ambition, and intrigue that welled so unfailingly from the mind of the new Aspasia. She knew all the gossip well enough to be aware when the lists for the Tribunate were being drawn up and sent her protégé around to see Bonaparte about nine o'clock in the evening. At eleven Constant was still arguing for a place; at midnight the favor was granted and the new Tribune departed without thanks in such a passion of delight that Bonaparte was left with a frown and a mental question as to whether the insult had been intentional.

It had not, of course; Benjamin Constant was merely enraptured at discovering himself in a place so perfectly suited to his talents that he could hardly miss greatness. The next day he met Chénier, Andrieux, and Daunou at de Staël's. They concurred perfectly that the tribunate was a pulpit from which they could expose liberal views under the very shadow and license of the government, without encountering those difficulties which are imposed upon orators in elective assemblies by the odious necessity of belonging to a party. "Government must be set free from parties, whose services are illusory and dearly bought," pronounced Constant; and at the same time, government must learn to do without "the intoxicating and destructive resource of arbitrary action."

The nature of a government that was neither that of a party nor that of a partyless arbitrary head did not concern him; he belonged to an Opposition secure against being forced to translate principles into practice, able to employ every act of those in power as an opportunity for the restatement of absolute principles: the natural rights of man— personal liberty, liberty of religion, liberty of personal expression ("A revolution is nothing but the citizens' criticism of arbitrary acts of government") ; and the rights of man in his social capacity—the absolute inviolability of property, liberty of industry, the right of petition.

The very first project of law submitted by the Council of State gave the new tribunes a chance to strike a note clear as a bell. It was a matter of procedure, regulating the process by which laws should move from one of the legislative bodies to another, a subject on which the constitution was silent, Sieyès being above such petty details. It provided that unless the Legislative Jury granted a special exception, the Tribunate should not discuss a law for more than three days.

Rœderer, who brought it in for the Council, explained that it was needed to keep laws from being merely talked to death, as so often happened with those submitted by the Directory to its legislative. Benjamin Constant to the tribune —the awkward, gangling youth who had begun a history of human religion on the backs of playing cards was by now become one of the handsomest men in France; his style had hardened and refined under the constant reading of Voltaire, he was now master of that combination of antithesis and irony always so appealing to Frenchmen.

—The urgency laws passed by the Convention (he said) were always bad; but we now have a government that proposes to give us nothing but urgency laws. Why is it that this government assigns to its only deliberative body the meanest of its public edifices, the old Palais Royal? Why is so much care expended in pushing everything rapidly through this body? Why are we considered so hostile that it is necessary to leave laws for the least possible time among us? All this leads straight to the false idea that we are nothing but a corps of objectors, with no function but that of contradicting the government, which must enfeeble our position in public opinion and subject us to the necessity of having every proposition flung past us on the wing, so that we are unable to seize it or to grasp its significance.

He looked around. "As for those who speak to us of the idols of fifteen days, let them remember that in these walls the Tiers État met and an idol of fifteen centuries was overthrown."

It was a splendid speech, thrown into higher relief by the fact that Honoré Riouffe, who made the reply, was prolix and dull, running off into a long panegyric on Bonaparte till the assembled Tribunes began to stamp feet, to whistle, and to shout, "Talk about the law!" When Constant reached de Staël's salon that evening she placed a laurel wreath on his head in a pretty little private ceremony, and called him "the second Mirabeau."

III

The First Consul did not take so amiable a view, nor were matters mended by the extravagant delight with which the

opposition newspapers welcomed the speech, all Paris talking of little else, and a *spectacle* made of it, which Fouché
had to suppress. Tribune Miot de Melito, coming in on
Bonaparte in the evening to report that in spite of Constant
the body had voted 56–34 to send speakers favorable to the
project before the Legislative Jury, found the chief thunder-
browed over his midnight chocolate. Miot protested that
Constant was a valuable man, much talent, only necessary to
attach him to the government . . . "My enemies deserve
from me nothing but steel," growled Bonaparte.

He was devoured by a terrible sense of urgency—the man
who said he might lose battles but he would not lose minutes.
"What I need is time," he told aide-de-camp Junot, "and
time is the one thing I cannot afford." He knew that any
method of procedure that did not absolutely hinder legislation would work as long as operated by reasonably honest
and intelligent executives, the kind less concerned with laurel
leaves and public prints than with the work they were doing.
As for Constant's reference of every action to principle—
bah! Where were the principles of his own craft when he
had led a column through the hostile batteries at the bridge
of Lodi and first attained the concept that destiny might
have something in store for him? Here as there, the necessity
was speed; France was surrounded by enemies.

On 5 nivôse, the day after the new government took office
(in costumes by David), identical notes had gone out to the
King of England and the Austrian Emperor—"France summons me to the first position in the state"—and can we not
have a soldier's peace, now that the untrustworthy old government of the Directors has been replaced by one with firm
roots in the nation? Already Austria's reply was at hand—
polite, conciliatory, meaningless. The English reply would
follow in a week and make it clear that for the Allies this
new government was no more than Barras in a uniform
jacket, a repetition on a ten-year theme:

> Greatly indeed would his Majesty rejoice whenever it shall ap-
> pear that the danger to his own dominions and those of his Allies,

has ceased; whenever he shall be satisfied that after the experience of so many years of crimes and miseries, better principles have prevailed in France; and that all the gigantic projects of ambition, and all the ruthless schemes of destruction, which have endangered the very existence of civil society, have at length been finally relinquished. The best and most natural pledge of the reality and permanence of such a change would be the restoration of that line of princes who for many centuries maintained the French nation in prosperity at home and in consideration and respect abroad. Such an event will at any time remove all obstacles in the way of negotiation of peace.

GRENVILLE

"I might reply that France will make no peace till England restores the Stuarts," sneered Bonaparte, but—*la patrie en danger*—and not less than in the days when a red banner flew over the Pont Neuf and the Convention decreed a levy *en masse*. Only General Bonaparte, gathering all the threads through the hands of that admirable military drudge, the Minister of War and Chief of Staff Berthier, could understand how great the danger was. When Danton flung to the coalized kings of Europe the head of a king, there had been within the breaking frontiers an inexhaustible reserve of Frenchmen who thought it bliss to be alive in that dawn, who needed only muskets and a song to march under any leader whatever in those dense columns of attack that had carried them from Valmy to the heights that slope down toward Vienna.

This is an older, colder cosmos, where people along the roads stare in hungry apathy and a brigade quits its post at the Alpine border to quarter itself in a region where the foraging is better. If the reserves of enthusiasm are running out, the physical reserves not less so. France's best army is marooned in Egypt, 30,000 strong with a sea full of English cruisers between. The wonderful Army of Italy has been beaten and beaten; its morale shaken, its soldiers starving and without ammunition, it lies pressed back to the Ligurian shore, no more than 36,000 men under Championnet, an officer who has no more confidence in his soldiers than they in him. He is faced by Melas of Austria, with his 60,000 and 20,000 more in reserve. In the background of Austria hangs that great Russian force under the invincible Suvorov who has already beaten the French from north Italy; and the Russ may even be bound for the Rhine frontier, where the prospects are as good as even but will not stay so under their weight.

Jean-Victor Moreau commanded there, esteemed the best blade in France, better than Bonaparte even; Sieyès had wished to use him rather than the corporal of Corsica in making his new state. Moreau had 100,000 men and those of the best; but across the dark stream stood equal strength under Archduke Karl Ludwig of Teschen, the ablest soldier Hapsburg ever produced, who had sent France flying into retreat the autumn before. In the background of the north loomed land-hungry Prussia, her Polish difficulties settled, ready to throw in Frederick the Great's perfect army whenever she might gain with little loss.

Fortunately, there was reason to believe that not all marched well among those Allies against France. From Italy General Championnet, from the Alps General Masséna, reported that Russian uniforms had not been seen since vendémaire, when the latter inflicted on Marshal Suvorov that appalling defeat at Zürich, the first in the old Marshal's life, which broke his heart. A tale floated in that the Austrian Empress had overnight become mad jealous of the beautiful princess of Hungary, daughter to the Tsar; forbidden her the court. Bonaparte sent for all possible men who knew Russians, that strange race who came so late to European civilization that they must be perpetually reassured that the rest of the world considers them a part of it.

There was no doubt: the Tsar who had sent him such peculiar communications when Malta was taken away from the moribund knightly order of St. John was quite mad; an undeveloped adolescent who had compensated for his dwarfish size, waddling gait, and ugliness by slipping back into the age of chivalry. Something might be made of that. Among the cities of Flanders were some 7,000 Russian prisoners, taken in the late campaign when the British tried to invade Holland. They had been specifically excluded from the cartel for the exchange of prisoners because England had too few Frenchmen behind the bars to feel able to ransom Russians at the price of her own men. But this refusal was capable of another interpretation and Bonaparte hoped the Tsar would reach it when he had the 7,000 fitted with new uniforms and arms and sent them back to Russia with a letter saying he could not keep in prison men who had fought so valorously. Moreover Malta (now under close blockade and siege by the British) was herewith freely ceded by France to Tsar Paul I, as Grand Master of the Knightly Order and sure shield of Europe against the heathen Turk.

Prussia was playing close companion of the Russ at the time, already vaguely linked with the Northern League against the Revolution which Tsar Paul had been forming. To that court the First Consul sent his personal aide-de-camp, Brigadier Duroc, "the best-beloved man in France"— brilliantly educated, who could make epigrams in three languages and had seen all the hard fighting in the Egyptian campaign. If Bonaparte's appointments were not all so good, it could be called a remarkably happy choice. The young Prussian King had reformed the bad, mad, mystical court of his father; dismissed the harem of thirty-four professional mistresses and all the singular political harpies who used to revel with them, deciding to rule alone like a true Hohenzollern. He had been brought up in the camp and his tastes were those of a military ascetic; when Duroc presented his credentials, His Majesty talked for an hour on end, all about the battle of Jaffa and the siege of St. Jean d'Acre, never a word of politics; and ended by inviting the new envoy to dine.

The dispatch about this reception reached Paris toward the close of rainy pluviôse. Bonaparte went to work on his military plans without further reference to Prussia.

THE WORM'S-EYE VIEW—III

. . . I am here to see Suwarrow on business, and am not sorry for the opportunity of seeing one of whom one has heard so many and such extraordinary things. Indeed, it is impossible to say how extraordinary he is. I must not on any account be quoted, but he is the most perfect Bedlamite that ever was allowed to be at large. To give some little notion of his manners, I went by appointment to pay my last visit, which I was told would be one of ceremony. I was fully dressed; after waiting a good while in an antechamber with some aides-de-camp, a door opened and a little old shrivelled creature in a pair of red breeches and his shirt for all clothing bustled up to me, took me in his arms, and embracing me with his shirt sleeves, made me a string of high-flown flummery compliments. We all got up yesterday at six in the morning to attend him at Mass. We saw him crawl on all fours to kiss the ground and hold his head on the ground almost a quarter of an hour with various other antics. The vocal music however was good and interested us.

After Mass we dined at about nine o'clock, and sat till twelve, by which time all our heads were splitting. Before dinner Frere and Casamajor were presented to him. The latter being extremely tall and Suwarrow very short, he jumped up on a chair to get at Casamajor's neck and kiss him. He began before we sat down to dinner by drinking a tumbler full of rololio or strong liqueur, the heat of which seemed to take away his breath. It is the sort of thing that people drink thimblefuls of. At dinner he drank a variety of strong things, among others a cupful of champagne, which went round the table; and as the bottle was going round, he held out his beer tumbler and had it again filled with champagne. Afterward a servant filled him a large tumbler of something which I did not know, but I presume was not water. He talked incessantly and unintelligibly, becoming more and more inarticulate. As I sat next to him, I was really bored to death. Such are heroes, and thus the world is led, and such is fame and name. It is a correct picture of this mad mountebank.

Lord Minto to Lady Minto from Prague

4

ARMY OF PHANTOMS

Paris, Genoa, Geneva: pluviôse—floréal, An VIII
(January–May 1900)

DIJON in Burgundy is famous for its cookery. The main road comes through from Paris and runs on across the mountains of Franche-Comté to Geneva, throwing off a branch in the valley of the Doubs to Mulhouse in Alsace. To Dijon, as soon as they were set free by the capitulation of La Vendée, Bonaparte directed the 20,000 men who had been brought down from the campaign in Holland to be the steel fingers within the velvet glove of his clemency. They were designated the Army of The Reserve, and the papers described their movement with loud adjectives. From that central position, they would either make Moreau on the Rhine irresistible, or enable General Suchet on the Var to break into the plains of Italy as Bonaparte had in '96. The new army would receive all the conscripts coming forward in such numbers. General Berthier himself was to command it, Bonaparte's staff genius; to replace him at the War Ministry, Carnot Organizer-of-victory was called from retirement and a sentence of deportation.

Paris was full of Austrian spies that winter. It could not be otherwise with so many émigrés returning. Most were inclined to agree with the anti-Bonapartist press that the optimistic statements about the Army of The Reserve repre-

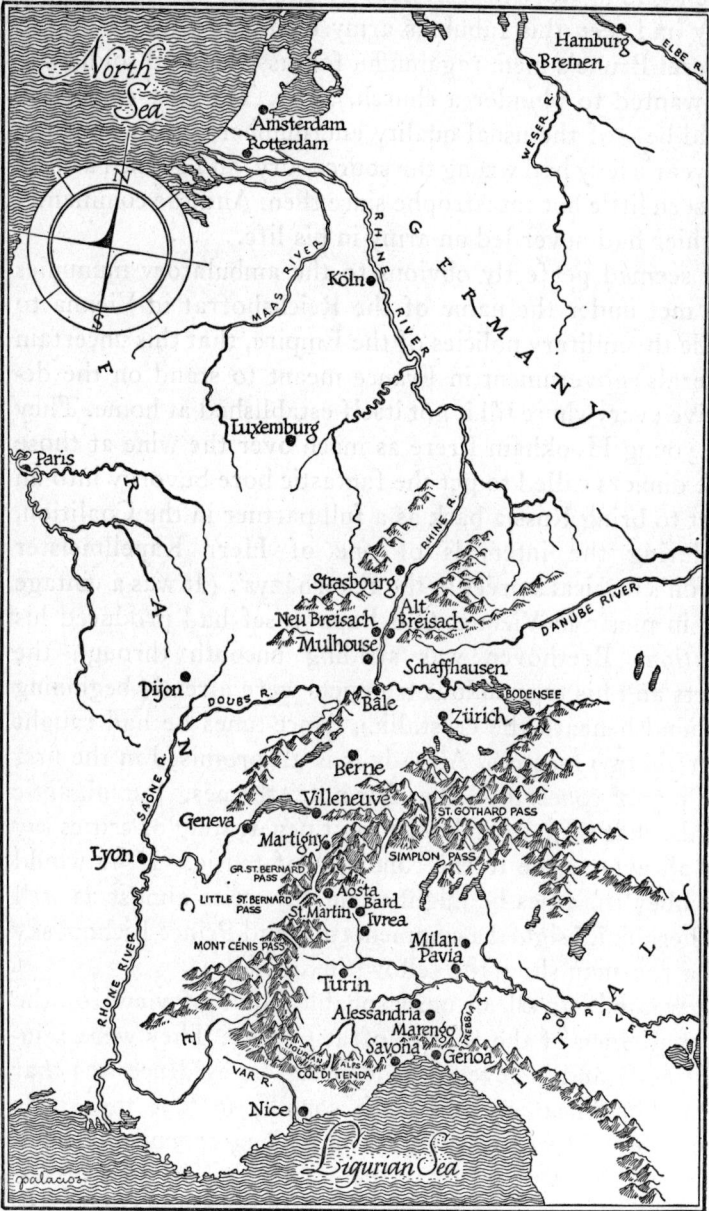

sented gilding for the clay feet of the idol of fifteen days. They had seen this fabulous army tramping through Paris, General Brune's men, ragamuffin fantassins, good soldiers if you wanted to plunder a church, alors. The new conscripts would be—of the usual quality and numbers, given that the last year's levy had wrung the sources dry, and French armies had seen little but catastrophe since then. And the command? Berthier had never led an army in his life.

It seemed perfectly obvious to the ambulatory mummies who met under the name of the Reichshofrat in Vienna to decide the military policies of the Empire, that this uncertain Generals' government in France meant to stand on the defensive everywhere till it got itself established at home. They told young Hookham Frere as much over the wine at those state dinners called to pet the fantastic bore Suvorov into an effort to bring Russia back as a full partner in the Coalition, or during the intervals of one of Herr Kapellmeister Haydn's musical soirées at the Esterházys'. (It was a vintage year in music in Vienna. Old Papa Josef had produced his *Creation;* Beethoven was striding uncouth through the streets and his tremendous trumpets were already beginning to sound beneath the crystalline dance-tunes he had caught from his two masters. Already it is all promised in the first two piano concertos—the few-note themes, the gigantic chords, that were to make the most penetrating of critics say that all arts aspire to the condition of music. "If he would only obey the rules he might some day write almost as well as Cherubini," sighed a commentator, and Prince Lichnovsky had a footman show the fellow the door.)

It was not at all an unreasonable point of view for the old gentlemen of the Reichshofrat to take. They were a judicial body and believed in evidence. The evidence was that Austria had beaten the French soundly in '99; the Gauls were in a state of disorganization, strung around the semicircle of Alpine passes that enclose the headwaters of the Po, their right wing on Genoa. Neither their disposition nor numbers were secrets at Vienna; there were two wings, under

Generals Suchet and Soult, the former holding the left of that sweeping curve from the Mont Cenis pass down to the Col di Tenda, where the mountains run north and south. Soult's command picked up there to carry the line east to Genoa along the crests of the Ligurian Alps. Suchet had a division 4,000 strong in the Mont Cenis under General Thurreau, all the rest much scattered, some back along the Var for sustenance, and all in bad shape physically, 18,000 together.

Soult has about 20,000 in the French right wing, with Division Miollis of 8,000 in Genoa, the rest among the passes. All are hungry and ridden with typhoid, for the Ligurian Sea is full of English cruisers and the normal mode of transport along that rugged shore is by water. All these commanders were names on a piece of paper to Austria, but the overall chief who came down to take charge of the Italian frontier as the old century closed was more than a name. He was André Masséna, the silent, dark, dour man who had begun his adventures as a smuggler in these same mountains and came to the day when Bonaparte hailed him on the plateau of Rivoli as "Enfant chéri de la victoire." A dangerous man; it was he who broke the stout Russians at Zürich last summer, and old Suvorov's heart. But a commander is only as dangerous as the instrument he wields, and this one is now hardly a menace against the 60,000 commanded by our General Melas.

Michael Friedrich Melas, who can be sufficiently dangerous himself on the field of battle. Seventy-one now, but all his life a soldier, a stout old gnarled oak from the seven mountains of Hungary, still full of sap as on the day when he won his first promotion in the field, by covering the retreat to Lugos with a single regiment of hussars against an entire Turkish army. He was in person among the bullets at Cassano and the Trebbia in '99; nothing on a battlefield ever escaped his experienced eye, and after the fighting was over, Suvorov embraced him publicly, declaring that it was the skill of Melas had made a drawn battle into a victory and a victory into the rout of the enemy.

This was good enough to win him a high command, but the old men in Vienna could not avoid suspecting that Baron Melas, so much less brilliant than brave, was nearly as much of a danger to his friends at the council table as to his enemies in the field. They therefore propped him up with a careful plan of campaign and a strong staff—Freiherr Zach for the chief of the latter, who looked like a conscripted schoolmaster and was said to know more than any other man in the world, with young Radetzky for adjutant, all fire and quick decision, "the darling of the army."

The Reichshofrat ordered a winter campaign, to capture Genoa first, then work into southern France with the co-operation of the British fleet and a force of 20,000 men the British would gather in Minorca. But Melas' supplies and ammunition did not come, neither did England, there was a heavy fall of snow in Liguria at the end of February, so he wisely kept his men in cantonment till April while the French froze among the rocks. By that month the troops were all afoot.

The divisions of Wukassovitch, Haddick, and Kaim, under command of the last, were left in the Turin region with much of the army's cavalry and most of its mobile artillery, to exercise continual pressure on the passes held by Suchet's men. They outnumbered the French 25 to 18. On the extreme Austrian left, General Ott was given 15,000 men to ascend the valley of the Trebbia in an attack whose main purpose was to keep the French from breaking out eastward. Graf Hohenzollern, with a force mainly cavalry, held the Scrivia Valley and the main road north from Genoa, making the connection between Ott and Melas' personal command, which was the main corps of battle, working from Acqui up to the sources of the Bormida around Ceva. Here a wing under Elsnitz split off into the broken country westward, forming a flank against the French from the Col di Tenda and the region of the Var. Melas with his 23,000 men would reverse through the same passes the direction Bonaparte had taken in his great campaign of 1796, fall on Savona, break the French line, and then lay Genoa under siege.

II

The countryside was anti-French, and Melas' orders to keep his preliminary troop movements secret were obeyed. The first notice Masséna had was on the morning of April 5, a rainy day, when Ott's column drove in his outposts on the watershed of the Trebbia. Hohenzollern attacked the same morning, but instead of putting all his force in to break down a flank as instructed, he spread wide, trying to get round both flanks and through the center all at once, according to the cordon system in which the Austrian army had been trained. Masséna's Division Gazan beat him off. At the same time all the church-bells in the region east around Genoa began to ring and the peasantry to turn out with fowling pieces for a shot at a Frenchman. Masséna thought Ott's must be the main Austrian attack he had been worrying about; shifted his reserve through the city during the day of the 6th and early on the morning counterattacked Ott and drove him from the hillcrests.

There was no pursuit. Before evening the French commander had the dreadful news that Melas had appeared on the upper Bormida with forces a division strong against every French battalion; had broken through at once and was in Savona across the communication line back to France.

Cut off.

Masséna had made energetic efforts to get more food into Genoa, but most of his corn convoys were still behind the Var. He instantly dropped a division to hold the eastern passes against Ott and turned back with his whole mobile force, Soult leading one column, himself another, to re-establish the line. One took the hill road through Sasello and Voltri, the other the normal coast route—an eccentric, but Masséna counted on bringing them together again by a

quick march across the hills to Montenotte, where Bonaparte won his battle in '96. Unfortunately this movement
bucked head-on into Melas' general offensive, and Masséna's
own column along the coast was beaten back under the drive
of four times its number of Austrians on the 10th. Soult in
the hills won a battle against Melas' flank guard round Voltri the next morning and there was savage fighting along the
slopes for three days more, but Melas kept pushing his big
columns in and the end of it was that the Ides of April found
Masséna completely locked in Genoa, requisitioning all the
grain in town, even oats, to make bread.

The ambulatory mummies in Vienna could permit themselves a certain amount of satisfaction. Back in January they
had called before them the Archduke Karl, the best soldier
of Hapsburg and of Austria, and he had told them the
French peace offer should be accepted. This was (he said)
high tide; for the coming campaign there would be sub-
tracted from their own side Suvorov and his Russians, while
to the other there would be added the mind and the sword of
Bonaparte; and neither did he like the look of that Army of
The Reserve.

The old gentlemen had looked somewhat sour on that,
and Baron Thugut, who was the head of them, thought
Karl's melancholy mood bespoke failing health. His Highness ought to (and did, in the upshot) give over command
of the Rhine army for a period of recruitment at his castle
in Bohemia. As for the Army of The Reserve, it was becoming increasingly clear that it existed only as an effort of the
French artistic imagination. Bonaparte was having trouble
with his press and had clapped a censorship down to silence
the windy little liberals of the Benjamin Constant type, so
news of troop movements no longer came through this normal channel. But just previous to the order of silence the
papers had reported a grand review and parade of the Army
of The Reserve at Dijon for the benefit of the First Consul
himself. There were Austrian agents at the review; they
were unanimous that it was a sorry performance, by not

above 6,000 green young conscripts and limping veterans. The 20,000 from Holland had apparently gone back there on some rumor of an English landing. General Melas was so advised, as he drew his lines along the hills that are the outer defense of Genoa, while the English fleet moved in to bombard.

III

To General Moreau:

The main body of the Army of the Rhine to cross the stream between 20 and 30 germinal near Schaffhausen, march on Stokach in order to turn the Black Forest and render null the enemy's preparations to defend its gorges, push the left wing of the enemy beyond the Lech.

The day when the Army of the Rhine passes the stream, the three first divisions of the Army of Reserve will assemble at Dijon from Châlons and Lyon and march on Geneva. The second three divisions will leave Dijon in the early days of floréal and proceed to Zürich. The towns from Strasbourg to Bâle will be the assembly points for conscripts and replacements, and these, with the garrison battalions, will guard the river against any forward movement of the enemy.

The depot at Geneva will be under the immediate orders of the Army of Reserve, and is to receive at once 100,000 bundles of rye, 500,000 rations of biscuit, 2,000,000 cartridges, and 500,000 rations of brandy.

By order of the FIRST CONSUL

There is the plan, simple and gigantic as a Beethoven concerto. (Not yet the full symphony—not yet the prolonged and intricate orchestration of all the instruments of war.) Moreau is to throw himself on the rear of the Austrian left flank with 100,000 fighting men, driving their army north of the Swabian highland and placing himself on the main road to Vienna. Even if they turned back from the Rhine in time to avoid disaster they must fight backed up to their line of communications, and with their front a prolongation of it, most dangerous of positions. Meanwhile the Army of Reserve, secretly assembled in the shadow of the glare provided by its overpublicity, would march through Geneva-Bern-Zürich, 50,000 strong (guarding Moreau's rear against counterattack during the process), and be projected past the flanks of the locked armies across the affluents of the Danube; straight on the heart and brain of the Empire at Vienna. Nothing that happened in Italy would matter.

But Jean-Victor Moreau refused. He was a big man with a flat face, as to his emotions at once envious and modest, so sincere a republican by intellectual conviction that he had held firm to the Revolution even when it guillotined his father. Believed that the office should seek the man; and had himself been sought by Sieyès to furnish the military arm, when the latter decided to overthrow the old Directory as the only means of saving the Republic. They were in consultation on the matter when a secretary brought in the news that Bonaparte was back from Egypt. "There's your man," said Moreau; "he will do it much better than I." That was modesty; but now the other mainspring began to operate and he refused point-blank to serve under Bonaparte, who reserved to himself command of the Army of Reserve and general direction of the movement.

France could not afford to dispense with a soldier of Moreau's ability, who moreover knew the Black-Forest-Swabian country where the campaign was to be fought as well as his own bedroom—better, for he had slept more in camps than at home. A new plan, then. Moreau's move should be as before, through Schaffhausen and Stokach, with one large corps of four divisions to cover his Rhine Army's rear. Half the Army of Reserve should push through to Zürich as before, then fall under Moreau's orders. When it reached station the four-division group would turn south through the St. Gothard pass toward Milan and central Italy, to be joined there by the other three divisions of the Army of Reserve, entering through the western Alps, the whole striking a blow against Melas, while Moreau operated along the Danube.

Berthier himself went down to Bâle to arrange matters.

He crossed the movement of Moreau's own chief of staff going to Paris with objection, objection, objection—he could not spare for the Italian project so large a detachment from his own force as four divisions, even in exchange for part of the Army of Reserve; the state of the roads, the position of the enemy and a dozen other things did not permit him to make a move so far to the flank as proposed. He thought he could more properly operate a crossing of the Rhine in the face of the enemy at Bâle, the Breisachs, Strasbourg and Kehl.

To General Moreau:

2 FLORÉAL

I have received, citizen General, your letter. The weather is good; your troops are numerous and well led. Our confidence in you is complete. Send us some enemy battle-flags and plenty of prisoners.

BONAPARTE

IV

Bourrienne came in to find Chauchard's big map of Italy unrolled across the floor. The First Consul was flat on his stomach over it, with the frog-faced Berthier squatted behind him, busily engaged in sticking in wax-headed pins—red for the Austrians, black for the positions and movements of the French. As the secretary watched, the black heads of the Army of Reserve drew together from its depots toward Dijon, moved across Vaudrey and Rissoux to Geneva, each pin a day's march, across the lake, then swung into the passes round the foot of Chamonix, between the summits called the Silvery Needle and the Red and so down past Aosta——

"Where do you think I shall beat Melas, Bourrienne?"

"How the devil should I know?"

"Idiot. Look: Melas has his headquarters at Alessandria with his magazines, his hospitals, his artillery, and his reserves. There he will remain till Genoa surrenders. Crossing the Alps here, I shall fall upon him, cut his communications with Austria, and meet him at San Giuliano."

Bourrienne smiled politely, making the inward remark

that this business of maps and pins was a rather silly game. Outwardly he said that he had come on some business connected with that estate of Villiers which the General was buying as a delayed wedding present for his pretty sister Caroline, who had three months before married Murat, the cavalry general. The First Consul called his secretary a fool, tweaked his ear amiably, and signed whatever paper was necessary. Everything connected with that marriage put General Bonaparte in a good humor these days. In more than one way it promised the healing of an ancient feud—one of those intrafamily contests which always give trouble in households living by the Italiote tradition that the fortune of any member is to be shared by all. For pretty Caroline had sought the appui of Madame Joséphine de Beauharnais-Bonaparte in obtaining consent to the marriage, after brother Napoléon, as executive head of the family, cried; "What! Shall he mingle his blood with mine? Why, he is nothing but the son of an innkeeper!"

But something clearly had to be done about the girl. The First Consul had permitted himself to announce in the official *Moniteur* that one of his sisters was to marry Jean-Victor Moreau, and pretty Caroline was the only one who did not already have a husband. Jean-Victor, who had not been consulted before the announcement, went to Bâle and the army headquarters instead of to the altar, and that made the Bonaparte family ridiculous; but by a system of logic which has never escaped the boundaries of Gaul, the stigma would be considered as erased by her marriage to another man. Besides, Joséphine asked it, a sign of reconciliation, one of those guarantees by symbolic action which are so important among Latins: a double guarantee. Murat had been her lover during the campaign of '96—if not her first infidelity, at least the earliest of which her husband had certain knowledge—and the personal coolness between the two officers lasted till Bonaparte saw the cavalryman's plume blaze among the Turkish squadrons at Aboukir, where he saved the army. The appeal for the marriage, then, was Joséphine's farewell to lighter years; she had no more to fear or to hope from lovers, she was concerned with the family.

The family who hated her so, and so sought to undo her. They had met the General on the road when he returned

Pulled from bed to add their cries to their mother's

from Egypt—Joseph, Lucien, and little Louis—producing a detailed account of his lady's infidelities and her intrigues with the Directory, precise as a ledger. An unpleasant scene, at the close of which the General went home to lock himself in his bedroom; while Joséphine, who had started too late

and had taken the wrong road in the effort to get her story
in before that of the vindictive relatives, sobbed and beat the
door till her lamentations filled the house where all Paris
had once hailed her as "Our Lady of the Victories." Her
maid found a way through it. "Bring the children," she said,
and little Hortense and Eugène de Beauharnais were pulled
from bed to add their cries to their mother's. At three in the
morning the door came open; at seven, brother Lucien was
summoned to see the reconciliation accomplished in spite of
him, and now—now she had repaid evil with good, and by
her services for pretty Caroline had found herself a partisan
in the very heart of the family that so cruelly wronged her.
Could the hand of friendship, thus offered, be refused?

. . . Bonaparte called Bourrienne a fool and told him to
roll up the map. The date was 15 floréal. That day there was
a clash between Moreau's outposts and the whitecoats on the
shores of the Bodensee.

V

The chief of engineers was named Marescot, one of those
men so precise that they obscure every statement with a superabundance of detail. It was by no means easy for an army
with guns to enter Italy through the western passes. He believed the arrangement for dismounting the light artillery
and having it pulled through the snow on sledges was sound.
With a hundred men to a gun, and considering the angle of
ascent, the factor of safety was of a mathematical order that
promised insignificant impediments, unless a fresh precipi-
tation——

"Can we get through?" demanded Bonaparte.

"I believe so; but with extraordinary efforts."

"*Eh bien, allons.*" He stood up and stepped into the next
room to change into a uniform from the common blue coat
he had worn while calling on M. Necker, the moth-eaten old
saint of finance—a disconnected interview. The banker had
lately taken to addressing himself as "magistrate of the

truth," and behaved as though he held a patent for that commodity, with a long prosy lecture on how the head of the French state must see that happiness could not exist unless the government met all its obligations, even including those swindling bonds of arrearage and of requisition whose existence had so disturbed the wall-eyed Gaudin. Bonaparte interrupted him with a counterlecture about imposing some sense of responsibility upon his daughter, the de Staël, who was getting dangerously close to Royalism. Both men promised and neither meant it, for they understood one another about as well as a Zulu and a Chinese, and they parted with feelings of mutual disrespect. "Very ordinary fellow," grumped the philosophical financier, and, "Wheezy old schoolmaster," said the General.

Now adieu to all that, blue coat and ambiguity. The troops are moving, the van is led by Jean Lannes, small, neat, with his rolling Gascon oaths and pomaded knot of hair behind, all covered with scars, for he has been wounded in every battle since Bonaparte saw him lead the whirlwind past at Dego. The corps of Victor has the rear—circular Victor, "Beau Soleil" for the jolly red face so frequently alight with wine, an old companion from the General's past of the days at Toulon siege and the Paris barricades. Murat has the cavalry, Marmont the guns. Guillaume-Philibert Duhesme commands the infantry corps of the center; a soldier who has mounted step by step the rungs of command on courage and a capacity for keeping his men under control, which is merely courage in another dimension among Revolutionary levies, who could appeal to the nearest commissioner and get a general guillotined. Duhesme has no head and it does not matter; a messenger from Lannes says the first Austrian outpost has been driven in, it is adieu to the old attorneys of Paris, and to family affairs and back to the honest life of the camp, with a bed in a cloak on cold stones or at some peasant's hut.

"What do you need to make you happy?" the First Consul asked one such, who was guiding through the snows the mule of this unknown but evidently important man, muffled in the longcloak.

"A mule like the one you are riding."

Two months later a commissioner of the French Republic brought him the animal with a deed to certain arpents of land, and tools for tillage.

Guiding through the snows

WRONG END OF THE TELESCOPE—II

Courier and Evening Gazette, London:

NEW CALENDAR.—A correſpondent, in a merry Chriſtmas mood, has amuſed himſelf with giving us a new ſet of names to the months, *a la Francoiſe*. They run thus, beginning with April:

Spring:	Showery,	Flowery,	Bowery.
Summer:	Moppy,	Croppy,	Pop-py.
Autumn:	Wheezy,	Sneezy,	Freezy.
Winter:	Slippy,	Drippy,	Nippy.

Commercial Advertiser, New York:

DIJON, APRIL 17 GENERAL BERTHIER is expected here from Basle to-morrow or next day. His carriage broke down twice or thrice: he continued his journey in one of the carriages of his suit, and sent his private secretary and young Visconte to Dijon. Generals arrive here daily; general Victor, Berthier's first lieut. generals Watrin, Chamberlhac, Harville, Mensmer, Riveau and Carnot. The conscripts arrive in crowds. Gaiety, youth, vigour, everything announces good and fine troops. The arrival of the chief consul, who is impatiently expected, has drawn to our town from 20 leagues round us persons who are curious to see him.

Sun, London:

STRASBURG, JUNE 9 WE receive, at this moment, the official news of a large Corps of Austrians under the orders of Prince Ferdinand, having attacked, on the 5th of this month, the Left Wing of the Army of the Rhine, in the neighbourhood of Ulm. Our troops received them in their usual manner. The Enemy was completely beaten, and was obliged to fly precipitately into the Fortifications of Ulm. We have made 1600 Prisoners, and taken eight Pieces of Cannon, Waggons, etc.—An Enemy's General, whose name we know not, has been killed.

Courier and Evening Gazette, London:

PARIS, MAR. 9 WHAT a change have a few months made in Paris. A Jacobin is not feen nor talked of, and the laft fubject we think of is politics. All the ladies vote it *degoutante.* "Ma foi," faid a lady to me the other day, "c'eft une chofe affez *ennuyante* que la politique! Memes mots, memes idées, point de varieté! C'eft auffi cruelle (this I fuppose was intended as a climax) c'eft auffi cruelle que d'avoir un mari toujours à nos cotés, au bal mafqué de l'opera."

Lord Minto to the Hon. A. Paget:

VIENNA, 27TH MAY, 1800 THE Campaign has been uniformly successful in Italy. A very masterly plan has been executed with great spirit, activity and courage, and is on the point I trust of being crown'd with the capture of Genoa & the extinction of Massena's army, which is all that remains of the Italian war since the remainder of the French army of Italy has been driven fairly across the Var. Melas after Nice was in his possession, determined to throw a considerable part of his troops, especially cavalry, to Turin, partly for meeting Berthier who was reported to be approaching Italy with about 10 or 15,000 men by way of Switzerland. Melas was under no uneasiness at this attempt to relieve Genoa; & can oppose a superior force to Berthier without diminishing that which invests Genoa.

5

SCENES OF YOUTH
REVISITED

Genoa, The Lombard Plain: 25 floréal—
23 prairial, An VIII
(May 15–June 12, 1800)

THERE are five passes through the Alps to Italy—
Mont Cenis, Little St. Bernard, Great St. Bernard,
Simplon, St. Gothard—and no roads in any, no
place where wheels can go. Bonaparte was using them all.
General Thurreau, with the left wing of Suchet's Var army,
pressed Austrian Kaim (of Elsnitz' command) in the Mont
Cenis, which leads direct to Turin, the enemy's forward base
—a diversion. Through the Little St. Bernard marched Division Chabran of Victor's corps, which would fall in on the
main body in the Vale of Aosta. Moreau was making good
progress with his campaign. Carnot had gone to the front in
person to give him positive orders for the detachment of a
corps of 15,000 under General Moncey to pass the St.
Gothard on Milan, meanwhile throwing a small wing into
the Simplon. Bonaparte and the main guard took the Great
St. Bernard, the route of Hannibal.

At Villeneuve, foot of the ascent, the troops were re-
viewed by the General in person, a review that was not a
ceremony, for he walked down the lines speaking to old comrades in person. "See that that man gets a new pair of shoes."
"You have a broken stock to your musket; Colonel Rapp will

provide you with an order on the depot for a new one."
Every detail checked by himself, a task that might have
wearied sleepless Argus.

Biscuit for a week's march was on each man's back and
a heavy supply of bullets. It would be a hard journey, but
veterans in the ranks told tales of that other stormy descent
on Italy, the glory of Montenotte when the light shook in
the skies, and the plunder thereafter: "Three battles in a
day and a dead march in between——" "When he held the
flag at the bridge of Lodi, ah, formidable!" "The day he
broke the Austrians' dishes!"

The bugles blew at midnight; the start was made within
two hours after, to avoid marching through the daylight
when the sun would melt snow and send avalanches crashing
down the cliffs. As the steep slopes began, all the drums beat
a *pas de charge* and the bugles echoed among the icy pillars.
The men began to sing, not ballads, but the fierce march-
songs of the armies of the Revolution—"Ça ira," "Sambre-
et-Meuse," "La Marseillaise"—tugging at the ropes to the
sledges that bore the guns and caissons till it was time to
change hands and the bugles blew again, thin in the Alpine
air. Toward morning they reached the hospice of St. Bernard, and here a surprise awaited them; the First Consul had
sent on provisions in advance and the monks placed tables
out along the route, from which they served to every man
bread and cheese, wine and eau de vie.

On downslopes the cavalry had it worst; they must lead
their horses and a false step by the animal took man and
beast both down into those terrific gorges—not many, but
enough so that there was less of song and more of cursing.
At Aosta on 26 floréal Chabran's division fell in on them
from the lesser St. Bernard; but three days later, the chief
being at Martigny to forward supplies, word ran in from
Lannes that he was blocked by a small fort on a projecting
spur between Chatillon and San Martino, the fort of Bard,
containing 800 stout-hearted Hungarians.

Bonaparte had expected something like this; that fort had

stood as the worst flaw in his plan ever since the survey that aide-de-camp Duroc made of the route during the winter. Again and again he had impressed on Lannes the importance of getting past the place early to seize Ivrea and the outlet to the plain—"The fate of Italy and perhaps of the Republic depends upon capturing it." From Martigny, on the 23rd, he wrote forward that Lannes was to get a battery on a dominating peak to shell Bard, with a pair of mortars on the road below—"Do not waste cartridges, the place is impervious to musketry."

But Lannes could not. There was no dominating peak, an escalade failed, the Austrians from their castle fired down into the town and blew up some of his ammunition. Bonaparte rushed Marmont and Marescot forward to see what could be made of the matter. The latter, arriving first, thought guns on Albaredo Mountain behind might shell it out, but when the pieces were hoisted up with ropes and muscle they proved too small, the balls would not carry, and bigger guns could not be raised.

Bard was impregnable, said Marescot; he was an engineer. Berthier, who was now up with the advance, sent word back for the divisions to halt in place, but Lannes (who did not recognize words with negative prefixes) found that the goat-track up which the too-light cannon had been dragged passed right on across Mont Albaredo. He threw every man in his corps into the task of improving it—steps cut in cliffs, walls built along ledges where the overhang might force men down, bridges beginning with tree-trunks, flung across breakneck ravines.

On the last day of floréal his men were pouring down around Ivrea, where there was another Austrian post, whose commander was now calling in reinforcements from all over north Italy; in a few more days he would have the way completely blocked. Lannes attacked at once, but was beaten off; no guns. Bonaparte entered his headquarters from a session of sliding down a slope for fun to fall in a fury and cry that he was served by idiots. But they were not all idiots; at that

same hour Marmont the gunner had hit on the happy expedient of carpeting the whole road through the town of
Bard and past the fort with manure laid on a bed of straw to
deaden sounds and dragging the cannon through by night.
As the fifth or sixth gun passed, the people in the fort woke
up and threw down firepots to see what the rumor of sound
below might mean; then began shooting by their light and
killed upwards of thirteen men. But they lacked material for
more firepots and had no ammunition to waste by shooting
blind. The guns slid through; on 2 prairial Lannes renewed
his attack on Ivrea with their help, captured the place, and
broke up its garrison. The passage was won, the great march
done, and 60,000 Frenchmen came rolling into the vernal
plain of Italy with Bonaparte at their head.

Near Pavia some of Murat's cavalry captured a packet of
Austrian dispatches. One was from Melas to his mistress in
that place—she was not to let herself be disturbed by a lot
of silly rumors; the Army of the Reserve was legendary, and
whatever of it was not could be taken care of by General
Kaim and his detachment.

II

On 20 floréal Generaloberst Ott sent a trumpet to the lines
east of Genoa to announce that he was going to fire all his
guns in celebration of a victory over Suchet on the Var.
Masséna was ignorant whether it was true or not that Suchet
had lost a battle (as a matter of fact it was not), but thought
that if the Austrians wanted to fire guns, he would give them
something to shoot at. Next morning he put nearly his whole
force into two columns of attack against their position on
Monte Ratti, northeast of the town, Soult leading one up a
concealing draw, Miollis the other, straight ahead. A ground
mist gave cover till with bayonet and "Vive la République!"
the hungry wild men went storming over the parapet. The
Austrians tumbled back among the ravines and the column
returned with 1,500 prisoners.

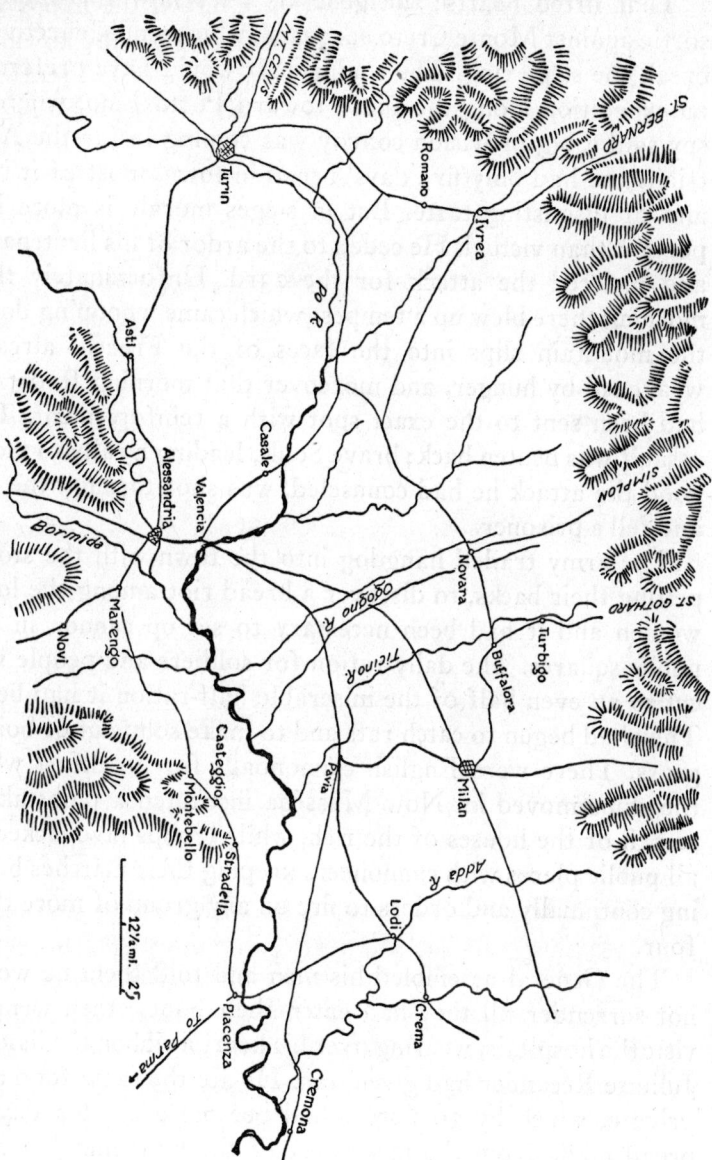

Campaign in the Po Valley

That lifted hearts; the generals were now for another sortie against Monte Creto eastward, which would effectively break the siege ring. The commander would have preferred an expedition along the shore toward Porto Fino, where a spy said a big provision convoy was coming in for the Austrians; he had only five days' bread in town, most of it bad and of disgusting taste. But in sieges morale is more important than victual. He ceded to the ardor of his lieutenants and ordered the attack for the 23rd. Unfortunately that morning there blew up a tempest which came whooping down the mountain slips into the faces of the French, already weakened by hunger, and moreover that morning Radetzky had been sent to the exact spot with a reinforcement. The assault was beaten back; brave Soult, leading a rally to make good the attack he had counseled, was shot through the leg and fell a prisoner.

The army trailed hangdog into the town with the storm pelting their backs, to discover a bread riot among the local women and it had been necessary to set up cannon in the public squares. The daily ration for soldiers and people was cut to an even half of the miserable half-ration it had been. They had begun to catch rats and to make soup out of boiled grass. There were English cannonballs for breakfast when the ships moved in. Now Masséna instituted a painstaking search of the houses of the rich, while troops bivouacked in all public places with cannoneers keeping their matches burning continually and orders to fire on any group of more than four.

The General assembled his men and told them he would not surrender till they had eaten their boots; then went to visit the hospitals, wearing over his heart a ribbon the lissome Juliette Récamier had given him. He ate the same food as a private, which by 30 floréal had become a crust a day of bread made from the mere dust of the bins, mingled with such unsavory materials as starch, hair powder, sawdust, and linseed. People were dying of hunger in the streets; the scarecrow soldiers on the perimeter had no strength to lift their cannonballs, it was impossible to hold out longer, but the indomitable scoundrel would not surrender, his single will against that of every person in the city.

The 30 floréal and a week; on the latter day Masséna's own aide, Captain Franceschi, swam ashore from a small boat with his saber in his teeth and English cannonballs bouncing around him. He had been Outside; the news there was that General Bonaparte had come down like an avalanche from the Alps. The day before, Lannes with the vanguard had won a battle at Romano. Masséna let a famished drummer beat up the chamade for a parley and managed to prolong negotiations for another week before the Army of Italy marched out with rolled standards. His hair had gone snow-white and Juliette Récamier would never love him again.

III

The state of mind of that stout warrior Michael Friedrich Melas (who would have done so much better in a breastplate than a uniform jacket) was afterward described as confused. It was nothing of the sort; he saw the position and what he should do about it with the greatest clarity, only most of what he saw was optical illusion. After Ott beat back the French sortie of May 15 (a good day's work, that!) he left that general in charge of the siege and himself went forward to the Var front to make arrangements for the invasion of France. There were reports of enemy movements among the Alpine passes, but it seemed to him that this was obviously one of those attempts at diversion of which French generals were so very fond. The Army of the Reserve (if it really existed) would be taking the main turnpike through Lyon and Grenoble presently to appear on the Var front. General Zach agreed; according to the science of war, the French would need a secure line of supply for the operations of so considerable a force, and though one might put a division through the passes, it would be impossible to support it with those roadless wastes of stone behind.

But on the 18th a Croat arrived who had been with the garrison at the Fort of Bard. He had slipped through and ridden hard with an oral message from the commandant, who all day long had been watching an entire French army defile past, outlined against the sky over Albaredo, without being able to do anything against them. Melas left Elsnitz with 18,000 to continue the Var operation and himself went to Turin, sending Zach on ahead to make an estimate of the situation around the St. Bernard exit, while 9,000 men were ordered up from the Riviera to form a nucleus under his own command.

On the 25th he was in the Piedmontese capital and encountered four pieces of news which conspired together to darken counsel. Generaloberst Haddick was at hand with the badly exhausted fragments of a detachment nine or ten thousand strong that had been covering the outlet of the St. Bernard along a small stream and a chain of heights at Romano. He had built his defense around a bridge and lost his guns when storms of French infantry forded the stream both below and above, at the same time slamming a column right across the bridge into the teeth of his cannon; tried to retrieve the day with a cavalry charge, which after initial success was shot to pieces among broken ground and vineyards. Ivrea had fallen to the enemy.

This looked like French in force in that direction, but if they were in strength their actions were very puzzling. They had not pursued Haddick, nor made any effort to follow up their triumph at Romano. On the other hand, the detachment under General Kaim, holding the outlet of the Mont Cenis pass at Susa, had been heavily attacked on the 20th and was holding its ground only with difficulty; the French were inching forward there with continuing pressure. A dispatch of Masséna's had been captured. His food would last till the 24th and he counted on being rescued before that time. General Wukassovitch, far to the east at the outlets of the St. Gothard and Simplon, reported that he too was being attacked.

The Army of the Reserve then did exist. Nothing else could explain the bold front France was showing. From the data in hand, however, it was possible to determine that army's line of action sufficiently to make counteraction possible. The account from the Fort of Bard of an entire army mounting the Albaredo could be dismissed as fantastic; an overwrought observer had exaggerated the number of men going past, as is not infrequently the case. General Berthier must be bringing the new army through the Mont Cenis pass for a direct thrust on Turin, in the expectation that Melas would be forced to abandon the siege of Genoa to meet the threat to his base. The other movements were diversions by a few men, designed to draw Austrian strength northeastward.

Well, Michael Friedrich Melas would not abandon the siege of Genoa. He had collected fewer than 20,000 in Turin —the local garrison and Haddick's refugees, not a force fit for field action. But Kaim was holding up well against that main French drive at the Mont Cenis. A brigade from Elsnitz, originally intended for Turin, was diverted to help him, and so was a division of cavalry from the magazine point at Alessandria. The 9,000 from Ott were to push on to Turin; 1,500 horse from the Tuscan garrisons to reinforce Wukassovitch at the St. Gothard and Simplon.

This reshuffle of forces was fairly complete by May 28. When it had been made, Ott still had 25,000 blocking Masséna in Genoa while he negotiated for the surrender. Elsnitz with 18,000 on the Var was engaged in reducing the bridgehead Suchet had kept on the east bank, while some 5,000 more behind him in Liguria were ready to move forward for the invasion of France or to support Melas' personal command at Turin. That command now numbered 24,000 and Kaim had another 12,000 falling back slowly down the valley of the little river Ripario to join them. They would hold Berthier and his Army of the Reserve at the foot of the Mont Cenis till he got in trouble about supplies and had to go back to seek a valid line of operations. Wukassovitch had upward of 10,000 to hold the St. Gothard and Simplon against the detachments there. As for the diversionary group that had entered Italy by the St. Bernard and beaten Haddick, it would be smothered in the gradually increasing resistance of the garrisons in Lombardy, 14,000 altogether.

These arrangements satisfied everyone but young Radetzky, who wished to assemble all the troops from the Riviera and—instead of merely starving the French force from the Mont Cenis into retreat—smash it in a battle. But these junior officers are always ambitious of flashy personal renown instead of the more solid glory of permanent service to the Empire.

IV

The order was for Lannes to stand fast on the stream he had gained. The other corps were to file past his rear, swinging off leftward toward Milan and the highroad that crosses the northern affluents of the Po. Murat's horse, which had been on that flank to guard against any movement of the Austrian Lombardy garrisons, naturally fell into the lead. General Bonaparte was much concerned with those questions of supply which Freiherr Zach thought insoluble for an army dangling at the end of a cord back across the Alps (75 per cent of the General's correspondence during the march deals with this question), and he had conceived a solution by changing his base to the Lombard quadrilateral. The Austrian communication line following the north bank of the Po was already severed. The change of base would have the advantage of making it easy to cut the other highroad, the one paralleling the river on the south, and at the same time opening the St. Gothard for Moncey's reinforcement.

The first of the south-running rivers is the Ogogno; Murat reached it at Novara on 9 prairial with Division Boudet of Duhesme close behind, and captured the place from a handful of Austrian cavaliers, who galloped off without a fight. They belonged to the cavalry command of Baron Festenburg, who was screening the country east to the Ticino River, which is deep and wide enough to be a true military obstacle, and is helped in that respect by a big canal which supplies the city of Milan with fresh water. Wukassovitch had Melas' orders to hold this river and canal line against what the latter had conceived as a small French detachment coming through the St. Bernard, and had sent his General Laudon down to Buffalora. He himself was deeply concerned over what appeared to him as the more important force of Moncey, coming down from the north.

The report of Festenburg's riders—that there were heavy French forces to the west—was a shock, but there was no time for Wukassovitch to improve his position, for the day after Murat reached Novara he was on the Ticino at Turbigo with Division Monnier, which had cut cross-country. Some of Festenburg's horse held the stream. Monnier planted guns which smothered an Austrian battery and got over, since the enemy cavalry could not work up momentum in the narrow tongue of land between river and canal. Laudon, marching from Buffalora to the sound of the cannon, arrived only in time to run into a stirring bayonet charge that stopped him dead; and then Division Boudet came through Buffalora on his rear. The Austrian command broke up with a loss of 1,500 men.

Wukassovitch, getting word from his cavalry (which did its scouting very well indeed) of more and more French in Lombardy, decided on instant retreat. He marched all night and most of the next day to get back across the Adda, sending off an express to Melas. On 15 prairial Division Loison of Duhesme, which had fanned out southeast in pursuit, reported from Lodi that the Austrians were moving back on Crema. Should the river be forced?

—Yes, answered Bonaparte from Milan; he wanted Wukassovitch pressed right back into Mantua, off the map, and sent Duhesme to lead the drive, which by 17 prairial had overrun most of the country up to the Mincio and pushed its cavalry vanguard into Cremona. Cremona also is on the great highroad south of the Po; the French were now sitting on both Melas' lifelines back to Austria.

But only with the most tenuous of forces, which could be easily brushed aside; and there was another, circuitous route through Piacenza and Parma across the hills, by which the Austrians might still escape if they marched fast. Bonaparte was not a little astonished by the speed with which Wukassovitch had escaped his trap—these were not the Austrians he had known in the An IV. If they all marched like that, it was more than ever important to cut their routes beyond possibility of repair so that Melas would have to come fight for his life. With the sour little observation that the decorations with which Milan was hung for his triumphal entry were the same that had been used to welcome Suvorov and the Austrians the year before, he slid Lannes to that general's left down on Pavia the 12 prairial and pushed Division Gardanne of Victor straight south to meet him there. Murat swung out of the advance toward Piacenza. These arrangements were completed by 16 prairial; the Austrian magazines were found at Pavia and grenadiers of France ate roast goose prepared for the tables of Imperial princes. Moncey was unpardonably slow in coming through the St. Gothard, alleging trouble about victual which, the General informed him, should have been cared for before he began his march.

On the 19th there were brought to Milan two packets of recent dispatches which Murat's horse had taken from couriers south of the river. One set from the K.K.Reichshofrat to General Melas informed him that it was now certain the Army of the Reserve did not exist; he was to push forward the invasion of Provence. The other was from Melas homeward and contained a detailed note of his dispositions.

V

After Lannes' little combat at Romano, Bonaparte himself had ridden to the outposts on that front and had been recognized by an Austrian officer who had been on the staff during the peace conference at Leoben four years previous.

The officer was absolutely certain in identifying his man when Melas talked to him. At the same time spies brought word that the force passing through the St. Bernard was much more imposing than Melas had at first believed, but that it had filed eastward toward Milan; and it became clear that the French in the Mont Cenis were not very strong. By May 30, accordingly, Melas had formed a new picture of the situation and a new plan that contained more of Radetzky than of Zach.

In this version Wukassovitch was to hold the enemy's advance on the Ticino. Kaim would reinforce Haddick with 6,000 men, while Ott sent eight or nine thousand up through Alessandria and Casale. The two latter columns together would throw themselves onto Bonaparte's rear, cutting him off from the St. Bernard and his communications. The orders were issued; but on the 31st, when the troops were moving into position, came Job's messenger from Wukassovitch, saying that he had been assailed by an overwhelming force from the St. Gothard, the Ticino line was already lost, and he doubted whether he could even hold the Adda. Now Melas—or Zach for him—understood; and both knew that an army, like a diver, can exist with its lifelines stopped only barely long enough to clear the obstruction.

Orders were issued for an immediate concentration at Alessandria—Elsnitz to drop the operation on the Var, coming back through the Col di Tenda to Asti; Kaim to drop 3,500 men in Turin citadel and also march through Asti on Alessandria; Ott to drop the siege of Genoa at once and head for the same place. The Governor at Alessandria, Skall, was given command of the general reserve, with the duty of holding open the line of communications along the south bank of the Po through Piacenza and Cremona or at least Parma. Ott's men, who would arrive first, were to push out along this route, fortifying and holding all bottlenecks.
. . . These were the arrangements described in the documents Bonaparte had captured.

At Milan the First Consul now had the vanguard of

Moncey and part of Duhesme. Murat was out in the direction of Piacenza, scouting and screening along the north bank of the Po; Lannes and Victor setting men over to the south bank by every available bridge and pontoon. There is a point on that south bank where a spur of the northern Apennines crowds valley and road almost to a defile, the town at this point being named Stradella, an ideal place to set up a defensive position against which Melas would sooner or later be forced to break his fists. But Bonaparte was not thinking of any such scheme as allowing the enemy to pile up before Stradella like a river at a dam. He put his dividers on the map, calculated that Melas' main concentration at Alessandria could not be formed before 24 prairial, June 13; but that part of Skall's reserve would be at Stradella by the 20th, June 9. Lannes, who had the advance, was ordered to push on, attack them and break them up—so many the fewer Austrians to meet on the day of the big battle.

It was a miscalculation; these Austrians, like Wukassovitch, had learned how to march since Bonaparte last saw them. Ott was already pushing for the Stradella defile at the head of 18,000 men. (The rest of Ott's troops were in Genoa, taking care of the prisoners; when he received his marching orders he tried to persuade Lord Keith of the British fleet to take over the place, but that noble beef-eater replied "it would be improper" for him to do so without orders from the military department—in London.)

Lannes, pushing out from Stradella, encountered the enemy at the village of Casteggio, where the valley broadens out a bit, in possession of the town, with artillery in its eastern outskirts and the stone houses made into strong points. The French command had only some 8,000 men, his own corps and a few of Victor's, but his information was clear, this was only a small group of Austrians. He deployed and attacked, with a small flanking party moving into the hills on his left.

The Austrian artillery beat his first effort into the ground. He organized a second, swinging a brigade out rightward along the river-bank to get round those guns, while the men in the frontal assault wormed forward, taking advantage of every obstacle, to shoot into the windows of the houses and kill the cannoneers at their pieces. A sudden rush carried several of the guns and brought the French right into the heart of the town. They were outnumbered and outpositioned, but they had fire in their hearts and Jean Lannes to lead them.

Ott's main reserve was back at the next village, Montebello. He was a good deal astonished at being attacked in this place, but not in the least dismayed. Reinforcing his center in the village, he put a whole division onto the high ground on his right (the French left) and about two in the afternoon carried Lannes' weak flanking party away and turned in on his center, which was now being counterattacked in front. The French were ejected from Casteggio and— as the Austrians came pressing on, slow but determined— were driven steadily back, leaving a long trail of dead and wounded across the fields. Only the most heroic efforts of Lannes himself and of his division leader, Watrin, kept them from breaking up. They were so closely held they dared not even retreat, but hung on, making every tree and copse a fortress, hoping for Victor or Murat.

At about four Victor did appear with his Division Chambarlhac. Instead of using them to sustain his quaking front, Lannes audaciously sent them up the hills against the Austrians who had turned in on his head of column, exposing their own flank as they did so. It was a Revolutionary attack, bayonet columns, with clouds of skirmishers in front; caught the Austrians on the loose and drove them from the heights. Watrin picked his men up out of their ditches and carried them snarling back into Casteggio, while Lannes, now out on the left, brought Chambarlhac down on Montebello in the enemy rear.

Ott had put in his last reserves to hold the attack at the river-bank against his own left, the French right. As the slow green Italian twilight settled over the smoky valley he had nothing left, was driven back in prone rout, his corps a wreck, 2,500 killed and wounded, 4,000 lost in prisoners when he failed to get out of Casteggio in time. Bonaparte himself had ridden to the front in some misgiving about his diagnosis of the Austrian movements. He arrived to find Lannes, wounded again, "covered with blood but drunk with joy," holding to the pommel of his saddle as smoke-blackened soldiers cheered him through the streets of Montebello. They had smashed an army half again as large as their own and closed the jaws of the trap on Baron Melas of Siebenburgen.

VI

Suchet, back on the Var, had done quite as well as Lannes.

The mountains run from north straight to the sea there, and Suchet held the one just east of the Var. Austrian Elsnitz was in possession of Nice city at its foot, except that he had not taken the citadel, which stands on a lofty almost-island of its own. From this citadel the French saw Elsnitz preparing for his attack of the 27th May and signaled over to Suchet by means of the ingenious telegraph system of Dr. Chappe. The French general massed his guns in the bridge-head east of the stream, set up concealed abattis and placed most of his infantry far up the line on his left, where there was a pass that ran eastward before cutting south.

Elsnitz' attack was broken, of course. As he put in more and more men to make it go, Suchet released his own column upstream, which broke through, throwing a fragment of Elsnitz back among the high summits and swinging the rest around with their backs almost to the sea. This took several days of slow hill fighting. By the time Suchet was ready to move again Elsnitz had his orders for the retreat on Alessandria. He tried to move by his right, but now Suchet poured greater and greater forces through the gap he had created, attacked by his own left again, broke the long Austrian line in two, and obtained possession of the Col di Tenda.

Elsnitz' men had to wander through hills, rocks, and snow with no food or guides; they died or came in to surrender by whole battalions. Their commander arrived in Ceva, well short of Alessandria, on June 7 with only 8,000 men, hungry, discouraged, unutterably weary, their uniforms in rags, after one of the most dreadful disasters of the war. In all these scattered combats Melas had lost nearly half the men with whom he started the campaign.

VII

It was Bonaparte's special excellence that in war as out of it he was a master psychologist of a practical stamp. After a few combats along the outposts, after tracing a few moves on the map, he could gauge with considerable accuracy the quality of an adversary's mind and the man's probable re-action to stimuli. In the present case he could not seem to make out that his opponent had more than a series of im-pulses. When Melas had tried to cut off the French rear from the St. Bernard, when he pushed Ott forward, he had been bold and decisive; in his concentration around Turin, in his instructions to Elsnitz and Wukassovitch, he had been (considering the state of his information) careful, precise, systematic. Bonaparte had the documents before him. He was of course ignorant of the fact that these fluctuations rep-resented the successive ideas produced by Zach and Radetzky upon a mind that worked for itself only in the heat of battle and as the result of personal observation. Seeking the com-mon denominator of the observed phenomena, the First Consul thought he perceived it in the moral cowardice which so often afflicts second-rate commanders (any Austrian offi-cer would be physically brave), and makes them avoid battle unless they have forces so overwhelming as to guarantee victory.

The pattern was a familiar one. Melas must now be severely shaken by Ott's defeat at Montebello and Elsnitz' among the mountains. He would try to escape. Instead of bringing Moncey down across the Po then, Bonaparte ordered the three divisions of this corps to switch west from Milan to the Ticino, with the small division of Chabran that had just taken Fort Bard, out forward on the road running north from Alessandria.

With his main body, Murat now taking the lead, the First Consul pressed straight forward toward that Austrian base. On 23 prairial (June 12) there arrived at headquarters from Paris his old friend, Louis-Charles-Antoine Desaix, just escaped out of Egypt, "quite an antique character, like a Roman." The General welcomed him warmly and instantly gave him command of a new corps, made up of two divisions from Duhesme, who was personally east on the Mincio. Desaix was to slant off from the main body to Novi and block the Austrians' path should they try to turn back down the main road to Genoa and make their escape in that direction.

The command to all units was forward; on 24 prairial the vanguard, with which Bonaparte, crossed the stream Sesia into the plain of San Giuliano, a place ideal for the use of the heavy cavalry in which Austria was so very strong. No cavalry there; an aide reported the bridge over the next river, Bormida, had been broken down, but some Austrian artillery was firing and the little village of Marengo burning so that smoke obscured everything. Evidently Melas had left rearguards to hold the river bank and had begun his march, north or south. Bonaparte turned back to the village of Garofolo, where he could sleep in a bed; the army was to push through Marengo and camp in march order.

6

SURPRISE

The Plain of San Giuliano: 25 prairial, An VIII
(June 14, 1800)

BUT Melas was not thinking of escaping in any direction; he was preparing to do the one thing he knew how to do without advice from anybody—fight a battle. There had been a council of war the night before, with the officers bowing stiffly to each other over their medals. They were cut off and it was not their fault, the old General said, but that of the Aulic Council, the Reichshofrat, which had given them such false information about this Army of the Reserve. Now it was their part to extricate themselves like soldiers and men of honor. Before them lay three choices: move north, cross the Po at Valencia, and reach a line of communications via Pavia; move south to Genoa and lean on the English fleet; or turn straight east across the Bormida and fight a way through. They had two bridges and beyond them almost the only plain in North Italy where cavalry could ride, unchecked by ditches.

The old man's manner left little doubt as to what his own choice would be; he was living again the days of the great retreat to Lugos, when he cut his way through the Turks. They all agreed, agreed, agreed, from young Radetzky, speaking first because junior, to grandmotherly old Zach. The enemy were farthest forward near Marengo village, where they had taken one of our outposts the night before and camped just on our side of a little marsh-edged brook. According to the reports of the scouts, this would be a forward flying wing; the French main body was across the more northerly of the two roads leading eastward, the one running to Sale. The powerful division of Ott, 7,000 strong, should attack this force, clutch and hold it. O'Reilly's small division is to brush the French aside from before Marengo. Behind it would march the divisions of Haddick and Kaim, with Morzin's grenadiers, main guard of the battle, then Elsnitz with the cavalry (that dummkopf could lead horse at least). These would swing through a great half-circle, falling on the flank of the French opposing Ott. We are 31,000 strong, with 200 cannon and 7,000 of the cavalry that are Austria's pride. The French cannot be more. The move for dawn.

Before dawn, however, news ran in that Suchet with his column had followed Elsnitz hard and was already at Acqui. It would never do to have him come down on the rear with a battle in progress, so Melas woke from sleep to detach 2,500 of his horse for holding Suchet in check, then listened for a while to the sounds of the men camped beneath his window before lying down again. The soldiers were in good spirits, talking slowly under the false dawn, a happy augury.

Daybreak is near six o'clock during June in those latitudes; at that hour all the trumpets blew and the troops began to move, O'Reilly leading against the French along the brook, where the fighting blazed up fiercely at once. Progress was slow; a difficulty had declared itself at the fortified bridge-head to the east bank, where only one exit had been provided, so the enceinte filled up with men pouring over the bridges, who could deploy only gradually. It was eight o'clock before Haddick got into line with O'Reilly, with a powerful battery playing on Marengo village. Melas rode up, a trifle impatient over ticking time; he sent Haddick in at once, without waiting for Kaim, or for Ott's attack to develop on the left. The delay was allowing the French to form. In spite of the fact that the attack was made with the greatest valor, the whitecoat soldiers throwing all sorts of material into the brook for stepping stones, Haddick was beaten off after an hour of hard fighting, the commander

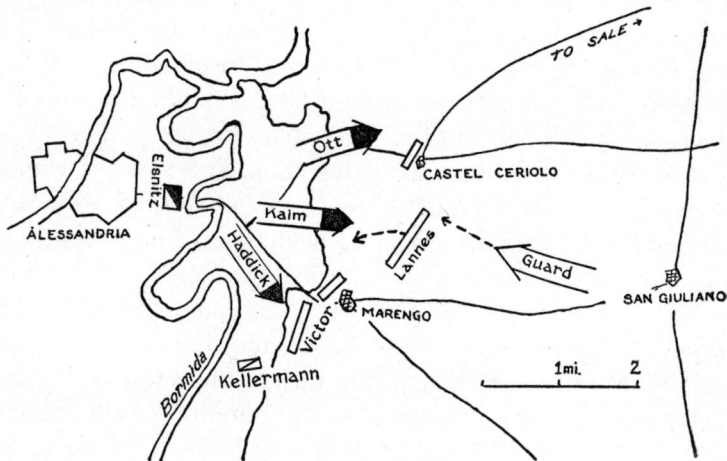

Marengo: the Austrian victory

himself mortally wounded, his division so broken that it had to fall back and re-form.

Kaim came through the tattered companies and attacked again, while Melas swung Elsnitz down to get around the French left, since their front was gripped so tightly they would have trouble extending in that direction. Elsnitz forced the brook but, as he tried to charge, was in turn charged by a small body of French heavy horse and stopped where he stood; nor could Kaim break through, though several of his battalions managed the brook and got bridgeheads beyond its marshes.

It seemed clear to Melas that the French were reinforcing from their right, where Ott had not yet begun his drive, but they were weakening. More guns were brought up, with Morzin's grenadiers in support of Kaim; and now Ott worked through the bridgehead gate and also attacked, taking the town Castel Ceriolo on the Sale road at about eleven in the morning from a stout defense. By this time Austria had half Marengo village, and it was evident most of the French were trying to stand around that point. Melas reversed plans, swinging Ott down onto the right of the enemy position. This new push encountered some reserves the enemy had brought up, who formed square and, in the most savage fighting of the day, stood Ott off for an hour— or until he brought some cannon up to break the squares, then charged them with cavalry. The French reserve was driven from the field a little after noon, and now the whole enemy line began to go back amid evident signs of disorder, leaving a good many prisoners behind, no longer fighting anything but an escape action in little groups.

Victory. The old General, who had come from a night nearly sleepless to take two wounds and have a horse shot under him, was very weary. He turned the pursuit over to General Zach, with infantry columns moving parallel along both roads eastward, and himself went back to Alessandria to write a dispatch announcing the first triumph his nation had ever gained over this Bonaparte—not so formidable a fellow after all, when hit hard by an officer who understood how to handle troops on the battlefield.

II

The corps of Victor had moved forward along the general line of the southerly road on the night of 24 prairial, and after a skirmish in Marengo village, camped at the edge of a little stream on a fairly broad front, with a brigade of 470 heavy cavalry under Kellermann (this is François-Etienne, the son of old Valmy Kellermann) between it and the Bormida. Lannes' smaller corps had been on the same road; it swung out to the right and night came upon it while slanting up into line with Victor; so that in the actual encampment it was somewhat echeloned back from his position. A brigade of Desaix, who had been on the northern road, reached the village of Castel Ceriolo, due north of Marengo. The Consular Guard, made up of some 800 veteran foot and 360 horse, went some several hours' ride to the rear with the General, to the tower of Garofolo.

Bonaparte had hardly begun to take his coffee in the morning when the guns began to boom; he gave orders that the Guard should be alerted to move at once, and, running downstairs, mounted to ride to the front. The sounds of battle rose louder and louder in the still Italian summer air and it was clear enough without messengers that Melas was across the Bormida and attacking. One aide was dispatched to recall Desaix from Novi; another, who had reported the evening before that the Austrians had no bridge, was called a coward for not having gone far enough forward to make certain, and the General rode on with a portentous frown. There were not more than 15,000 men at the front; if the Austrians knew their business they would eat up the whole army.

It was nearly eleven o'clock before the scene of action was reached. By that time Victor in Marengo was beginning to go to pieces. Kellermann on his left flank had stopped the Austrian cavalry, and Lannes on his right, northeast of the village, had proved a model of constancy. But the latter had been forced to inch gradually leftward from his original position in support of Victor's flank, his last man was in against Kaim and the Austrian grenadiers, and now Ott's big battalions were pouring down onto a wing that floated in air. It would be hours before Desaix could arrive.

The General ordered Victor to hold the outskirts of Marengo at any cost, prevent the Austrians from debouching through it against Lannes' left flank. The Consular Guard infantry was rushed forward on the latter's right and formed square; its little body of horsemen rode with loose rein against the sustaining cavalry of Ott's command. High on the right, Division Monnier of Desaix, which had been so far behind on the march to Novi that there was time to bring it back early, was ordered along the road to Castel Ceriolo to menace Ott's flank and rear.

For a time these measures succeeded. At the center the Guard infantry broke one attack and Monnier reached the outer edge of Castel Ceriolo. But it was now nearly noon, the Imperials had been granted time to get all their forces through the bridgehead and into line, especially their numerous cannon. Fifty of them were brought to bear on the squares of the Consular Guard, while the menace of some hussars kept it closed up as a target. About noon this artillery blew the square apart under heavy casualties, while Ott's reserve smashed Monnier out of Castel Ceriolo. Victor was fought out; there were more and more signs of disintegration. "The plain was covered with fleeing men, some of them even crying 'Sauve qui peut!' "—the old wild yell when fear stands at the brink of panic. There was nothing to do but order a general retreat, and it was made in no good form, the men hangdog in small groups, the officers in blood and dust with few words.

III

At dawn of day Desaix had heard the distant repeated shock of guns, ominous in the north. His own scouts had already investigated Novi and found no enemy there. This must, could only, mean that the battle was being fought back there were the Chief was. Before Bonaparte's message reached him, he had already turned the whole force around and, with the drums rattling quickstep, was marching along the road that leads from Novi to Sale. It would be nearly two o'clock when he reached the village San Giuliano, a place set in a valley with gardens and hedges around and a fold of ground hiding it from the plain. Victor's men were still streaming past toward the rear, a few of them being halted among the houses. Desaix left orders for his own solid demi-brigades to form, facing west at San Giuliano, and rode farther north with the General to where Lannes' corps, in almost as bad shape as Victor's, was coming back across the plain, and Division Monnier, still in fairly good order, was covering the road out of Castel Ceriolo.

"Well, what do you think of it?" asked Bonaparte.

Desaix produced his watch. "The battle is completely lost; but it is only two o'clock—we have time to win another."

Both staffs were rushed in every direction to assemble the little groups of men who had begun to coalesce wherever there was a good officer. At San Giuliano Marmont had managed to save five guns from the early rout, Desaix brought five more and there were eight in the reserve; he placed them on Desaix' right. Kellermann and his cuirassiers were brought round and put into the center, between the guns and Lannes. The General rode among the troops, haranguing them: "Far enough back for today. You know it is my custom to sleep on the battlefield."

All this took time; but time was granted since Zach, who was heading the pursuit in route-march column along the Marengo highway, was halting every few minutes to close up his parade order. The Austrian cavalry—what there was of it, now they missed the men sent to Acqui—was spread across the farm-dotted plain, linking with Ott's column on the other road. Kaim, also in column, followed Zach at several hundred yards' distance; the remainder of the Austrians similarly followed Kaim.

It was nearly six o'clock when Zach's head of column reached the backslope concealing Desaix. That general saw them. It was a moment of inspiration. "Tell the General I am going to charge," said Desaix, and charged. "Bid Kellermann attack," ordered Bonaparte. At the same moment out blazed Marmont's guns, loaded with canister, into the tight columns as Desaix burst from cover against them with a cheer.

The first fire killed him; the 9th Regiment went mad when they saw their beloved leader fall, and, heedless of firing, flung themselves on the artillery-shaken Austrians with the bayonet. As Zach's rear ranks tried to spread and crowd forward, Kellermann's big armored horsemen cut right through them; from the rear Victor's men took heart of grace and joined the rally, there was a brief confusion of shooting and shouting, and then Zach, trapped between Kellermann and Desaix' wild men, had surrendered with 2,000, while the re-

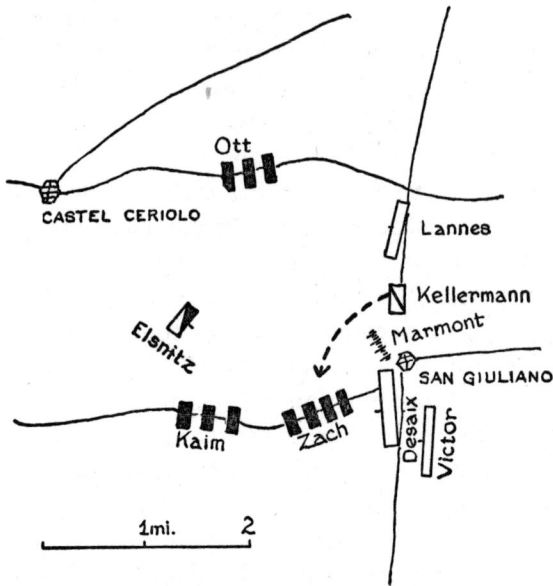

Marengo: counterattack

mainder were running back toward Kaim with French bay-onets in their backsides.

It would be about this time that the Austrian horse in the center began to get themselves disengaged from the vine-yards and come down, but Kellermann's men had open ground in which to work up steam. With the remnant of the Guard cavalry they fell on the Austrian squadrons as fast as they appeared and dispersed them. Elsnitz completely lost his head and was the first to ride from the field.

Kaim's group was already unsettled by the disaster to Zach, there was now no commanding general to give orders and their guns had been left behind. As Desaix' storm hit them in the fading light, they broke; Lannes swung into the attack, and in a tenth of the time it had taken to cross the plain eastward in the morning, the French were back across it, through Marengo (where a brief effort at a stand was broken up), and battering at the gate of the bridgehead. O'Reilly, not involved in the general rout, could hold there only long enough to let Ott through, then broke the bridges behind him. Night found France in full possession of the line of the Bormida and 3,000 Austrian prisoners; 7,000 more of the Imperials were dead or wounded, their organization broken and communications beyond repair.

IV

After they had something to eat, Bourrienne the secretary sat down to write the bulletin of the battle to Bonaparte's dictation.

"Here we are, just as you said, on the plain of San Giuliano. It is marvelous! You ought to be satisfied."

"Satisfied, yes. But Desaix! Ah, it would have been a real victory could I have embraced him on the field of battle."

There was silence for a moment and Bourrienne thought he saw tears at the edge of Bonaparte's eyelids, then the dictation went on, which had to be run through quickly in order to receive a trumpet and a flag of truce from Alessandria. There had been another council of war; Baron Melas of Siebenburgen offered for Austria to evacuate all north Italy and turn over to the French the keys of the fortresses, if they would let his men march back across the mountains, not to fight in that land any more. Accepted: on 28 prairial the General reached Milan and two weeks later was in Paris, leaving Masséna to handle the details of the capitulation of Italy, which he had done so much to win.

WRONG END OF THE TELESCOPE—III

The Sun, London:

GENERAL MELAS has united under his Command all the Troops garrisoned in the different Towns of Italy, and intends to give battle to General Berthier. During the absence of the Austrians, the Citizens must do Garrison duty. We expect shortly to hear of a decisive battle in that quarter, of the success of which we entertain no doubt, as our Army ardently wishes to engage Berthier.

Another Army of Reserve, of 30,000 men, is to be formed at *Laybach.*

The Sun, London:

FRENCH THEATRICALS

THE theatrical rage in Paris at this moment is introducing on the Stage well-known and celebrated Characters. Hogarth and Garrick have lately afforded a Plot to a French Dramatist, who has introduced them in a Musical Piece entitled *The Portrait of Fielding.*

The Painter is representing as being passionately enamoured of his Ward *Sophia,* and as being beloved in his turn. He considers himself as criminal for this passion, as his friend *Fielding* left a natural daughter, with an earnest request on his deathbed that *Hogarth* should marry her. This daughter, however is not to be found, nor is there any clue to direct the search of her. *Sophia* receives orders to go and join her mother in the County of Somerset. *Mr. Watson,* her protector, a rough man, arrives from Bath in order to carry her off, and only delays his departure in order to be present at a feast which is the same evening to be given in honour of the deceased *Fielding.* The same motive brings *Garrick* to *Hogarth's* house: the two friends express great regret at not having any portrait of the Author of *Tom Jones,* who would never suffer his likeness to be taken. In the mean time some one comes in and announces that a pretended portrait of *Fielding* is to be sold. The Painter hastens to go and look at it, and the Player forms the design of bringing *Fielding* to life again. He enters a closet where *Fielding* used to dress himself at the house of his friend, and where the clothes were preserved as relicks. The Painter returns disappointed, and sits down to make a sketch from recollection, when he hears a sepulchral voice from *Fielding's* dressing-room, calling him *Hogarth come and paint me, you have but a moment.* The voice strikes him it is that of Fielding himself, who appears at the door. He approaches, and in his enthusiasm takes a perfect likeness—*Sophia* is more affected by it than any one; it corresponds with a miniature which her mother had given her, and which she wears at her bosom. *Sophia* proves to be the natural daughter whom *Hogarth* was requested to marry, and thus he is able to reconcile his love and his friendship.

Mr. Lock, Consul at Naples, to the Hon. A. Paget:

THE post of yesterday brought us particulars respecting the disastrous condition of the Austrian arms.

The French under Berthier after being worsted by Melas on the 14th near Tortona, attacked the Austrians unexpectedly next morning before daybreak, & defeated them with great loss, among the prisoners said to be Melas and his *Etat Major.* The misfortune is ascribed in great measure to the treachery or cowardice of a Brigade of 3000 Cavalry commanded by General Nobile, which opened the way to the Enemy by falling back upon the Infantry & throwing it into disorder.

Talleyrand to Bonaparte:

GENERAL, I have just returned from the Tuileries. The audience of ambassadors could not have been more brilliant, and I will no more try to depict the enthusiasm of the French, and the admiration of the foreigners, than the sentiments that filled my own breast on reading the letter you wrote to the consuls. What a beginning and what a climax! Will posterity be able to believe all the prodigies of this campaign? There has never been an empire not founded on the marvellous, but here the marvellous itself is truth.

J. Russell's Gazette, Philadelphia:

FOREIGN INTELLIGENCE

THE Firſt Conſul, during his ſtay at Milan, wrote to all the Cures of the city, to aſſure them, that religion and its miniſters ſhould be reſpected, and protected, and adviſing them to recommend by their precept and example, obedience to the laws. Since the departure of Bonaparte, there has been publifhed a very long difcourfe, fuppofed to have been addreffed by him to the Cures. The Firft Conful is made to fay, "that he is perfuaded the Catholic Religion, Apoftolic and Roman, is the only one which can afford real happinefs to fociety. That he regards its minifters as his deareft friends—that the Catholic Religion develops in a fpecial manner, the principles of democratic government, and fupports its rights—that France, grown wife, has learned from her misfortunes, to adhere to the anchor which alone can fave her in the midft of the tempeft." Neither the author nor the editor of this difcourfe are known. The police of Milan has made inquiry, but hitherto in vain. It has been printed at Genoa, where it is generally confidered apocryphal.

7
FAMILY MATTERS

Paris: messidor, An VIII–frimaire, An IX
(July–November, 1800)

To the Faubourg St. Antoine, where the street merchants cry "Fru-its! Fru-its!" like piping sea-birds, the news was flung just before dawn of 2 messidor from the back of a horse by a messenger bearing dispatches. People began to turn out at once and to place candles in the windows. Mme. Permon and her daughter, who had spent the night in the suburbs, came home along an alley of two hundred bonfires, around which people were dancing with shouts of "Vive Bonaparte! Vive la République! Vive l'armée!"

The demonstrations elsewhere were more restrained but hardly less heartfelt. On the Bourse funds shot suddenly from 29 to a new high at 37 and M. Talleyrand ordered a reception at the Tuileries for the official announcement of the happy news to the foreign ambassadors. The intensity of his relief can be judged from the fact that it was a full month since that famous evening when he appeared at the Vaudeville with Fouché, and the affair that grew out of that meeting had reached the point where it could no longer be concealed. The two men had dined together and later passed the evening at the Hôtel Marbeuf with Sieyès and Cambacérès; of course the subject of the new constitution came up,

99

and nobody was surprised when the conversation turned on
its radical defect in providing no means of succession for the
head of the state. What if the General were cut in two by a
cannonball down there in the Italian plain? For that matter,
what if his army were driven in defeat, as had happened to
generals before?

The questions spread among the salons that spring in ripple after ripple, always rebounding to Talleyrand and
Fouché after having touched the shores of the political
world. These were the figures at the center, equally necessary
to the new régime, equally at the heart of its policies because equally in the confidence of its chief. Fouché, who alone
could control the Jacobins, intimate of Tallien, Barrère, and
Carnot, even of Benjamin Constant and the de Staël; Fouché
with his police, who knew all the secrets of France and could
have sent any man in the country to Cayenne—loyalty is a
word so difficult to define when the government has not even
been loyal to itself, and today's treason becomes tomorrow's
orthodoxy. What could Talleyrand give beside this? The
support of birth and all that implied for a régime which had
inherited the Revolution. "It is evident," remarked the ma-
jor-domo at the first Consular reception, back in nivôse,
"that very few of these people have done much walking on
parquet floors."

True. Whatever their abilities, Gaudin, Cambacérès, Rœderer, Sieyès himself, were little men, lacking not so much in
social graces as in that wholly indefinable aura which sur-
rounds something worshipped even after the rational reason
for the worship has disappeared. Talleyrand had that aura
and attracted others who had it; when he opened his new
house with a soirée on 6 ventôse, the names among the guests
were La Rochefoucauld, Crillon, de Lameth, de Ségur and
de Coigny, the last of whom had been the familiar friend of
Louis XVI, and the first, his Master of the Royal Wardrobe.
Garat sang; he was wearing one of his ridiculous cravats.
La Harpe came out of retirement to recite some verses from

his translation of *Gerusalemne Liberata,* and Bonaparte was never so happy in his life.

The two men were indispensable to the régime and they knew it; but they were also indispensable to each other and knew that too, standing together, the only weight capable of counterbalancing the sullen Corsican figure of Lucien Bonaparte, Minister of the Interior, who early in the intrigue became aware that there was a succession question and injected himself into it. It was, in fact, impossible to keep him out; as a powerful speaker with a following of his own and a man who had demonstrated political ability under stress, he was one of the more obvious candidates as heir-apparent to his brother. Talleyrand regarded him with horror as a mere club-jack, who possessed all of Napoléon's capacity for violence without the controlling intellect. To Fouché who, so far as he had any principles, held those of republicanism, Lucien with his abilities represented the danger that the Consulate would become a dynasty. Moreover the great policeman had already attached himself to Mme. Joséphine as the surest liaison to her husband ("More men are bound by passion than by interest," he used to say), and Lucien detested the woman. The hand of friendship, offered through pretty Caroline, had been utterly rejected, for Mme. Générale had a fault that to Lucien's Italiote mind rendered her forever unacceptable—barrenness. His brother should get another woman.

Talleyrand, foot and mind in the old régime, by no means shared Fouché's dislike of the dynastic idea—for the future, and provided Lucien were not Crown Prince. The diplomat had the best of reasons for knowing that Fouché's spies watched everything he said and did, even the very secret conversations with a certain Abbé Montesquiou, agent in Paris of Louis XVIII; and that best of reasons was that he could read. The diplomatic representatives of France are provided with armed guards; when dispatches from Fouché to the First Consul were on the road, it was a simple matter for such guards to transform themselves into temporary bandits, who rifled the valises and (having read the documents) abandoned them as brigands will who find useless papers instead of money.

The two ministers were thus in the position of professional gamblers who play a game in which each knows the other is cheating. They co-operated in a good-humored manner with assurances of mutual respect, went to the Vaudeville together, and (both being of a classical turn of mind) formed a triumvirate to save the state from Lucien in the event of his brother's credit being demolished by defeat or his head by a bullet. The role of Crassus was played by an old senator of bloated wealth, Clément de Ris; he kept all the papers and burned them later, on becoming involved in another business so obscure that it was known only by the name of "la ténébreuse affaire," so there are no certain data on how far the triumvirate proceeded, or in what direction. But they seem to have gone at least to the length of determining that the choice of a successor lay between the Marquis de Lafayette, just released from captivity in Olmütz, and Carnot, organizer of victory.

It was a choice from which Talleyrand, at least, was profoundly happy to be absolved. Lafayette's principles were pure, but the same could not be said of his intelligence, and against him lay the objection that he failed to meet the indispensable requirement of a leader of the Republic: He had no Capet blood on his hands, had not been a *votant;* would lie under the inevitable fear and suspicion of those (the majority of the government) who were, and would almost certainly be driven into the arms of the monarchist reaction by that opposition. Carnot was a *votant* of premier crû, but so far in that direction that an administration with him at its head would be downright Jacobin. Only under a Bonaparte presidency could a meeting ground be found for old and new worlds—and moreover, Charles Maurice de Talleyrand Périgord, who made a profession of insincerity, was obliged to confess in the privacy of his cabinet to an emotion that he would have been the last to admit in public. He loved Napoléon Bonaparte.

Not that he was a homosexual, like Cambacérès. ("Hic, haec, hoc," Talleyrand used to call the three Consuls, with the masculine for the General, the feminine for Cambacérès, leaving poor Lebrun the neuter.) It was a love of intellect for intellect, Platonic or Spinozan. With this added, that in the other each recognized, under whatever veils, a spirit that would also serve the state. "Bonaparte is not thinking either of giving up his place or of making it permanent," the diplomat told the Royalist envoy. "He wants peace, but more in order to improve the government than to conserve it; he is an independent character, more avid of glory than of the titles of grandeur."

Of all ambitions, that for glory requires the most co-operation from others and yields the most to them.

II

The First Consul reached Paris on the night of 13 messidor, very late, and was immediately closeted with his leading ministers, who came seriatim to bear tales against each other. Lucien could easily be excused his part in the succession intrigue as a member of the clan, to whom the patrimony of the Bonapartes was a matter of legitimate interest, whatever form that inheritance might take. Talleyrand seized the occasion of the national holiday over the fall of the Bastille on 24 messidor to give a magnificent private fête following the public one at the Invalides. The de Staël wrote to beg the minister "in the name of our ancient friendship" for an invitation; he replied begging her in the name of their ancient friendship to stay away. But every class except the ideologers of the Tribunate was thoroughly represented—soldiers, writers, artists, mathematicians, financiers, and, best of all, not a small assemblage of seigneurs from the court of Louis XVI. Talleyrand was so perfect a host that it was easy for him to persuade these last to mingle on familiar terms with the nouveaux riches and little men who had come up from the administration; and after that it was easy for him to persuade the Chief that his obscure negotiations with the Royalists (of which Lucien and Fouché complained) had been for the purpose of drawing these malcontents into the light of the rising sun.

Clément de Ris disappeared into the stews of "la ténébreuse affaire" and Fouché was accordingly left to bear the blame for all. He tried to exculpate himself by shifting it to Carnot, where some mud stuck indeed, but not enough to avoid that for a time there was a marked coldness between the policeman and his master.

It is probable that with Cambacérès as Second Consul, attention would sooner or later have been directed to the second major defect of the constitution in any case; but the autumnal atmosphere around Fouché directed attention to the fact that during the hurry of those last days of constitution-making the judicial setup had been neglected. The great policeman was in fact conducting his arrests and imprisonments on a system very little removed from the arbitrariness of the defunct monarchy. Indeed, the judges did not know what the law was in many cases; and a great legist of Toulouse would not even have a clerk's knowledge in Picardy. The hazy statutes of the Revolution had abolished feudal law, but for all the rest, France was still ruled by the ancient collection of status, customary, and parlement law; and this was often different from district to small district. For that matter, a good many of the Revolutionary statutes were inconsistent with each other; any jurist who wished to render a Bridlegoose verdict could find some law to back him.

Intolerable. Bonaparte appointed a committee to make a draft code and sat down to look out his window at the world, with a view to obtaining the peace now so much needed for the stabilization of France. To the north the mad Tsar had his soldiers back; he wrote a letter almost of adulation for the First Consul's knightly conduct, changed his Northern

League from one against the Revolution to one against English commercial exactions, and challenged to personal combat with lance and coat of mail any monarch who would not join. There were no battles; the Regent of Denmark did not have to be persuaded, since he had a grievance against England anyway, the islanders having destroyed one of his frigates with many dead, and captured the whole convoy she was covering, when the ships did not wish to be searched —and on the high seas! Prussia joined readily, with an eye on rich Hanover; so did the Swedes, and all's well in that quarter.

To the south lay Egypt and Malta, the latter under so close a blockade by the fleets of England that there was clearly little to be done. The relief of the Army of Egypt was also a naval problem, and since the dreadful night of Aboukir, France had no Mediterranean fleet. The First Consul had been not a little shocked when he took office to learn how poor was the state of the ships in the major squadron, the one at Brest—how short the arsenals were of stores like masts and cordage, even of provisions and system. It was one of the reasons why he had placed an engineer in charge of the Ministry of Marine. But wars are not won by waiting for perfections; already in nivôse the General had conceived a combination to reproduce at sea his favorite military method ashore of multiplying mass by velocity. Honoré Ganteaume, reputed the best seaman in France, was sent down to Brest. As soon as the inevitable storm-wind from the east blew the English blockaders clear, he was to run out at the head of nine fast line-of-battleships loaded with munitions and reinforcements, and to make for Egypt. The coast there was so long that the rosbifs could not possibly keep it all under observation.

Something of the kind had been tried during the previous year, and it had not succeeded; therefore there was set up at the same time an effort to cure the worst difficulties of the Army of Egypt by infiltration. Frigates and little brigs were fitted out in the southern ports to carry ammunition, medical

supplies, wine, special troops, and even a company of co-
medians through the blockade. Peace was made with the
American States whom, under the old Directory, Talleyrand had imprudently antagonized by asking their embassy
for a bribe. Their ships, being neutrals, could be hired for
the transport of wine and medical supplies, and the skippers
were not above doing a little smuggling of more definitely
contraband articles if the price were right.

These were palliatives, designed to keep the Army alive
till a general peace could be negotiated with Egypt still
partly in French possession. Since the night just after Talleyrand's fête, when a batch of dispatches steeped in vinegar
against the effluvium of the plague arrived at two in the
morning, Bonaparte had known that hope of a real conquest
there was gone. Bourrienne saw the General's face fall when
he read them; for the dispatches said that Jean-Baptiste
Kléber, Commander of Egypt, the heart of gold and one of
the best officers of France, had been assassinated. The command had fallen by seniority to Menou, a terrible booby,
who was high on the army list only because he had made the
conciliatory gesture of renaming himself Abdallah and embracing the Law of the Prophet. Ganteaume's ships had
lacked too many things to sail with the winter storms; now
it was summer, with the winds onshore, so there was little
chance he could run out before another six months had
passed.

Yet the chance of a general peace seemed not small that
summer. The agents in England said that the hitherto irreducible hostility of Pitt was tottering along with his government, Britain was worried over the Tsar's League of the
North, and in burning thermidor there arrived at Paris a
messenger from His K.u.K. Majesty with proposals for an
immediate continental armistice. It was the Graf St. Julien,
who had been taken prisoner in Desaix's charge at Marengo
and later carried the surrender proposal to Melas. Bonaparte liked him and knew he possessed the Imperial confidence. A suspension of hostilities for all armies was at once

agreed upon and Talleyrand sat down to talk things out with him.

What were the conditions to make it a peace? The two men named those their governments regarded as essential—confirmation of the left bank of the Rhine for France; for Austria, the line of the Mincio in Italy and recovery of the fortress of Mantua. There were details, but no fundamental conflict. The controlled visage of the ex-bishop of Autun cracked into a smile, and he observed that there was no reason why they should not sign the preliminaries of the peace then and there—subject, of course, to ratification by the consuls of France and His K.u.K. Majesty.

Graf St. Julien shifted uneasily in his chair. He was a soldier, new to diplomacy, and, with the Frenchman's steady eye upon him, was finally driven to admit that he did not believe his instructions from the Emperor permitted him to take so grave a step. Talleyrand already knew that; the Graf had not arrived before advices from French secret agents in Vienna that on the very day the news of Marengo reached that capital a new treaty with England had been signed. It bound Austria, in exchange for two millions sterling, not to make a separate peace; and a good part of the money had already been spent. But Austria dreadfully needed the months until spring to recover from the effects of the Italian defeat and to meet the attacks of Moreau in Schwabenland, and St. Julien had really come to gain time without committing his government to anything definite. The French diplomat, as he developed the argument, allowed no hint to escape that he knew the other's purpose. If St. Julien was not there to sign a peace, why had he come at all? After all, his credentials, signed by the Emperor's own hand, inquired of France "if the basis on which you wish to propose for a peace are such that one may flatter himself with arriving at that desirable objective." M. Talleyrand proposed merely an answer in the affirmative, signed by the two together.

St. Julien allowed himself to be persuaded, and they began to talk terms—a game at which his specific soldierly mind permitted him to make a somewhat better showing. Here M. Talleyrand was more reasonable than anyone could have believed possible, considering the military position. In five days the Austrian was posting back to Vienna with the draft treaty, accompanied by the supple Duroc.

The storm signals began to fly as soon as they reached the zone of the armies; the Austrian commander there said they were still at war and refused to pass Duroc through. The nearer he got to home the less Graf St. Julien liked his prospects; and he was perfectly right, for when he reached the capital, both the Emperor and Thugut his minister cried they were disgraced in the eyes of England and the world. They disavowed everything St. Julien had done and exiled him to a bat-ridden castle in the remotest parts of Transylvania. Still, the fat was now in the fire; the alternative to denouncing the armistice and fighting at once (which Austria was by no means prepared to do) was an effort to arrive at terms.

Lord Minto, at Vienna for England, helped by saying that his country would not object to a peace if she too were made a part of it (privately writing home that nothing could exceed the villainy of these Germans). Bonaparte jumped at the chance. Very well, said he, let us make it an armistice general, by land and sea; ships to circulate freely while the congress of accommodation is sitting. Naturally, the British saw through this device; it would permit the resupply of the French forces blockaded in Malta, the key of the Mediterranean, and of those in Egypt, the key of the East. A sea armistice by all means, they replied, but only on condition that one provision ship a fortnight be allowed to visit Malta and Egypt during that armistice, the ships to be checked by the blockaders to see that their cargoes contained nothing but food. This would do very well for Malta, but Egypt was the granary of the East, able to feed half Europe besides itself; the need there was for men and munitions. Bonaparte said no; there were more proposals and counterproposals, but the question always boiled down to this: Could England

be persuaded to accept anything, anything at all, in exchange
for leaving Egypt in French hands?

No, said the British, and time was running out toward
winter, when there could be no campaign in Germany. One
last question to Austria: Would she make a separate peace?
No, said the Empire, and as frimaire came, which the un-
liberated nations call November, the armies were ordered to
march. On the shores of the Baltic, Tsar Paul sequestered
all English ships and had their crews driven a hundred miles
inland under the knout; the fleets of Sweden and Denmark
were given a rendezvous with the Russians for early spring
when the ice broke; Prussian armies moved on Bremen and
the German rivers were closed to the trade of England. It
meant the end of Egypt, but the First Consul already had a
project in train elsewhere to give France the colonies, sea
power, and commerce she needed.

8

SAUL SLAYS HIS THOUSANDS

Paris, The Valley of the Danube: 5 floréal,
An VIII–12 frimaire, An IX
(April 25–December 3, 1800)

THE Austrian method of war had been slowly built up during a century and a half of fighting Turks in the east and Protestants among the Iron Mountains of the north, where local resources are few. Food and munitions were collected in magazines at fortified towns well behind the front, from which they could be moved up along the Imperial postroads. At the front itself the armies fanned out in a cordon, whose parts were (ideally) equidistant from the nearest magazine. These detachments advanced abreast, so that when one made contact with the enemy there was always another within supporting distance. If they were forced to retreat, they did it together; an enemy found himself enmeshed in forces which continually concentrated and moved nearer to their sources of supply; and there were many opportunities to strike at the opponent's flanks. So had the Austrians circled round Masséna at Genoa, so had they struck down his sally.

In the north Kray von Krajova was their commander, the Hungarian with the polished face that made him look like a living statue; vain of his reputation, a friendly man of some culture, who made observations on philosophy and wrote charming letters to his brother. A corps general under

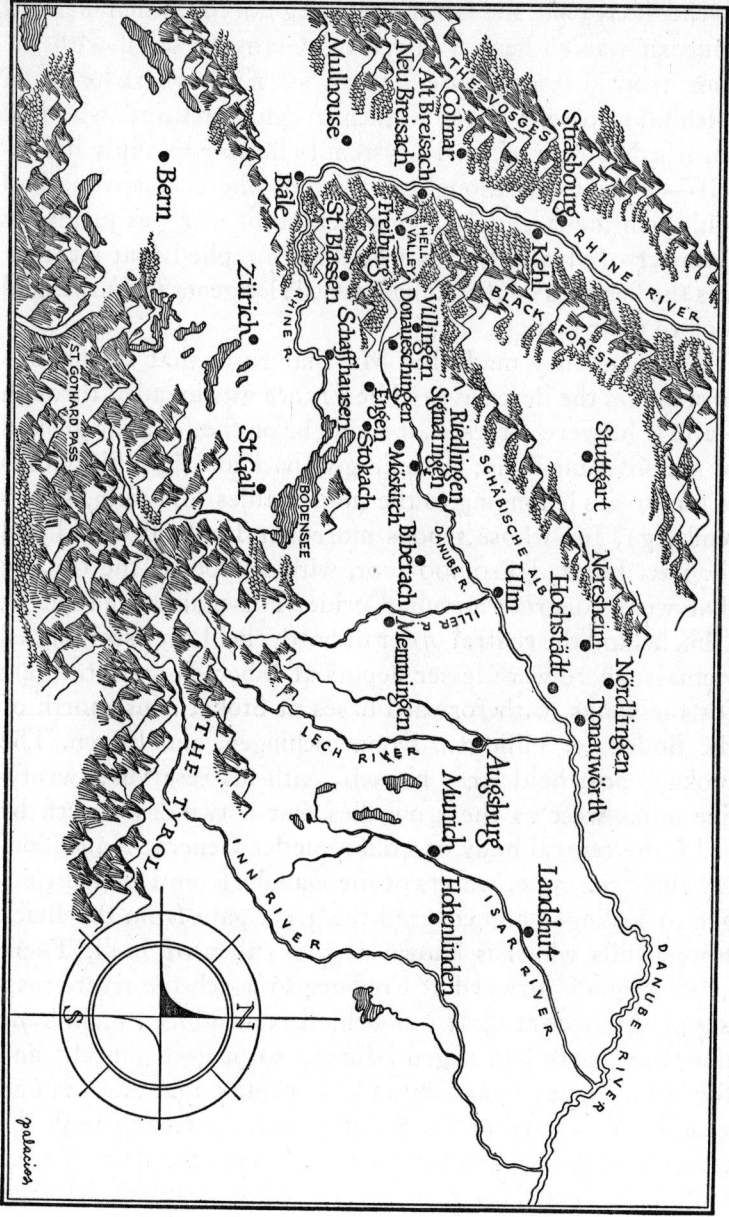

III

Archduke Karl in the latter's campaign of '95, when General Jourdan was so beaten in central Germany; then with the main army in Italy before Suvorov's arrival, where he won a splendid victory over the French. A good tactician, who had absorbed enough of Karl's system to be able to apply it himself—or so it was thought at Vienna where, if anyone had told them the Archduke's new method of war was primarily a matter of strategy, they would have replied that strategy was the business of the Aulic Council; let generals in the field look to their tactics.

The plan they made for Marshal Kray that spring was to stand on the defensive, while France was invaded through Italy. If he were attacked, it would be on the familiar ground of the old campaigns; he could give back and fight his battles in territories belonging to the subject allies (Bavaria, Württemberg), for whose troops moreover England would find the pay. He had 110,000 foot, with 25,000 of the cavalry that were Austria's peculiar pride. His main magazine at Ulm, behind the central order of battle, held over six months' victuals; there were lesser depots at Biberach and Stuttgart for the wings, with forward bases at Stokach just north of the Bodensee, Villingen, Donaueschingen, and Engen. The Stokach post held Kray himself, with his reserves; twenty-five miles west as the crow flies, but a two-day march by road, the central body of 40,000 under General Nauendorf lay along the upper waters of the Danube from Donaueschingen to Villingen and covered the great gate from the Black Forest hills which is known as the Valley of Hell. There was a brigade forward at Freiburg to watch the river-crossing of the Breisachs. It was behind Nauendorf's main body that Bonaparte had urged Moreau to project himself, and the latter made the understandable protest that Austria had a strong vanguard in the Rhine valley, protecting both the crossing and the little-used road north into the Black Forest from Bâle. Austria was thus at the center of an arc; Moreau would have to concentrate by marching around it, and if they caught him during the process, it would go hard.

The Austrians also had a flotilla of gunboats on the Bo-densee under an English sea captain. From this point down through the Tyrol to guard the eastward outlets of Switzer-land lay Kray's left wing under the Prince of Reuss—25,000 men, of whom a goodly proportion Tyrolean mountaineers who knew the country and fought for their homes besides. General Kienmayer with 15,000 held the northern debouches of the Black Forest country; General Sztarray with 16,000 more was close up to the Rhine, north of Kienmayer till Frankfurt was reached, which place was strongly garrisoned. Kray had the odd arrangement of no fewer than three chiefs of staff—Schmidt, who had held the same office under Arch-duke Karl and was supposed to bring an element of his think-ing into the conversation; with Chasteler and Weyrother, who had shown much talent in the complex business of plan-ning moves on a map and having them work out in practice.

Kray's own plan was to simulate an attack on the west-flowing Rhine near Bâle, then take the French in the rear by shooting the Prince of Reuss into the wild Swiss country round St. Gall, south of the Bodensee; but the Aulic Council said no—main battle in Italy, we will hold here.

II

The Austrian arrangement was somewhat peculiar for the system under which it was made, with the main strength poised well back and the fan-spokes of the cordon touching the Rhine only at the extremities of the area they were de-fending. There was a sound reason for this: the French held three strong fortified bridgeheads on the right bank at Bâle, the Breisachs and Strasbourg-Kehl. If Kray were not to at-tack them, he could be sure that Moreau would attack from two of them in such force as to pinch out and destroy any formation that tried to hold the river line. As a matter of fact, Moreau was planning to use the southern pair of bridgeheads only, with a feint to the north to draw Austrian reserves in that direction. When he fled from pretty Caroline down to his army at the beginning of frimaire, he found it still under the old divisional system of the Revolution and promptly reorganized it into four main corps, the better to conduct this system of attack.

Claude-Jacques Lecourbe had the corps of the right wing, 40,000 men; he was from Besançon, where the pics of the Jura stand against the horizon, and all his early experience had been gained in that region, as one of the elected officers of the old National Guard, though he rose up the ranks during the wars in the north. A famous mountain fighter, who had gained great glory in Sambre-et-Meuse, and greater still when, with only 1,500 men, he held Suvorov and the tough Russians among the Alpine passes a year ago until Masséna smashed them. His wing was in Switzerland along the Rhine from the lake to the curve at Bâle; at the latter town stood Moreau himself with three divisions, 28,000 men, of the army reserve.

29,000 constituted the corps of the center, holding the line from Bâle to the Breisachs; this was Gouvion St. Cyr, known for his frigid politeness and still more for a cold, intelligent nerve that never cracked. When brave Joubert was killed in the dreadful defeat at Novi in the An VII and everything seemed crashing down, two generals surrendering with all their men, St. Cyr held his troops together, made good the retreat, and beat off the pursuit. He had been an artist, and had a wonderful eye for topography and proportion. With a heart equal to his head, he would be commander-in-chief next, and had held the post briefly during the winter, but dour technicians of his stamp seldom impress in a polity where war is the first business and all army appointments are partly political; Moreau obtained the reputation of being the better soldier by being the better man.

Lecourbe and St. Cyr are worth remarking, for they will be met again. Left of them stood Gilbert-Joseph Ste. Suzanne, with 20,000 men in his corps, holding the river down to the Main, and there is little enough to say of him. See how the weight of the French was to their right, around Bâle, well closed up to the river. They could march faster and farther than Austria, and such magazines as they had were up in the front line, but there were not many of these, for though Moreau thought in terms of the strategy that had ruled all Europe since Prussian Frederick, he was also a General of the Revolution, whose commissary was so inefficient he had to live off the country.

Carnot had been up to the line himself and seen that all the men had new uniforms and were in good spirits. Their drill was precise; they were called "Messieurs of the Rhine" to mark them from the rowdy citoyens of Italy, who marched all day behind Masséna on glory and a biscuit.

On 5 floréal they broke camp. (Bonaparte and Bourrienne were looking at their map.) Ste. Suzanne concentrated rapidly and began pouring his men across at Kehl at four o'clock in the morning. There were spies about; Moreau had counted on that, and had done his best to deceive them by renting a new house at Colmar and coming down with his staff so that the whitecoats would be convinced that the true attack was here.

The Austrian tactical system was a reproduction of the strategic; Ste. Suzanne easily broke through the light infantry formations of the cordon round the bridgehead, and by evening of the first day had not only beaten one of Kienmayer's reserve formations, but was also solidly in possession of the north-south highway along the right bank of the river. Kienmayer and Sztarray were split, except as they could unite over the mountains to Stuttgart, sixty miles to the rear.

On that same day St. Cyr debouched from the Breisach bridgehead, broke up the screen opposing him and, pushing one division toward Freiburg and the head of Hell Valley, pivoted another under his best tactical officer, General Ney, northward as though to establish communications with Ste. Suzanne. Kray had reports from his field commanders the next morning, which would be 29 April, and as the Austrian light cavalry had done its usual good scouting, the not outrageously inaccurate estimate of 40,000 Frenchmen across the Rhine was arrived at. The Austrian reacted according to pattern, countering the expected blow against his right center at Villingen via Hell Valley by sending 7,000 men from the reserve to Kienmayer and bidding Sztarray attack southward along the main Rhine highway.

That same night Ste. Suzanne got his orders to pull back across the river, covering his retirement with a chain of posts; St. Cyr to shoot out his right with all the artillery and baggage toward Bâle, where the three heavy divisions of Moreau's personal command were. Moreau's infantry pushed along the route into the Black Forest against Kray's vanguard; a formation of heavy horse moved north to meet St. Cyr, with the Rhine on its left.

The combats were everywhere affairs of outposts, the Austrians always overwhelmed by numbers. By 10 floréal, April 30, Moreau with the vanguard of his reserve had edged across the hills to St. Blassen and was linked with St. Cyr; Ste. Suzanne was coming through Hell Valley on the left rear of the movement. Kray was demonstrating how hard it is to give up a notion once formed by ordering Sztarray to reinforce Kienmayer and drawing from his left flank along the Bodensee to reinforce his center, where he now was. He was thus completely off balance rightward the next morning, when Lecourbe surprised a crossing at Schaffhausen and began to march on Stokach and its magazines, while Moreau, throwing the weight of his personal command to the right, pointed on Engen.

On May 3 Lecourbe struck Stokach; he had 25,000 men up, and the only Austrians before the place were 9,000 under Prince Joseph of Lorraine who, in view of the importance of the magazines, tried to hold on. Frenchmen poured in on him from every wood-path and valley, and he was badly broken, with the loss of 4,000 prisoners, all his guns, and the great Stokach magazine; the remnants of the command were thrown back northeasterly toward Möskirch. Kray did not hear of the disaster till the next day, but in the meanwhile disquieting reports from his southern flank had caused him to countermand the reinforcement to Kienmayer and to shift his main body southward to Engen, which the troops reached May 4, very tired.

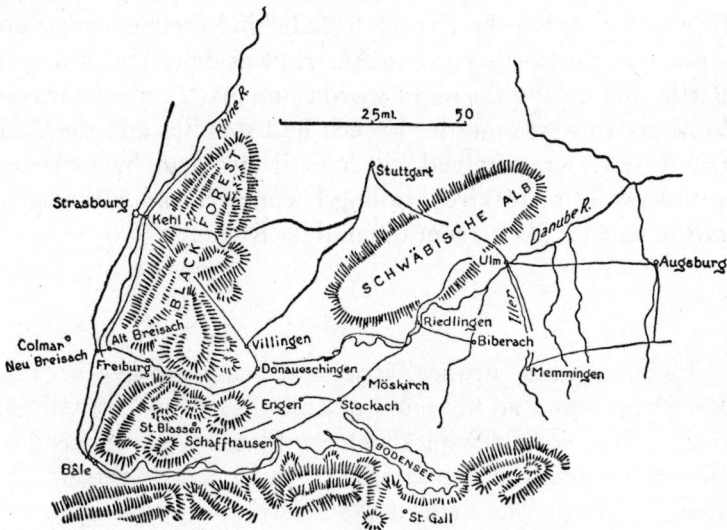

Moreau's summer in Germany

The result now stood that Moreau had sent Kray's right wing out on a tangent, severed the communications between the Austrian center and left, and had 50,000 of his men in hand, facing that center, reinforcements close behind, while Kray had 45,000 and no near reserves. But the country was rugged and heavily wooded, there were no maps, the roads were mere tracks where two could pass, and the hostile peasantry told lies when asked where these tracks led. On its march to Engen, Division Ney of St. Cyr thus became engaged in a series of blind valleys. The wagons were left behind; then the division reached a place where guns could be put through only by engineers' making road with hoes and bayonets, all other tools being back with the train. This resource also failed in time and Ney arrived for the battle with tired men who had to borrow ammunition.

Under such circumstances the clash for the position at Engen turned into a patchwork, swaying affair of regiments and divisions appearing from obscurity to attack the natural fortresses of hill, wood, brook, and village. On the southern flank a charge of Austrian grenadiers at twilight, sustained by cavalry, drove the French back behind their morning positions; at the northern wing Austria was driven in. A drawn battle; but during the night word came that Lecourbe was in Stokach, so that now the French had supplies and the Austrians few. Kray solved his logistic problem by ordering withdrawal to Möskirch, calling Kienmayer and Sztarray to fall in on that place from the middle Rhine.

III

First round to France; it missed being decisive because Lecourbe, who had the mind of an old sergeant, waited for orders, and, not receiving them, went into bivouac instead of swinging around on Möskirch to cut off Kray's retreat. As soon as Moreau learned of the Austrian movement, he ordered Lecourbe's three divisions up against the new enemy position, himself with the reserve moving eastward across Lecourbe's rear, to keep pressure on Kray's left flank and crowd him up against the Danube. Just beyond the river in this region lies the Schwäbische Alb, a worn and barren highland that is the watershed for the two great European river systems. Kray would find hard marching there if he were forced across; St. Cyr slanted north from Engen, picked up the main highroad paralleling the Danube, and moved toward Möskirch along this line, with Ste. Suzanne behind him.

It was a cordon-system advance, which Kray met with a cordon-system defense at Möskirch town, where the turnpike and the route up from Stokach draw together at the crest of an open plateau. The town was strongly held by Joseph of Lorraine, with artillery covering all the exits from the wood of Rumbach, where the road from Stokach leads

up slopes. Rightward of Lorraine was General Nauendorf
with a corps, echeloned forward through the village of Heudorf and the woods behind it. There was an Austrian reserve
in the rear, but the other troops of that nation were scat-

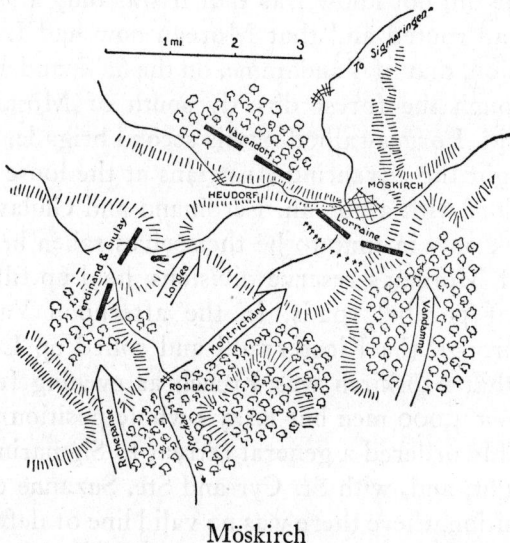

Möskirch

tered along the postroad westward (where General Giulay
and the Archduke Ferdinand had command) and up toward
the Danube, including a division of Bavarians under their
General Wrede.

Moreau approached this position along the Stokach road
on the morning of 16 floréal (6 May), with Division Montrichard of Lecourbe in the lead. The division attacked at
once; was beaten off by Lorraine's batteries and lost most
of its own guns when it tried to get them into position to reply. Lecourbe's second division, Lorges, had now arrived.
Moreau filed it leftward for an attack on Heudorf, and the
leading brigade carried the outer houses of the town in a
rush. Lorraine's battery from the center fired into the flank
of this brigade, however, and at the same time Nauendorf
released horse and foot from the shadows of a wood and
struck back hard. Lorges' brigade went back in a state re-

sembling rout, and Kray, who had seen the whole thing, imagined he had complete victory. He ordered Giulay and Ferdinand to come in on the flank and rear of this broken formation.

What he did not know was that it was only a single brigade he had routed and that Moreau now had Lecourbe's third division, that of Vandamme, on the field, and was filtering it through the forest directly south of Möskirch, the Klosterwald. Lorges rallied on his second brigade, attacked again, caught the advancing Austrians at the loose and carried Heudorf with a hurrah. Ferdinand and Giulay arrived on his flank only in time to be themselves taken in flank by the first of Moreau's reserve divisions, held up till now by the lack of parallel roads. In the afternoon Vandamme worked through the Klosterwald and rolled up Lorraine's flank, so that Möskirch was French as evening fell. Each side had lost 4,000 men but Kray's whole position was now confused. He ordered a general retreat to Sigmaringen during the night, and, with St. Cyr and Ste. Suzanne crowding in on a position where there was no valid line of defense, was forced to slip across to the left bank of the Danube and the edge of the Schwäbische Alb country.

Moreau's strategic objective was now secured. He had pushed his opponent's main force across the river and away from the main east-west highroad, "The Boulevard of Germany," that leads into the heart of Bavaria across the north-running affluents of the Danube—had cut Kray's communications with the Reuss force of 25,000 in the Tyrol. Now Jean-Victor operated by his right, to drive Reuss still farther south and to project his own centralized mass of maneuver still farther east, so that Kray would either have to march by a long circuit to face him or be thrown altogether off his line of operations and back on the mountains that bordered Bohemia.

Kienmayer's corps fell in on the main Austrian command the night the latter crossed the Danube, and there was a council of war, at which the disagreements among all those chiefs of staff brought out the fact that the Imperial army was trying to accomplish mutually contradictory objectives. It was seeking to cover the Tyrol against any attack from the north that would jeopardize the communications of Melas in Italy, and at the same time to protect the minor states north of the Danube, which furnished a good third of the Imperial troops—men who would be withdrawn if the French swallowed up their countries. There was also the question of bringing Sztarray and Reuss in on the main body to build up its strength to the point where a battle against Moreau's mass could be undertaken. All might be accomplished (they decided) by a retreat to the river country along the line of the Boulevard, but this was a region of gorges, where Austria's horse could hardly hope to hold head against the active infantry of Gaul.

There was thus no decision on the overall question; but while they were beating it out, messengers from country people and the cavalry screen began to come in with news which made it clear that Moreau was edging south of east toward the big Biberach magazine. As the Austrian army had not been smashed at Möskirch, only pushed back, it was possible and obvious to undertake a speed march to the rescue.

Austria moved therefore, downstream to Riedlingen, crossed past the peak called Bussen, and made a forced march to Biberach, arriving on May 8, to the great astonishment of the French vanguards, who were themselves just beginning to arrive before the town. It is covered by a stream, not wide, but flowing between deeply bitten banks, the Riss. For some reason only himself knew, Kray had directed that 10,000 of his men should constitute a kind of foreguard on the left bank. As they reached position, tired and straggling after their hard march, they were sharply attacked by the light troops of Division Richepanse of Moreau's reserve, and then by St. Cyr's whole corps. Kray could save his vanguard only by forming well to the rear behind Biberach and letting them be driven in on him. St.

Cyr rushed the bridge, while Richepanse gained another crossing lower down and flanked the whole position. Kray lost 2,000 men, had to retreat hastily cross-country to Memmingen on the next river, Iller, and the Biberach magazine was in French hands.

There was no pursuit, St. Cyr's position as a rival aspirant for command being too delicate for him to make one without orders, and Moreau being unable to give them because he was at the rear, reviewing the corps of Ste. Suzanne. This allowed Kray time to evacuate the stores from Memmingen before the French bicornes began to appear among the hills. When they did, he retreated down the Iller to the great Austrian center depot at Ulm, while the French brushed aside the stream-guards, won a passage and a footing on the great Boulevard, whose head is here.

The Austrians were now above Moreau's left flank, and might fall on his communications if he attempted to move along the highroad, but this worried Jean-Victor not a bit, since in the various combats he had whittled the enemy's strength down so far below his own that he could make ample provision for his endangered wing. He was going to march on Munich and Vienna. Unfortunately just at this moment War Minister Carnot arrived with the positive order of the government that 20,000 men be sent through the St. Gothard into Italy, the corps that became Moncey's. There were some hard words said around headquarters about the interfering salaud of a Bonaparte, not even a Frenchman, but old Terrorist Carnot could be as grim as any man alive, and the troops must march.

IV

At Ulm Kray was joined by most of Sztarray's men and a reinforcement of Bavarians that brought his numbers up to equal Moreau's again. This meant that in a hostile country, where every peasant was an Austrian spy, the French lacked force to deceive and push past their opponents; they must maneuver Kray out of his position or besiege him in it. There was small chance of the latter; Ulm was an extensive entrenched camp, with immense quantities of artillery, and everyone remembered how a great Austro-Russian army had gone to pieces before just such a camp of Frederick the Great's at Bunzelwitz in '61. Moreover, Ulm lay astride the river junctions, controlling the only bridges; it could not even be blockaded without the risk that the Austrians would rush heavy forces through the town and overwhelm whatever troops were on one of the peninsulas among the impassable streams.

Moreau received a sample of this on 23 floréal (May 13) when he closed up to the fortress with the corps of Ste. Suzanne coming down Danube's left bank. Kray attacked this single corps sharply with those of Kienmayer and Sztarray. Ste. Suzanne was in trouble when rescued by the appearance of St. Cyr's dense columns, visibly moving toward Ulm along the right bank, the good countenance of his own men, and the fact that a Graf all hung with decorations had arrived in Kray's lines to warn him in the name of the Aulic Council against making any attacks—his mission was defense.

Now the pace slowed down. Moreau concentrated on the right bank, pulled back south of Ulm, and threw Lecourbe's corps out toward Augsburg, in the hope of drawing Kray from his hole to fight a battle; but the Austrian's service of information told him this was only a lightweight feint, and he never stirred. The French were not finding it easy to provision; had eaten out Biberach magazine and made such severe requisitions on the country that a guerrilla movement began to grow up along the lines of communication. Moreau judged the fault lay in his own ranks; shot a couple of exacting commissioners and sent home several generals, including St. Cyr and Vandamme, thus planting an acorn from which an oak would grow. Meanwhile, under the abundant rains of prairial, while Bonaparte was thundering through the Lombard plain, the army was reorganized.

The new arrangement gave Moreau a corps of the center, under the General's personal command; one "of the right" under Lecourbe, and another "of the left" under Paul Grénier, a kind of epauletted sergeant who had come up through the ranks on courage, and who knew how to obey orders, but very little else. Richepanse had a separate command—an oversize division of cavalry and light infantry for fast movement. Ste. Suzanne was sent back to the Rhine, in charge of recruiting depots and the suppression of guerrillas. A patchwork of formations was put into the heads of the Swiss valleys as protection against any move by the Prince of Reuss, and since that officer was as great a booby as Austria possessed, the task did not have to be taken seriously.

On 21 prairial, June 10, the troops began to move (Jean Lannes was storming Montebello at the head of his grenadiers)—Richepanse pulling back up the Iller to cover Memmingen and the line of communications, the three fighting commands fanned out and pushing toward the Lech on a front fifty miles broad. They struck that river all along the line on 24 prairial, mopping up the Austrian guard detachments there, and driving through Augsburg. Kray's service of information was smothered in an overaccumulation of detail from so many points at once; and as it went blank, Moreau's whole army pivoted on Richepanse and swung up toward the Danube, with the right wing from south of Augsburg marching fast, fast, a trick at which the Revolutionary levies could always outmatch the world.

Kray had strong forces watching all the Danube crossings from the north bank, with the corps of Sztarray on the south side. The latter's early reports had spoken only of Frenchmen marching eastward past, and his orders were to do nothing till he could surely fall on the rear of such a movement, so he had done nothing at all. But as he waited, his loose chain of posts was struck on June 15 by Grénier's whole corps with the French reserve cavalry, and what was left of Sztarray retreated to the north bank at once. Kray was still uncertain where Moreau was; as a matter of fact most of the French army was up to the stream and well east of Ulm.

The next three days Moreau spent in tapping here and there for a passage. The bridges were down clear to Donauwörth, all boats had been destroyed, but on the 19th June, 30 prairial, Lecourbe set up a big battery at a ruined bridge near Höchstädt, drove off the Austrians on the farther bank, and, under cover of some light infantry who swam the stream, his engineers repaired the structure rapidly enough so that all his men were across by nightfall and Moreau's corps of the center by midnight.

Now Kray had information at last, but it was the information that his lines of communication along the Boulevard of Germany and those along the Danube were alike severed. Ulm had become untenable; the only way out lay northeastward toward Bohemia. The very next morning he took up the march, through Neresheim on Nördlingen, with 50,000 men; 4,000 had been cut off and captured in Moreau's crossing. The Austrians lost still more at Neresheim on June 22nd, when Lecourbe and Division Ney of Grénier, after a day of torrential rains that halted the French on their cross-country route, caught up with Kray's rearguard and overwhelmed it.

At Nördlingen Kray gathered his men around him on the 24th and held another council with his three chiefs of staff. Attrition was eating up his numbers and the troops were so desperately tired that there was reason to fear the result of a battle; but he had been forced back on a line of retreat that could end only in Bohemia, where no reserves of food had been prepared, while Moreau was in possession of all the main highroads to Vienna. Word had come through of Marengo and the armistice terms in Italy; he sent a flag of truce to the lines, to say that a general armistice was being signed, and, while Moreau was digesting this information, made a forced march to Neuburg and Ingoldstädt, recovering his homeward route.

The ruse was a success in saving Kray from attack, but a failure in another sense, since the French general rushed his troops forward pell-mell to gain possession of as much territory as possible before the armistice should become effective. Lecourbe was shunted south to gain the passes toward Italy, while the other corps moved on and through Munich. For two weeks thereafter, there were shufflings among the plains of central Bavaria; then simultaneously Moreau began to run out of victual again, and the Graf St. Julien came through the lines on his mission to Paris. Moreau granted a general armistice on the terms of French troops holding the line of the Lech, with Austria to keep the Danube fortresses, being allowed to reprovision them once in two weeks. Himself, he posted to Paris to look at the political situation.

v

It was the thermidor of the fêtes and jockeying for position. The de Staël was at Coppet, where they talked of nothing but the victories of Moreau, the incorruptibly republican general, and were horrified at the news from Marengo. "The good of France, of humanity, demanded that there should have been defeats there." The lady's new book was a declaration of her personal war on the government—in its form a disquisition on literature, in its content a philosophical act of faith, the credo of the liberals. Without absolute independence of thought and speech there is no true glory, no morality, no progress. It is necessary to believe in the perfectibility of man, to labor unceasingly toward that goal; no revolution is ever over till philosophy be enthroned, in the form of writers and orators who will elevate public spirit above self-interest. In France republican institutions had outrun the spirit of republicanism. We are sunk in the lukewarm hell of Dante, with parties quarreling on grounds that have no reference to philosophical principle. A long period of education under men of the word would be necessary before the formation of that great moderately liberal body which alone would be able to govern in the name of pure philosophy and without the use of force.

The time for publication was singularly ill-chosen. However Platonic this statement of principles, no one could miss the fact that it was a public rejection of what the de Staël had privately rejected before—any accommodation with the Consulate. Bonaparte had sent his brother Joseph to see her, who used to be an habitué of her famous salon. "The First Consul is discontented with you. Why are you so opposed to the government? What is it that you want?"

"It is not a question of what I want, but what I think."

The reply was a proud and even a splendid one, but it would have sounded better if she had in fact been demanding nothing from the head of state. Actually she had covered reams of paper and employed dozens of messengers in making requests: a tribunate for Benjamin Constant, a this for X, a that for Y, and above all, ever repeated, two million francs for old Papa Necker, the wheezy schoolmaster of Geneva, who had personally loaned that amount to the late Citizen Capet. On the highest principles of moral and political philosophy, the de Staël considered that the sum should be refunded to the daughter of the lender by a government that made it impossible for the royal family to discharge the debt.

It was characteristic of Germaine de Staël (and of the intellectual liberals who had done little but annotate her doctrine) that she should be astonished when Bonaparte expressed indignation over hearing her denounce as a tyranny the government from which she was demanding extralegal favors. As far as she was concerned, the two sets of actions belonged in different intellectual departments—like that "sensibility" then prized as evidence of a truly noble nature: the sensibility which consisted in a sympathetic anguish over the victims of misfortune, the purity of the emotion being ruined if anything practical were done to alleviate the unhappiness. De Staël was hurt when Talleyrand refused her a card for his fête to the First Consul, and mortified at receiving eleven notes of regret on the morning following her coronation of Benjamin Constant as the second Mirabeau. Why (she demanded) this adventitious connection between the expression of ideas, which dealt in absolute principles, and the daily conduct of life, which merely furnished raw materials from which principles were developed?

It never occurred to her (for instance) that the prefects might be giving that disinterested service* she demanded from the coalized philosopher-kings. She was not aware of prefects; for her as for Sieyès, they were mere executives, inarticulate; contributed nothing to that vocal enlargement of the human spirit which was the highest good. If she and her entourage had given these appointments any attention, they would doubtless have expressed toward them the same revulsion the liberal interest felt toward the men named to the great offices of state. Prefects and councilors alike were ex-Jacobins, ci-devant Royalists, executives; not an orator or a man of letters on the list, no one at all who could contribute to that process of education in philosophical principle.

To Mme. de Staël, to the liberals, such a series of appointments was an outrageous act of betrayal on the part of the man whose accession they had hailed with delight as having brought to the support of enthroned political philosophy in the person of Sieyès the force and civic virtue of the victorious armies. They found it vile that the resultant government should be concerned with the material welfare of Frenchmen at home and the position of the nation abroad.

Worse; Bonaparte had instituted a censorship which abridged the right to criticize the government in the light of those principles on which all hope of perfectibility rested. For the censorship which began by concealing the movements of the Army of Reserve had developed into an instrument frankly political, with the number of dailies in the capital

* "Enthusiasm" the age called it, in a word which has so completely changed its meaning that writings of the period are often incomprehensible to moderns.

cut to thirteen and the suppressions falling most heavily on precisely those liberal publications whose columns expressed the views of Constant and de Staël. From the Tribune this brought the memorable phrase that there was in France "only servility and silence—a silence to which all Europe is listening"; from Fouché, the last brought a request that Mme. de Staël would wait on him.

The First Consul (he remarked), "doubtless ill informed," suspected her of exciting M. Constant against the government.

"M. Constant is a man of too superior a spirit to take his opinions from a woman!" she cried.

Fouché bowed, with a slight smile on his bloodless lips. He considered Mme. de Staël's health in need of recruitment; perhaps it would be as well if she spent a few weeks in the country.

There was more in it than the old formal conflict between thought and action, between today and tomorrow. Intellectual liberals frequently encounter financial difficulties; it is not a paying profession. The de Staël liberals rejected the support of parties; the violence of the Jacobin assaults on *De la Littérature* was equaled only by the acerbity of the Royalists: "She writes on metaphysics, which she does not understand; on morality, which she does not practice; and on the virtues of her sex, which she does not possess." It was natural enough, in view both of the opposition from the regular parties and of the de Staël's connection with the financial markets through her father, that she and her liberals should have sought the support of the one group whose hostility to the new régime, to Bonaparte himself, was irreducible—the bankers.

It had not been forgotten that the First Consul was the man who, four years before, when he was General of the Army of Italy, had shaken the whole structure of international finance by tapping the tills at Leghorn on the ground that they held English gold and France was at war with England. It was not forgiven that Gaudin's financial pro-

gram had spoiled some very promising investments, by re-
funding the bad government paper, then mostly in bankers'
hands—or that under Carnot, Minister of War, it was impossible to arrive at those profitable little arrangements in
connection with supplying the armies. The voice that spoke
through the suppressed journals was the voice of liberalism,
progress, perfectibility—in general terms, with specific reference only to the departures from principle made by the
government; but the hands that paid the bills were those of
Récamier, Ouvrard, Necker. There was no sense of guilt
involved in this alliance of high principles and high finance;
the philosophy was purely political, and economics had not
been invented. When Bonaparte declared that if he did not
bridle the press the government could not remain in power
for three months, they called him an "ideophobe" and turned
like sunflowers toward Jean-Victor Moreau, a General who
thought of politics in terms of letting it be run by orators.

The question of whom the victorious republican General
would consort with when he reached Paris was thus a matter
of importance. He arrived somewhat unexpectedly, just as
Carnot was handing Bonaparte a superb pair of gold-
mounted pistols, studded with diamonds. "You brought them
at just the right moment," said the First Consul, and instantly presented them to Moreau, an act of generosity
which was lent additional point by the fact that at the close
of the Italian campaign the Consul had distributed "weapons
of honor" to soldiers who had especially distinguished themselves.

The General of the Army of the Rhine was invited to
dinner, and over the coffee cups heard with lowering and
beefy countenance a proposal that he should unite himself
in marriage with Hortense de Beauharnais, daughter to
Joséphine, and a little less than half his own age. He replied
that marriage was the farthest thing from his thoughts;
what other excuses he made, we do not know, but a couple of
nights later, dining at a house of liberal—that is, anti-Bonaparte—persuasion, he was heard to remark: "Bonaparte

wanted me to marry into his damned family; but I managed to get out of it."

General Moreau was, however, not quite done with the damned family. Ever since the bad fright on the occasion of her husband's return from Egypt, Mme. la Première Consule had been on her best behavior, and she was sufficiently pleased with her new dignity to make a genuine effort toward increasing its importance. Creole society is pretty much a unit, regardless of the island of origin, and she was acquainted with a certain Widow Hulot, who had a daughter of ravishing attractiveness, with a considerable dot, as the defunct M. Hulot had been treasurer of the Ile de France. Joséphine assembled the Widow Hulot, the Widow Hulot's daughter, and General Moreau. The thing took fire at once, for Moreau's modesty made him awkward and embarrassed in company, as his ambition made him later regret lost opportunities, and in the Hulots he recognized a pair of women who would run his life, furnishing for him that *appui* in Paris he had heretofore lacked. Joséphine arranged everything; within a week from the time Moreau announced his pleasure at escaping one marriage, he was contracting another, and General Bonaparte gave the pair a sumptuous present.

VI

A midwinter campaign in central Europe is next to impossible; therefore the First Consul directed that the French armies should make one, being confident that Carnot's supply organization would stand up better than the Austrian under conditions of foul weather and worse roads. Moreau would have the main attack, of course, but Bonaparte had learned his lesson about offering plans to that officer. Jean-Victor was merely reinforced up to 90,000 men and told to operate in the valley of the Danube. Far to his right the Army of Italy, now under General Brune (who had done so well in Holland and the Vendée), was to strike across the Adige around Verona and up the highroad of the hills as taken by

Bonaparte himself in the An VI. General Macdonald had a small corps in Switzerland; in spite of winter weather "which made the inhabitants of these regions themselves seek the shelter of the valleys," this body was to push through the passes at the headwaters of the Adige onto the Austrians' right flank in the south and Brune's left. General Molitor commanded 20,000 men on the northern wing of the Tyrol, where the Prince of Reuss had stretched his lines perilously thin to hold communication between that country and the main Austrian force. Molitor was to pierce these lines and sweep out the Tyrol. General Augereau to lead a force along the Main into Franconia against the Austrians still operating there. Bonaparte himself would go to Italy and take over from Brune as soon as affairs at Paris permitted.

Thus our side. On the other, Austria had fortified the passes of the River Inn; Archduke Karl from Bohemia had sent down 10,000 men; Bavaria doubled her troop complement under the alliance; at Budapest, Herr Haydn's new tune of *Gott erhalte Franz den Kaiser* was played through the streets, and Kaiser Franz himself appeared to rouse again that "revolt of the Hungarians" as in the days when Maria Theresa rode up the Mount of Kings with her baby on her arm and a sword against the four quarters of the world.

Kray was removed; 65,000 of the main army along the Inn were placed under the command of the young Archduke Johann, only eighteen, but educated within an inch of his life and supported by a good chief of staff, General Lauer. There was no hope of an offensive toward Italy; therefore the Aulic Council approved a plan for a winter campaign in Bavaria, which would much surprise the French, who never fought in the winter because their supply system would not stand up under the pressure of muddy roads and rainy weather. The good chain of magazines we have built up during the armistice will give us every advantage in this respect, and the lay of the ground will give us still more. Let Johann move across the Inn and Isar via Landshut, while General

Klenau gathers the garrison troops from the Danube fortresses and the new men from Bohemia at Regensburg, to
strike into Moreau's left flank, deep behind the Isar. If the
Frenchmen stand, good; we fight a battle, hitting them front
and flank together. If they retreat, again good; we gain
winter quartering in Munich and the Jacobins are forced
back behind the Lech into rough country, where they will
find it hard enough to eat.

Operations commenced on November 28, which was 7
frimaire for the French, under a continual gale that was
snow-ice in the Alps, but in Bavaria a windblown rain that
froze as it fell. Neither commander had an idea as to the
position or intent of his opponent, and the weather made
scouting so difficult in the wooded country between the Isar
and the Inn that Austria groped forward blind. The first
division of Kienmayer's right wing corps reached Landshut
the next night, and threw out scouts to connect with Klenau.
This was the day set for the main guard, with the Archduke,
but under the corps command of General Kollowrath, to
cross the Isar. The piercing rain had so drowned the roads
that it was almost impossible to move artillery. Next morning the march began again, but at Ampfing the vanguard of
the center struck a strong French formation, and there was
a fight.

The Archduke had nearly 30,000 men in presence and
drove the enemy in, but his scouts reported that behind their
retreat the French had come to a stand and were bringing
up artillery about ten miles south and west, in the Ebersberg
forest, a wide region of trees, defile, and marsh which sur-
rounds the main highroad to Munich. This meant that the
enemy must have serious forces under the cover of the forest.
The rains were continuing uninterruptedly, with still further
delays for the baggage-train and guns. The headquarters
council that night considered that to continue the march toward Landshut and the Isar with all that French infantry
close on the flank and rear of the slow-moving column would
be dangerous. The plan was changed: the main guard would

follow the Boulevard direct to Munich, Kienmayer was
called from the flank to follow a parallel road, and Klenau
to move down on the French communications at or behind
the Bavarian capital, while the Archduke was fighting them
along the front.

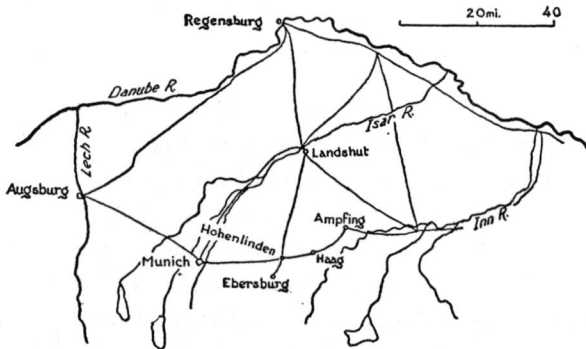

Campaign of Hohenlinden

How correct this decision was became clear on the next
morning, December 1, when the French were found in position on a plateau near Haag, easily outflanked and driven
away. The weather cleared a little that day, and cavalry
began to get around. Before night their reports were in that
all through the Ebersberg and along the upper waters of the
Inn the Gauls had their backs to Austria, marching, marching, evidently in general retreat toward Munich. Bulletins of
good cheer were dispatched to Vienna. General Kienmayer,
who had made a fine march down from the Landshut region,
was pushed along a road toward Munich paralleling the
main highway on the north. The corps of Riesch, which
formed the left wing, similarly moved on a parallel track to
the south; and Kollowrath's main guard took the Boulevard,
through Hohenlinden, aiming on Munich. This was the only
road that would carry cannon and trains; they were accordingly placed behind the fighting formations, with some thirty
squadrons of horse, under the Prince of Liechtenstein as a
rear guard. That afternoon, December 2, a heavy wet driving snow began, and continued all night.

VII

The Inn is little inferior to the middle Rhine in width, rushing between precipitous banks over a succession of boulders past old gnarled forests where the kobolds dwell. It is a major military obstacle, and the reports that reached Moreau's headquarters before the armistice was denounced were that the Austrians had fortified every place on the lower stream where a crossing might be won. If crossing were made among the upper reaches, a roadless country of mountain lakes would be encountered, while the curve of the stream exposes any movement from Munich down to the Danube to a ruinous counterattack in flank.

The problem seemed insoluble; but Chief of Staff Dessoles thought that the Austrians might be tempted from their fortress river by a move forward that would change to a retreat when contact was established. Thus they might be drawn into a battle among the defiles of the Ebersberg forest or in the marshes of the Isar. On the resumption of hostilities, therefore, French columns moved out toward the Inn, slowly because of the atrocious weather. Grénier with the corps of the left wing took the Boulevard through Hohenlinden, Haag, and Ampfing; Moreau's center corps pushed toward Wasserburg, and Lecourbe toward Rosenheim a little ahead of the rest, as though the army were still operating by its right as in the previous campaign. In the rear Ste. Suzanne, with a newly raised corps of 20,000, covered the debouches from Regensburg.

On 9 frimaire Grénier's leading formations encountered powerful Austrian forces at Ampfing, and promptly retreated to Haag, where there is a good defensible position. The Austrians were pushing all around it by next morning; General Ney, whose division held most of the line, wanted to fight them, but Moreau was present in person, and ordered a retreat on Hohenlinden, calling in the center corps and Lecourbe toward the same place.

At the town a road springs off in a northerly direction, skirting the Ebersberg wood. Grénier's three divisions took position along this road on the evening of 11 frimaire under a pelting snowstorm. They were north of the town, facing east and covering the issues from the forest on their side of the Boulevard. Division Grouchy of the center was echeloned slightly forward south of them in some open ground to hold the outlet of the close and perilous defile through which the postroad reaches Hohenlinden, and there were tirailleurs out among the trees. A good position; but Moreau had plenty to worry about that night. The Austrians had been drawn and were coming along for their battle, but he still had only 33,000 men in position, with his divisions Richepanse and Decaen out to the south on foundered roads. Lecourbe's entire corps was still farther away. Overreached?

Weather and country had not permitted reconnaissance, but it was clear that a good part of the Austrian strength must follow the highroad through the defile to where Grouchy blocked its exit just east of Hohenlinden. Richepanse's men were accordingly turned out before dawn to drink their soup shivering amid snow still falling so thick they could not see ten meters, then to make a speed march to fall in on the highroad by means of a little track that crossed the hills, gaining it, then dropping back on Grouchy before the Austrians arrived. Decaen followed.

Austria also was early afoot that morning, and the fact that they marched on a better road soon carried the troops of the main guard under Kollowrath and the Archduke some miles out in advance of the other columns. About eight in the morning they reached the exit of the defile, where they were received by hearty—and surprising—salvos of artillery through the falling snow. The vanguard was halted; the Archduke put a couple of regiments of Hungarian grenadiers into the trees along the slopes, formed a column of attack, and tried to charge home on the guns of what he took for a rearguard. Grouchy countered with clouds of light skirmishers who among that snow and murk were more than a match for the Hungarians; the cannon cut the Austrian advance to pieces after about two hours of effort. In the rear of this fight the Austrian trains began to pile up. At an hour before noon there was only a little bickering of musketry going on before Grouchy; in the defile was an increasing tangle of men, guns, and wagons, unable to move, and anxious officers conferring.

The only decision they could reach was to wait for the flanking columns of Riesch and Kienmayer to get around those French, but instead of Riesch from the south, there now came an ominous growl of cannon, and then bullets began to whistle down from the snow-hidden heights.

It was Richepanse, though as yet with only two of his brigades. The third, that of Drouet, had strung out somewhat to the rear along the rough tracks, and as the first two approached the highroad, Riesch's vanguard ran into Drouet's flank. The Austrians were more surprised than the French and took time to set up a formal attack, which allowed Drouet to deploy and prepare to sell himself high. Richepanse with the other brigades pushed on as previously ordered, the more since the sound of guns from Hohenlinden told him he was needed. Riesch finally was in order, but as his attack came on, so did Decaen, on *his* flank, striking hard and carrying this Austrian corps right out of action.

At about the same time Richepanse reached the point where the hill-track fell into the highroad. There were Austrians below. His men began to shoot; just at this moment the snowfall ended, and he could see the whole main body of the enemy army bunched in an inextricable mass of men and guns and wagons, with a regiment of cuirassiers closest, dismounted and waiting. Richepanse had only a handful of horse with him, but he promptly flung these forward in a charge, while his infantry spread along the heights, shooting down into the mob. The cuirassiers surrendered; Richepanse got his artillery into position and every minute his infantry poured in a hotter fire.

Down at the exit of the defile, General Moreau had

ridden anxiously to the front line. Now, with the eye of a
true captain, he noted, instead of preparations for a renewed
attack, a kind of uneasy floating movement among the enemy,
like a boiling beanpot.—Richepanse has come (he deduced

Hohenlinden

correctly), and swinging Division Ney out of line from north
of the town, he ordered both that force and Grouchy to
charge.

There were no harder hitters in the armies of the Republic, and the Austrians were now in utter confusion, raked

the length of the defile by Grouchy's guns, riddled from the heights by Richepanse's musketry, bottled in by their own trains. Men threw down their muskets and climbed over each other in the effort to get away. Whole battalions surrendered; it was only with the greatest difficulty and through the sacrificial charges of the Prince of Liechtenstein's cavalry that they got the Archduke himself clear of that mad rout.

Kienmayer came on the scene farther north while the main body was collapsing, and he also was well beaten; by another night the French were flowing forward along all the roads to Vienna, sweeping the Imperial army before them, minus its artillery, minus 12,000 prisoners, minus some 5,000 dead, with the Bavarian corps destroyed.

"I am glad," remarked His Imperial and Kingly Majesty to the Queen Mother Maria Louisa, "that your son saved *half* my army"—the type of politeness one might expect at an Austrian court. But nothing could alter the fact that Austria must now make peace on whatever terms France chose to give, and regardless of what the paymasters in London might say.

It had been the greatest of all the chess-game campaigns of the eighteenth century—and it was the last.

WRONG END OF THE TELESCOPE—IV

The Sun, London:

EXTRACT FROM LETTER FROM PARIS

I HAVE learned through a certain channel that, in the conference which *Duroc* has had with General *Kray,* the latter has formally declared, that until a Monarchy be established in France, neither Europe nor France can calculate on peace. *Bonaparte* has two lines of conduct to pursue, either to make a king, or to become one himself. The Army of Italy appears to be in these intentions. Immediately after the Battle of Marengo, it was in agitation to declare *Bonaparte* king. The Army of Germany, it is said, is inclined towards a Prince of Bourbon. *Moreau* has very frequent communications, not only with General *Kray,* but even with the court of *Vienna.* This Court has proposed simply to re-establish *Louis XVIII. Moreau* has transmitted this proposition to *Bonaparte.* I cannot say what the Chief Consul may have in his head, but it is certain that he plans fresh changes. Before long you may expect a new and great Revolution.

The Sun, London:

HOUSE OF COMMONS, MONDAY MR. *Jones* took the opportunity of noticing the current report of the day, that an Armistice had been concluded between the *Emperor* and the French. He wished to know if His Majesty's Ministers knew how the fact really stood; more particularly as it was only on Thursday last that a Subsidy of three millions had been voted to the *Emperor* for the purpose of carrying on the war, and he hoped it would not be too much to ask whether we had any chance of being included in such an Armistice, or in those Preliminaries of the Peace which might be entered into in consiquence of it?

Mr. *Pitt* answered, that the question was one which he was not called upon to answer.

American Citizen and General Advertiser:

YARMOUTH, DEC. 16 THIS morning arrived the Diana Packet, Capt. Ofborn, with feveral paffengers, and a meffenger from Vienna, with difpatches for government. Report ftates, that the archduke John has defeated the French and taken 2000 to 3000, fome fay 9000 prifoners, befides feveral pieces of cannon.
Star

Half paft one o'clock. We have juft heard a report, that the meffenger whofe arrival from Cuxhaven we have announced in a previous column, brought an account of a fubfequent battle on the 5th, in which the victory was on the fide of the Auftrians, who fucceeded in taking Munich. At the late hour at which we heard this rumor, it was impoffible for us to afcertain upon what grounds it refts, or whether it is entitled to any credit.

Three o'clock. We again ftop the prefs to fay, we learn a letter had been received at the Secretary of State's Office, dated the 5th, afferting that the French are flying in all directions, in confequence of their defeat on the 4th and 5th.

Courier

AUGSBURG

The battle which took place in Bavaria was very bloody. The Auftrians are at Ingolftadt and Preyfingen. They fay there are feveral thoufand of the French made prifoners. Wafferburg, which, on the retreat of the Auftrians, was taken poffeffion of by the French, was afterwards burned by the former. Moreau has his headquarters at Hohenlinden; thofe of the Archduke are at Muhldorf.

Gazette of the United States:

FROM LATE LONDON PAPERS THOMAS Paine refides in an obfcure lodging in the fuburbs of Paris. He is in the laft ftage of a decline through intemperence.

Thomas Campbell to Dr. Robert Anderson:

MY journey to Ratisbon was tedious, but not unpleasant. The general constituents of German scenery are corn-fields—many leagues in extent, and dark tracts of forests equally extensive. Of this the eye soon becomes tired; but in a few favoured spots, there is such an union of wildness, variety, richness and beauty, as cannot be looked upon without lively emotions of pleasure and surprise. We entered the valley of Heitsch on the frontiers of Bavaria, late in the evening, after the sun had set behind the hills of Saxony. An incident apparently slight heightened the effect produced by external beauty. While we gazed up at the ruined fortifications, that stretched in bold, broken piles across the ridge of the mountain, military music sounded at a distance. Five thousand Austrians, on their march to Bohemia (where the French were expected to penetrate), passed our carriage in a long broad line, and enchamped in a wide plain at one extremity of the valley. As we proceeded on our way, the rear of the army, composed of Red-cloaks and Pandours, exhibited strange and picturesque groups, sleeping on the bare ground, with their horses tied to trees; whilst the sound of the Austrian trumpets died faintly away among the echoes of the hills.

Anonymous Broadside Published in London:
HOHENLINDEN

*Dedicated to the Rev. Mr. Alison by his most
respectful friend, the Author*
[By Thomas Campbell]

On Linden, when the sun was low,
All bloodless lay the untrodden snow,
And dark as winter was the flow
    Of Iser, rolling rapidly.

But Linden saw another sight
When the drum beat at dead of night,
Commanding fires of death to light
    The darkness of her scenery.

By torch and trumpet fast arrayed,
Each horseman drew his battle blade,
And furious every charger neighed
    To join the dreadful revelry.

Then shook the hills with thunder riven
Then rushed the steed to battle driven,
And louder than the bolts of heaven
    Far flashed the red artillery.

But redder yet that light shall glow
On Linden's hills of stainèd snow,
And bloodier yet the torrent flow
    Of Iser, rolling rapidly.

'Tis morn, but scarce yon level sun
Can pierce the war-clouds, rolling dun,
Where furious Frank and fiery Hun
    Shout in their sulphurous canopy.

The combat deepens. On, ye brave,
Who rush to glory or the grave;
Wave, Munich! all thy banners wave
    And charge with all thy chivalry!

Few, few shall part where many meet!
The snow shall be their winding-sheet,
And every turf beneath their feet
Shall be a soldier's sepulchre.

THE WORM'S-EYE VIEW—IV

. . . A young lady *émigrée* had gone to Augsburg with her child, believing that the French would never trouble her there. When their army unexpectedly began to approach, she attempted to fly from the city, but making an error as to the direction of her exit, ran right into the French outposts. As soon as she discovered her mistake she fainted. General Lecourbe, much moved, furnished her with an escort and ordered that she be taken to whatever city she wished. Unfortunately, the child was forgotten, and the unhappy mother, in her state of near-collapse, did not notice it. A grenadier found the child; in-formed himself as to where she had gone; and being unable to take it to her at once, had a leather knapsack made, in which he carried the infant about. Whenever a battle was near, he dug a hole in the ground where he deposited his charge, and when the fighting was over, came back for it. At the armistice the grenadier took up a collection which reached the figure of twenty-five louis; placed them in the child's pocket and returned it to its mother. The whole army applauded, but no one was able to tell me the name of the virtuous grenadier.

Chevalier C. L. Cadet de Gassicourt—Voyage en Autriche, en Moravie et en Bavière

THE WORM'S-EYE VIEW—V

. . . Now here I am on the same road taken by all the other army leaders in this war, Duke Albert, Prince Koburg, Clerfayt, Wurmser, De Vins, Beaulieu and Archduke Karl, the last of whom could not even be saved by the fact that he was the Kaiser's brother. Last night I was informed by a courier that I might return to my Hungarian estate to wait there till His Majesty should decide what other orders to give me. Who will replace me, I do not know. Some say an archduke, others the FM Josef Colloredo. Today I am informing the Hofkriegsrat that I am giving up the command of the army, so I am turning it over temporarily to Graf Karl Kolowrat.

Don't be concerned about my troubles, since I have constancy enough to be my own consoler; the only thing I regret is that just as I began this letter, General Moreau's adjutant came in with news of an armistice, under which there will be no more hostilities till September 10. Tomorrow morning I will leave here by Branau and Linz, not going through Vienna, but direct to Pest, where I will leave my baggage and then on to pleasant Topolya, to arrange everything so I can pass my last days in quiet loneliness.

Feldmarschall Kray von Krajova to his brother

9

DETECTIVE STORY

Paris: floréal, An VIII–28 nivôse, An IX
(May 1800–January 18, 1801)

JOSEPH FOUCHÉ was accused of believing in nothing. It was false; he believed in everything, including the de Staël's inherent perfectibility of man and the broadest liberty for the individual—provided only that the individual complied with certain standards of human conduct, which standards happened to be those dominant in contemporary mœurs. Back in the days of the Terror, ferocity had been the fashion; Fouché proclaimed that "the Republic must march to liberty over corpses." Where others used such language out of conviction, like sea-green Robespierre, or in fury against long-enthronèd wrongs, like Marat, Fouché did it because everyone else was doing it. He aroused considerable disgust by becoming one of the grimmest proconsuls of the Terror and conducting the "fusillades" of Lyon when the Convention had voted to have the inhabitants of that city shot in a row beside their mass grave, and at the same time expressing himself as unconvinced on the justice of the step.

The disgust came chiefly from people who did not know or did not appreciate the fact that Fouché had been a member of the Oratory of St. Philip Neri, most egalitarian of monastic orders, in which the prior takes his turn with the rest at

145

serving table and the government is not from Rome, but
from within, on the lines of a clerical club. The themes of
freedom of thought and limitation of expression he had
learned there made an antiphony throughout the career of
the Minister of Police; and he was a pitiless, fearless executive.

It was not for his services in abolishing the old government that the new one had confirmed him in the ministry.
Bonaparte rewarded services with money or an estate and
considered the past as holding no mortgages on the future.
Neither was it alone because Fouché could bring to the support of the régime the extreme regicidal Jacobins. The presence of Carnot in the War Ministry furnished all necessary
guarantees to that group. Fouché's claim to office was that,
as an executive, he displayed in their highest development the
qualities which are the peculiar property of the Oratory—
the calm, rational, almost free-thinking consideration of
every question in the light of pure reason, divorced alike
from passion and from any received ideas beyond the fundamental dogmas.

The papers of the Central Bureau of Police, when he sat
down to them, showed a department badly organized from
materials so inferior that good organization was almost impossible. Ministers of Police had succeeded each other rapidly under the Directory, hardly having time to realize that
the public police were not really under their command, but
under a variety of leaders, the heads of the other departments. Authority over the secret police had been scattered
among the five Directors, who did not allow their police
minister even to read the reports. "Secret" was, moreover,
not a descriptive adjective; everyone knew them, a collection of old delators from the days of the Terror, broken-
down nobles and unfrocked priests, who haunted the gambling houses, unsuccessful prostitutes, and ticket-of-leave
convicts. "Functions which are always difficult, they rendered revolting," arresting anyone they pleased for any
reason at all.

To these Fouché applied the besom that had brushed Lyon, mass dismissals, and a pair of drastic blanket orders, one retroactive and one administrative. No arrests would henceforth be made by the secret police without written authority from a prefect; and every person in the Paris prisons was to present a written statement of his case to a board of visitors appointed for the purpose. Three hundred new secret police were recruited in Paris alone; the royalist agency there reported across the frontiers that it was impossible to recognize them or to escape their attention, and the agency must cease this correspondence for a time.

For the public police a Prefect of the Seine was set up; he was a magistrate and had charge of all regulatory business, including passports, the survey of transitory domiciles, and censorship. The other big cities received similar magistrates, appointed by the départemental prefects, but responsible to Fouché; they were held in line and the whole system was linked together by a system of traveling commissioners. Under the authority of police prefects and commissioners fell both the old gendarmerie and the new National Guard. As soon as the new administrators were in office a campaign as systematic as that of an army was undertaken against the irreducible Royalists of the west and the brigands of the Midi. The man with the big moustachios who rode beside one in the diligence was likely to have a brace of pistols under his coat; the man he caught was instantly translated before a military tribunal and was probably shot the following morning. By the date of Marengo the Paris Prefect had nothing to signal and wives of soldiers in Italy found they could travel down to visit their husbands, the roads having become miraculously safe.

The roads were safe, but Fouché himself was not. Given that so many émigrés were returning—Fouché himself enormously helped the process by one of his best and ablest public documents, advising that whole classes be stricken from the émigré lists, instead of the current system which forced each émigré to bring a lying witness to the fact that he was not an émigré at all—given that so many émigrés were returning, it was inevitable that a party of reaction should form. It was also inevitable that this party should attach itself to a minister; this is how parties function in the absence of representative government. It may seem somewhat surprising that the minister of the reactionaries should be Lucien Bonaparte, of the Interior.

Surprising because it was an alliance between the most ideologically Jacobin member of the inner councils and the partisans of a throne that had been torn down by Jacobins. But on the personal side, Lucien was as much interested in finding the support of a party as they were in discovering a leader; and the reactionaries could discover no one else who combined a position that might be useful to them and a susceptibility to flattery from people bearing the oldest names of France. The parties to the unsigned contract found less difficulty in reconciling their ideas than might be supposed; they met on the common ground of preference for arbitrary rule, which had always been a part of royalism's intellectual baggage, and to which revolutionists from below always come as the only means of controlling the forces they have released. In spite of his Jacobin allures, Lucien was not a *votant* or anything like one; he now pronounced himself in favor of a life dictatorship for the head of the state, as the only means of assuring stability to the national institutions, and the bargain was struck.

II

The *point d'appui* against Fouché was the religious question. Bonaparte clearly meant to bring back the papal legate; he had told the Vendéans as much. Fouché, who so rarely committed himself to anything beyond recall, was by his very origins determined against a Catholicism in strict bonds to Rome. Jacobin, Terrorist, Minister of Police, Oratorian, executive; believing that the stability of the new government depended less on its form than on freedom from exterior

influence during the delicate period while forms were harden-
ing into institutions with traditions of their own—everything
led him in the same direction. He was in the closest of relations with Périer, Bishop of Clermont, head of the "constitutional" clergy set up before France went atheist under
Robespierre—the Constitutional clergy which had sworn allegiance to the Revolution and to principles which Rome considered incompatible with sound doctrine, especially on the
key questions of the escheated church properties and the control of the priesthood from Italy.

The whole post-Revolutionary government, the whole
structure of the society that supported it, were in a sense
founded on the confiscated properties. Adroit and subtle
though he was, Fouché could not conceive a permanent
settlement that would return the Church to France without
returning the properties to the Church—which meant taking
them from their present holders and reversing the Revolution. He considered that a temporary recognition of the *fait
accompli* might be possible, but beneath that theme the
Rhine-daughters of the clergy would be perpetually singing
for their treasure—that is, for the return of the Bourbons,
who would give it to them for the asking, since their cause
was already bound up with the return of the other confiscated
lands to the nobility.

Fouché was a *votant* and a counterrevolution would certainly cost *votants* their heads; but, to give him only the
credit due, it is doubtful whether this factor had as much
influence with him as with those other relicts of '93, who had
thrown out the results of every election since that date as
soon as it became apparent that the electors had decided
against a government of *votants*. He was sufficiently certain
of his ability to follow the prevailing intellectual fashion to
believe that he could even ride out the storm of a restoration.
But he was an executive, a Police Minister, to a degree an
Aquinan; he disapproved of revolutions, even counterrevolu-
tions, and believed in order as the key to a full life.

This had led him into the rather curious position of tenderness toward the Jacobins as the partisans of order, and detestation of the Royalists as the party of anarchy. Lucien made the most of the fact that in the earliest days of the new government, Fouché released from jail all the prisoners held for their share in the old conspiracy of Babeuf (four years ago, and now it was ancient history!). There was an argument in Bonaparte's cabinet, with Lucien pointing out that these were no ordinary Jacobins, but men of the true fanatic left, who had pronounced their belief in perpetual revolution. He succeeded in adding a new word—"anarchist" —to the vocabulary of his brother, the General; the General who had set up his government on the ruins of one in which Jacobinism was dominant. The next step was to talk of the necessity for this new government to reconcile itself with the Second Estate, the Estate of the Church. While the First Consul was preparing for the Marengo campaign, it seemed to a good many that Fouché was tottering and Rœderer did not hesitate to announce himself publicly as the enemy of the Minister of Police.

The ex-Oratorian was saved by one of the factors on which his adversaries counted most heavily—the alliance between Lucien and the reactionaries. A certain proportion of the latter were realists, to whom it did not matter whether the king were called Capet or Bonaparte, as long as he brought back the old times; but behind them was a hard core of positively venomous hostility to anything but the return of the exiled house. When these last saw Bonaparte winning over their very emissaries, when they saw their party fragmenting in the direction of Lucien, when they saw vanish all hope of the restoration of the old régime through the resignation of the new, they quite logically went underground and began to conspire. It is not necessary to suppose they recognized their secret war as a struggle between Bourbon and Bonaparte. The General was not the head of a rival house; he was merely a kind of regent who had the bad taste to refuse a dukedom. The whole cast of their thinking was around the theme of a government in which everything flows from a single individual. When the head of such a state changes, everything in it changes, as it had changed when the "Despotism tempered by epigrams" of Louis XIV had been succeeded in an hour by the complacent oligarchy under the regency of the Duc d'Orléans. The "essential object" of which they spoke in their letters was removing the present head of the state in favor of one who would crack more easily.

Fouché read the letters. Already at the end of the second month in office, his new secret police had discovered most of the Royalist secrets. It diverted him to let the plot develop until there were involved a certain Chevalier de Coigny, a certain Chevalier Joubert, a pair of hedge-priests, and Hyde de Neuville, who had come to offer Bonaparte the dukedom —till their correspondence with Georges Cadoudal, leader of the Chouans of Vendée, was established and through him with the British Cabinet—till the plans were laid for kidnapping the First Consul as he drove out to Malmaison for a last visit among the spring flowers before departing to join the Army of Reserve—till the British government had offered ships to bring over the royal princes, and highly practical lists had been drawn of who should have the plundering privileges on what millionaire buyers of estates seized from the nobility and the Church. In floréal, just before the Malmaison visit, the axe fell. Joubert, de Coigny, and the priests were arrested; the papers were published in the official *Moniteur* which, on Fouché's ingenious suggestion, called the business "The affair of the English agency."

"After such services," Bonaparte wrote publicly to his Police Minister, "anyone would be above calumny, and it is unnecessary to add more, to demonstrate the complete confidence I have in you."

III

The letter and the feeling it expressed were among the influences that led Talleyrand to form an alliance with the

Minister of Police. It was a somewhat uneasy alliance, since Talleyrand regarded Mme. Bonaparte as a real danger, and Fouché had attached her to himself even more closely than the identity of their interests against Lucien demanded. The means was finding money for her extravagances—that matter of the magnificent collection of pearls, for instance, said to have been at one time the property of Marie Antoinette. They were in the hands of Foncier, the jeweler, and Joséphine felt she could not live without them—the queen's gems on the neck of the First Consul's wife, how appropriate, how symbolical! The money was found and the husband's suspicions lulled by telling him they were the necklace presented by the Cisalpine Republic. But it was necessary to take Bourrienne the secretary into the scheme in order to have someone confirm to suspicious Bonaparte that these were indeed the Cisalpine jewels, and Bourrienne told Talleyrand, with whom he was very intimate.

It seems to have occurred to the great diplomat that, valuable ally though Fouché might be against Lucien, the pearl business showed him as appropriating too many of the attitudes of a first minister for one who was, after all, a mere director of hired bravoes. What followed is as shadowy as *la ténébreuse affaire* itself. The partisans of the Left always contended that the business was engineered, a case of *agents provocateurs*. The indubitable facts are that in fructidor, at about the time of General Moreau's marriage, a pot-valiant cashiered major named Harrel showed up at the Tuileries with a story that the First Consul was to be murdered.

Bourrienne, to whom the tale was told, repeated it to Bonaparte (and Talleyrand). The General advised him to give Harrel some money, but to say nothing to Fouché. Something over a month later, on 19 vendémaire, there were arrested in the lobbies of the Opéra a half-crazy sculptor, Ceracchi; a wholly crazy painter, Topino-Lebrun; and two persons without professions, who had been minor public functionaries in the days of the Terror, Aréna and Démerville. Two of them had false facial hair and all had poignards. On examination they spouted the most violent Jacobinism and admitted they wanted to stab the First Consul. Harrel was put back on the army list and was made governor of the prison at Vincennes.

It is not at all impossible that Harrel himself had worked up the whole "plot" from some of the drunken debates of a pair of penniless tavern republicans, who went on because they did not know how to turn back. (They even lacked the money to buy daggers; that came from the man they were going to assassinate.) It is possible that Bonaparte was fully conscious of this, and encouraged the intrigue in order to have an opportunity to make a peculiarly forceful declaration against "anarchy." He normally took a long view, and, on the long view, the people whose conciliation the government most required were those reactionaries, those Royalists, whom Fouché could combat, but not win. Before they would make peace with the Consulate they must be convinced that this was not a Jacobin government, that their lives and property would be safe under the Jacobin Minister of Police who had conducted the fusillades of Lyon. The Jacobins themselves required no such pampering; they were wedded to the Consulate by the fact that the alternative to it was a Bourbon restoration.

But if Talleyrand and Bourrienne promoted the affair to discredit Fouché, they failed spectacularly. The man who resigned on the "anarchy" declaration and the wave of anti-Jacobinism that went with it was Carnot, Minister of War. Fouché was permitted to extricate himself by a statement in the *Moniteur* that the official police had discovered the whole conspiracy, and that it was not really directed against Bonaparte, but had been conceived with the design of making the police appear reactionary because they arrested Jacobins. This was backed up in less than three weeks by Fouché's discovery of a perfectly genuine anarchist named

Chevalier, so far to the left that even the Jacobins had dis-
owned him, patiently fabricating an infernal machine in his
garret.

In fact, the Opéra plot was so much more absurd than
dangerous that it could not possibly have dragged Fouché
from his pedestal, even if he had altogether failed in connection with it. Actually, his men made the arrests; and before the Police Minister's opponents could improve any
advantages the affair gave them, the matter of the *Parallel
Pamphlet* began to send its seismic shocks along the galleries
of the Tuileries. It is impossible to say that Fouché lacked
any given piece of knowledge at any given time, but his
first official cognizance of the pamphlet was when he began
to receive copies from the provincial prefects. Considerable
quantities of the publication (they said) had been received,
bearing the stamp of the Minister of the Interior, M. Lucien
Bonaparte, with a letter requesting they be given the widest
possible distribution. As matters of publication and censorship fall within the jurisdiction of the Police Department,
they were applying to him to know whether the document
really did represent the official policy of the government. It
had already produced the most unfortunate effects among
those who had read it.

The pamphlet in question, when Fouché came to examine
it, was without signature and bore the title *Parallel among
Bonaparte, Caesar, Cromwell, and Monck.* In the style which
had passed for eloquence among the provincial Jacobin clubs
of ten years ago (and which Juliette Récamier had found
inadequate for the expression of tender emotions) it declared that France was in danger as long as her future depended upon the life of a single man. The greatest of men,
to be sure; he united glory abroad with sound administration
at home, as Cromwell had in England and Caesar in Rome.
But not immortal—"Where is the system provided for the
purpose of maintaining the great example he has given and
perpetuating the work of his genius? The fate of thirty millions hangs on the life of a single man!" . . . "Remember

how at Rome, when the greatest of men was basely assassinated, he was replaced by a Nero, a Caligula, a Claudius!
Unhappy France! Will you also become the prey of such as
these?" The remedy? Obviously, to pass a law of succession,
to—here the pamphlet became coy, but no one could miss
the implication—make certain that the hero was succeeded
by another of the same family.

Fouché said he already had half a dozen complaints from
the prefects about this extraordinary production. Clearly
Lucien had written the thing in his own interest, and the effect was thoroughly bad. In the one direction it practically
confirmed the already prevalent opinion among the public
that the Opéra plot was a government-promoted fake; in
the other it was an invitation to assassinate the First Consul
before any real law of succession could be passed. Bonaparte's face did not change during the speech, but nobody
likes to be reminded that he may die with his work half done.

When the policeman was through, Joséphine, who was
present, came over to sit on her husband's lap and to rumple
his hair. "I implore you, Bonaparte, don't make a king of
yourself. That dirty Lucien is trying to push you into it, but
don't listen to him."

The First Consul frowned, disengaged himself, and sent
for his erring brother. The pamphlet? Lucien would not
deny that he had circulated it; the actual writing had been
done by a literary hack named Fontanes, to whom he had
merely supplied some ideas and who (now that one saw the
whole thing in type) had clearly exceeded his instructions. At
this point Fouché seems to have permitted himself a snort.
No matter how the instructions had been exceeded, the
Minister of the Interior remained responsible. The affair of
the pamphlet was of a piece with the way in which his department was conducted generally—rotten with waste and
peculation (Fouché supplied details that made Lucien's head
swim), while the Minister himself was conducting almost
public orgies with Mlle. Mazzeroni, an actress of low repute
(more details).

Lucien, however he may have suspected, was certainly not aware of the extent to which his activities had been under the surveillance of Fouché's men. He could defend himself only by a rather desperate counterattack, in which he accused the Police Minister of being a cutthroat Jacobin who enriched himself by blackmailing gambling houses.

The other Bonaparte, who had sat silently through tirade and countertirade, shooting quick glances from one contestant to the other, now emitted a few phrases to the effect that the *Parallel* contained some valuable ideas which he himself shared, but the last pages were the work of an idiot, and sending the thing out for distribution under an official stamp was the act of a madman. He was obliged to demand his brother's resignation.

It was Talleyrand who cushioned the fall, rather astonishingly at first glance, but not when one remembers that he had an alliance with Lucien against the Beauharnais. He asked for the disgraced Minister's services in the diplomatic department and sent him to Spain as ambassador, though referring to him as "nothing but a barroom bouncer."

"But who will be back stronger than ever, because his brother thinks so much of him," said Rœderer, to whom the remark was made.

"I think not," said the diplomat, and turned away.

IV

Fouché was now impregnable and he used his position to warn the First Consul unceasingly that no real conquest of royalist opinion was possible, that, try though he might, he must soon or late face the fact that the old régime had lost too much ever to accommodate itself to the new, and would be satisfied with nothing but wiping from the slate all that had happened since 1792. It was a choice between a government of *votants* and a Bourbon restoration.

Bonaparte took this counsel very ill, which is not surprising since his whole theory of government was involved. He usually replied that the real danger came from the opposite direction, from the purlieus inhabited by those whose technique it was to fish for power in the seas of disorder, across whose surface run waves of unbridled oratory—the left and the crypto-left, the de Staël and the heirs of Robespierre.

The debate was dropped and taken up at intervals all through the last weeks of the attempt to find a formula for peace with England which did not involve the only condition laid down as indispensable by Lord Grenville a year before: a Bourbon restoration. The negotiation broke down, the drums that drummed to Hohenlinden began to beat along the Danube—and on 3 nivôse in cold, frosty weather, General Bonaparte decided to go with his suite to hear Herr Haydn's new oratorio *The Creation* at the Opéra. Joséphine was not dressed in time and the General, who was tired and a bit cross, set out before her, taking Lannes, Berthier, and Third Consul Lebrun in his carriage. The coachman had been protecting himself against the weather with potations; he set out at a brisk trot and when one of those one-horse watercarts pulled across his way in the rue St. Niçaise, instead of waiting for it to pass, he cracked his whip and went round it on two wheels, executing a magnificent *vrille* at the next corner.

At that moment there was an explosion which shook the whole city. The coach was lifted bodily from the ground, struck, and went reeling on, with shattered glass showering its passengers. Back in the rue St. Niçaise the fronts of buildings were torn out, over twenty people were dead, over a hundred injured were screaming; Joséphine's coach, not far behind, picked its way through an appalling scene. Bonaparte calmly entered his box at the theater and asked for "the book of the opera"; he had been shot at before.

In the morning all the functionaries of state appeared at the Tuileries to congratulate the First Consul on his escape. He gave them a homily: "Nobles, Royalists, priests—they had nothing whatever to do with this; this is the work of the Septembriseurs, men of blood who traversed the Revolution in crime; the Terrorists. France will never be peaceful till she is delivered from these wretches . . ." with a great deal more, and one visitor after another piling fagots on the blaze.

An explosion which shook the whole city

It was a public ratification of the scene on the previous evening, when Bonaparte returned from the theater to greet Fouché's arrival with: "Well, I suppose you suspect the Royalists of this piece of work."

"To be sure I do; and what is more, I will prove it."

The remark had been received with a sneer. Now the policeman entered in the midst of this denial of everything he had said, looking silently from eyes far apart under his wide, low, pale brow. One of the councilors went over and shouted at him to know why he made no defense of himself.

"Because I have no intention of speaking until I know what I am talking about." Talleyrand remarked amiably that Fouché ought to be shot.

The Foreign Minister doubtless felt he could afford a few extravagances at this point. Fouché had just furnished an admirable justification of the Talleyrand principle that success in intrigue can be erected only on a solid foundation of laziness. Himself, he had done nothing to eliminate Lucien, and the busy Fouché had done it for him; he had not bothered to eliminate Fouché, and Fouché had now eliminated himself.

M. Talleyrand might not have been quite so self-satisfied had he known what Fouché's activities were up to that moment. The Police Minister had rushed to the rue St. Niçaise as soon as he heard of the explosion, accompanied by his assistant, Réal. Among the débris they found a leg of the horse that had pulled the fake watercart which really contained a barrel of powder. They set a guard over it so it should not be lost, and, after looking round, subjected it to examination. The hoof had a brand-new shoe of rather peculiar design, and at the very moment when councilors were shouting at the decaying Fouché, his police were conducting a tremendous *rafle* of all the blacksmiths of Paris to find the man who had applied that shoe. They discovered him within three days; he recalled having shod the horse for a short man with an old scar over his left eye, dressed so and so. Enough of the cart remained to permit finding the man who owned it; he had rented it to a person of the same description as that given by the blacksmith.

Moreover Fouché recognized the description; the scarred man would be a certain Carbon, messenger, servant, and companion of Limoëlan, an ex-Vendéan who had been drawing money from the English government, and who had had some obscure connection with the kidnap plot of the previous spring. A recent report on Limoëlan had come in, to the effect that he had reached France in a small boat some weeks before, with another Royalist named St. Régeant. They had been under surveillance of Fouché's agents, who found them practising in a park with an air gun, when one of the agents made a blunder, got himself shot, and the two conspirators disappeared.

Fouché and Réal were now fairly sure of their game, but no one would listen to them, and the Minister was only nominally still a member of the government. He was not removed; merely ignored. Reports from the prefects no longer reached his desk, but went right on past to the First Consul's cabinet. Nobody informed him about meetings of the Council of State, and when that body did sit, it was to hear Bonaparte ask for a law of proscription against the Jacobins:

"Blood must flow!" he cried. "As many culprits must be shot as there were victims of the explosions, and twice as many deported. Any government must lose the confidence of its people if brigands like these are left unpunished. I am ready to sign their death warrants with my own hand. It is not for myself I care; I have faced danger enough and Fortune has preserved me."

This speech so encouraged de Bourmont, the royalist leader who had once tried to buy Bonaparte for the king, that he offered the services of two hundred "former" Royalists to hunt down the Jacobins guilty of the outrage. Fouché, working against time, and alone save for a handful of assistants, thought the offer indicated too close an acquaintance with royalist groups. He instantly had de Bourmont arrested and put the screws on him. Yes, the prisoner reluctantly admitted, there were certain places where people assembled who thought France ought to have a king. He named them; within three hours Fouché's handful of agents were on guard at every such place.

Bonaparte meanwhile had failed to get his Jacobin-proscription law through the Council of State, too many of whose members had been on proscription lists themselves to trust any government with such an instrument. Talleyrand ingeniously suggested a quasi-executive decree on the model of the *senatus consultum* of the early Roman Empire, which would be passed through the Senate as a measure required to preserve the Constitution, of which the Senate was official guardian. Talleyrand prepared the document, Cambacérès greased its way past the Senators, and Bonaparte drew the list of proscribed—130 men who had been Terrorists eight years previously, as Fouché himself had been. Now all the measure required was the signature of a responsible minister, and since it concerned police action, specifically the signature of the Minister of Police. Fouché knew very well that the men were innocent, but understood quite as well that a refusal to sign was equivalent to resigning, and he never would find the guilty parties.

He signed; and the hundred and thirty were sent to Nantes for deportation to Cayenne. Three days later, Carbon was in the toils, telling everything he knew, and the following morning eighty more Royalists, including all the plotters but Limoëlan and St. Régeant, the latter being in a hospital with a breast-bone broken in the explosion. Of course there had been no Jacobins at all involved; it was murder in the name of Louis XVIII, and Georges Cadoudal was the man behind it. The money for the powder came from England—England's reply to a refusal to make peace on the terms that she laid down.

Nobody but Colonel Rapp, the General's aide, remarked that everyone seemed to be trying to push Bonaparte to arbitrary measures. Nobody but Talleyrand remarked that a new method of legislation had been found, by which the ordinary chambers could be by-passed; and nobody but Fouché noted how official concern with the private life of the Chief of State had come to resemble that of a court.

THE WORM'S-EYE VIEW—VI

To Citizen Talleyrand:

PARIS, 22 GERMINAL, AN IX
I REQUEST you, citizen minister, to send to Citizen Otto the attached note. You will let him know that after having presented this note he will try to have Du-theil and Georges arrested, and that if they are not turned over to the French government, they should at least be held under arrest for transportation to America.

PARIS, 22 GERMINAL, AN IX

THE undersigned has received the order of his government to present to his excellency Mr. Addington the following:

Europe has rung with the event of 3 nivôse. The crime which, in attempting the life of the First Consul, has compromised the innocent population of a part of the city of Paris has a character of horror almost unexampled in modern history.

The First Consul is very far from believing that either the old or the new ministry would be capable of having paid for or ordered a crime which would be disavowed among the most uncivilized races.

Nevertheless the persons named Dutheil and Georges, both in England and under the pay of the British government, ordered this crime and numerous others which have had the result of killing unhappy people. Two journalists on the government payroll have, at London, offered apologies for this crime and expressed their regret that it did not succeed.

The state of war which exists between the two peoples has no doubt broken some of the bonds that unite neighboring nations. But are England and France, even at war, less than civilized and European nations? And international law, which softens the evils of war, does it not prohibit according protection to monsters who dishonor human nature?

It is the place of His Britannic Majesty to act in this case according to the dictates of his conscience, the laws of his religion, and the principles of his policy.

As to the First Consul, he declares energetically that, if a similar crime had been committed in London, he would hasten to arrest and to turn over to English justice the perpetrators of that crime; even more, if a person, after having attempted the life of the prince or of one of his principal ministers, had sought refuge in France, the First Consul would have behaved like Fabricius with regard to the King of Epirus.

BONAPARTE, *First Consul*

10

SWEET PEACE

Paris, Lunéville, Amiens: ventôse, An IX—
vendémaire, An X
(February 1801–October 1801)

T O CONTEMPORARIES watching from the outside, the
treaty of peace with France signed by Austria on the
9th of February, 1801, seemed a guarantee that,
after an interlude of revolutionary madness, Europe had
returned to the sane stability of the eighteenth century. It
was a hard peace, to be sure, but no harder than those
Frederick the Great had given the same Austrians after
beating them in battle a half-century before. It made territorial readjustments, but not so violent as those made in
the extinction of Poland.

The document was drawn in a fashion quite typical of that
century of logical illogic and Lockian inconsistencies for the
sake of a *modus vivendi,* by negotiators who discussed clauses
with the utmost aplomb, while Richepanse marched and
Moreau's artillery thundered in the snow-scarred passes of
the Ebersberg. Not so had the embassies of the terrible revolutionary Republic conducted their business. "Sign," one of
them had cried, "or we will smash your Empire like this!"
and hurled a tea service to the floor, ordering the armies to
march before dawn.

Even the personality of the French peacemaker contributed to the idea that reason once more ruled the world. He was Joseph Bonaparte, the General's older brother—tall, amiable, easy-going, with those airs of a country squire which the eighteenth century so perfectly understood; liked nothing better than to put on an old hat and stroll through his estate at Mortfontaine, discussing the health of cabbages with kindly wrinkle-faced peasants. The fact that he was so much a nonentity that every serious question had to be referred to Paris was only another guarantee of stability. France had passed from the state where boobies had their heads cut off to that in which they received government appointments, provided only that they belonged to the right family. This Revolution, of which everyone had been so much afraid, was after all working out as a change of dynasty, a type of event with which the eighteenth century was familiar.

Yet the appearance was factitious; the document that issued from the old diplomatic town of Lunéville in Alsace was actually more revolutionary than the Revolution itself. The latter had been an upheaval confined in its effect by the fact that Europe refused to consent to it, and sent the armies marching to Valmy to put it down. At Lunéville the Emperor not only shook hands with the devil (under pressure of defeat, one had made peace with the obnoxious Vasa of Sweden in the past); he also agreed to assist in the destruction of the system that produced the Empire.

That Austrian Empire was decidedly Catholic; the long wars against Turk, Swede, and Prussian could be viewed without too much strain as an extension of the Crusades. It was not feudal, but quasi-feudal, dynastic, composed of a series of small principalities so intensely complex, both as to legal right and as to boundaries, that only through the central chancellery at Vienna was administration possible at all. The cement was the system of ruling families overlying this diversity. The Duke of Modena (for example) also ruled estates in Jülich on the lower Rhine; the Prince of Luxembourg was a gospodar in Hungary, and neither of these lords was able to think in any terms but those of the widest interests of the Empire. Moreover (though it is easy to exaggerate this feature for ears attuned to more modern musics), the Imperial system was to a degree an economic unit with England, whose manufactured goods and overseas imports entered by way of the Netherlands in the north and Leghorn in Italy for exchange against Continental raw materials.

The Treaty of Lunéville attacked this system fundamentally and at every point. It conceded the whole left bank of the Rhine to France, with Holland as her client state, shutting off access to northern harbors except for goods passing through French hands. It placed other French client states in all western Italy, and cut Austria off in that direction. In all the renounced territory from the Adige to the North Sea, it swept away the checkerboard of princes and replaced them with prefects. Nor was this a mere eighteenth-century transfer of territory; it was a basically changed system, which was, by the Austrian act of acceptance, frozen permanently into the European structure.

It is true that there had been a somewhat similar acceptance at the Peace of Campo Formio in 1797. But that had been a truce with an armed brigandage, whose hold on its own country was tenuous; a truce intended to be broken, as was evident from the warlike acts of the French ambassador who took the ratification to Vienna. The signature of that truce had been accompanied by no change in the Austrian policy-making bodies. From Lunéville emerged a peace which everyone regarded as stable, a peace which even in London was held to be the basis for the long-term settlement of Europe, as soon as England should have concluded her outstanding business with regard to Egypt, the colonies, and the League of the North.

All this might be forgotten. It related to the acceptance by Austria, under military pressure, of the acts of others, as she had accepted the terms of Campo Formio. The true change was that the earlier peace recognized the principle of "indemnification" on a national basis, while Lunéville put it on an internal basis—at the specific instance of Joseph Bonaparte, bolstered by letters from his brother. In the 1797 treaty the Empire had received the lion's share of the territories of the Republic of Venice, extinguished in order to provide indemnifications. There was room in those territories for a dozen, or twenty, or a hundred of those minor lordships which were the building blocks of empire. The arrangement of setting them up was begun almost as soon as the treaty was signed, some of them going to the few, the very few, princelings who had lost their lands in territories ceded to France.

Lunéville ejected all the petty lords from a triangle of territory along the left bank of the Rhine, beginning in Lorraine and ending at the Hook of Holland. It dispossessed many in the north Italian territories that passed from Austria to France, including one quite important central Italian potentate, the Grand Duke of Tuscany, whose lordship included Leghorn. He was a member of the Imperial house; and when at the peace table Graf Cobenzl for Austria asked that this prince should at least be indemnified in Germany, he was no little surprised to receive a French reply that the Republic would be very happy if the treaty not only permitted but actually enjoined such indemnification—and not for His Highness of Tuscany alone, but for all the other disinherited magnificoes as well.

II

The approval was conveyed in that diplomatic language whose purpose is always to mask the speaker's real sentiment under its opposite; but it is unlikely that Cobenzl, who had a good deal of experience in diplomacy, was deceived as to the genuine alacrity with which the French received his indemnification proposal. For all brother Joseph's soft façade, the Bonapartes were recognized as sharp bargainers. Cobenzl attributed their yielding in the matter to a genuine desire for peace, which made them willing to give him something to

tąke home and exhibit as a diplomatic victory, provided there
was no direct cost to France involved. This would be the
Bonaparte method; it was the General who had thought of
the device of indemnifying Austria with the spoils of Venice
at the close of the last war. This time is was equally clear
where the indemnification was to come from, though the
Lunéville treaty said only "from within the body of the
Empire." The Empire had nothing with which to indemnify,
except by secularization of the great churchly principalities,
the bishoprics. The Austrian diplomat was quite happy to
achieve indemnification by this route, only asking that it be
forced upon him by the treaty, so that he would have an
unanswerable argument with which to beat down those of the
Church.

To him, the whole process appeared as merely one of those
complicated, ingenious arrangements by which the Austrian
Foreign Office so frequently achieved the results its seldom-
victorious armies failed to gain. His old preceptor and
leader, Baron Thugut, could have told him better. The
Baron had a far clearer idea than his pupil of what the Austrian Empire really stood for. Thugut was, so to speak, an
alien who had adopted it as a way of life out of profound
intellectual conviction from the date when, as a page boy so
obscure that no one knew the name of his father, he had
been brought up in the incredible establishment of Prince
Kaunitz, with its indoor riding ring and hundreds of meow-
ing cats. Cobenzl himself knew Kaunitz only as a name at
the foot of a document, or a bent figure glimpsed during
youth, toddling stiffly across a columnated vista. There was
no communication of ideas, except at the second remove,
through Thugut; and Thugut was so secretive, so determined
never to raise up a rival for himself, that even to his most
trusted subordinate he communicated nothing but method.

He, Thugut, seemed to assume that he would always be
present, at least behind the scenes, to control those broad
lines of policy which he had caught from Kaunitz, and
which the other councilors of Austria understood by instinct

rather than by intellect. The assumption had been perfectly correct down to the months following Marengo and the armistice on the Danube. The armistice, however, represented the very antithesis of the policy with which Thugut had identified himself—co-operation with England and implacable hostility to the Revolution. (It is interesting, though not altogether exceptional, that the one ruling figure in Austria who came up from the bottom should realize that the whole Imperial system depended upon making such careers as his own impossible except to the utmost talent.) When the armistice was made Thugut demanded to be dismissed. Cobenzl was his logical successor at the Foreign Office, the best man in the Empire. He had to go to Lunéville for those negotiations that went on simultaneously with the winter fighting, and the technical direction of foreign affairs fell into the hands of a verecund old soldier, Graf Colloredo, while the actual leadership remained with Thugut.

But the latter, universally detested (behind the scenes he was blackmailing half the Austrian nobility), was maintained in power only by his successes. The dreadful day of Hohenlinden crushed not only the Austrian army, but also Thugut's policy. His retirement became genuine; the Archduke Karl forced the appointment of another soldier, Graf Trautmannsdorff, in association with Colloredo. As neither of them had experience or self-confidence in diplomacy, Cobenzl at Lunéville became the actual foreign minister, writing his own directives, submitting his achievements to himself for approval. The greatest of these achievements, almost the only one, was his success in keeping the princes happy by indemnifying them through secularization.

Graf Cobenzl failed to realize that his victory was purely technical. Secularization deprived Austria of her position as the defender of the Church and joined her with revolutionary France as its despoiler. It made the Empire the accomplice of the Revolution, and by adopting the Revolution's system as the basis of the permanent peace froze that system not only into the structure of Europe as a whole, but into that of the Empire itself. There was now no logical basis upon which the whole French method, including the dispossession of princes as well as prelates, could be protested. Although the Emperor had signed this peace as head of the confederation of German States, he had in effect abdicated that rule, he no longer represented the intricate system of the Holy Roman Empire, only the dominion of Austria.

III

The heritage of the Revolution on the Continent was thus made secure, and a general peace which would allow consolidation of its gains required only the assent of the one power still in arms against France—England, now threatened with ejection from the general European system. As soon as the Austrian armistice was signed, General Murat led a corps down into southern Italy, where he terrified Ferdinand the Burglar of Naples into making Taranto a French base and excluding British ships from its harbors. A similar act of exclusion from her ports was procured from Austria. Bonaparte arranged a naval combination by which the Brest fleet should ride through the British blockade on the winter gales and pass to the Mediterranean. With all bases in that inland sea closed against the enemy, it would be strange if their naval forces were not pushed out beyond the Gates of Hercules, as they had been in 1796.

At the same time His moonstruck Majesty of Spain was persuaded to find something wrong with the conduct of Portugal, and to send his armies across the frontier, with the design of closing that country's harbors also to British ships of war and commerce—the latter more important than the former. It was the First Consul's observation that the British, a shopkeeping nation who did not understand honor, could be far more effectively dealt with by a threat to their pocketbooks than by one to their national integrity.

M. Otto, the agent in London, reported that the irreconcilable government of Pitt had fallen on the news from the Mediterranean, and had been succeeded by one of more pacific disposition, headed by a man with an unpronounceable name, of whom no one had ever heard—Mr. Addington. A similar exclusion of English commerce from the north, the First Consul felt, might stir this gentleman to seek peace, in spite of those phrases of a year before about making no composition that did not include the restoration of the Bourbons. To achieve such a result an instrument was already in existence—the Tsar's League of Northern Neutrals which, by giving it something other than a defensive focus, might be transformed from a madman's fantasy into a real alliance of interests. Defensive alliances, as Bonaparte once remarked, have no force till physical contact has taken place, and not very much then, while a combination in which each member expects to turn a profit will find unshakable adherents.

. . . It is necessary to remember that for the vast bulk of Europe, the French Revolution had been a peripheral event, affecting only the western rim. In the countries of the heartland it meant only an influx of dancing masters with considerable skill at borrowing money. The great movement of the period for them was the downfall of Poland, which had demonstrated that powerful states could become still more powerful by engulfing their neighbors of the second rank. That Polish collapse let loose a torrent of what was politely called "land hunger"—though it is fair to observe that nobody but a certain obscure Professor Kant at the University of Königsberg regarded land hunger as an urge to brigandage.

To assume that a national desire for more territory was looked upon as morally wrong at St. Petersburg, Berlin, and Vienna is to accuse generations of quite able and sincere men about those courts either of diabolism, of a deliberate predilection for evil, or of the inability to rationalize their actions. Ideologically those men, those courts, were living in an atmosphere perfumed with Leibnitz, Newton, and Voltaire. (One of the reasons why England was frequently incomprehensible to the Continent was that she was already far gone in empiricism.) They believed in human happiness through an orderly world in which every individual had his place on a hierarchic stair leading up to a throne; the only question was—which throne? It seemed to them a sweet and decorous act to have destroyed the anarchy of Poland, where any individual could paralyze all the rest, prevent any action whatever for the common good, by pronouncing the fateful *liberum veto*.

There was another such anarchy abroad at the turn of the century. "The Ottoman Empire cannot last much longer," pronounced Bonaparte—and was heard from Schönbrunn to the Winter Palace. Russia should have Rumania and Rumelia, with the reversion of Constantinople when that place fell into Christian hands; Austria would gain Bosnia and Herzegovina; Prussia would be compensated with the illogical English appanage of Hanover. As for France, all she asked was an outpost in Egypt and common action toward a just and general European settlement.

Can a league be made on these terms? Specific steps: the northern powers to set their navies afloat and bar Britain from the naval stores of the Baltic; the Tsar's troops with the help of a French corps to make a campaign against India through the Hindu Kush; the Prussians to seize Hanover. It was an enormous scheme, but it entered the domain of the practical while Brother Joseph was still arguing clauses with Cobenzl at Lunéville. Tsar Paul sequestered all the British ships in his harbors and marched their crews a hundred leagues inland. Prussian troops entered Hamburg and closed the great rivers that led to central Germany. The Danes already had a serious cause against England for stopping their corn-ships and forcing them to sell in British markets at prices fixed by the British government. At precisely this moment, what did the maladroit islanders do but halt a big Danish convoy in the Channel, shoot up the frigate that was covering it, and kill many of her men? Denmark equipped a fleet; General Masséna, the best mountain-fighter of France, received orders to lead a corps on the long walk halfway round the world to India.

Dazzling prospects! Which came down crash on the news that arrived six weeks after the Lunéville signatures. The British fleet would not be pushed from the Mediterranean again, but held Toulon under close blockade, the Brest ships arrived too badly battered by storm to make another run. Egypt surrendered; another British fleet had gone to the Baltic and destroyed the Danish navy in a terrific battle; and, to crown all, Tsar Paul was assassinated.

IV

General Bonaparte himself dictated the note on the occasion that appeared in the *Moniteur:*

"Paul I died on the night of the 24th of March, and an English squadron passed the Sound on the 30th. History will reveal the connection that exists between the two events."

The note of bitterness was not due to the downfall of the grand plan for a Continental union against England. When a plan failed, the General's method was to make another, without useless regrets or that annoyance which interferes with clear thinking. His rancor was over the fact that the evidence showed pattern, and the pattern was one of an English government engaged in those dirty devices which render all government unstable—and at the very moment when Bonaparte was straining every nerve to eliminate anarchic forces from France and from Europe. The money that bought the explosives of the rue St. Niçaise had come from England. An English doctor was an eyewitness, if no more, to Tsar Paul's murder, and the murderers were let go unpunished by the new pro-English Tsar. An English fleet had fallen on the Danes without a declaration of war, destroyed their property and killed some thousands of them. The conclusion was inescapable: if the English could not have a world arranged for their peculiar benefit, they wanted no world at all, a reign of perpetual war and anarchy. Indeed, this state of perpetual war was manifestly to their advantage. Through war they had gained the Dutch colonies and some of the French and Spanish. Thanks to the fact that their warships held the sea, they were able to exclude not only France, but also the neutrals, from the carrying trade and all that it implied, and peace would end their advantage.

Bitterness is not, however, an instrument of practical politics. The First Consul recognized instantly that with the Northern League broken and the French out of Egypt there was no longer any material gain possible to either party in the Anglo-French struggle. The nominal objective of England's war in the first instance had been to keep Belgium and the mouths of the Scheldt out of the hands of France, which had opened them to commerce (contrary to old treaties) and so endangered England's monopoly of the Continental carrying trade.* The issue had prevented the signature of a peace back in 1796, when the First Coalition collapsed. But the Belgian issue was hopelessly lost to England at Lunéville, when Austria abandoned everything to the left of the Rhine. Indeed, it had been in anticipation of Austrian failure to hold out for the recovery of Belgium that Grenville had made his tactless reply to Bonaparte's peace note of a year before— that England would make no peace which did not include the restoration of the Bourbons. He was required to find a better reason than the Scheldt for continuing the war.

Now, in a sense, the Bourbons had returned; that is, the guarantee of stability of which the Bourbon name was the symbol. One of the articles in the Treaty of Lunéville, the

* It is perhaps necessary to explain that although France had plenty of other seaports, all lacked water communication with interior Europe, and that in 1800 goods could be transported efficiently only by water. In pre-Revolutionary Europe, Antwerp had been closed to overseas trade with the entire goodwill of Austria, whose flag flew there. The Rhine and the Maas were as effectively shut to trade by the fact that their mouths were Dutch, and goods entering by that route had to hurdle two or three customs barriers. But English ships and goods could enter the Continent by the free port of Hamburg and so reach Hanover which, being both an English possession and a member of the German Confederation, permitted English-carried goods to reach the central Continent without paying duties and with a minimum of handling.

specific one which required the indemnification of the Duke of Modena, was for the establishment of a new kingdom of Etruria in central Italy, carved out of the Modenan territory and the old States of the Church, with Leghorn to give it economic validity. The king was the young prince of Bourbon-Parma, husband of one of the Spanish Infantas—or to put it otherwise, Bonaparte had succeeded in reconciling even some of the Bourbons to his régime. Moreover and decisively, if Mr. Addington's government was to improve on its predecessor, it must do so by making peace. No other difference in policy was possible; it was a government by the same party, embracing many of the same men.

M. Otto waited on Lord Hawkesbury at the English Foreign Office, while along the Channel Admiral Latouche-Tréville collected gunboats and built barges for direct attack on England (with orders not to press matters too deeply). An English adventure against the Isles of Quiberon was beaten off, and the Spaniards (*mirabile dictu!*) broke up an attack on Ferrol, and Lord Hawkesbury invited M. Otto to dinner. England wanted Ceylon—but yes, very well, on due consideration, would return the Cape of Good Hope to the Dutch Republic in exchange. England wanted the French out of Egypt. France wanted the English out of Malta— very well, it should be returned to the ancient knightly Order. England wanted a large West Indian island—Trinidad or Martinique. No on Martinique, Bonaparte had plans for it. No on Trinidad, as well; it belonged to Spain, he would not negotiate away the territory of his allies, this peace must be genuine and general, no lost causes left hanging in the air.

A French corsair was run aground among the Seychelles, the new theatrical season was not brilliant, Mr. Pitt read Horace over a quart of port in his retreat, and General Bonaparte wrote a letter advising the "Count of Provence" not to call himself Louis XVIII. Minutes were written, couriers rode in an atmosphere of important secrecy. One of them was from Madrid with the news that His Most Catholic Majesty had ceased operations in Portugal and was demanding a general peace without delay.—So? Give them Trinidad, then, wrote Bonaparte.

On October 2 M. Otto hung in his window an illumination bearing the word CONCORD. A mob led by a British sailor,

M. Otto hung in his window an illumination

who thought the Frenchman meant to claim that Britain was conquered, forced him to take it in. It would be only two or three days later that Talleyrand called at the Tuileries with his usual package of notes for signature and reports to be read. Working with his usual speed, Bonaparte discussed each with the cold-visaged diplomat and disposed of them all in an hour.

"Now I have something for you," said Talleyrand, and

produced from his pocket the treaty, signed. For a moment the First Consul was mute, then:

"Why didn't you tell me that at once?"

"Ah, you never would have listened to me about the rest. When you are happy, you are unapproachable."

He was right. Bonaparte jumped up and ran out of the room. He had pacified and organized a Europe that at last had room for the French Revolution.

WRONG END OF THE TELESCOPE—V

Republican Watch-Tower:

It is ſaid in a French paper, that a violent diſpute lately happened between Lucian Bonaparte and his brother-in-law, General Murat, which terminated in a meeting at the Bois de Boulogne. The parties fought with piſtols, and the General is ſaid to have been wounded.

The ſame paper ſtates, that Carnot was in complete diſgrace before his removal from the war department.

Republican Watch-Tower:

The Pariſian Journaliſts have been ſome days endeavoring to find out where Lucien Bonaparte is gone. One ſends him to Germany, another to Italy, a third gives him important buſineſs to Ruſſia, and a fourth to England and now they know not where he is gone. Theſe journaliſts are not the only perſons whom the journey has cauſed to make falſe conjectures, for the matter is yet a profound ſecret.

Cobbett's Weekly Political Register:

The Difinitive Treaty is at last arrived, and sorry we are to say, that it contains nothing to compensate for the delay, which has taken place in the negotiations. From the length of time spent at Amiens, one might have expected that the Noble Marquis had, agreeably to the hopes held out by ministers, obtained some condition tending to arrest the fearful progress of France, and to secure His Majesty's dominions, together with the trade and commerce of his subjects, against the effects of that progress; but, for such conditions we have looked in vain through the articles of the treaty which, by the courtesy of the First Consul, we have been enabled to lay before our readers several weeks sooner than we should otherwise have been called upon to discharge that melancholy duty. We cannot help observing briefly—Not a word is said about the Italian Republic, about Louisiana and Florida, or even about the island of Elba.

The Malmesbury Diaries:

On the 12, a Frenchman, called Lauriston, occasional aid-de-camp to Bonaparte, brought over the ratification. A Jacobin saddler in Oxford-road saw him pass in his way to Otto's, who lived in Hereford Street; he assembled the mob, persuaded them he was Buonaparte's brother, and Lauriston was drawn about by them in a hackney-coach to all his visits. Government did not know in time, and John King, (Under-Secretary of State,) when I met him, treated it very lightly; yet it was a most disgraceful circumstance, and a sad precedent.

11

THE LAW AND THE PROPHETS

Paris: 11 nivôse, An IX–An XIV
(January 1, 1801–1804)

I T WAS a new France, strange as Cathay. The curtains
drew back; travelers rushed across the Channel and
in from Germany to see the small figure at the center of
the stage, surrounded by those odd barbarians who had cut
off the head of an anointed king and seemed prepared to do
without one. A new France; statistic—suppose a peasant of
Burgundy or Auvergne to have 100 francs of income. In
Bourbon times he had paid in taxes to the seigneur 14 francs,
to the Church another 14, to the state, 53. Under Revolution and Directory, he paid whatever the commune thought
he ought to pay, and the figures are vague; but if he ran a
profitable farm, the amount became so high that most men
preferred poverty. Under the Consulate and Gaudin's new
system of assessment the figure was 21 francs to the commune on the same 100 francs of income; nothing to the
other agencies.

Where Chateaubriand's homecoming had been through a
land smitten by God, with women dragging plows by ropes
across the hungry fields, Mr. Charles James Fox found
"agriculture extremely flourishing and the peasants relieved
of their burthens." The English Liberal went on to the Industrial Fair at Paris and admired the new cloths and
porcelains. Behind him, the great mills of Roubaix had

begun to spin—"To Citizen Biard, for the invention of his method of weaving cotton, 12,000 francs from the government"; and funds had run from the 21 of the morning of brumaire up to 80.

These were the outward signs of an inner order, painfully achieved and still in process. Englishmen saw life taking on the ease of a settled country, and Dr. Brodum sent over from London his gilded coach to advertise "the virtues of his incomparable syrup." In the streets were Kemble the actor, an American painter named Fulton, James Watt, and Lord Elgin, fresh from the task of mutilating the Parthenon to preserve its statuary. They approved—approved the new pictures, the universal gaiety, the fact that at eight in the morning a breakfast was offered, consisting of soup, fowl, a superb paté, and fruit.

Behind this was labor. The commissioners to codify the laws of France were Tronchet, Portalis, Bigot de Préameneau, Maleville; they brought in their first report on 11 nivôse of An IX, when the town was in a turmoil over the infernal machine plot, and it was slipped off unobtrusively to the courts of cassation for comment. By fructidor, when the negotiators were meeting at Amiens, the draft was back. The legislative section of the Council of State looked it over and, in parts called "Titles," submitted it to the full Council and the legislative bodies. Portalis had charge, grave, reverend, a philosopher logical as Leibnitz, who had advanced irrefutable objections to Rousseau, the intellectual leader of the commission. The process went slowly, chiefly because of this personage. "He would be the most eloquent orator of the Council if he only knew when to stop," said General Bonaparte.

It was nivôse of An X before the Titles were ready for consideration by the Tribunes and Legislative, and by nivôse of An X the Tribunes had reached the last degree of irritation possible to men who talked very well without persuading anyone to listen. They had become excited over the special courts set up to try the infernal machine conspirators,

Daunou going so far as to conduct a scandalous altercation with the First Consul, calling the head of state names not usually permitted in public; but they had not succeeded in rousing a corresponding degree of excitement among the people. They had tried to establish the Tribunate as a factor in international relations by finding defects in the peace treaties, but they had been laughed at for their pains when, after several days of impassioned oratory, the most serious criticism they could advance was the use of the word "subjects" instead of "citizens" in the accord with Russia.

But most were lawyers and nearly all were littérateurs in some form. This Code was the business of ideas and the words in which they were expressed—their business. It happened that the first Title was that in which general principles for the new Code were laid down. "There exists a universal and immutable Law, the source of all positive laws; it is nothing but natural reason in so far as it governs man."

This Ciceronian and stoic theology (it is almost a quotation from the "True law is right reason" passage of *The Republic*) was very far from expressing the concepts of a generation that had been stewing in the romantic juices of Rousseau under the dry skeptic atmosphere of Voltaire; or of fulfilling the desires of practical executives who had been overdosed with general principles during the past eleven years. The malcontents of the Tribunate easily carried through their own body a motion to send orators unfavorable to the proposition before the Legislative. They complained that the Title was nothing but a series of moral maxims, incoherently arranged and in many cases tendentious. For instance, it contained a prohibition against retroactive laws. This would (said they) permit a man born under the old royalist laws of primogeniture to claim that the Revolutionary law of inheritance was retroactive in his case, and therefore void. The Legislative was so impressed by the need for avoiding moral maxims that it threw the Title out.

It was the first real victory the Tribunate had gained over

the government, and it was followed by another within the week, when the second Title, on the enjoyment and loss of civil rights, came up. All the bandogs barked at it—Siméon, Daunou, Andrieux, Chénier, and always Benjamin Constant, with the de Staël in the background, clapping her chubby white hands. The Title was incomplete, incoherent; it needed greater length and precision of phrase. For instance, it did not state specifically that a man born of French parents

The malcontents of the Tribunate

in a French colony was a Frenchman. Not all the objections were like this; so many of them were so well founded that the Legislative agreed with the Tribunes and threw out the second Title. The same day of this vote Tribunes and Legislators were each to present the name of a candidate for co-option to a vacant Senate seat. After a period of fierce lobbying, both bodies presented the same name—that of Daunou.

It was more than a declaration of anger with the executive. It was also a warning and an effort to delineate spheres of action, an attempt to keep the First Consul in his place as a mere executive. The Abbé Sieyès himself came out of retirement to help against the Titles and to vote for Daunou. That so extreme a means as that of abolishing the new laws before they could be enacted should have been found necessary, that an actual as well as an implied threat should be made to throw out every Title of the Code which France so desperately needed, that most of the exceptions to the Titles should have been taken on grounds so frivolous, had nothing to do with the codification itself. The true reason why the liberals felt it necessary to pull down the "Robespierre on horseback" was that he was threatening the very foundations of philosophical liberalism.

He was restoring the public practice of religion in its most repulsive form—the Roman Catholic Church.

II

The philosophical liberals were not trying to abolish religion. They were sincere Deists as Voltaire had been a Deist, or pantheists like Rousseau. They had objected quite as fervently to the public practice of irreligion by the Robespierre on foot as they now objected to the religion of the Robespierre on horseback. In their eyes religion simply was not a social function. The proper concern of society was to regulate the relations between a man and his fellows; to make religion a part of this relationship was to turn the state into a policeman for the priests, an indecency as gross as that which Bonaparte had committed in toying with his wife's charms while an aide was with them in the coach. Religion and sex were alike private matters. National decisions on a basis of philosophical principle could never be brought forth where religious passion was the midwife.

Now Bonaparte, like most mere men of action, was apt to appeal to passion instead of reason. He had begun this game just after the battle of Marengo, when he attended a *Te Deum* Mass at Milan, a horrible thing for a Revolutionary general to do. That Mass was one of the reasons why the de Staël declared that the good of France and humanity "demanded that there should have been defeats in that quarter." The very phrase she employed demonstrated how far the philosophical liberals were from being under the same compulsions as the General. They took a long view—so extremely long that they were willing to see Frenchmen die and France defeated, rather than have victory and tranquility with an accompaniment of priestcraft. In the delineation of spheres of action which they were attempting to enforce, the executive's business was to save the state in accordance with principles laid down by philosophers. If he could not do it that way, he was an incompetent executive.

The possibility that popular support might not be forthcoming for a state founded on their principles entered the heads of the liberals only as a matter connected with that long period of education under rulers devoted to philosophy which de Staël had called for in *De la Littérature*. The possibility that during the educative process a state without internal shoring might collapse under exterior pressures never entered their heads at all. In any case, it would hardly have mattered to them. That brilliant little group of talkers, where everyone had the purest principles and money enough to support them (courtesy of Banker Ouvrard), were internationalists. They could and did contemplate with the utmost calm the idea of flying to one of the minor German states or Switzerland or Sweden, there to begin anew their discourses on principle. France to them was less a homeland than a laboratory; not for them Vergniaud's passionate cry of *"Périsse notre mémoire, pourvu que la France soit libre!"*

They were, no doubt, laying the foundations of a better future, but they were some distance from the specimens in the laboratory, who lacked their freedom of motion; and from Bonaparte, who was concerned with the (to them) trivial matter of providing France with a system strong enough to resist exterior attack from the forces opposed to the Revolution. The religious argument was one of the strongest in the arsenal of the Bourbons, in favor of those forces; for the Revolution had been intolerant. In the name of freedom to worship as they pleased, publicly, with the administration of the Catholic sacraments, the peasants of the Vendée had been in arms for a decade and those of Saintonge and Auvergne had joined the Companies of Jesus and the Sun. There was a priest in every conspiracy; every war against Revolutionary France had some of the aspects of a crusade, and now that the wars were over, a deep growl of discontent ran through the country, perfectly audible to the attuned ear in the Tuileries.

Nor was the discontent without reason. The Revolution first required priests to swear to a clerical constitution which they could accept and still remain in some kind of communion with Rome; and then, under Robespierre, abolished religion altogether. There resulted two sets of persecuted priests. They hardly dared emerge from hiding until the Consulate replaced the capricious Directory. The latter had kept the antireligious laws on the books, even though enforcing them only when there was some special point to be made.

The juring priests, the "Constitutional clergy" (as they were called) who had accepted the earlier Revolution, now remained in possession of such churches as retained their religious character—but they had come to preach to empty pews. A good many of them had been ordained by bishops who were themselves really elected to episcopal office by Jacobin clubs; they had a name for bad character, and their preaching dealt more with politics than with the word of

God. The nonjurors, still fully in the Roman communion, held services in their homes, and these services were preferred by the orthodox, who constituted the immense majority of Frenchmen. But the nonjuring bishops had either mounted the scaffold or joined the émigrés during the Terror. The places of those who had died by violence or in bed had been filled, but not according to the ancient practice of the Gallican Church, through election by the chapter and confirmation by the Pope. The interim method was direct appointment by the Holy See.

It is necessary to add that the occupant of the See at the time was Pius VII, an obstinate man, who owed his election to Cardinal Maury of France, friend and helper of the Bourbon princes; and that the election had taken place in defiance of the Revolution, which had held Pius VII's predecessor a prisoner till he died, and had forbidden the papal institution to be continued. A Pope of such background could hardly be expected to name bishops favorable to the new government, nor could the bishops he appointed and the émigré bishops he maintained be expected to look with favor on any priest who was not an active agent for the counterrevolution.

This was the situation when General Bonaparte rode home to ovations from the field of Marengo, devouring during the journey every volume on church history or canon law he could get hold of. Behind him he left orders that General Murat, commander of the Army of Lower Italy, should kneel before the papal throne, and in turn order the troops of the Neapolitan kingdom to quit those parts of the Papal States that had not been incorporated into the Kingdom of Etruria. Murat also carried a request that the Pope would send a negotiator to Paris to discuss all outstanding questions.

Now Pius VII had been given a powerful impulse in the direction of his papacy by the French Royalists, but his election had been at least as much due to that party within the Church which was willing to go a long way in recovering France for Catholicism. Besides, he was badly in need of another strong Catholic power to balance Austria, which was exhibiting an appetite for papal real estate only exceeded by the Revolution itself.

He named Monsignor Spina, a Genoese priest with much experience in diplomacy, and the latter arrived in Paris on November 5, 1800, which was good speed, considering the state of the roads, the age of the man, and the natural delays in this sort of business.

III

The negotiation dragged. His Holiness was suspicious of Bonaparte's good faith, and had instructed Spina to draw things out until it was discovered how the new ruler of France stood on the question of returning Etruria to papal sovereignty and the church lands of France to their rightful owners. Moreover, the Austrian winter campaign was just opening and, if it succeeded as well as expected, the French usurper would be in a position where real concessions might be had from him.

Nothing that the Monsignor found in Paris removed the suspicions or urged him to an unseemly haste. Of course he encountered the liberals and was given to understand they exercised wide influence. Talleyrand, with whom the churchly envoy had to deal, treated him with a coldness that was easily enough explained by the fact that the ex-bishop was living with a certain Mme. Grand on terms of public intimacy. The Foreign Minister's position with regard to past and present would become quite impossible if the Church were re-established; but in spite of the personal background, it was an official coldness and entitled to be noticed as such. Fouché was openly against any Roman accord whatever, on the ground that Rome and the Revolution could not live in the same house; seized the occasion of Spina's visit to enforce the laws against nonjuring priests in their utmost rigor, and looked at the Monsignor in a way that made the latter write to his Pope: "That man makes me shiver."

Talleyrand and Fouché were appointees who could be dragooned into line with a threat of dismissal, but Mgr. Spina's service of information can hardly have failed to let him know that they were not alone, not even alone with the liberals. The scientists on whom General Bonaparte depended so much for advice—Monge, Laplace, Lagrange—only smiled and quoted Voltaire when the First Consul spoke of restoring religion. They replied to his irrefragable demonstration of the necessity for religious order and the elimination of priestly plotters by asking him why he did not set up a Gallican church on the model of the Anglican, with himself as Henry VIII; a new Protestantism.

The General himself seemed the only man in Paris who was in favor of an agreement. He might be lying; and he wanted a Concordat on terms that made it easy for Spina to execute his instruction for delay, on the ground that there were items which required the personal consent of His Holiness. The reduction of the bishoprics from 158 to 60, for instance; no political powers for the clergy; no more Church lands, and the Pope to recognize the national ownership of those already seized; priests to receive a regular salary from the government, which would nominate the bishops, subject to papal confirmation; clergy to give a promise, though no oath, that they would obey the national laws; the whole order of bishops to be revised by the resignation of those now seated and the appointment of new; the clergy to be responsible to the civil authorities for their civil actions. It was, in fine, the solution the early Revolution had tried to make, rejected by most of the priesthood at that time—but with modifications that could make it acceptable to Christ's viceregent. (Bonaparte had read well his church history and canon law during that trip.) So acceptable that Spina himself would have signed at the end of the third week; but word came back from the Curia that he was still to delay, that the only conditions under which he might agree at once were the restoration of the French church lands and the Etrurian provinces.

The negotiation dragged. Austria went down at Hohen-linden, the infernal machine went up in the rue St. Niçaise, the mad Tsar died and so did England's fever for war, all was peace but with the papacy, and now it was Bonaparte's turn to suspect bad faith. He sent a diplomat named Cacault to Rome (since everything apparently had to be decided there, anyway) with instructions to press matters, though in the most respectful way, "behaving toward the Pope as though he were in command of 200,000 men."

Cacault was as friendly as could be wished; Pius VII as anxious to reach agreement as any Frenchman could desire. But the papal treasury was desperately empty, His Holiness needed the support of taxes from the lost temporalities, and at every step, the ancient immovable forms required that a precedent be found and the proposed action submitted to a full congregation. Thus the chancellery had to go back to the fourth century to discover that all the bishops of Africa had once resigned their sees in a controversy over the Donatist heresy, with failure entailing the special sin of "detestable irreverence." Most of the other precedents ran as deep; it was 23 floréal of An IX (May 13) before the rough agreement was on its way from Rome, signed at last.

It crossed an express from Paris. Bonaparte's uncertain temper had given way. In a cold, dry, cutting voice, he told Spina that he would confer immense benefits on the Church, but they must be accepted at once; the Curia was quite evidently playing the game of the royalist émigrés—oh, through no fault of His Holiness, of course. Cardinal Consalvi, the Papal Secretary of State, was responsible. *Eh bien,* it was time to finish; all treaties, all existing agreements with the Pope were at an end. "If Henry VIII, who had not one-half my power, could break with the Pope, I can manage very well without him." Talleyrand had been authorized to summon a general convention of the Constitutional clergy.

François Cacault was a diplomat of that pre-Revolutionary school which measured success less in terms of positive results than in those of extracting admissions against interest from the other side. There was an odd interview at the Vatican: the Pope, Consalvi and himself present, the two churchmen not troubling to hide their melancholy and chagrin.—I am now bound by my new instructions (said the diplomat) to demand instant acceptance or rejection of Bonaparte's terms, but since you, Monsignor, are named the author of these difficulties, I suggest that a more favorable arrangement can be had only if you go to Paris in person.

They tossed the idea back and forth for a bit, Consalvi frankly fearful about entering the furnace of Revolutionary iniquity into which so many churchmen had disappeared. He had spent all his life about courts, save when the French had thrown him into prison on the capture of Rome a few years before, and apparently he expected to find Paris streets full of Sansculottes, wearing breechclouts and carrying clubs. His Holiness was reluctant to part with the man he regarded as the mainstay of his administration. Cacault tried to reassure the two timorous men, but was unhelpful about other suggestions. At last the Cardinal, with a sigh: "Since there must be a victim, I will make the sacrifice, placing myself in the hands of Providence."

IV

The trip took twelve days, which we may believe to have been spent in honest prayer. Consalvi reached Paris on June 20 (1 messidor) and had barely finished his dinner when he was informed that the First Consul would receive him on the morrow, a haste which contrasted so wildly with the slow politeness of the oldest diplomatic office in the world as to confirm all his fears. It is probable that he spent an uneasy night.

In the morning a master of ceremonies called for him with a carriage, but unescorted, another barbarism; but there the savageries ended and the surprises began. As the Cardinal entered the Tuileries and crossed to the wide staircase, all the balconies and balustrades were crowded and packed with people, not Sansculottes with hair in their eyes, but well-dressed, polite; ladies who whispered behind fans. His foot touched the first step; there was a word of command, a bugle, and a sharp roll of drums carried him to the head of the stair.

Was carried up the steps by a roll of drums

Beyond he passed a tall, empty apartment, expecting (we have his own word for it) to be ushered into a cabinet, where he would have one of those private interviews with the head of the state in which Roman diplomats were so skilled. Instead, double doors were thrown wide, and the travel-weary Consalvi found himself in a vast chamber, its walls lined with men brilliantly dressed and dazzling with the gold lace of the state uniforms Jean-Louis David had designed—the Senators of France, the Tribunes, the Councilors and Legislators; and facing them, in a long rank, the Foreign Ministers, glittering with stars, and all the generals of the first army of Europe. From the window below came crash on crash of

drums. The most simply dressed man in the room stepped
forward:

"I know why you have come. I desire the negotiations to
open immediately. I allow five days for them. If they are not
ended without delay you must return, for I have arranged
everything with a view to such an interval."

They commenced the discussion then and there, before the
world. There was hardly even a question of returning the
church lands, the point on which Fouché said Rome would
be adamant. On July 15, a Concordat was signed, substantially on Bonaparte's original terms. Later, nineteen of the
émigré bishops refused to resign and had to form their own
little church in England, which lasted till 1893. Two of the
Constitutional bishops also refused to resign and had to be
more or less forcibly ejected; but the schism was over, the
new bishops were all Frenchmen living in France, and part
of them Constitutionals, in accord with the First Consul's
constant idea of fusing the old France with the new. As for
Talleyrand, ex-bishop of Autun, an adjunct to the Concordat
absolved him from his vows, but he had to marry Mme.
Grand within the month afterward.

V

The First Consul had wished to celebrate 18 brumaire,
the second anniversary of his accession to power, with a fête
of universal peace, beginning with a *Te Deum* at Notre
Dame and the consecration of the new bishops. Two things
prevented it—the Papal Chancellery, with its customary
dilatoriness, failed to send the necessary powers of consecration in time, and the philosophical liberals made trouble in
the Tribunate.

A legislative act was necessary to ratify the Concordat,
and in language that might have come from the days of the
Terror they swore Bonaparte should never have it. The First
Consul pushed the ratification through his Council of State,
but Pius VII, though with the best will in the world, was

forced to ask for something better, since he was having his own difficulties with the Italian Cardinals, who thought too much had been conceded.

It was at this juncture that the first Titles of the new Code were brought in and thrown out. Probably most of the Tribunes and a good many of the Legislative thought they were taking this action on the merits of the Code itself, and possibly some of them actually were; but the liberals who followed de Staël and Benjamin Constant made no effort to deceive themselves or anyone else. They were drawing a line in the sand, which the executive would cross at his peril. Let him now bring forward his Concordat; they would talk it to death. The country was at peace, there was time for that process of education toward moderate liberalism, and how better could the instruction be accomplished than through leisurely debates in the legislative assemblies?

Bonaparte was often conscious of time-pressures others failed to feel, but in this case the hours really were marching on with no laggard stride. He would doubtless have indignantly rejected the idea that time lacked because of the invincible hostility of England to an economically autonomous France, and the hatred of Austria for a France that challenged her system of a federation of princes. He was honestly convinced that these issues had been settled forever at Lunéville and Amiens. The urgency came from within France. His government had come to power because Frenchmen were tired of living under a régime which, whatever its principles and its exterior achievements, was an anarchy so far as it affected their normal social life. Such conditions may be borne briefly while a bad world is being torn down for the construction of a better, but when peace is signed the ordinary citizen wishes to move into the new house and be let alone there. The liberals had miscalculated; the Consular régime might not be built on the best of principles, but it was tolerable, more tolerable than that of the perpetual debates on form, infinitely more tolerable than the monarchy. School was closed; graduation day had arrived.

Yet for the moment, for a brief period following the rejection of the second Title, while the liberals were contemplating with relish the prospect of disavowing Bonaparte's executive act in making the Concordat, they were more powerful than he. They held the Tribunate, on the issues that counted they controlled the Legislative, and in the matter of Daunou's nomination they had shown they could infiltrate the Senate. Behind and beyond all these they had enough of the Army to say they had the Army—in a state that owed its life to the Army, one that had seen four military *coups d'état* in less than six years.

Bonaparte had come from the Army and was adored by it, but was now so highly placed that he must deal with it through the chain of command, that is, the generals; and generals are always conservative, even in their radicalism. Officers like Brune, Lecourbe, Jourdan, Masséna (the best general of all), Lannes, Richepanse, Souham, had gone to war as young men, when a liberalism slightly to the left of the bygone Girondins was the intellectual climate of the day. They had never left camp since, nor had they any contact with others who did not share this political view; they clung to the old orthodoxy. Bernadotte was an avowed Jacobin; Augereau had already been the leader of one leftist *coup d'état*; and Moreau—Moreau had been captured body and soul by the intellectual liberals.

The Creole marriage that Joséphine planned gave her a rival instead of an accomplice. Mother-in-law Hulot was as ambitious as Lucifer; why should not her daughter's general occupy the political place of the Corsican, as she and her daughter had tried to push into the physical place reserved for Joséphine at one of the fêtes? To achieve eminence, Moreau needed only a party; the liberals not only supplied him with one, but also with an epigram—*"Il n'y a que deux parties en France, les moraux et les immoraux."* From their point of view it expressed the case precisely; Jean-Victor appeared at gatherings private and public, his bovine jowls set in an expression of classical repose, his Breton silences suiting him admirably to the role of Cincinnatus. He really had very few thoughts of his own beyond ordering up another brigade of cavalry, but that did not matter—the entourage of de Staël was only too happy to do all the talking.

The combination thus formed was far more dangerous than surface appearances or subsequent events would indicate. The philosophical liberals perceived it as a combination against political immorality, and thanks to their powers of articulation, they made their views prevail abroad, both then and later. To Bonaparte it was a combination for by-passing the new constitution and restoring the anarchic system of the Directory, with its administrative chaos and an executive paralyzed by a too-powerful, ever-disputatious legislature composed of fraction parties. "They want to make a Great Elector out of me!" he cried, harking back to Sieyès.

Fortunately the constitution itself offered a means of dealing with this attempt to nullify it in favor of endless debate. Twenty of the hundred Tribunes, sixty of the three hundred Legislators, were to be replaced yearly. The instrument of government provided that when the system became fully operative the retirement would be by seniority, but there was no provision for the interim replacements. Cambacérès went before the Senate and persuaded it to vote (by the same process of sénatus-consulte used in the infernal machine cases) a list of the Tribunes and Legislators who should remain in office. Benjamin Constant was of course not on that list; neither were Chénier, Andrieux, Daunou. "They have taken the cream off the Tribunate!" cried Mme. de Staël furiously, and there is certainly something to her remark that the government could only choose between opposition and utter subserviency—for the Senate now adopted the shabby subterfuge of declaring that it had received no nomination for its vacancy from the existing Tribunate and refusing to co-opt Daunou.

But "Lice!" said Bonaparte, "I brush them off my clothes," and the public business went forward. The Code was withdrawn from general legislative consideration. Title by Title it was submitted to the legal section of the Tribunate, which made its comments to the Council of State, with Bonaparte presiding to expedite matters; the Council revised it and took the product before the Legislative. The Concordat was ratified just in time for a *Te Deum* in Notre Dame on Easter Sunday. Mme. de Staël locked herself in her room and closed all the shutters that she might not have to witness the "odious spectacle" of the procession; Generals Lannes and Augereau tried to jump out of the carriage when they found it was taking them to church and stayed only because of a formal order from Bonaparte, but revenged themselves by talking loudly all through the ceremony.

"What did you think of it?" asked the First Consul afterward.

"Nice-looking piece of banality," replied General Delmas, to whom the question was addressed. "Nothing was wanting but the million men who perished in pulling down all that."

VI

Perhaps; there would be among the million a good many not in agreement that the destruction of religion or even of the Church was the thing for which they died. The liberals had miscalculated; the Revolution was not a revolt against the Church, but against the Second Estate. The revived institution was received with delight by the men who had pulled down the old establishment; it was no longer necessary for the Tribunes to sit in secret session for fear of popular reprisals, as they had been forced to do when debating how to break the Concordat.

Most of all, the Code could now go forward. We have a description of the process: the council-chamber was in the Tuileries, to which Bonaparte either came down, or in from Malmaison, with a few vivats and lifted hats to salute him. At the door soldiers presented arms with a flash of metal, the drums rolled along stairways, the doors sprang open and in he came—young, small, dark and intense, as David painted

him, the councilors in their robes rising in greeting. There
was a place for him on the dais between Cambacérès and Lebrun. He took it: *"Allons, messieurs, commençons!"* and
someone read the Title or part of Title under consideration.

The debate was free, energetic, decisive. Grave Portalis,
Rœderer and Bigot the erudites, stately Tronchet with his
white hair, Maleville the world's authority on the law of
Rome—they gazed in astonishment at this soldier half their
age, whose sole legal background was the Institutes of Jus-
tinian, read while he was in barracks confinement for a prank
while a young lieutenant of artillery. His language was anti-
legal; "Stupid ass" was the least expression he used, but
without minding compliments to himself in similar vein. Not
infrequently it was necessary for the old lawyers to call him
to account with a reminder that a certain solution had been
tried and found a failure; and as often as not he yielded.—
Society being composed of individuals theoretically equal
(Bonaparte said once), social life is the concern of all society; that is, of the state. Any institution that interposes between the individual and the state should be deliberately en-
feebled—the family, for instance.—He had to yield that
point; but when he debated, the debate took fire, the question at issue emerged from the dusty rolls and touched life.
He could resolve two hours of qualification into a phrase—
let someone else work out the language of the law. On the
second Title, of citizenship:

"When I hear a man doubt whether a Frenchman born in
the colonies can be a Frenchman without specific law, I ask
myself whether I am going insane. Can there be such a question?"

Shall the courts be allowed to determine doubtful paterni-
ties? "Society has no interest in the propagation of bastards."

Shall alimony be permitted? "Would you allow a father
to drive a daughter of fifteen from his house without provision? Parents owe their children maintenance."

Or that sparkling exchange with Portalis, who had set his

face like iron in favor of divorce for adultery only. Bonaparte: "You would permit no divorce, for it comes to the same thing to make it so degrading to apply for it that none but a man with a face of brass would do so. That's your scheme, isn't it?"

Portalis: "If we were dealing with a new people, I would not admit divorce."

Bonaparte: "To make marriage indissoluble is to promote ennui and set the village curé above the law. If the marriage is unhappy, shall not the civil law, which has no cognizance of the lofty sacramental theory, provide for the happiness of individuals?"

Portalis: "Man is social and marriage is in nature."

"I deny that! Marriage does not derive from nature, but from society and morality."

The question is settled: divorce by mutual consent shall be the law.

At every point, the sharp succinct epigram, the logic from so broad a base that Tronchet, *aetat* 75, "the Nestor of the assembly," must say—"Now I understand the meaning of the word genius."—Tronchet, who had nothing to hope or fear from flattery, a man beyond years and ambitions, who had dared defend Louis XVI on his life trial before the Convention. Nor was debate all; the First Consul could toil more terribly than Walsingham at tasks that left even those who knew them heavy-eyed and with attention flagging. When he presided, the session never rose before midnight; at two in the morning he could cry, "Come, come, citizens, wake up! We must earn the money the French people pay us."

Fortunate conjunction! Portalis with his learning, Maleville and his tradition from the marble peace of Rome; Tronchet and Bigot de Préameneau, the practical working advocates under the custom-law of Teutondom; Bonaparte with his first principles—behind all, the frogs' chorus of the other Councilors and the legal section of the Tribunate. Of all the corporate products of the mind of man, none was produced in so brief a space as their Codes, save only the

American Constitution; none has remained so long as a rule by which men live and can live. It was not Bonaparte's alone, though it came to be called by his name. Maleville has left his signature on the law relating to families, Portalis is in the law of wills, Tronchet has his finger deep in the criminal code, and set it down that the distinction between facts and law is "a dream, inapplicable in practice."

They produced four separate codes—a Civil Code, a Code of Civil Procedure, a Criminal Code, a Code of Criminal Procedure—with a Commercial Code to be added later, the whole making up the single great Code. What was it? A wedding of north and south, of tradition and document. A union of proved experience and logical argument from the natural rights of man, the most permanent piece of construction to emerge from the French Revolution. Behind it lies a single principle: to lay down clear, precise, general rules within which the administrative officers—judges, juries—determine where the line of justice lies in the individual case.

It is a principle that will never be admitted by Anglo-Saxon or German jurists, nurtured as they are in case-law, precedent, and the idea that there is no such thing as a legal case to which some previous decision does not apply. The Code converts every case into a suit in chancery, even criminal cases. Under it the jury does not pronounce harshly, "Guilty" or "Not guilty," but replies to a series of questions —"Did A assault B?" "How much damage was done to B?" "Did B offer unbearable provocation?"—with the judge deciding what penalty A receives if any, by the light of the jury's answers.

This feature, more than any other, has brought upon the Code the criticisms of Nordic legists, who complain that it gives no specific information that will allow an attorney to advise his client how a case will fall out; that, for instance, the law in illegal contracts reads only: "Laws relating to public order and morals cannot be derogated from by private agreement." Of course the Code gives no specific information in such a case; it is the whole point of that vast document that in the individual case the court shall decide whether a contract is contrary to public morals. The Code was made for men and not for lawyers. "Men have bowels and the law has none," said Bonaparte.

There are other criticisms, better or worse founded, according to one's view of absolute justice and public policy. In the Civil Code the position of woman is distinctly low; she cannot give, sell, or mortgage real estate, cannot act as a guardian, cannot inherit from her husband till the children are satisfied. There is no provision for *habeas corpus* in the Criminal Code; no protection for labor in the Commercial Code. The Code of Civil Procedure is badly arranged; has the air of miscellaneous provisions thrown together anyhow. The Code as a whole favors the subdivision of property. The drafting of enactments is often clumsy, done by men who had more of the First Consul's devotion to principle than of the legalists' taste for precision.

Grant all this; grant that a gust of passion could blow into the structure such an institution as that of civil death. The vast edifice stands firm; the critics are dead. In the civil law all men are truly equal for the first time in European history (no, England is not an exception—England still had entail and the privilege of the House of Lords); the family is protected even against the government, property is secure, religious freedom cannot be impugned, the procedure of the courts is quick. The oft-repeated statement that under the Criminal Code "a man is guilty until he is proved innocent" is false. On the contrary, every agency of the state is required to search out evidence favorable as well as unfavorable to the accused, and failure to do so is a reversible error —precisely the error that led justice to an ultimate triumph in the Dreyfus case a century later, when all the dice were loaded against the prisoner.

Beyond this, the Code had an importance never attained by any other instrument of law. It followed the flag—to Germany, Holland, Switzerland, Austria, Italy, and beyond the

Atlantic to Louisiana. In the European lands the French Revolution had hitherto appeared as a horde of Sansculotte soldiers who talked about liberty, but who stabled their horses in the church and took away the best cow in exchange for some money printed on waste paper. But with the coming of the Code, those elements of human happiness that are represented by tranquility, security, and disinterested justice were no longer in conflict with the elements represented by liberty of thought and action. The seigneur, the Graf, were no longer necessary. Twenty years later a reminiscent Bonaparte was more proud of the Codes than of all his victories in battle.

WRONG END OF THE TELESCOPE—VI

Columbian Centinel:

AMONGST the moſt memorable events of the preſent age, the converſion of BONAPARTE from MAHOMETANISM to Chriſtianity, may be allowed the foremoſt rank. As evidence of his former faith, and recent converſion, we have reinſerted his famous proclamation in Egypt, and his late letter to the Miniſters of the Holy Catholic Religion in France.

Report of the Prefecture of Police, Paris:

On the appearance of the work entitled "The English People, puffed up with pride, beer and tea," certain English visitors said yesterday in the cafés adjoining the Palace of the Tribunate, that the French government was ridiculing their nation and doing everything it could to force a war. One of them, who had a copy of the book, said he was going to bring it to the attention of his ambassador.

Lady Bessborough to Granville Leveson-Gower:

CALONNE, just returned from Paris, was very entertaining, tho' mortified at not having seen Buonaparte, but the account he gives is extremely interesting. Buonaparte's life, by Calonne's account, is as extraordinary as all the rest. He bathes every Morning for an hour, during which time a man chose for that purpose translates the English Papers to him. When there is anything he dislikes he frowns very much, and knocks the side of the bath with the rope he has to get in by, faster or slower in proportion to his anger, but he never speaks, except once that, on some strong assertion about him, he call'd out very loud: "Il m'en a menti!"

Miss Berry's Journal:

LEFT Calais between eight and nine o'clock. The first thing that must strike anybody who knew the appearance of this part of the country formerly, is the improved state of cultivation, all the land looking clean, well cropped, and neatly ploughed, and the cottages cleaner (on the outside at least) and infinitely more comfortable than formerly. The people, the children particularly, struck me as looking much better, fatter, fairer, and better fed. The only buildings that wear a melancholy and ruinous appearance in the country are the poor churches, all of which, even in the little villages, have their windows broken, the tops of their spires knocked off, and most of them their roofs falling to pieces.

It was near eleven o'clock before we got to Madame Fouche, the wife of the Minister of Police, who had an assembly that night, and to which Mr. Jackson had announced our coming. All the company were leaving when we entered the room; luckily we found Mdlle. de Contuela, whom we knew, and who presented us to a fair vulgar-looking woman in a yellow wig, with a very fine lace handkerchief, which fell down like an apron before her. This was Madame Fouche.

Anne Plumptre's Narrative:

THE whole country of Picardy, which we had now traversed from north to south, reminded me so extremely of Cambridgeshire, that I began to think I had gotten back to England again by means of magic, without being sensible of it myself. It is a flat open country, but well cultivated, and interspersed with a number of villages, knee deep in mire, and composed of miserable clay cottages, from where are poured forth a swarm of ragged inhabitants. It is impossible not to notice an abuse which has been frequently mentioned, and which can never be too severely reprobated; I mean the intolerable number of beggars by whom travellers are assailed.

Mr. Jackson to Mr. Abbot:

THE great dinners at which I have assisted are a bad representation of a bad dinner in a great room at the London Tavern, or Crown and Anchor; only that in the latter the appearance of the waiters, as well as of the company, would be infinitely better than what we have here. What do you think of Lord Cornwallis, with all his dignity of decorum, dining the other day at a table of thirty covers with the kept mistresses, and being obliged *ex officio,* to hand out the ugliest and frailest of them, because she was in keeping of the Minister for Foreign Affairs? I am going to dine today with Fouche de Nantes, the ingenious and human inventor of the *Mariages Republicains,* under Robespierre. He is the new Minister of Police.

A Few Days in Paris (Anon.):

THERE has always seemed something in the character of the French people hostile to any decisive progress in painting. It is by no means a picture Country. I speak of the Northern Provinces of France, and remarkably deficient in cottage scenery; And the City life, to which everything is sacrificed, restrains them in those bold excursions among the wild and irregular, but sublime and artless compositions of nature, which at once give vigour to the imagination and supply materials for the fancy.

The Palais Royal is little less infamous than its late owner. It is one of the principal curiosities of Paris, and exhibits a scene of extravagance, dissipation, and debauchery, at every hour of the day and night. Shops of millinery, jewellry, clothiery, booksellers, clock-sellers, print-sellers, china-houses, coffee-houses, bagnios, money-changers and gamesters, all unite in amicable rivalry. Let a man walk under these arcades and he will never want food, either for meditation or amusement. The concourse of people in the Palais Royal is never at an end; its public is the most numerous as well as the most brilliant, of any of the places of resort in this city.

King's Letters from France:

THIS noisy, bustling distracted city resembles what it has been for the last century; the Revolution might occasion some little interruption; but like an elastic energy, the people's temper has reverted to what it was; cookery continues a principal science among these gourmandizing people. The Parisian ladies walk with a quick short step, graceful and alluring; but they seem always in haste; coaches drive furiously; cabriolets go at full trot; people gesticulate and speak vociferously; the streets are narrow and the noise resounds all over them; there seems incessant confusion and riot. The wines in France are more genuine and wholesome than in England, and provision at half the price. There are few highwaymen and bold robbers in France; but pilfering *bourgeois* and tricking trademen out of numbers; they have improved in cheating.

Maria Edgeworth's Journal:

THE country appeared one vast flat common, without hedges, or ditches, or trees, tiled farmhouses of equal size and similar form at even distances. All that the power of monotony can do to put a traveller to sleep is here tried; but the rattling and jolting on the paved roads set Morpheus and monotony at defiance. Dunkirk is an ugly, bustling town. Strange-looking *charettes,* driven by thin men in cocked hats,—the window-shutters turned out to the streets and painted by way of signs with various commodities. A variety of things, among them shifts, petticoats, and corsets, were fairly spread upon the ground on the bridges and in the streets.

Consular Decision:

THE minister of marine proposes the approval of a sum of 10,000 francs for the account of the American citizen Fulton, to permit the same to make a complete trial at Brest of the submarine vessel *Nautilus,* and to allot him certain sums as a recompense.

Decision: The First Consul agrees to this arrangement.

BONAPARTE

Placard in Rome on the announcement of the Concordat:

Pio VI per conservar la fede
Perde la sede
Pio VII per conservar la sede
Perde la fede

12

THE SUBTLETIES OF BROTHER JOSEPH

Paris: 28 germinal, An X–9 frimaire, An XI
(April 18, 1802–November 30, 1802)

THE *Te Deum* at Notre Dame on Easter Sunday of 1802 signalized at once the re-establishment of peace in Europe and of France's special peace with the Church; but in connection with it there was a very peculiar incident. Citizen Joseph Bonaparte refused the place that had been reserved for him in the cathedral, close to the First Consul; coming in instead with the Councilors of State and sitting well to the rear among them. This might have passed for a piece of becoming modesty, except that in that case— why did Joseph bother to attend at all? His brother knew how much Joseph loved to strut, preen, and wear coats of many colors on public occasion; and knowing this, was moved to make inquiry into the cause of such uncharacteristic behavior. Fouché probably conducted the business, but even this is uncertain, because everything about it was carefully hushed up.

There was an excellent reason for this suppression. The facts that were presently laid on the First Consul's desk amounted to this: that there had been a conspiracy to confer upon the head of state "the apotheosis of Romulus" during that solemn mass—that General Bernadotte, commander of the Army of the West, was close to the head of the conspiracy and had worked his soldiers to the sticking point by telling those Revolutionary veterans that the priests were to come forth from the cathedral to bless the military standards—that Bernadotte had given Joseph at least a very clear intimation of the project, and Joseph had done nothing but place himself beyond the range of whatever weapons were to be employed. The plot broke down because of the firm and good countenance of that small group of élite and devoted soldiers, the Consular Guard, entry into which had been made a reward for bravery in the field.

Now one of the reasons why the First Consul had fought down Portalis and Maleville to put divorce by mutual consent into the Code was his belief in family honor; believing this, he could hardly bring his own brother and his brother's brother-in-law up on charges. But the incident pointed out the fact that if he had enormously increased the security of every other man in France, he had done so at the expense of his own. If so, the stability of the country as well. There was no replacement with the necessary prestige except Moreau, the captive of the intellectual liberals. There was no possible substitute for the Consular government but one dominated by Jacobins or Royalists; even a Moreau government must become one or the other, or it would lack any roots in popular esteem.

The situation may be seen in one direction as the foundation of that "contempt for men and respect for their achievements" which was later so marked in Bonaparte; but in another, it was a call to set some keystone into the arch he had so laboriously built. It is unnecessary to accuse the First Consul of a more than normal desire for personal power at this stage. The accusation has been made, but it is based on hindsight and will not stand up under the contemporary evidence. One of the reproaches made against him at this time was inconsistency, of having no settled policy with regard to his own powers. Colonel Rapp remarked how often it was necessary to cut down the enthusiasm of the Consular lieutenants, who wanted to give him thirty millions when he asked for only twenty. The First Consul calls Berthier a dolt for suggesting that he make himself king, and laughs when told that he is spending more time over his meals than in the first Italian campaign—"Already! The corruption of power!"

Bonaparte's interest was in fact that of the good workman who is concerned with seeing his work stand. The silent conspiracy of Bernadotte revealed to him that all the labor of stabilization rested on a very insecure basis when a shot in a cathedral could bring back the days of the Bourbons or of the Terror. The Consular government, with its whole program of finance, industry, reconciliation, and reconstruction, by no means possessed a fixity corresponding to its achievements, or the credit it enjoyed in the country for those achievements.

The more nearly the fusion of parties was arrived at, the more irreconcilable became the factionaries—Jacobins, intellectual liberals and Royalists alike, who insisted that only in their way of life was life desirable. The state was now so organized that they could attack it only at the head; but against that head, they would continue to try legislative paralysis or musket-balls during High Mass, as long as they saw any chance of gaining their end by such means. With a small proportion of these factionaries, reconciliation was probably forever impossible, but these doughty spirits could be dealt with by the police. The rest, the majority, still only required to be convinced that the revolutions were over, that the new government was permanent.

There resulted two measures. One, passed as a *sénatus-consulte* in prairial, a week after the reconsecration of Notre Dame, was a general amnesty to "all persons guilty of the crime of emigration," provided they returned to France before 1 vendémaire of the new year. There would be restored to them such of their estates as had not been sold under the escheat laws of the Revolution, save only the nationalized forest lands.

It was a *sénatus-consulte* because there were so many *votants* among the Legislative that to submit the measure to this body would have aroused the Tribunal opposition once more; and it was passed partly to cut the last ground of self-interest from beneath the Royalists, partly to end the scandals by which the removal of a name from the official émigré list had become a matter of petty bribery—but most of all, to bring to the support of the new state a group of vague but extensive financial and social influence, who had everything to hope from the Consular government (the forest lands) and everything to fear from either intellectual liberals or Jacobins.

The second measure was the long-term Consulate. Its origins go deep, and precisely to what point cannot be said with accuracy. The conversations on which the question pivots had no recorders, and were set down by various memorialists in the light of the interpretation they wished to give the words. It is certain that at least as early as the Peace of Amiens, Talleyrand was urging Bonaparte to make himself king—the step would double the value of France's diplomatic position, furnishing to the rest of Europe the guarantee of stability and order without which any peace was likely to be uneasy; and internally the tradition of France was profoundly monarchist, the Washington formula had no attractions, as Lafayette had discovered.

To the influence of Talleyrand must be added that of Brother Joseph, who treated the matter as a foregone conclusion, and discussed everything on the basis of the First Consul as permanent and almost absolute chief of the state. There was a good deal to discuss, for Brother Joseph had gained by experience a certain amount of skill in dealing with diplomatic questions. His calm good sense and moderation gave his mind an almost English quality, which Bonaparte found as valuable as the logic of the three mathematicians to whom he so frequently submitted his ideas. The effect of constant contact with a mind which approaches such a question as the assumption of permanent power only along the line of seeking the means can be extraordinarily persuasive. Talleyrand could be as convincing as any man on earth, yet in the long run it is doubtful whether he and Joseph could have drawn the First Consul to their side without a third influence, the strongest of all.

It came, at first sight rather surprisingly, from the old Conventionals, the *votants,* the regicides. By the nature of the later years of the Revolution, they had been left as the only unified body of able, experienced men near the sources of government. It was not concealed from them that, as the Revolutionary fire burned lower, they were leaders without a party, and in deadly danger. The return of the Church and the universal pleasure with which it had been received, the return of the émigrés under the amnesty law and their acceptance by society, portended for the *votants* the return of the royal family; and the return of the royal family meant Death. "My poor Cambacérès," Bonaparte used to taunt his Second Consul, who was of the regicides, "when the Bourbons come back, you are the first man they will hang."

The jurisconsult did not need the pleasantry to tell him that, nor did any other of the *votants.* Since the Day of the Sections, back in the An IV, when the cannon of a captain of artillery blew the Revolution to tatters, their group policy had been consistent in one thing only: By no means, under no circumstance, must a régime come to power that would lead to a restoration. They had clung to the control of the government through four violations of the constitution by *coup d'état,* not so much because they wanted power as a thing in itself, but as a means of self-preservation; and they possessed the political skill, the influence, the control of administrative organs, that enabled them to remain in office. Bonaparte's program of fusion and reconciliation left them cold; but if they could administer, they had failed to govern, and their only hope now lay in rendering the First Consul's government so permanent, his régime so strong, that it would be a barrier against the reaction. Thibaudeau, prefect of the Gironde, expressed the thought of all when he wrote to Bonaparte:

"The men of the Revolution, no longer able to oppose a

counterrevolution, will help you make one, hoping no more than to find in you a guarantee."

In the midst of every discussion of the consular powers and the necessity for extending them, there had sat one figure

The old legalist trots past without daring to look round

from the *votant* group—Jean-Joseph-Régis Cambacérès, who had begun as something of a figure of fun and ended as one of the most trusted counselors of all. Who can forget the picture left by a visitor, of Bonaparte writing at a table in his cabinet, a rather large room, when the Second Consul is announced?

"Let him approach," says Bonaparte, writing away without looking up; then—"No, I'm too busy now." Then the pudgy old legalist, who has already started across the parquetry, trots past and out the opposite door without daring to look round, a sheaf of papers in his hand, face red and queue bobbing in an agitated manner at the back of his neck.

He was gluttonous, vain, and ugly, but his voice was always for moderation, always for the legal means. His learning was immense and he possessed one of those rarely orderly minds which can instantly perceive the relations between a series of apparently random ideas, and as instantly place them in a logical order. In the debates on the Code, he nearly always spoke after Bonaparte, lending solidity to the First Consul's uncontrolled epigrammatic sallies, showing how easily and smoothly the latter's ideas could be fitted into the pattern of law. Cambacérès was pre-eminently a man of the Revolution; had been President of the great Committee of Public Safety; but was so much without personal ambitions (except those of setting the best table and keeping the best wardrobe in Paris) that he had altogether escaped being involved in the convulsions, and was only the most capable, most conciliatory legal mechanic of the Convention.

The same qualities had now gained him something like complete domination over the Senate, where he both flattered the members and obtained all Bonaparte wanted by providing the legal details for Talleyrand's invention of the *sénatus-consulte* on the occasion of the infernal machine plot. The members were, indeed, delighted to find the question so grave that it could not be resolved in any body below their own.

Now Cambacérès had seen Bonaparte hesitate, doubt and blush like a maiden sought by her lover, under the urgings toward royalty of Talleyrand and Brother Joseph, himself saying never a word. But when the Amiens Treaty was presented for ratification, he persuaded the Senate to offer the First Consul "a signal pledge of the gratitude of the Nation for his services."

It is significant that the old Conventionals, who had received the amnesty proposal with averted eyes, voted the "signal pledge" by acclamation. The Tribune Siméon was

one—a member of the Revolutionary left, who had joined
the liberals in the attack on the Code. He headed the delegation which the Tribunate sent to request that the Senate
vote the gratification. When the general project had carried,
some of the Senators were naïve enough to ask whether this
expression of gratitude should take the form of a monument
—or perhaps a sum of money and a fine estate? Cambacérès
could do no better than suggest a deputation to ask the First
Consul what he would like.

Bonaparte declined to say—a piece of modesty which was
then and later the subject of much useless speculation, but
which had the effect of greatly perplexing Cambacérès, who
could then obtain from the Senate nothing more than a vote
that in view of General Bonaparte's outstanding talents his
Consulate should be prolonged for ten years.

On the essential point of securing the stability of the
régime, this was about as useful as though the monument
had been voted, and Bonaparte was disposed to be angry
until Cambacérès called. He had already warned the First
Consul that something of the kind might happen unless the
Senators were told clearly what was needed, but the Second
Consul was far too clever a man to bring up bygones. The
present question, he said, was not one of irritations, but of
technique. He proposed the form of Bonaparte's reply to the
Senate—that while he was delighted with this token of esteem, his powers as First Consul derived not from that body,
but from the Nation as a whole; any alteration in those
powers must come from the citizens. Bonaparte would then
retire to the suburban residence at Malmaison, and Cambacérès, as pro tem President of the Council of State, would
carry through that body a motion to put the question of extended powers to a public vote in a form that would provide
everything necessary.

It was so arranged; the First Consul never hesitated long
over anything and by this time had made up his mind what
he did want and need. On 20 floréal, Council of State, Tribunes and Legislative, successively passed (with only one

dissenting vote, that of Carnot) through a form of question
to be voted on by all Frenchmen:

"Shall Napoléon Bonaparte be Consul for life?"

It was the first time that the clanging vocables of his
Christian name had been used in a public document; and he
had received a lesson on the value of modesty in dealing with
public assemblies.

II

Of course, the proposition carried—by three and a half
million votes to eight thousand, the only opposition being
from the philosophical liberals, most of whom stayed away
from the polls. But the event raised almost as many questions
as it settled, and one of them was the question with which the
First Consul was peculiarly unanxious to deal, as evidenced
by his peevish unwillingness to have the second question of
the plebiscite submitted at all. It read: "Shall he have the
right to name his successor?"

The addition had been suggested by the ingenious Brother
Joseph and instantly approved by Cambacérès, who saw in
it a means of assuring the exterior world that the consular
régime would continue indefinitely, a concept at least at this
time foreign to Bonaparte, who saw his personal government and his personal life as coterminous.

The view was assuredly not shared by Brother Joseph. He
told his secretary that Napoléon was aiming at setting up
a dynasty and founding an empire on the ruins of Austria.
He (Joseph) and Brother Lucien were in disagreement as
to whether the First Consul ought to choose his successor by
primogeniture (Joseph was the elder) or for political skill
(Lucien was the more active), but they were united in feeling
that only the dynastic basis had any permanence—and also
in feeling badly used. Joseph thought he should have been
offered the presidency of the Cisalpine Republic of Northern
Italy; Lucien, that he should have received one of the offices
of State. ("They talk as though it were a question of the

estate of the late king, our father," growled the First Consul once.) Both the Corsican brothers knew exactly where to place the blame for the failure of this relative who had struck it rich to live up to his family obligations. The fault lay with the Créole, the childless, light-minded, unfaithful wife, to whom the First Consul was inexplicably devoted.

Against the best interests of Bonaparte himself (as the brothers saw it), against all the interests of the family, Joséphine remained immovably antidynastic. A dynasty would ultimately mean one thing to her—divorce. Bonaparte's insistence on writing an easy divorce law into the Code in the face of so much opposition filled her with tremors. It was a disturbing indication that the idea was hovering at the back of his mind that one day he might want an easy divorce himself. Even the words (reported to her by Fouché) in which he had rejected such an idea were less an assurance that such a thought had never entered his mind than a statement that the reasons were not yet adequate. "Why should I separate myself from this poor woman because I have been fortunate? Had I failed, had I been thrown into prison, she would have stood by me. Besides, if I did think of another marriage ——"

Joséphine's effort to achieve the reconciliation of the family in the matter of pretty Caroline's marriage had broken down completely, followed as it was by the affair of Lucien's pamphlet, and his dismissal from the Interior Ministry. There was a Corsican family brawl that night in the Tuileries, with everybody screaming. Old Mme. Letitzia, mother of all the Bonapartes, naturally could not see that Lucien had done anything but advance the family interest by suggesting that his brother set up a dynasty. She tried to defend him, and when that proved unavailing, turned furiously on Joséphine, crying that she was taking money from Fouché (which was true) and that she was trying to alienate Napoléon from his brothers (which was not).

Joséphine won that round by bursting into rivers of tears and persuading the First Consul to come to her defense, but the breach was unbridgeable, the brothers knew they could obtain real security and honor only by getting rid of That Woman. Not only was she antidynastic herself—Lucien used to tell her to hurry up and manufacture a baby if she wished to keep her husband after he had obtained the life tenure—but her link with the sinister Fouché continued; Fouché, with his crocodile smile and his files, in which everything the brothers had done was set down. It could only have been through Fouché, the letter-opener, that That Woman had learned how Lucien from Spain had written to the First Consul, advising him that if he divorced Joséphine, he might aspire to the hand of the Infanta Isabella. The dissolution of a mere civil marriage would not be repugnant to the principles of the Most Catholic King.

"Shall he have the right to name his successor?" It promised nothing to the First Consul but an intensification of the wretched wrangling which took up the hours he wished to give to the Code, or the reorganization of the army, or Gaudin's new budget. He was sufficiently an idealist, enough an honest craftsman, even enough of a patriot, to be determined that whatever obligations the Corsican family system imposed upon him, he would not be pushed into making a crown prince of either soft Brother Joseph or violent Lucien. To do either would be to sacrifice the stability of the régime, the thing for which he had striven so hard. Moreover, it would be an invitation to either Royalists or Jacobins to assassinate the Consul for Life. No member of the family would be stable.

At this point Joséphine, whose grace and social sense were making her more and more an indispensable member of the entourage, produced a plan. It did not promise to heal these internecine feuds, but it would at least mollify their effects by giving a more equal balance to the parties within the family. Her daughter Hortense was seventeen, marriageable age; she had been carrying on a mild flirtation with Duroc, the handsome aide, who used to slip up to her room, leave a letter within the secret drawer of her desk, and then signal

Secretary Bourrienne, who whispered to Hortense over the evening game of billiards that the letterbox was filled.

(Poor Bourrienne! He sighed in vain to play the leading part in the little romance for himself, but Hortense wrote in her diary that he was of "advanced age"—he was thirty-two—and laughed when he mooned under the trees at Malmaison or translated for her heart-rending passages from Young's *Night Thoughts*.)

The children thought their intrigue was a delightful secret, conducting it in what they imagined to be the best court tradition, with side glances in the drawing-room, the language of flowers, and conversational allusions that only two could understand. Of course, the First Consul knew all about it; when he sent Duroc to congratulate Alexander of Russia on his accession, the aide was made a general of division—in view of the importance of the mission. "He's a fine fellow, and now that he has won his promotion there is nothing against this match."

It is possible that the new general looked less enthusiastically than Hortense on the project of ending this charming game with a wedding. Bourrienne says so, and his credibility is not much damaged by her denial, since the forms required her to deny. Something like an unwillingness by Duroc to carry the matter through is necessary to explain the events of 14 nivôse, when Bonaparte stepped into the cabinet where Bourrienne was working, his face set in the pout that always followed a domestic quarrel. He asked for Duroc and, learning he was abroad, told Bourrienne to go find him; tell him he could have Hortense with a dowry of 500,000 francs and command of the 8th Military Division for himself, but he must marry her at once, within two days. Otherwise Hortense must marry Brother Louis.

"Will she like that?"

"She will have to."

Duroc was not located till half-past ten in the evening, and his response to this proposal of shotgun marriage was to tip his hat over his eyes: "Tell him that he may keep his daughter for me. I'm off to call on some whores."

So Joséphine had her wish, and three days later her daughter was married to young Louis Bonaparte, who passed as good-hearted because he never took part in the family rows. The bride wept all through the ceremony, Joseph and Lucien watched in silent gloom, and everyone agreed it was a dull occasion. It was also the first of the family marriages that had been made for reasons which had nothing whatever to do with human affection.

III

Joséphine had now won a victory of major proportions, the extent of which is clear from the First Consul's remark at the sober-second-thought family conference on the morning following the scene over Lucien's dismissal to Spain: "There is no longer any need of worrying about my heir. I have found one: Louis. He has none of the defects of my other brothers and he has all their good qualities." The Louis-Hortense marriage was thus a notice to Joseph and Lucien that they might as well make the best of the Beauharnais connection, it had been built permanently into the leadership of the house. But Joséphine's luck could not hold out forever against opponents so skillful as Brother Joseph, so vigorous as Brother Lucien—particularly as she was swimming against the stream of time.

The first difficulty was Louis himself. He caught his wife up on phrases, criticized her dancing and clothes, the fact that she received an officer guest with the cordiality of artless eighteen, made a terrible scene when she instinctively pulled a robe round her as he came into the bedroom one day when she was dressing. She was miserable, and within two months of the marriage she was pregnant. Without bidding her farewell Louis posted off to Joigny, where the regiment of which the First Consul had made him colonel was cantoned. Military life suited him no better than it had during the previous year when, after a month of bloodless campaigning along the Portuguese-Spanish border, he had secured a leave of absence on the ground that his health was bad. Two months at Joigny brought on another decline. The doctors (he wrote his consular brother in a letter which did not even mention the name of Hortense) advised him to take the waters at Bagnères-de-Bigorre, since his constitution was breaking down. The house that brother Napoléon had bought for him in Paris was to be sold; he was unhappy and it was better that he should not return.

The child was born in vendémaire of An XI, which is October 1802, a boy—to the infinite contentment of the First Consul, the only second-generation male in the family. In the absence of the father, he saw to the christening, naming the baby Charles-Napoléon, "after his grandfather and his uncle" officially, which failed to conceal from the salons and pamphleteers the point that the doubled name combined those of Charlemagne and of the First Consul, of the two men who had led the armies of the Franks to the conquest of Lombardy and the Rhine. The infant was immediately declared, not publicly indeed, but in family councils, the heir of the house—for by the date of the christening, it had almost become a House, Fouché and Joséphine had lost their game, and it was clear that the Byronic hypochondriac Louis had even less to offer the future than the two brothers who had in effect conspired to make their baby nephew a dauphin.

The tide-set toward dynasty was, in a sense, Fouché's fault. He should have known more about what was going on in the house kept at Auteuil by Cabanis, one of the ejected tribunes. It is even possible that he did know, but kept his mouth shut for reasons of his own, one of them a republicanism sincere only to the extent of believing that where there were many masters, the police power was master of them all. The men who met with Cabanis were, after all, proposing and doing nothing more illegal than the Tribunes who had secured the rejection of the first Titles of the Code. If de Staël and her group were in those gatherings, so were the few but very respectable political-theory Senators who followed Sieyès, so were a good many financiers, and a still greater number of the generals who flocked to Paris on the conclusion of the peace. One of this last group, General Bernadotte, was the center of the whole combination. The language these ill-assorted co-workers used was often rather free—they were fond of referring to General Bonaparte as "the Sultan"—but it would appear that the means they proposed to alter the scheme of things more nearly to their hearts' desire were constitutional. The generals proposed to obtain for themselves a *sénatus-consulte* dividing France into a series of military districts, each governed by an officer, with Bonaparte remaining in charge of the district of Paris.

One wonders what the philosophical liberals would have said about this scheme had it reached the operative stage. The memoirs they wrote about the period later are singularly mute on this point, though at the time the de Staël described Bernadotte as "the true hero of our age." The plan was never more than an outline for most of the participants, however, since on 30 floréal a servant was arrested at the Paris barriers, as he was bringing some horses and baggage to the city from Rennes in Brittany for General Simon, chief of staff to Bernadotte. The baggage proved to consist of a number of placards addressed to the army:

"Soldiers! You no longer have a country. The Republic has ceased to exist. A tyrant has seized upon power and that tyrant is Bonaparte"—with a great deal more in the same or an even more violent key. When the matter was followed up, it was found that similar packages of placards were waiting transportation to every city and military headquarters in France.

How deep the affair went, who was involved, we shall never know. The First Consul suppressed the whole thing and had all the papers destroyed. Perhaps even Brother Joseph had a finger in it somehow; there is quite a period here in which the air around him radiates chill. Simon was dismissed from the service without a trial; Bernadotte was

informed that the state of his health required him to resign
the command in Brittany, and to take a long rest at the
waters of Plombières. Mme. de Staël, who had gone to the
family summer place at Coppet near Geneva, was told that
she need not bother returning to France. She settled down to
write an exquisitely sensitive diary of exile—a rather curiously chosen theme, considering that she was a Swiss by birth
and a Swede by marriage, who had never acquired French
citizenship.

The point was that the unraveling of what came to be
called the "generals' conspiracy" or the "placard plot" came
not through Fouché, but through Dubois, the prefect of
Paris, and through General Davout of the military police.
During all this period the great detective, with his legion of
spies, had been unable to discover anything but a mad plan
by a pair of disgruntled lieutenants, half-crazy and usually
more than half-drunk, to assassinate the First Consul as he
drove abroad in his carriage. Lucien and Joseph were not
slow about pointing out Fouché's failure; on 28 fructidor
the Ministry of Police was abolished, with a message to the
Senate announcing that Citizen Fouché had been nominated
to its membership.

General Bonaparte to Laplace the scientist, 9 frimaire,
An XI:

"Friendship is only a word; I love nobody; no, not even
my brothers. Perhaps Joseph a little; but even there it is a
matter of habit; it is because he is the elder. I know perfectly
well I have no real friends, but as long as I remain what I am
I shall have as many as I need, so far as appearances go."

13

LOUISIANA

Madrid, Paris: 1801–May 22, 1803
(An IX–2 prairial, An XI)

IN THE tall corridors where voices were never raised and
rats scuttled behind the tapestries that pictured the
deeds of barbarous kings, figures stirred among the
perpetual shadows. The First Minister of State was drunk.
He lifted his vapid and meaningless face from the papers on
which he had been slobbering and, with his single eye wandering toward an angle of the ceiling (he was afflicted with
a horrible strabismus), inquired whether the embassy of
France had come yet? A bowing footman replied that he
had, but was closeted with Her Majesty.

Belowstairs, the King's glance wandered from one to another of the little group before him. He had been summoned
from the forge, where he had been engaged with his blacksmith in the fascinating task of making a pair of greaves,
and he found it somewhat difficult to fix his attention on
other business. The emotion he desired to express was
pleasure; so far as could be made out through the layers of
paint that covered the rocky protuberances of her face, his
harridan wife was being gracious. Anything that produced
such a result was entitled to the dim gratitude of Carlos IV,
King of Spain, Emperor of America and the Indies. But the
jutting Hapsburg lip and his inability to control his counte-

The First Minister of State was drunk

nance gave His Majesty the aspect of a small boy, pouting at the edge of tears.

To be sure, it seemed to Don Carlos that he had just been told by this uniformed lackey from Paris and his frog-faced coadjutor—what was the name? Berthier—that he must hypothecate a part of the Empire of Spain, what dishonor! The dosage was more than adequately sugared for His Majesty by France's request to recall to court his own good friend, that delightful Don Manuel de Godoy, Prince of the Peace—but how could this be pleasant to Her Majesty, who had dismissed the young man as a lover three years before, after his numerous infidelities to her? Royal Carlos wagged his head as the voice of Alquier the envoy droned through the polite inanities which diplomacy employs to permit the recipient of a message time to prepare a reply. Ah! there was the point (he recognized)—there was to be a new kingdom of Tuscany, with Luis of Bourbon-Parma as king and his own daughter, the Infanta Maria Luisa, for queen.

Was this not the plan he had rejected three years before? No, now he remembered—his confessor had said only the other day that it was a matter for the conscience of Don Luis and not for his own, if the former wished to rule a nation built on estates stolen from the Church. It was true, as M. Alquier was saying, that Trinidad was half English and the territory of Louisiana more than half French, a pestilential swamp which produced expenses instead of bar silver. Besides, Her Majesty was pleased—and the French could not take possession of New Orleans until the exchange of ratifications, which could always be delayed till minds changed . . . His Majesty's mind wandered off slowly beneath the words to the shaping of his greaves, his head nodded till a bell began to toll and it was time for prayers.

The First Consul had given France an empire.

II

It was an empire she had held before, but under circumstances how different! In those days Lally and Dupleix were wrangling with England for the Indies, the great adventurers were running the woods of Canada to produce a usufruct of precious furs. Louisiana (as Don Carlos observed) yielded nothing but expense and the scandal of M. Law. Its strategic use as a *point d'appui* for the encirclement of the English colonies disappeared when Quebec was lost, and no visible sacrifice had been involved in keeping it out of the hands of England by permitting Spain to add it to those American dominions too strong in mere bulk to be attacked.

That sacrifice had been made by a government still under the ideological domination of Louis XIV's Colbert, who believed that there was only so much commerce in the world, and that what was obtained by one nation must be taken from another. There was still a trace of this in the restrictions Bonaparte leveled against goods of English manufacture. But only a trace; the point of emphasis was now changed, the objective sought in his new arrangement was not so much to deprive England of anything within her own system, as to set up a French system economically valid in its own right—a system not dissimilar to the England-India complex, in which the manufactures of the home country were exchanged against the raw materials of the colony, leaving surpluses at both ends for cash sales to foreign account.

It was no part of Bonaparte's intent to invade the English market with goods produced either in France or in the French colonies. For the present he merely wanted to escape the grip of the system which, in the years before the Revolution and even during it, had forced France and Spain alike to buy English or English-colonial goods for cash and thus, in their own overseas enterprises, to seek only for Golcondas. The English plenipotentiaries at Amiens tried repeatedly to get a tight trade agreement into the treaty and Bonaparte as steadfastly refused. There is a sufficiently startling resemblance to Thomas Jefferson in the First Consul's remark that "Agriculture is the soul, the foundation of the kingdom; industry ministers to the comfort and happiness of the population. Foreign trade is the superabundance; it allows of the exchange of the surplus of agriculture and industry. Foreign trade in its results is infinitely inferior to agriculture; it ought to be the servant of agriculture and home industry."

In this, as in his program for the conciliation of all parties, the First Consul's basic idea was not particularly original. He was once more the beneficiary of the national experience —in the current instance, the experience of having seen the vast treasures seized from Church and nobility by the Revolution flowing gradually and by devious routes into London strongboxes. But, as in the political case, his method and breadth, his ability to forget prejudice, to concentrate on the technical detail of achievement, made all the difference. During the conferences that followed the wars of the eighteenth century, it had been the custom to argue violently and long about the possession of the rich islands. Bonaparte conceded two of the richest, Trinidad and Ceylon, without turning a hair. He was interested in relatively poor, relatively populous (50,000 Europeans) Louisiana.

The general reason was no secret. "France must have ships, commerce, colonies"—to relieve her of English financial domination. It is the specific point of why Louisiana was made the centerpiece of this structure that has interest. One would have expected the choice to fall on Saint-Domingue, the revolted colony, in which two-thirds of all the exterior commercial interests of France were concentrated before the blacks massacred their masters under the spur of the Revolution.

To contemporaries, it seemed that Saint-Domingue was in fact the main focus of interest. The ink was hardly dry on the treaty of Amiens before Bonaparte was assembling a fleet in the western ports under Admiral Villaret-Joyeuse. 20,000 men made up an expeditionary army, under General Charles-Victor-Emmanuel Leclerc, to whom, as a bon voyage present, the First Consul gave the hand of Pauline, loveliest of the Bonaparte sisters, already at sixteen a creature of singularly voluptuous allures. "Rid me of these gilded Afri-

cans and we shall have nothing more to desire," said the
head of state, as the expedition sailed away through an intense glare of publicity.

It was a light as factitious as the over-illumination that
had attended the organization of the Army of Reserve. Several things show it. In the first place, there was a raging inconsistency between Bonaparte's indifference to the other
rich islands and his concern over this one. In all probability
the place would have to be reconquered from the Negroes.
It would have been child's play to transfer this thankless
task to the British when they asked for a large Caribbean
island at the peace-table, and instead take Ceylon for France
—Ceylon, to which the French historical claim was quite as
good, possessed of far more easily tapped wealth, and with
the inestimable advantage (General Bonaparte always attached great importance to such symbols) of recalling to
every Frenchman that there had been a day and place when
the red cross of St. George fled before France on the sea.
Ceylon had seen the great Bailiff of Suffren come into harbor
"smoking and glorious," with captured British battleships
in his train; Saint-Domingue possessed no traditions but that
of a lazy life and the recent one of a servile war.

There was a second expedition to the Americas, prepared
in a silence which contrasts strikingly with the blare of trumpets round Leclerc. The latter was a good enough officer, but
of no special distinction, and had never commanded anything as large as a division. The second expedition was
headed by Beau Soleil Victor, who led a corps at Marengo;
and under him were Augereau, who had been a corps commander in the first Italian campaign, and that able St. Cyr,
who quarreled with Moreau. The army was 30,000 strong,
half again as large as that for Saint-Domingue; and its destination was New Orleans.

While it was preparing, letters were going to Madrid.
The Infanta's kingdom of Tuscany should be enlarged by
the principalities of Parma, Piacenza, and Guastalla if Spain
would cede useless Florida, or even Mobile and Pensacola,

to France. The addition would make young King Luis by far
the most considerable power in Italy, and would give the
Spanish family control of the Po crossings as well as of the
Leghorn port of entry.

. . . Parenthetically, this was not the dangerous increase
of Spanish influence it might appear. While the Leclerc expedition was on its way, Bonaparte invited the 24-year-old
king to Paris, partly to demonstrate that even Bourbons
could be reconciled to his new government, partly to look
over this new neighbor of France. Fouché's men watched
everything the new monarch did, and their reports were
illuminating. He burst into tears at receptions, trembled
when a gun was fired at the hunt, and, when allowed to
choose his own diversion, opted for a game of hide-and-seek
in the garden . . .

Even as the letters were going out, Barbé-Marbois the
treasurer was drawing a memorandum demonstrating from
various chancellery references that the ill-defined boundaries
of Louisiana should of right extend from St. Mary's on the
east coast of Florida around to the Rio Grande, with all
the hinterland to the Great Lakes and the Pacific shore. Unfortunately both for the demonstration and for the proposition to exchange territories, the ambassador at Madrid by
this time was Lucien Bonaparte. On the signature of the
earlier treaty, royal Carlos had presented him with twenty
paintings and 100,000 crowns' worth of diamonds; the ambassador simply could not see his way clear to pressing this
great and good friend for an augmentation of what was
usually understood by "Louisiana." But this was a side issue;
the main point remained that Saint-Domingue was a way-
station on the route to Louisiana, as England had Gibraltar,
Good Hope, and Mauritius as way-stations on her route to
India.

General Bonaparte was a soldier and thought in strategic
terms. He wanted colonies; but the trouble with those under
the French flag was that the British took them away in war,
and if recovered, they were usually in a state of nonproduc-

tive disrepair. In time France might be able to challenge the British naval supremacy that made this possible. But the sea challenge would have to be a product of the land Bonaparte proposed to open up; the commerce not only of Louisiana itself, but also of the trans-Appalachian territory of the American Republic, already sending through New Orleans goods to the value of 8,000,000 francs a year, nearly as much as went through Leghorn, the first port of Italy. All that trade would fall into French bottoms, and in a time so brief as to make the movements of England and Spain look slow, the colony would be beyond the power of any expedition the British could send against it.

In the meanwhile, until the foothold was thoroughly established, it was necessary to have the way-stations, Martinique and Saint-Domingue, where squadrons of less than battle force could lie and render it impossible for the English to slip past with a convoy of troops large enough to assault New Orleans. It is an old axiom of strategy that the best place to deal with an army is on the sea, where it cannot fight back.

III

Brilliant dream! Which, if carried out, might have spared Europe many years of war at the price of transporting the conflict to America. "At the moment Louisiana becomes a French possession, we must marry ourselves to the British fleet and nation," said Jefferson, again paralleling Bonaparte. (The two men thought almost alike on every question where their backgrounds permitted.) The prospect was defeated by an insect and an obstinacy.

The insect, of course, was *aedes Aegypti,* the common mosquito. Under the tropic sun of Saint-Domingue, thoughts and emotions that are clean as an arrow in the fine air of Paris suffer a heat-warp. The First Consul's instructions had been perfectly specific: General Leclerc's force was sufficient to beat down any opposition, but he was to land in peace. There was to be no question of the restoration of slavery.

The black leaders, especially their brilliant military commander, Toussaint L'Ouverture (who had had the temerity to address to Bonaparte a letter "from the first of the blacks to the first of the whites"), were to be sent to France.

On the basis of what happened later, it has been assumed that this was an exquisite treachery, leading to imprisonment sentences passed in advance. But it is not an attempt to defend the instructions on moral grounds to say that treachery is by no means provable on the immediate contemporary evidence, which is the kind that counts. Bonaparte always sought personal contact with present, past, or potential opponents. He possessed, and consciously used, a singular charm of manner, had a lucid, logical mind, was almost invincible in debate. He had seduced Jacobins (Français de Nantes, Barrère) and leaders of the royalist party (Bourmont) to the support of the government, to the disinterested service of France, and there were to be cases still more striking, including a former first minister of Louis XVI. He never inquired what factory made a tool that would cut. It is not at all impossible—at least there is nothing to contradict the idea—that the order to send the black leaders to France was less a *lettre de cachet* than the first step in a program of missionary work.

Upon only one point Bonaparte was obstinate. Saint-Domingue, the essential protective base for Louisiana till it reached self-support, must not remain in the hands of a government that controlled its own foreign relations. Such a government might turn indifferent or hostile when England reacted to the establishment of a French-colonial system by a war to preserve the dominance of her own—as she was not unlikely to do. Under Toussaint's régime the great colony had opened its ports to the North Americans and had stood neutral during the last conflict. This must not be repeated; and though there might be a number of means of bringing the colony's foreign affairs under French control, violence and treachery were those of last resort.

They became the first resource under the irritant sun of

Saint-Domingue, so clear but so uncandid. Leclerc found himself ranged against an obstinacy equal to Bonaparte's own. Toussaint, the greatest statesman of his race, so recently a slave, perceived that only an administration completely controlled by blacks offered the necessary guarantees against the return of the detestable institution.

"Beware," he said to Leclerc's emissary, as he scattered a handful of white corn over a great jar of black kernels and shook it violently: *"Où sont les blancs?"*

It is not recorded what the officer replied. General Leclerc replied by quarreling with his admirals and putting one of them under arrest, then splitting his expedition into detachments for simultaneous landings at all the major ports of Saint-Domingue. Toussaint had foreseen this; his orders were to burn the towns as the French advanced, burn the plantations and take to the hills. The program was carried out at the great city of Cap François. At most of the others local leaders, jealous of their own prestige, tried to make a stand and were beaten in battle, not without difficulty. It would be the sun that gave the French leaders the unhappy inspiration of massacring their prisoners. Even Toussaint was not unaffected by this fury; his fierce general Dessalines spoke the spirit of all the rest—"War for war, crime for crime, atrocity for atrocity"—and the occupation turned into a social war of a character not seen since the days of the Tatars.

The campaign lasted down into May 1801. Toussaint's generals began to desert, he was being driven in, and the island was being devastated. He might have carried on a guerrilla war; he surrendered under a safe-conduct with the honest objective of sparing his country. Leclerc promptly placed him in arrest, had him bound and sent to France on a battleship, where he coughed away his life in a cold stone cell among the mountains of the Jura; and this left the leadership of the blacks to Dessalines with his crime for crime, an intelligent savage where Toussaint had been an intelligent man.

Enter *aedes Aegypti,* carrying agent for the yellow fever, then in its grand climacteric throughout the Caribbean. When Toussaint surrendered, the jungle campaign was already costing the French not far from 200 men a day and Dessalines had marked the fact—marked also the rising tide of fear and resentment among his own people, as Leclerc put into force the plan he had worked out to disarm the blacks. The new Negro leader was intimate enough with the whites to note among them the rise of that reckless humor which enters any group when early death must take all but a few, and those few chosen not by any virtue but by lot. He renewed the war, more fiercely than before. By September Leclerc was writing home that not one-seventh of his effectives were left, and ordering that part of the military chest be spent on a splendid service of plate for Pauline—for what mattered, when tomorrow we die?

Thus the second expedition dribbled out into reinforcements for Saint-Domingue. Victor, Augereau, and St. Cyr never sailed, the reinforcements died as they came in; so did Leclerc. Dessalines massacred every white and mulatto he could reach, and the command fell into the hands of a fat little sadist named Rochambeau, who gave soirées at which Negroes were eaten alive by wild dogs for the amusement of ladies in evening dress.

IV

By this time events in Saint-Domingue no longer mattered. The clock had run to 1803, and it was clear that England would never permit the establishment of a French colonial system. The juridical causes of complaint were insignificant but instructive. Every English visitor to Paris, including most especially Charles James Fox (received with the distinction due the man who, throughout the war, had enunciated the French point of view in the Houses of Parliament), remarked how the phrase "infernal machine" sooner or later managed to crawl into the conversation when the

First Consul gave an audience. It was the one act of all those done against him and France that Bonaparte would never forgive or forget; and he remained convinced that the plot had been hatched in the English Cabinet.

He knew that two of the leading plotters, Georges Cadou-dal and the pamphleteer Peltier, were living comfortably in England, and the best of his information was that the former was receiving a dole from the British government. There seemed to him no reason why a government that wished to deal honestly with France should permit the brother heir-apparent of Louis XVI not only to live in close association with the English Court, but also to attend official reviews and receptions in the uniform of a force that must be forever at war with the heirs of the Revolution—the French Royal Army. Bonaparte did not in the least understand the English tradition of free speech; it seemed reasonable to him that if the British government were really amicably dis-posed, it would do something about those sections of the press which were attacking him with a violence that had few parallels. He even asked that such attacks be suppressed. England replied honestly that her laws did not permit any such thing; Bonaparte made it a condition of the trade treaty which England kept asking for that she do something about his bill of complaints, including Cadoudal and the Princes as well as the press.

In view of the First Consul's efforts toward an autoch-thonous French system, it is doubtful whether the treaty would have been granted in any case. The clause the British wanted to put in it was one permitting British ships to handle the trade between France and the French colonies, but deny-ing French vessels any similar privilege within the British system. But the question of whether, under other circum-stances, the treaty would have been granted is one of purely speculative importance. There was no trade treaty; the bank-ing and commercial classes who controlled a good part of the British press redoubled their attacks on what they de-scribed as outrageous interference in the affairs of a neighboring nation. It indicated the First Consul's aggressive intentions. He had similarly (they pointed out) interfered with the affairs of the Cisalpine Republic of northern Italy. All the resources of eastern France were being devoted to the construction of two great highways over the passes of Simplon and Mt. Génèvre. Alessandria, where old Melas was beat, had been turned into a great place of arms, and in the districts round it, veterans of the French army were being settled, marrying Italian girls, and constituting an organized reserve, which drilled twice a month. The Cisalpine had chosen Bonaparte as its president; and now the man was interfering in Switzerland.

An explanation circling fairly well back is necessary. Before the Revolution, the government of Switzerland had been centralized in the hands of a fat, lazy, contented financial aristocracy, ideologically of that Voltairean amoral agnostic cast so well pictured in the memoirs of Casanova. Politically it was Athenian-liberal, on the lines de Staël and Benjamin Constant had caught from the former's father, the "prosy old schoolmaster" of Geneva—liberty by all means, but peasants must know their places. Economically, this aristocracy was the link between the banking houses of north Italy and those of England, through similar establishments in Hamburg. The perpetual neutrality of Switzerland gave them a peculiarly favored position.

Much of the wealth that fell to the French state under the Revolution had eventually drained into London coffers through the hands of this group. When the Directorial government got into financial difficulties during the An V, it exported revolutionary doctrines and received in return the contents of the treasury of Bern, by which the expedition to Egypt was financed; but the members of the old firm in Switzerland had never acquiesced in the rape.

The general peace gave them an opportunity to recover. It provided for the withdrawal of French troops from the cantons, and within two months of the signature the troops were in fact over the frontier. The event happened to coincide with the presentation to the Swiss by their provisional revolutionary government of a new and considerably more democratic constitution. The money-men financed a campaign for its rejection. (It is a curious footnote on the history of communications that they could conduct this campaign in the mountain districts by assembling people in the churches and telling them that the real reason the French had left was that the Austrians had won a great victory on the Rhine, and that an immense army of Russians was besieging Bonaparte in Milan—not a word about peace; and that the deception could succeed.) The constitution was rejected, and Switzerland was now without a government.

The country was full of disbanded troops, members of the regiments that had been in service with royalist France and the Italian princes. It was easy to hire them for a counter-revolution "for Swiss liberty and the restoration of the ancient constitution." The Austrian Emperor, who was a seigneur in Switzerland by virtue of an estate he owned at Bazuns in the Grisons, sent officers. The provisional government, which seems to have been composed of well-meaning sheep, fled to Lausanne in a panic and wailed to Paris for help.

It was instantly accorded. Within the day Bonaparte ordered a division of 6,000 men from Huningen on Bâle, two more divisions, 12,000 strong, through Geneva, and another from the Cisalpine up through the Simplon pass. The counterrevolution collapsed. Swiss delegates met in Paris and formed a new, federal constitution, which gave each canton control of its own affairs and put an end forever to the country's internal quarrels.

It was a burning disappointment to the London financiers, who had looked forward with pleasure to the restoration of their old banking connection, and the English papers made the most of the affair. The presence of French troops in Switzerland possessed an irresistible double appeal to idealism and the sanctity of contract, to fear and nosiness. In the English view, when a treaty had failed to cover new conditions, the proper step was to negotiate a new instrument. Nobody listened for a moment to Bonaparte's statement that the French troops had not gone back into Switzerland to stay, and that he could no more suffer a government avowedly hostile to France and maintained by Austria to lie across his lines of communication with Italy than England could permit an inimical régime in Ireland.

Public subscriptions were opened in London for the heroic Swiss, struggling against a foreign despot; there was enormous indignation against Mr. Addington's government for permitting such things to go on in the world; and neither the fact that the heroic Swiss were uninterested in being defended by London, nor the rapid retreat of the French received notice. Mr. Pitt, riding with Lord Malmesbury in the park, intimated that although he had retired from politics, the violence of this creature across the Channel might make it necessary for him to buckle on the armor again. Mr. P. thought it not unlikely that Bonaparte would assume the presidency of the Batavian Republic as he had that of the Cisalpine; apply the commercial laws of France there also, and bring to an end that intercourse with the Continent upon which rested the prosperity of Old England.

Mr. Addington's government actually was not so supine as its opponents represented. In the Admiralty department it had tough old Lord St. Vincent, brought up in the eighteenth-century tradition that a Frenchman was something between a devil and a tailor's dummy, whom it was lawful to despoil. St. Vincent had been very much shocked by all those naval movements in the Caribbean, and still more so by the news that the French navy, so completely crushed in the late war, was building 53 ships of the line of a new and very fine model. It seemed to him that the things done in Switzerland and Italy were evidence not only of aggressive intent, but of Bonaparte's intention to clear his land flank before devoting all his energy to the sea, in a new contest for empire.

To him, this quite clearly meant a struggle for the Mediterranean, since the fates of North America and India were already decided. The Treaty of Amiens called for the evacuation of English troops from Egypt and Malta, and England was the soul of honor with regard to international obligations; yet in view of the threatening attitude of France, he could not but advise that the evacuations be delayed. Moreover, there was within the treaty itself clear juridical ground for such delay. The article for the restoration of Malta to its ancient knighthood said the step should be taken under the guarantees of the major powers, and the signatures of Prussia and Russia were still wanting to such a guarantee. As for Egypt, the Ottoman Porte (under a little judicious pressure) had requested that the British troops remain there to preserve order.

V

The total forms an interesting exercise in opposite methods in tearing up a scrap of paper, but for the Addington government keeping the peace had now become a wholly secondary consideration. It was under fire in Commons for its bumbling finances, its failure to increase the British navy, above all, its failure to halt France on the Continent; and the fire was being directed by the best speaker the House ever saw, Mr. William Pitt. At this juncture Bonaparte furnished him with fresh fuel by publishing the report of Colonel Sebastiani, one of his aides, who had been on a tour of the Near East. It said that the Turks and local Mamelukes were squabbling fiercely in Egypt; that the English showed no intention of leaving, but that they were an ill-armed, unorganized, dissolute rabble, so much detested by both Turks and Mamelukes that in another war 6,000 Frenchmen would be enough to repossess the whole territory.

The sensation this produced in England forced an instruction to Ambassador Lord Whitworth to take a stiff tone in Paris. His reply on Malta was that the Treaty of Amiens had been based on the principle of mutual compensations. Since France had made such enormous gains in Piedmont and Louisiana, England felt she had a right to be compen-

sated with Malta. Just as this message was being delivered
the new session opened in London, and Mr. Addington tried
to undercut his opponents by inserting in the speech from
the throne: "In view of the warlike preparations in the ports
of northern France and Holland, His Majesty has judged it
expedient to adopt additional measures of precaution for the
safety of his dominions. Though these preparations are
avowedly directed toward colonial service—" they probably
had another and less innocent objective.

It was the most offensive possible means of stating an un-
truth. The "warlike preparations" were in fact the third
reinforcement for Saint-Domingue, consisting all told of two
frigates, one ship of the line and five transports. Lord Whitworth realized the implications as soon as he saw the Ga-
zette, and hurried round to smooth out Talleyrand, whom
he judged (correctly as it happened) to be in favor of peace.
Talleyrand waited on the First Consul; there was a long interview, with Bonaparte pacing the floor and finally promising he would restrain his irritation. For two days he did;
then came the 13th of March, a Sunday, when by old usage
the diplomatic corps was received at the Tuileries. Of
course they were all waiting to see how the hot-tempered
First Consul would take the insult flung at him from across
the Channel.

As he entered and looked round the circle of controlled
vulpine faces, Bonaparte's brow knotted. He stepped over
to Whitworth:

"Milord, so you want war?"

"No, General, we are too sensible to the advantages of
peace."

"We have already had fifteen years of war."

"It was too many."

(Louder) "Well, I shall give you fifteen more; you are
forcing me to it. I don't know of any real differences between France and England; I only know that the island of
Malta has not been evacuated in the time prescribed by a
solemn treaty."

Talleyrand made one last effort, persuaded Bonaparte to offer mediation by Tsar Alexander, how sincerely one cannot say; he may merely have wished to keep the record straight, though the evidence favors the idea that he thought peace was still possible on the basis of minding one's own business. Offer useless: before it could be delivered in London the Addington government was tottering to its fall. England replied merely that the Tsar would certainly not accept the mediation of such a question as Malta, and offered the counterproposal of England's evacuating Malta in exchange for France's evacuating Holland, Switzerland, and Piedmont, militarily, economically, politically. Lord Whitworth's instruction told him to describe this as an ultimatum; it met another:

"Malta or war," said Bonaparte coldly.

VI

There remained a detail. Since the half-idiot Carlos put his name to the document making Louisiana French, there had been in Paris a certain American, M. Livingston, who wearied Talleyrand with his importunities about the River of the West. The settlers beyond the mountains of his own callow republic had no ready means of transit to take their goods to seaboard markets, and had early fallen into the habit of floating them down the river to New Orleans. The Spanish Governor of Louisiana had formed with them an arrangement of mutual profit by which these goods could be placed under bond without duty till picked up for transport overseas. The Intendant of New Orleans fell on a quarrel with the Governor and cancelled the arrangement. To quiet the storm that blew up among his western people, the American President had sent M. Livingston with a proposal for the purchase of New Orleans. The idea was absurd, of course, but Talleyrand kept him in play, because a negotiation that has not been definitely closed may always be useful in exerting pressures elsewhere.

A couple of weeks after the wrathful interview with Lord Whitworth came the news of the impending arrival of a second American negotiator, M. Monroe, with a new proposal. If not New Orleans, the Americans wished to buy a site for a new town on the lower Mississippi, together with a slice of Florida—Spanish territory, but the two ambassadors had a shrewd idea that the real estate agent in Paris could arrange a deal for them. The matter was reported to the First Consul, who received it with a noncommittal grunt, but on Easter Sunday he called in Barbé-Marbois the treasurer, and Decrès of Marine and Colonies to ask them for advice. Could Louisiana be defended in the event of war? Both men knew that Bonaparte had already answered the question and was merely summoning them for ratification. No defense, they chorused; General Victor's troops had not yet reached the colony, orders had already gone out for the recall of the fleet in the West Indies, since the English horizon was become so threatening.

Bonaparte: "I contemplate turning it over to the United States. Even a short delay may leave me nothing but a vain title to transmit to these republicans, whose friendship I seek. They are asking me for but a single city of Louisiana, but I already regard the whole colony as lost, and it seems to me that in the hands of this rising power it will be more useful to the policies and even to the commerce of France than if I attempt to keep it."

Barbé made some slight objection to selling "what the Germans call souls."

The General laughed. "Send your doctrines to London. I am sure they will be the subject of great admiration there. I direct you to negotiate this affair at once, tomorrow. Do not even wait for M. Monroe." Then his face cleared and (it is to be remembered to his credit) he told the treasurer to insist that all Louisianans become full citizens of the American Republic from the date of the treaty. The interview ended.

Someone—probably Barbé—told Brother Joseph, who told Brother Lucien, and both were horrified. They had accepted without reserve the First Consul's doctrine of a French system with commerce, colonies, and colonial products, and neither of them possessed anything like their brother's resilience and flexibility of mind. Conversation with each other brought both into a fine Italian fury. *"Parbleu,* before he can accomplish anything like that, our Napoléon will hear from me," cried Joseph finally, and they went round to see the First Consul, whom they found in his bath. The interview turned stormy, Joseph shouting that the Legislative chambers would never consent, the General that he would get a *sénatus-consulte,* and then Joseph, with his face aflame:

"Well, General, I can tell you that you may get ready to join those poor devils whom you have so legally, so humanely, and above all with so much justice transported to Cayenne!"

Bonaparte leaped furiously from his tub, flinging perfumed water all over the elder brother, while the younger, already in some disgrace, tried to pacify both; and the next day when Livingston called on Talleyrand with once more the old plea to buy a piece of Louisiana, the American was startled half out of his wits to be asked whether he did not want the whole territory. "No," he said at first, thinking it was probably one of Talleyrand's diplomatic maneuvers— and besides, he had no authority, and thought such a purchase repugnant to his country's constitution. Talleyrand forbore to press him; but Monroe arrived within the week, who had known Barbé-Marbois in days past.

The Treasurer went round to see them both with clear, definite, specific proposals for details of the sale, and arguments on how great it would render the Republic of the West. In the beginning as tentative as men experimenting with their first olives, then with waxing enthusiasm, the Americans let themselves be drawn along. On April 30 the draft treaty was ready; on May 22 the ratification was signed and the United States pushed to the Pacific and the Gulf of Mexico. General Bonaparte flung down his pen and said:

"I have this day given England a maritime rival who will sooner or later humble her pride."

Even so, he did not know how little time would pass before Baltimore privateers were running the chops of the Channel. That same day Mr. Addington declared war.

WRONG END OF THE TELESCOPE—VII

The Farington Diary:

G. Smith has been in Paris 7 months, and is returned extremely disgusted with the State of Society.—No morals.—No integrity. Characters of the lowest kind abounding in wealth, which they expend in a licentious way.—There appears to be an indifference to everything but pleasure. No principle remains.—The Government may be said to resemble that of the Pretorian bands in Ancient Rome. The military power awes everyone; Bonaparte is very unpopular, and not respected, and his abilities not rated high.—Moreau has more of the public opinion. . . . He thinks a person may live in Paris at half the expence of England.

Cobbett's Weekly Political Register:

By turning to the state-papers in this number, our readers will find the treaty, which was concluded between France and Spain, on the 21st of March last, and which is now just published. The motive for keeping this treaty so long from the eyes of the world, evidently was to prevent the ratification of the cession of Louisiana from being known, 'till peace was made between France and Great Britain. This cession is of the greatest importance, whether considered as to the facility it gives the French of invading Mexico, or of domineering over the United States of America.

Miss Berry to Miss Cholmeley:

What think you of the *man Buonaparte?* absolute King of France, quietly established in the Tuileries! For my part I admire him, and think, if he can keep his place, he does his country a service. Nothing ever gave me so desperate an opinion of our Ministers and their yet more desperate projects than the abuse which is daily vomited forth in all the ministerial and soi-disant impartial papers against Buonaparte and the new order of things. I confess that, as a citizen of enlightened Europe, after all the various tyrannies under which the French have laboured, I should really be sorry to see them return to their old original worn-out tyranny under the Bourbons.

The Columbian Centinel:

NOTWITHSTANDING the prefent popularity of Bonaparte, it will not be a matter of furprife, if before a year has expired, (fhould he efcape private affaffination) he fhould be denounced and executed as a *traitor* and *tyrant;* and his name be held in general detefta-tion throughout *France.* We are far from wifhing fuch an event. —We feel a veneration for the man, who has fhorn the locks of jacobinifm in *Europe,* and of courfe in *America:* and who has brought the reftlefs fanfculottes of *France* to a fenfe of allegiance due to a government which protects them in their frivolity.

Lady Bessborough to Granville Leveson-Gower:

HERE are some more Paris stories. Buonaparte question'd Mr. Fox concerning Windham, saying he understood his talents were mediocre, and that he was an unfeeling, unprincipled Man. "C'est très bien pour vous qui n'avez que quelques démélés publiques. Mais pour moi je le déteste, lui et ce Pitt qui ont tout deux attenté à ma vie." Mr. Fox stared. Bte. went on saying he would have forgiven open enemies in the Cabinet or the field, but not cowardly attempts to destroy him, such as *subornéing* his own Guard and setting on foot the Infernal Machine. Mr. F. again with great warmth assur'd him he was Deceiv'd, that Mr. Pitt and Windham, like every other Englishman, would shrink with horror from the idea of secret assassination. "Vous ne connaissez pas ce Pitt," said Buonaparte.

Livingston to Madison:

THERE never was a Government where less could be done by negotiation than here. There is no people, no legislature, no counselors. One man is everything. He seldom asks advice and never hears it unasked. His ministers are mere clerks, and his legislators and counselors parade officers. Though the sense of every reflecting man about him is against this wild expedition, no one dares to tell him so. Were it not for the uneasiness it excites at home it would give me none, for I am persuaded that the whole will end in a relinquishment of the country, and transfer of the capital to the United States. Their islands call for much more than France can ever furnish.

Lord Malmesbury's Diary:

MR. JACKSON, who was sent as Minister to Paris during Lord Cornwallis's Negotiation at Amiens, was with me: he said, "That impressed as he was on going to Paris with the ideas of the character of the present French nation, yet their attempts to deceive, their duplicity, their bad faith, insolence, and vanity, surpassed his utmost belief." That the way in which they treated everybody of every description dependent on them, was unsupportable; that Buonaparte's manners were sarcastic, vulgar, and impertinent, but certainly with a degree of cleverness and *esprit*: that Talleyrand (the Minister of Foreign Affairs) was the most barefaced teller of untruths he ever met with; and that no one but Barbé Marbois had even a desire of passing for an honest man.

Lady Bessborough to Granville Leveson-Gower:

ROBINSON is arriv'd, with the most perfect wig à la Brutus you ever saw. He says Ld. Brome gives a melancholy account of Paris—that Buonaparte never dares show himself or go out, that he joins in no amusement but now and then yᵉ Theatre, and that his being there is only known by his guards, as he is entirely conceal'd in the box by a sort of screen put up before him, and that the constant expectation of attempts upon his life ruins his health and temper (I do not believe a word of all this), that the society in general is very bad, as all the rich people are mauvais ton and the bonne compagnie are too poor to assemble much, that Mad. Buonaparte is very amiable, and that her parties us'd to be pleasant till B. desir'd her to invite all the officers wives &c., which has spoilt them.

LOUISIANA

The Columbian Centinel:

MISSELANEOUS FOREIGN ARTICLES

(From London Papers by The Late Arrivals)

Mr. ADDINGTON, according to the papers, has thrown off his coat and waiſtcoat to challenge BONAPARTE. The First Con-ſul ſeems to have lowered but one garment in return to the defiance; and *that* neither his coat *nor* waiſtcoat.—Whether the altercation will terminate in *kicking* or *kiſſing,* ſeems yet to be as problematical as ever.

The Farington Diary:

I DINED at a Restauranteur adjoining the Thuilleries gardens, (not Very's) which was frequented by respectable people, but chiefly such as studied economy, the expense being much less than in many other Houses of the same kind. The first circumstance that I remarked was that there were a great number of tables as in the English Coffee Houses, at which parties were dining; but upon no one was there a table cloth, and under each plate, according to the number of persons, was a *napkin,* which the person to whose plate it belonged might put under his chin;—upon his knees; or make a small table cloth of it for his own purpose; and in each way I saw them used, which produced a whimsical effect. To these places respectable women go witht. remark. I saw a few dining at their ease in this large assembly of eaters.

14

PREPARATION FOR
AN EVENT

Paris: to 30 ventôse, An XII
(March 21, 1804)

IF THE war was not particularly popular with most Frenchmen, it was still less so with the First Consul. Everything had been done, but nothing; the machinery of re-
generation had been built and was operating smoothly, but
the products had hardly begun to come forth. The point is
missed if one treats as a mere exhibition of masterful bad
temper the incident of Bonaparte saying, "English muslin?"
and tearing a lady's sleeve at the Tuileries.

He could tell the difference: the English muslins were
better. The irritation that thus expressed itself in a piece of
torn cloth was not only over seeing the nation's carefully
gathered cash resources drained off for the benefit of an
enemy, but also because French goods could not compete
with British even on their own ground. Until they did, escape
from the British commercial system was impossible, and that
meant either submission to it or wars into the infinite future.

The industrial revolution had reached England in a singularly unlovely guise; the stuffs on which her booming prosperity was founded had been produced by the exertions of
tots below the age of puberty, who labored twelve hours a
day and were rewarded with the barest living, plus free religious instruction on Sunday. Neither Bonaparte nor anyone

else could encourage commerce by setting up such a system in France. The abolition of various forms of peonage had been precisely one of the things the Revolution was about, and though the liberation of labor it proclaimed was something less than complete in the eyes of subsequent generations, it was real enough to be a blessed new way of life to the people most concerned.

The First Consul accordingly sought to make use of the devices he employed when outnumbered in a military campaign—rapid movement and technical superiority. The instrument, the army commander in the war for economic independence, was Jean-Antoine Chaptal, Minister of the Interior in succession to Brother Lucien. He was a short, bandy-legged man, with a broad face, who thought very highly of himself—"The first lecture I gave was extremely brilliant" runs a characteristic entry in his diary—but nowhere near highly enough; for Chaptal was, like Gaudin and Tronchet, one of the true makers of France, and even beyond them, of the modern world. Among the family documents are letters from Franklin and George Washington, both of whom tried to capture him for their new republic of the West.

He came from a southern family of rich proprietors, in which the custom was for the eldest to inherit the land, while the cadets went in for law or medicine, which was easy as they lived near Montpellier, the most famous medical faculty of Europe. Medicine was Jean-Antoine's choice, or rather, for him, that of the distinguished physician his uncle, who became the lad's guardian when his father died. Jean-Antoine went up to Paris to study the profession with the then young Cambacérès in '76, and fell in with the group of gay intellectuals who hovered around the Comédie Française; wrote poetry and acquired a taste for sleeping with actresses. This was only to keep up with the fashion; he had met the great Lavoisier and discovered his true love and vocation in the fascinating new science of chemistry.

Three years later he was back in Montpellier, lecturing on

the subject, wrote a book about it, bought some buildings with a princely wedding present from his uncle, and began to make hydrochloric and sulphuric acids on a commercial scale for the first time in history. The process was his own invention—sulphuric acid, note, which is more important to modern industry than any other substance save iron alone. It was Chaptal's view that science is useless unless applied. He says so in his book; when the Revolution came along, they cut off the head of the pure scientist, Lavoisier, but they sent a special mission to rout applied scientist Chaptal out of his hiding place among the mountains of the Midi and make him inspector of saltpeter.

For the coalized kings were across the frontiers. It was Monge and not Chaptal who discovered the precious ingredient of gunpowder under the manure-piles of France; but it was Chaptal and not Monge who invented the process for purifying it from the raw material in three days instead of five months, and so supplied the burning lips that spoke from the heights of Valmy. The Directory, which had no need of scientists of any kind save those who could extract gold from strongboxes, sent him into retirement again. He employed his time by writing a book on how to make wine, which remained the standard work for over a century and has never been entirely superseded. When Bonaparte came to power, old friend Cambacérès looked Chaptal up. The First Consul had half an hour's talk with him, tried him briefly in a subordinate post, and then made him Minister of the Interior.

There has rarely been such a ministry. With his quasi-medical background, Chaptal naturally started on a system of hospitals, the first organized public enterprise of the kind in France or the world, each with adjunct schools for nurses, obstetricians, and midwives. There was a shortage of drugs, most being imported from Holland or England; Chaptal set up laboratories and made them himself, inventing the processes. Linens, blankets, bandage-cloth were unobtainable; he founded factories to make them. The factories were ineffi-

cient; he imported mechanics from England to build spin-
ning-jennies of the British Arkwright type. At their best the
processes and stuffs were only as good as the English and
the quantity produced was small; Chaptal set up a "Society
for the Encouragement of National Industries," with manu-
facturers actual and prospective as members, and laboratories where pilot models of the machines were installed.
Through a monthly bulletin fat cash prizes were offered for
inventions and improvements which became free for all to
use without patent and without fee.

Bonaparte wanted agriculture encouraged; Chaptal sent
to the prefects of every département for samples of the local
soil, himself submitted them to chemical analysis, advised
the local authorities what would grow best on them, appointed a host of traveling experts who moved from one end
of France to the other, preaching and demonstrating the doctrines of crop rotation and organic manures, many decades
before such a thing was heard of in any other nation. A century and a quarter later France was the only country west of
the Dnieper that did not have to import food; it was due
(fundamentally) to Chaptal. Education fell in his province;
he summoned the heads of the academies and told them their
system of instruction was hopelessly bad, that pupils in
geography (for example) learned only by repetition of
words, and might as well be concerned with some imaginary
country on the moon. They must use maps, models, and pictures, bring their subjects to life.

Everything done that authority and good will could do to
convert the political Revolution into a revolution of intellect, custom, and economics. Chaptal had a world to make
and he made it, an orchard to plant and he planted it—but
it would take a generation for the trees to bear fruit and
England declared war, so that it became necessary for the
Ministry of the Interior to become a producing instead of an
expending organization.

One night as Chaptal and his master were working late, a
valet opened the door and stuck his head in to announce

Mlle. Bourgoin of the Opéra, the minister's mistress. She came in, swinging her reticule, a little blonde. The First Consul glanced up, remarking that he would be with her in a moment, would she wait in the next room? Not a word from Chaptal, but he began gathering up his papers at once and resigned the next morning.

II

Even the technical means for an English war were unready. Forfait, the engineer Minister of Marine, had been relieved by a professional seaman, Denis Decrès, whom the First Consul had met during the Egyptian campaign, and who was vastly more efficient at the discharge of administrative detail. The change was less a demotion for Forfait than a recognition of his qualities as a builder. Under his leadership thirty new slipways for ships of the line had been set up, well scattered to take advantage of local supplies of labor and materials. Three battleships were laid down at Flushing, two at Nantes, three at Bordeaux, two at Marseille, three at Brest, three at L'Orient, six at Rochefort, four at Toulon, two each at Genoa and St. Malo. Nearly all the ships were of a new standardized model, 80-gun vessels, somewhat heavier and much more habitable than the 74 which was the normal British and previously the normal French ship of the line.

As turned out they were better-knit and often faster than their British opposite numbers, since Forfait was not only a good designer himself, but also had the wit to copy the hull form and planking jointure from one of those wonderful American heavy frigates, the finest warships in the world, when she put into Toulon for repairs. The exceptions to the 80-gun-ship rule were one of the Brest vessels and one at Rochefort. These were of the huge three-deckers which are the mainstay and fortress of every battle line at sea, and the fact that there were only two of them indicates the difficulties under which the whole program labored. Only Rochefort, Brest, and Toulon had built major warships before, and at the last port materials were short. In the new yards construction had to be carried on by house carpenters, apprentices, anyone willing to swing a hammer; and the work went so slowly that at the declaration of war there were barely 42 French battleships ready to oppose a British marine that carried 111 on its lists. 25 more were building, but only two of these would be ready soon.

As with the ships, so with the men. The seamen of the regular navy had gained comparatively little experience in the late war, and though some of them had improved their skills during the campaign of Saint-Domingue, their number was insignificant compared with the huge reserves of Britain. None of the admirals knew their business as tacticians, hastily promoted as they were when nearly all the officers of the old, experienced Royal Marine had gone émigré. The captains were habituated to defeat, they thought in terms of breaking away, saving their ships, rather than of beating the enemy. New men, like new ships, were only beginning to appear.

The inferiority was hopeless, French commerce was deleted from the seas at once, as Bonaparte had foreseen when he peddled Louisiana, and it seemed impossible to attack a state that so completely controlled all means of access to its vital parts. Back in the days when he had been merely General Bonaparte under the Directory, the First Consul had barely escaped being dismissed the service for reporting that the problem of a direct attack on England was insoluble, and flatly refusing to take command of an army destined for so foredoomed an enterprise. The event justified him; dazzling young Hoche, his rival, had lost life and reputation trying to carry the project through.

But in a military sense things were not as bad as precedent indicated, or so the figures appeared to say. They seldom are when a unified concept directs war, or victory through concentration on an essential point of contact would be impossible, and conflict could be decided by statistics, without recourse to artillery. The essential point of contact in this case was clearly the English Channel. Once let the battle-experienced, well-led soldiers of France be passed across that gap and they could make short work of ill-trained, incompetently headed levies who fought for King George. "Masters of the Channel for six hours and we are masters of the world!" said the First Consul.

Strategically the Channel amounted to a guarded defile. The attempt to force it by main strength in the days of the Directory led to defeat with heavy loss at the Battle of Camperdown, the normal result in such cases. But the Directory had also left the heritage of another and more genial plan, the leading feature of which was to decoy the guards away from the defile for long enough to permit the passage of an army—as was frequently done in the type of warfare with which Bonaparte was most familiar, as Bonaparte himself had done when he broke through the Ligurian Alps against Austria in his first campaign. The effort at decoy and diversion failed in the case of England chiefly because of another and conflicting strategy imposed upon that of the Directory by—General Napoléon Bonaparte, who had very skillfully managed to drive British ships out of the Mediterranean, whither the Directory was trying to decoy them.

In the normal conduct of maritime affairs during war, England already had severe temptations toward diversion from the essential point. These temptations Bonaparte planned greatly to increase in order to whittle down the marine reserves Britain could bring to the essential point at the time of contact. England had to protect the sea-borne commerce, especially to India, on which her life and empire depended. Bonaparte let loose against this commerce a swarm of privateers and public raiders which would call for the employment of many of the 111 battleships in ones and twos on convoy work, and backed this up by ordering the small squadrons at L'Orient and Rochefort out on heavy raids against institutions like the Newfoundland fisheries and the sugar fleets of the West Indies; forcing the British to make large detachments against these corsair battleships or see valuable assets go up in smoke. A squadron of Dutch ships in the Texel similarly had no function but that of keeping a British force standing off the harbor; it had nine ships.

The key element in the plan, the one feature that persevered through all subsequent alterations, was that the British force which came out to blockade one of France's two main fleets, that at Toulon, should be decoyed off to Egypt. The French Toulon fleet would thereupon make for the Atlantic, raise the blockade of Brest (the two French squadrons together would be far superior to the British off the latter port), and become masters of the Channel for long enough.

Dismissing to Egypt a British fleet hardly likely to take his orders did not strike Bonaparte as at all a chimerical project. In fact, his own previous conquest there made it relatively easy; the British were peculiarly sensitive about that Near Eastern area as a possible route to their treasure-house in India, and the garrison was weak. The least gesture in that direction would cause them to take action, and Bonaparte arranged a very decided gesture.

Toulon cannot be blockaded closely because of the prevailing winds and the shape of the coast. Let the French fleet steer south going out, till sighted by some British cruiser, then avoid him by cutting sharply west at night with lanterns extinguished. Let one or two light craft arrange to be captured, with carefully faked papers and trusty men who would tell the tale of Egypt; let rumor and the Italian papers speak of the same thing. The British would surely make for Egypt and the Toulon fleet could reach the Atlantic without pursuit.

One or two details were added to this framework when war came so suddenly that a squadron of nine battleships returning from Saint-Domingue could not reach Brest; five had gone to Spanish Ferrol, one to Spanish Cadiz, three to Rochefort. This left the French fleets and their opponents lined up as follows—14 French in Brest, watched by 15 British; two French in L'Orient and five in Rochefort, with a British squadron of five covering both ports; five French in Ferrol with six British on guard; at Toulon 11 French watched by 12 British. The Toulon squadron was thus not strong enough to fight the Brest blockaders unaided, and there was no means of communication that would let the ships in the latter port come out at the right moment for a combined action. It was therefore ordered that on its voyage north the Toulon fleet should pick up the single ship at Cadiz, release the blockade at Rochefort-L'Orient, and add the seven ships in those ports to its strength before standing in toward Brest.

The plan had three visible inconveniences. The British at the gate of Brest, being the stupid bulldogs they were, would almost certainly fight in the face of numbers. Some means must be provided for transporting the army across the Channel within the very brief period between gaining control of it and the arrival of British reinforcements. The transports must be given protection against the swarms of enemy light craft which continually operated in the narrow seas. All three points had been considered and provided for.

Back in the days when the Directory was planning its invasion of England, someone—we do not know precisely who —conceived the project of backing the major invasion forces aboard the great ships, with a wing carried direct to Duke William of Normandy's landfall in small, light, shallow-draft vessels which could be easily built, as they would have but one voyage to make. When he became Consul, Bonaparte inherited the project and a little matériel that was being languidly assembled. After Hohenlinden, when England was the only enemy left in arms, the idea of sneaking an invasion force across the Channel under cover of night or fog was erected into a major operation. Forfait designed several classes of flat-bottomed craft, which could carry a number of soldiers, the largest, called praams, mounting 12 guns of battleship caliber. An assemblage of these would have something very harsh to say to anything less than a squadron of ships of the line, that is, a major sea-going fleet.

It may be questioned whether the First Consul intended to use his praams for an invasion rather than as pawns in the diplomatic game of obtaining a peace. The forces assembled along the Channel at the time were not impressively large. But the English took the threat seriously enough; shop windows filled up with pictures of giant invasion rafts driven by windmills, Mr. Pitt in person drilled a company of militia, a regiment of lawyers presented themselves before His Majesty, George III, and England sent her greatest seaman, Nelson, to kill the dragons in the egg by attacking Boulogne with a squadron of frigates and brigs. The thing was tried twice; both times Nelson was driven off with loss.

Forfait's invasion craft were, then, secure against the lighter types of British warships. The First Consul came back to them for his real invasion plan in the An XII, but with this difference, that instead of the 250 light vessels assembled in the An IX, an order of fructidor An XI provided for over 2,000, to be built in every port from the Hook of Holland to little towns far up the Loire. They would concentrate at Boulogne and along the coast at either side of that town by breaking through the offshore British frigate squadrons, and they would be numerous enough to transport an army of 100,000 men, outnumbering all the soldiers of England. Batteries would protect the invasion craft as they lay waiting in harbor.

The original plan for the employment of the 2,000 vessels was so hedged round with alternatives that it is hard to be precise about it; but fundamentally it seems to have been intended to use these invasion ships alone, stealing a crossing as one would in establishing a bridgehead beyond a wide and deep river. Fog, storm, or a long winter night would make it possible.

The surprise-crossing feature dropped out of the plan quite early. The construction of the invasion craft went much more slowly than expected; in brumaire of An XII there were still only 100 of them at Boulogne, and those built in the other harbors along the coast were finding it next to impossible to work their way to the concentration point in the face of the close British blockade. Behind this disappointment lay the fact that Forfait's experience had been mainly with canal-boats and similar craft for still waters. When the wind blew strongly enough to move the heavy, clumsy praams, they could not work their guns, and the oar propulsion that might have served them in crossing the Channel during a calm was inadequate for the longer run down the coast.

In the second place a miscalculation in seamanship developed. It would take more than six hours, more than a single night, because there was not time enough in that space to move the invasion craft out through the narrow exit of Boulogne's inner harbor to the roadstead beyond. On 13 brumaire of An XII Bonaparte himself went down to Boulogne to investigate. All the praams and gunboats in harbor passed out and formed in line, as for battle or movement. The process was not complete by dark, and a division of English cruisers discovered what was happening and ran in for a cannonade. There was no particular damage to either side, but that night, before the boats could be brought behind the breakwall again, a storm blew up, five of the craft were wrecked and most of the rest dispersed along the coast when one foundered in the channel to block the rest.

On 4 germinal and on 22 germinal the experiment was tried twice more. Each time winds dispersed the squadron, and the best estimate now was that five days were not too much for the flotilla to load, to exit, form, and make the run to England, even if more than one port of embarkation were used.

Now it was manifestly risking the loss of the army to leave part of it in outer roadsteads aboard praams and gunboats for two or three days while the rest prepared to make the sudden mass movement necessary to stealing a bridgehead. No surprise possible.

Eh bien, the alternative—which seems to have been lying at the back of Bonaparte's mind all the time, and for which he began to issue orders on 11 frimaire, less than a month after the brumaire storm—the plan for the union of Brest and Toulon fleets in the Channel. The remaining inconvenience was the discovery of an admiral. To understand how great this difficulty was it is necessary to remember that a battle off the rocks of Brest in which the forces would be not much more than equal was probable. On land, where the French had for eleven years been producing soldiers who could win victories, there were not above three men whom Bonaparte could trust to fight battles in his absence—Moreau, Masséna, and one completely unknown, but of whom something will be heard, Louis-Nicholas Davout. On the water our leaders are Ganteaume, a wonderfully capable seaman, but with no stomach for battle; Bruix, a driving executive, but when it comes to taking risks, full of excuses; Villeneuve, a good head, but weak in the guts, will do nothing unless ordered. On the faces of all these lies "the shadow of the Nile," the memory of that dreadful night when a French fleet was wiped out; even their conversation shows an inner consciousness that France will never beat England at sea. Of the junior admirals there are Rosily and Missiessy, old men, tired, inexperienced in large commands; Magon and Gourdon, strong characters both, but of so little skill that they cannot handle four ships without falling into collision; Allemand, a good raider who thinks in terms of corsairs, of damaging without fighting.

One real possibility, alone—Louis-René-Madeleine de Vassor, Comte de Latouche-Tréville. He was the sole admiral in service to stay with the Navy when the Revolution came and had sat with the Third Estate; but Robespierre threw him into prison, with the intention of taking off his head because of his title. Robespierre's own head fell first; Latouche-Tréville emerged from his cell to a retirement which was broken only when Bonaparte called him out to command the Boulogne flotilla in the An IX, both because he was an experienced naval officer and because he was a noble. He had thus missed all the defeats; his mind was formed in the American war, when British ships not infrequently struck their flags to the lilies.

It was he who gave Nelson's frigates their bloody repulse. The First Consul placed him in charge of a naval division in the expedition to Saint-Domingue, where he showed both courage and a tactical ability that made the latter-day admirals gape. The orders that went out in frimaire, when it was clear that there would be no surprise crossing, included one for him; an order to Paris. He went, and by the First Consul himself was told the plan, in which Admiral Latouche-Tréville, with the Toulon fleet, was to evade Nelson's blockaders, release the Brest ships, and cover the invasion.

Latouche-Tréville, who knew something of Bonaparte's objections to allowing other officers command of crucial actions, asked what he should do if the British blockading squadron declined to quit Brest on his appearance.—Fight, said the First Consul, watching his man,—the blockaders of Brest will be in no good shape to deal with Ganteaume's ships after a battle with your fleet. Latouche-Tréville's face expressed nothing but pleasure; he posted down to Toulon at once, where he found the fleet in wretched shape, half the men lying drunk ashore, most of the officers spending their time at *bals,* many of the ships not even rigged, and the belief quite clear in all conversations that the only way for France to achieve anything by sea was through raiding commerce.

The new admiral made the men stay aboard their ships, sent the ships into the outer roadstead, and on a day in prairial when Nelson incautiously bore in toward the port without having all his force present, suddenly hoisted sail and moved out in line of battle. It was only a brief brush, but the Neptune of England, the invincible seaman, was actually forced to turn in flight.

III

If the First Consul had experienced difficulty in finding means to throw his strength against England, the British Cabinet was having quite as much trouble in attacking France. Austria, Britain's late Continental ally, was extremely sympathetic and even willing to go to war (provided there were enough money in it), but her army was being reorganized and was not ready to fight. Prussia, the classic ally, was too secure behind the shield of the best army in the world to consider the French a menace, and would be interested only in acquiring territory. There was none within the English gift but Hanover, which George III would never think of abandoning, and over which the English now had a juridical rather than a possessive right, since a French corps had seized the province as soon as England declared war.

She therefore had to carry on alone. There is nothing to prove, in the legal sense, that the British government was concerned in the effort that followed to make war by means not usually recognized as legal among the politer nations. On the other hand the indirect evidence is fairly strong. Mr. Addington's Government, manned by busy nobodies, was fighting for its life against the attacks of Mr. Pitt, and that able speaker found it easy to demonstrate that England stood still while Bonaparte's preparations moved on apace. Something more positive was demanded of the Government than the erection of Martello towers at the mouth of the Thames and the appearance of the Prime Minister in Commons, with his long limbs somewhat ungracefully togged out in a volunteer's uniform.

Now the only apparent means of positive action against France lay in the presence in London of a host of irreconcilable Vendéans, with the Comte d'Artois, brother of the man they recognized as king, for titular leader. The real head, and the distributor of the subsidies furnished by His Britannic Majesty's Government, was Georges Cadoudal, the brains behind the infernal machine plot of three years before.

Not long after the declaration of war, there appeared among these pensionaries of the past a man with a hangdog chin and charming manners. His name was Mehée de la Touche, his record of opposition to Bonaparte was irreproachable (he even had a prison past), he had been traveling from one end of France to the other, and he told the émigrés and Mr. Addington's people what they most wanted to hear—to wit, that the Jacobins and republicans of conviction really outnumbered all other parties put together, that they would prefer a Bourbon restoration to the tyranny that now had them in its grasp, and would be glad to co-operate in overthrowing the weak and bad Consulate.

The exile of de Staël proved where the republicans stood. Mehée de la Touche produced some very convincing letters from the Jacobins, with whom he had been connected. All the émigrés became very excited, Mr. Addington's people hardly less so, and the projects that had been only the subject of drawing-room wishful thinking began to be discussed at the practical level. Mr. Hammond, under-secretary of the Foreign Office, addressed himself to Spencer Smith, Minister to the court of Baden, and to Mr. Francis Drake, who had been promoted from espionage to the embassy in Bavaria, and they in turn to their connections in France. It was not a question of buying information alone; the sums laid out by Drake and Smith ran high into six figures of sterling and were so placed as to secure the maximum support for a grand plan.

That plan, so far as H.M. Government was officially concerned, lay within the bounds of legitimate warlike enterprise. It embraced a rising in Languedoc, where the anti-revolutionary Companions of the Sun were still active; they would be joined by the unrepentant Jacobins. There would be a new rising in La Vendée; a landing in France by a Prince of the Blood, to be leader and rallying point; and—a feature not found in any similar previous arrangement—a rising in Paris. Cadoudal—simply Georges without surname to all Frenchmen—took personal charge of the last, the most dangerous and most important element in the plan. A British warship set him on the coast near Dieppe on the night of August 21, 1803, with a few companions and a million francs (compliments of Mr. Addington) in a money belt.

Of course his own project was nothing so inconsequential as a mere rising. There was only one way of changing the policy of a state where so much power was concentrated in a single person, and that was to dispose of the person and see that the power was used in a desirable direction by his successor. Georges proposed to accomplish this by assembling a hundred or more men around the First Consul's carriage as he drove from Malmaison to Paris one day and killing Bonaparte as he resisted—an act of war, not of assassination, as Georges was pleased to remark.

As the plotter lived in hiding and among people of his own persuasion, he would hardly have learned that the prospects of a Jacobin-Royalist fusion against the Consul were hardly so rosy as Mehée had pictured them; but one thing was obvious from the beginning—not even a revolt accompanied by the assassination of Bonaparte was likely to succeed unless the adhesion of the Army were gained. In fact, with France at war, with the Army forming so large a proportion of the nation, a general was the only possible successor to the present head. There was only one general who would do—Moreau, clearly the second man of the nation as Bonaparte was the first, known to disagree with the Consul's policies, bound to change them, the candidate of the intellectual liberal republicans, who would (according to Mehée) fall in with the counterrevolution.

How to reach Moreau? There was in London at this moment a certain General Lajolais, a small, pimpled man, lame of one foot. Old friend of Moreau's during the wars on the Rhine. He had also been very intimate with Jean-Charles Pichegru back in the An III, when that officer tried to sell out to the Austrians. When Pichegru was found guilty and banished to Cayenne, there was no direct evidence against Lajolais, but so much of an indirect character that he was dismissed the service. Bonaparte had refused to reinstate him, so he had gone to London, where he was presently joined by Pichegru himself, just escaped from the dry guillotine of Sinnamari. Pichegru, of course, now had no hope but in the Royalists; Georges sent for him and for Lajolais, and they both arrived in Paris on 25 nivôse, An XII, whereupon Lajolais at once went round to call on Moreau.

The republican general was delighted to see his old friend. They had a long conversation, which Lajolais led round to the subject of Pichegru, of whom Moreau spoke in terms of warmth rather surprising from a man who had once publicly accused that general of treason. He had (Moreau said) always doubted the guilt of that soldier of France. The evidence against him was very bad: those d'Antraigues cipher dispatches had come through the hands of that pig of a Bonaparte, who had probably faked them or deliberately misread the ciphers in order to remove Pichegru as a possible rival. (Here Moreau apparently forgot that he himself had furnished to the courts the documents that produced the conviction in Pichegru's case.) This made it easy for Lajolais to say that the wronged man was in Paris and would like to renew acquaintance with Moreau, but as his status was that of a criminal escaped from prison, the matter would have to be handled with caution.

The meeting took place on 2 pluviôse. Pichegru, cold and intelligent, unhappy over the company he was keeping, went to the heart of the matter at once. There was a proposal to overthrow the Consular government and restore the Bourbons; was Moreau interested? (The means of overthrowing the Consulate do not seem to have been specified, but lay understood beneath all this conversation.) Moreau was much interested, but not to the extent of restoring the royal family. He himself (he said) had a considerable party in the Senate and the Army, who were justly indignant over the treatment accorded to him by the First Consul. Why, the man had even refused him admittance to a state dinner because he came in civilian clothes instead of uniform! If France were delivered from the Consulate, the government would certainly be placed in his (Moreau's) hands. He went on to specify how he would use the power thus attained. Pichegru could not move him in the direction of a restoration this time, but made an appointment for another interview by night in the Boulevard de la Madeleine, and left, murmuring to his guide; "So he's ambitious enough to want to govern France. Poor fellow! He couldn't govern for twenty-four hours."

The night of the next meeting was bitterly cold and very dark. In the Madeleine, Moreau was surprised to see the recognition signal he had concerted with Pichegru alone being given by one of a considerable group of men. As his friend stepped forward Jean-Victor ventured some remark about so large an assembly.—Nothing to worry about, said Pichegru, they are friends of mine; and motioned one to come forward and be introduced. The collar of the man's greatcoat fell back, and Moreau found himself looking into the piercing eyes and florid, handsome, thin-lipped countenance of Georges Cadoudal, murder conspirator and agent of England. In the black night he saw the deeper shadow of the guillotine; hesitated, stammered, would say nothing definite, not even repeat his former words.

"This is going badly," said Georges, after they parted.

IV

Even Georges did not know how badly. For the letters from Jacobins that Mehée de la Touche presented as pieces of conviction had been written in Fouché's cabinet; so were the documents for which Drake and Spencer Smith had paid all that money. The ex-chief of police had found public office too desirable to be sacrificed for any private opinions; all his senatorial salary, all the income from the estate Bonaparte had given him, went into the hire of private agents, of whom

Mehée was one. The conspiracy had been followed through every step, the movements of its members marked down, and the First Consul read the reports. When Moreau became involved (of course neither Bonaparte nor Fouché knew his attitude, only that he had been seeing Pichegru) it was clearly time to act before things became any more serious. The gates of Paris were shut to all who did not have military passes, and the official police were placed in touch with developments.

On their own account, they had already picked up several of Georges' small fry, including one Quéval, who confessed that Georges was in Paris and a royal prince was expected. Moreau was arrested and a house-to-house man-hunt began. On 9 ventôse it caught up with Pichegru; nine days later Georges was taken as he pistoled an agent-police, while trying to escape the city in a cabriolet; and within another week, all the rest were in the toils. Nineteen of them, including Georges, had their heads cut off. Pichegru committed suicide in prison, or was strangled there by order of the government for fear of the revelations he could make, according to some, who do not bother to say how any revelations of his could have affected the government. Eight were pardoned, all members of the old haute noblesse except General Moreau.

He was a national hero, the victor of Hohenlinden, and, besides, the evidence that could be brought to bear against him was weak; but he was so ready to play stalking horse for the next band of conspirators that his very presence constituted a danger. It has been said that Joséphine pleaded for his life and Bonaparte gave it to her. Perhaps so; the indubitable fact is that Moreau sailed for exile in America during prairial, when things had quieted down. The papers on Francis Drake and Spencer Smith were turned over to the courts of Bavaria and Baden, which had no course but to request England to withdraw the two plotting diplomats. Their fall aided that of the Addington Government no little.

Yet there remained one capital question with regard to

this most extensive and involved of all the conspiracies, a question resulting from the fact that Fouché's private agents were so few and the official police so weakly handled that not all the threads had been gathered in. Who was the royal prince, focus of the revolt and leader of the plot? Where was he? On his examination, Georges stated sharply that such a prince was to be in Paris and to give the actual order for the assassination of the First Consul.

Who? Bonaparte and Talleyrand went over the lists of the princes and their whereabouts. Not Louis XVIII, lying at Warsaw in pudgy comfort. Not the Comte d'Artois, who had discussed and arranged the thing with Georges in London—Mehée had seen him and was quite clear that d'Artois considered the royal blood of France too precious for so deadly a risk. Moreover, after the Paris gates were closed on 11 pluviôse, men were set to watch the smugglers' landing place where Georges and Pichegru had come ashore, and there had been no sign of d'Artois or any of his sons.

The only clue was the correspondence of Mr. Francis Drake, who had been paying such astounding sums for information that the fleets at Brest and Toulon and the camp at Boulogne were only feints, the real French war-plan was a descent on Ireland and the setting up of a pretender on the throne of Scotland. In that correspondence Drake mentioned "gaining over a general" (this would clearly be Moreau) and, through him, obtaining for one of the conspirators the command of a fortified city in eastern France, say Strasbourg or Besançon, where the royal prince would raise his standard—if necessary, without waiting for Georges' Paris rising.

Now there was one member of the Condé or junior branch of the royal family, living at Ettenheim in Baden, not two leagues from the Rhine frontier, the young Duc d'Enghien. The file on him said that he paid frequent visits to Strasbourg in disguise; that he was closely linked with an Englishman named Colonel Smith (Spencer Smith had some kind of colonelcy) and with Dumouriez, the traitor-general of the

Revolution. On 19 ventôse, the day after Georges' apprehension, Bonaparte called the two other consuls together
with Talleyrand, Fouché, and Régnier, the Grand Judge.
They agreed that the expected prince could only be Enghien;
and on the night of 23 ventôse a detachment of cavalry
secretly passed the Rhine, pulled the young duke from his
bed, and carried him back to France.

Mark the date. It is important, for by this time most of
the conspirators had been taken and a good many of them
had blabbed all they knew, with general agreement that the
arrival of the hourly-expected sprig of royalty was to be the
signal for action. There was another meeting of the heads,
Bonaparte's voice very hard. At last he had possession of one
of those Bourbons, who found it so easy to order infernal
machines and daggers for others and to laugh when their
dupes were caught. It was time to bring this process to an
end by an act that should strike the smiles from their lips.
He ordered that Enghien at once be placed on trial for his
life before a secret military tribunal.

The trial took place at Vincennes on the evening of 29
ventôse—an evening that closed in gloomy, with dark spring
clouds blowing across the sky. It was Holy Week; the First
Consul shut himself up at Malmaison and played chess with
one of the ladies, his forehead locked and nobody saying a
word, for there had been a long painful scene with Joséphine when she pleaded her prettiest for the young duke's
life, and refusing anything to her always left the Consul
tense and irritable. In the gray stone prison the colonels who
were the court met and bowed to each other for the first
time and Enghien was brought in. He was handsome and
proud, saying in answer to the interrogation that he had no
connection with any plot. Yes, he had served in the armies
fighting against France in the last war, and had installed
himself near the Rhine frontier to serve in others and in the
same way.

The old soldiers who composed the tribunal murmured
and stirred at this, and the president of the court pointed out

to the accused in what a position this statement placed him; but Enghien stuck to his point, then demanded to see the First Consul in person. He was refused and led back to his cell. The court began its deliberations in an atmosphere of cruel uncertainty, for if the young prince's admissions evidently placed him beyond the law, his courage and candor had impressed them all, and the evidence connected with the specific charge was dubious.

As men will under such circumstances, the colonels took refuge in the technicality of the formal phrases setting up their court. It had been written and signed by Bonaparte himself, and it said that the business must be concluded that night. The only man authorized to delay matters was M. Réal, Prefect of Police (the same who had worked with Fouché on the infernal machine plot), now under instructions to question the prisoner at length and make a report. The colonels knew of it; it offered them a convenient escape from responsibility. They passed sentence of death and sat down to wait for Réal to overrule them.

But Réal did not come. For forty-eight hours he had been questioning members of Georges' group, trying to feel his way through the inconsistencies in their statements; had gone to bed in the afternoon, completely exhausted, leaving word that he should be wakened for nothing. At three or four in the morning he woke and found the order for the Enghien interrogation. At once he hurried to Vincennes, but on the road met Colonel Savary, coming in the other direction with the news that under a leaden false dawn, by lantern-light, the young Duc d'Enghien had been shot beside his grave in Vincennes courtyard.

General Bonaparte, First Consul of France, had added himself to the list of *votants.*

WRONG END OF THE TELESCOPE—VIII

Ministry of Justice—
Report of the Situation of Paris; 29 germinal:

Spectacles.—The first performance of "The Battle of the Pyramids" brought a considerable crowd to the Théâtre Porte-Saint-Martin. The execution did not hold up to the subject; the piece was continually whistled at. This disorder continued right up to midnight. One actor wounded himself in the left hand with his own pistol. On the contrary, "Jeanne d'Arc," given yesterday for the fourth time at the Gaité, a piece in which appear white flags, fleurs-de-lis and other emblems of royalty, enjoyed great success. Englishmen in the audience made themselves noted by their applause whenever the royalist flags were displayed.

The Columbian Centinel:

NO NEWS

WE have not had a late arrival from *Europe* for ſome time. Nearly ſixty days have elapſed ſince the date of our laſt accounts from *London* or *Paris,* and the papers by the mails are uncommonly dry; furniſhing neither intelligence nor ſpeculation. This ſtate of things cannot laſt long.

The Columbian Centinel:

THE *Fame* arrived here yeſterday, from *Bordeaux,* which ſhe left the 19th *April*—She confirms the report ſome time ſince circulated, that GEN. PICHEGRU had ſtrangled himſelf in priſon with his handkerchief. Upwards 500 gun-boats had been built at *Bordeaux,* for the invaſion of *England;* the greater part of which had left the river for the northern ports of *France.*

Mr. Secretary Arbuthnot (Foreign Office)
to the Rt. Hon. A. Paget:

NOTHING has taken place since you left us, except the sad result of all our fine Projects for the re-establishment of the Bourbons, & of the particulars of the discovery you must know more than we are as yet acquainted with. We have only learnt from the *Moni-*

teur that Moreau is arrested, & that Pichegru is in flight. You may easily figure to yourself the consternation spread among Pichegru's friends by this melancholy intelligence. I am told that Monsieur is, if possible, still more wretched. They will still however persuade themselves that the game is not lost, but I own it is impossible for me to join with them in these sanguine Expectations.

A Few Days in Paris:

WILL it be believed that the National Institute is busying itself with the following subject for a Prize Poem for the year Eleven: It is taken from Montesquieu, and was proposed by Citizen Le Brun (not the Consul of that name) in these terms: *"Si la vertu est la Base des Républiques."* Le Brun is a very old man, and ought to know better: He has been one of the *dashing Poets* of the Revolution. However, the subject was immediately adopted by the President, who said it was a "fort beau sujet," and the only difficulty was, whether it should be handled in prose or verse; and if in the latter, whether the candidates should not be limited to three hundred lines.

15

DRUMS FAINTLY HEARD

Berlin, Vienna, St. Petersburg: March 21, 1804–
August 10, 1804

"IT WAS worse than a crime, it was a blunder," said Talleyrand, a remark which Fouché tried to steal for himself
when he had reached the age of realizing that a man is
more remembered by his epigrams than by his actions. It is
true that the execution of Enghien produced an immediate
and final cessation of royalist plots against the Consulate,
and gained for General Bonaparte, whatever he cared to
do, the unswerving loyalty of the children of the Revolution.
His cause was now identified with theirs; and his clemency
to Royalists while striking at the House made the event a
complete success in the field of domestic policy.

But Charles-Maurice de Talleyrand Périgord had traveled in foreign parts; understood far more clearly than either
Bonaparte or Fouché the current system of political ideology
—a system difficult for the children of any revolution to com-
prehend, in which an act against a hereditary monarch is in
some sense an attack on organized society itself, a proclamation of anarchy. Even Rousseau and Kant, from opposite
poles, are agreed upon this; and it early developed that General Bonaparte had shot an innocent man.

The facts could not be concealed—that the young duke
had visited Strasbourg, not to stir up a revolution, but to

spend some time with his mistress and to see a good show—
that the "Dumoriez" he kept near him at Ettenheim was
not the traitor general, but a German servant's mispronun-
ciation of the stupid old Marquis de Thuméry's name—that
the "Colonel Smith" friendly with the young prince was only
a German valet named Schmidt and given the military title
in jest—that the whole idea of seizing Strasbourg or Besançon had originated with the gullible Francis Drake.

It is not necessary to find behind the Foreign Minister's
remark more than an occupational prescience, as in the instance when he wished Bonaparte to become a king in order
to make diplomatic negotiations easier. The difference was
that this time occupational prescience provided him with the
wider view. Talleyrand perceived that there had been in
reality two wars: the serial struggle with England, which
had been in progress for nearly seven centuries, and in which
the late and current wars, with the interlude of Amiens,
were only incidents—and the war of the Revolution against
the kings, in which a peace had been signed at Lunéville.
The blunder worse than a crime was that of renewing the
second conflict and making certain that its objectives should
be confounded with those of the English commercial war.
The point is observable in the difference between the English and the Continental reactions to the execution—or
"assassination," as it began to be called abroad almost immediately. Beyond the Channel there was some acrid comment from Peter Porcupine to the effect that this was what
might be expected from Bonaparte. Lord Malmesbury
thought the man had gone mad, like Tsar Paul. The clumsi-
ness of Mr. Drake at Munich produced far more comment
and more tension.

But beyond the Rhine, the diplomatic structure which
Talleyrand and his master had so carefully built up blew
apart with volcanic violence. Remarking that "as for Prussia
it is only necessary to give her a bone to gnaw," the First
Consul had only just achieved a practical alliance with that
irascible and greedy entity, the basis of which was that the

Prussians should have Hanover on the conclusion of a general peace. It was a sound business arrangement, for the interests of the two powers were nowhere in conflict, their united armies were powerful enough to give laws to a world, and by reason of a secularization of church properties more complete than anywhere but in France itself, the Prussian monarchy had become in some sense the representative of the Revolution in eastern Europe.

It is true that the road to the perception of these facts had not precisely been a boulevard. It had taken nearly seven years to demonstrate how right the King was when he said at his coronation; "No, no, let the title be Frederick William; Frederick is for me unattainable"—seven years during which there gradually grew upon the consciousness of the lovely young Queen Luise the need and desire for setting up something like a rival administration. Not that there was any disagreement between the two; His Majesty was too uxorious to make it possible, and had too thorough an infusion of Hohenzollern arbitrariness to make it profitable. But the advocates of a harder policy toward France were aware that a weak man may be used for strong purposes, and in the beautiful Luise they had discovered a counter-revolutionist whose devotion to the cause was all the more intense because she herself was a Cinderella princess—the almost-orphan daughter of a pocket-handkerchief dukedom, whose father had abandoned everything to stagger tipsily from aleroom to aleroom across the world after his wife died. Not a few émigrés had come to the Prussian court—naturally, since it was the most Gallic of Europe; Frederick William always spoke his native tongue badly and that of Voltaire very well—and with the French occupation of Hanover their voices were reinforced by that of the Minister of Trade, Baron Stein.

Heinrich Friedrich Karl, vom und zum Stein. He was a Freiherr, that is, both proprietor and hereditary ruler of one of the thousand or more tiny knightly states or estates (it was never legally settled quite which they were) forming the groundswell of the Holy Roman Empire. He had been educated for the law at Leipzig, where he was intimate with Goethe the poet, and spent much time in the study of English history, for whose orderliness and consistency he conceived great admiration. On graduation he went to Wetzlar, where the Imperial law courts were; the pettiness of their proceedings disgusted him beyond measure, for he had an active mind, an immense capacity for the absorption of detail, and the ability to arrange it in significant order.

Some friend told him there was another such mind in Europe. He took service under Frederick the Great of Prussia, as a referendarius in the mining department of the Royal Domains; worked up rapidly, built canals and roads and founded industries in the County Mark (which is a good proportion of the modern Ruhr), making that district into one of the few paying propositions owned by the poverty-stricken nation. He toiled contentedly at his ditches and forges all through the turmoils of the Revolution, which he called "Metapolitics" and regarded as beneath the attention of a constructive thinker. Middle-aged squat came to him early; in 1804 he looked like a frog, with an incongruously sharp and pointed nose; and his reports said that the presence of the French in Hanover had brought down on the Elbe and Weser a British blockade that was extremely bad for Prussian trade, threatening to unbalance the finances.

Down to the date when young Enghien was shot, his arguments convinced nobody but the wrong people. Then, overnight, the Queen conceived a violent hatred of Bonaparte, began to listen to everything Stein said, and to pass his views, with a great many more of her own, to Frederick William. The subtle pressures which Luise had by this time learned how to apply began to build up, and the King, perhaps himself not quite sure how or why he did it, made the Franco-Prussian alliance a dead letter even before it was ratified. In fact, it never was really ratified; it died in the signing stage, when Frederick William insisted that the alliance carry a provision to admit English ships peacefully into the

German rivers. A little later Prussia was applying to the Tsar to know whether Russia "would stand by her in case of need."

II

This was doubtless partly the fault of Talleyrand, who found it so easy to avoid pressing any issue that lacked his personal interest, and whose personal interest lay in the direction of maintaining tradition—since he had reached the heights by flouting it. Among attainable alliances, he preferred that with Austria—the glitter, glory, formality, politeness which spoke of ancient renowns without suggesting the vulgarities by which they had been achieved. Yet when Talleyrand let parvenu Prussia (ideologically and geographically the natural ally of post-Revolutionary parvenu France) go by default, he could obtain nothing from traditionalist Austria, once the Enghien case revealed France as not yet beyond vulgar violences.

This was unfortunate; for in spite of ancient rivalries and accumulated torts, Vienna had been at the edge of seeking a French alliance. It was chiefly the doing of that ablest Hapsburg, the Archduke Karl, to whom Kaiser Franz had confided the War Ministry after Hohenlinden. The princely minister had spent nearly three years since that date in maneuvering for position as against the Aulic Council, cutting down its authority and extending that of his own office by the method of accumulated minor detail.

In March 1804, about the time Georges Cadoudal was laid by the heels, the Archduke turned in a memorandum. France could draw soldiers from a population of 40 millions (he included the Low Countries and north Italy) ; Austria had but 25. An ally was necessary if the Empire were to recover the lost lands in Italy or find others in their room, and what ally would it be? In the last war the Russians had demonstrated their undependability, Prussia had no quarrel with France and her ambitions lay in the same direction as those of Austria, Britain could give only money and not enough of that, for no subsidy she would be willing to advance would meet more than a quarter of the cost of war to a state whose present financial structure was insufficient even to support the peacetime establishment. Conclusion: let us stay home, reorganize the fisc, marry ourselves to France and her mighty army as a protection against anything that can hurt us.

The memorandum was rejected. Aside from the fact that it was obligatory for the doddering old councilors to oppose any idea put forward by an archduke so concerned in reducing their authority, the plan encountered that vein of militant romanticism that ran through the Austrian character into such expressions as the trumpet-calls beneath the ¾ beat of the new waltzes and the crowning of Hungarian kings on horseback with sword in hand. It has been said that no régime without a basic philosophy behind it can long exist. The system of ideas behind the strange Empire of Austria, despite its time-serving and frequent greed, was the philosophy of the *Minnesinger,* the knight with a song, joyously giving service to his lady and his lord. Honorable councilors could not but admit the force of the Archduke's realistic reasoning, but they were ashamed to agree with him, they fell on a long debate over the project for a French alliance; and, as they debated, news came from France of Enghien's execution, followed by news from St. Petersburg that Russia had broken off diplomatic relations with the executioner.

III

The rulers of Russia can only be described in the terms of abnormal psychology. The young man who collapsed in tears at the news of his father's assassination, and had to be carried to his room, was less an exception to this generalization than he seemed. Alexander I was handsome, gay, possessed of a degree of charm that would have made any woman long to be his mistress had he been a carter instead of an Emperor. In a short meeting he had completely won Luise of Prussia, who had never imagined so much heart and mind could be united in a person born to high place. She wrote him long sentimental letters, full of a schoolgirl adoration that is utterly unlike anything else she ever said or did.

It is not true that the Tsar planned the murder of Paul I, but he certainly knew it was going to take place, for Count Panin had explained to him the necessity "of putting an end to the reign of a madman" as the two took the air on a beach the summer before the great event; and Alexander nodded a cold, handsome agreement. After it was over, after a disheveled lieutenant burst into the Tsarevitch's apartment to greet him for the first time with the title of "Your Majesty" —the new autocrat promoted General Bennigsen, "the murderer-in-chief," to be head of the cavalry service, and kept the rest of the conspirators at court, including that Zubov who jumped on the dying man's belly "to drive the soul out."

Everything about Alexander was the same tissue of irreconcilables. His wedding was a royal love-match—"the union of Cupid and Psyche"—but he openly spent more time with his mistress than with his wife; yet only the Tsarina could draw him from those gloomy meditations into which he sank behind locked doors. He had been brought up by La Harpe, an old Swiss disciple of Rousseau, the choice of Great Catherine when Alexander was a lad; he educated the boy by making him copy such maxims as: "Jesus: a Jew from whom the sect of Christians takes its name." La Harpe taught him the phrases of Encyclopædist liberalism; he repeated them in a manner to charm dragons out of caves and made an intimate of the young Polish Prince Adam Czartoryski, who believed in "the liberation of the human race" —he did not say from what. So much an intimate that an affair between Czartoryski and the Psyche of the perfect royal marriage was encouraged without jealousy at any point of the triangle.

With a little kitchen cabinet of other liberal thinkers, Czartoryski persuaded the new Tsar that the world expected great things from him in the way of reforms—they did not mention the type. There was in Russia an institution called the Senate, as formless as all institutions are in an absolutism where everything existed only as long as the will of the master sustained it—a Senate founded by Peter III, a kind of club of superannuated officials, to whom the title of Senator had been given in lieu of a pension. It never met as a body, never thought or did anything. The best way of proving Holy Russia to be a stronghold of liberalism (the liberals said, with Czartoryski carefully holding himself aloof, because he knew his Alexander) was to make this Senate an organ of opinion. Charming thought! The Tsar issued an ukase requiring ministers to report to the Senate, and allowing it to debate their reports.

Alas, there was only one debate, the result of this a deputation to protest some minor Imperial decree about the amount of time officers of noble birth must spend with their troops. Alexander received the group with compressed lips and so coldly flashing an eye that they bowed themselves out of the room backward without completing their mission, and next day there was another ukase restoring the Senate to its ancient position of sinecure. Czartoryski entered the incident in his papers with the remark that Alexander was delighted with the liberation of the human race as long as everyone in it did as *he* pleased; and, having been brought forward to the portfolio of foreign affairs, began to look about Europe for channels into which the Tsar's liberating energy could be directed.

France offered the obvious occasion. France alone was making changes in the European structure; she had occupied Hanover, an obvious violation of liberalism, and had sent troops to Taranto, another. There was already some cause of disagreement between the two governments. At the beginning of the reign Alexander had brought from retirement the old Count Markov, almost the last of Catherine the Great's officials, and sent him as ambassador to Paris, a mark of special honor both to the diplomat and to the government which was receiving him. It was a mistake. Markov had never dealt with anyone but lying Turks and shifty Poles; he dealt with the court of the First Consul of France as though it belonged in the same category, expressing himself in favor of England at public assemblies with so much energy that Talleyrand was forced to demand his recall.

This was also a mistake, in a way, though it is hard to see what else Talleyrand could have done. The imperious Alexander's delicate sensibilities were injured. Instead of a recall, the Grand Cross of St. Andrew was sent to Paris for Markov—whereupon the ambassador resigned with the public remark that he was afraid that if he stayed in Paris he would be poisoned.

The news of the Enghien execution reached St. Petersburg before he did, on a Saturday. One can picture the impact upon Alexander's cloudy humanitarianism, upon his feelings about the sanctity of members of ruling houses. One can imagine the obscure drive to dissociate himself from the feelings of that other day of assassination, when a new Tsar lay weeping on a divan in the arms of his wife. On the Sunday, as he emerged from Mass into the salon where the foreign diplomats waited, Alexander paused to speak with each, save the representative of France, whom he did not even see.

That evening an ukase dressed the entire court in black; Czartoryski was instructed to prepare a note, demanding from the First Consul in the sharpest terms a clear and satisfying explanation of his conduct in the Enghien affair. It was delivered in Paris by Markov's successor, clad in deepest mourning. The Russian embassy did not have to wait more than two days for Talleyrand's reply. It remarked that France had demanded no explanation when the late Tsar Paul had been assassinated; and as for seizing Enghien on foreign soil, Bonaparte had done no more than Alexander himself would, had he sent a troop of cavalry across a neighboring frontier in pursuit of the murderers of his father.

In view of the actual position at Petersburg of the assassins of the late Paul, that was worth a break in diplomatic relations.

THE WORM'S-EYE VIEW—VII

. . . Stepping a hundred paces or so away from the imperial chalet with Zinovieff, my eye fell on a young peasant girl of surprising beauty. I pointed her out to the young officer and we started toward her; but light and graceful as a fawn, she fled toward a hut at a little distance and went in. Following her, he found her father, her mother and several children, as well as the beauty.

Zinovieff who, parenthetically, is the same who later was for twenty years ambassador at Madrid, talked with the father for a long time in Russian. When we were outside again, Zinovieff told me he had asked whether the father would give me his daughter as a servant, and that he had replied he would like nothing better, but that he wanted 100 roubles, as she was a virgin.

"And if I am disposed to pay so much?"

"She will be your servant, and you can do anything you please with her except kill her."

"And if she does not wish to?"

"Oh, that never happens; but you can beat her."

"And how much must I give her a month?"

"Nothing, except enough to eat and drink and let her take a bath on Saturday, so she can go to church Sunday."

"And when I leave Petersburg, can I make her come with me?"

"Not unless you obtain permission and post a bond; since this girl, in becoming your slave, does not cease to belong to the Empress."

The next morning at nine we went to the hut together, where we found father, mother and daughter. Zinovieff having explained, the father thanked St. Nicholas for the good fortune that had come to him; then said a word to the daughter, who looked at me and pronounced a "Yes" which I understood.

Zinovieff told me that I ought to assure myself that she was intact, as the contract would state I was buying a virgin. He added that the girl would be mortified if I did not, and that I would afford a great pleasure to her in demonstrating to her parents that she had been good. I went through with the matter as modestly as possible. Zinovieff handed the hundred roubles to the father, who gave them to his daughter; she only took them to hand them to her mother. My valet and my coachmen signed as witnesses.

The girl, whom I called Zaïre,

climbed in the carriage and we went on to Petersburg, where I took Zinovieff home and then returning to my own house and shut myself in for four days, without leaving her for an instant, until I saw her dressed in the French fashion, not luxuriously, but decently. I suffered from not knowing Russian, but in less than three months Zaïre had learned enough Italian to say anything she wished. She was not long in learning to love me, and then became jealous.

One night Bomback made up a faro bank which lasted until daylight. As I entered my own door I had the unheard-of good luck just barely to dodge a bottle Zaïre threw at my head, and which would certainly have killed me had it struck me. She threw herself furiously onto the floor, which she beat with her forehead. Filled with pity I ran to her, lifting her up and asking what was wrong, for I feared she had gone insane. She quieted down into floods of tears, but meanwhile called me assassin, traitor and all the other hard names that came into her head. To convince me she knew about my conduct, she showed me a layout of twenty-five cards in which she had read how my night was spent in debauchery.

I told her that I had spent the night with Bomback, but denied everything she imputed to me; then, needing repose, I went to bed and to sleep without giving her the smallest caress, though she lay down beside me to convince me of her repentance and obtain my pardon.

I woke after five or six hours, and finding her still asleep, began to dress myself, thinking over how I could get rid of this girl, who would probably kill me sooner or later in her jealous fury. Presently she woke and came to fall at my feet, weeping and assuring me of her repentance, imploring my pardon and promising she would never again tell fortunes with cards if I would only keep her with me. The conclusion was that I took her in my arms and did not let her out of them till I had given her the most evident marks of continued tenderness.

Two things contributed powerfully to make this girl love me violently: one was that I often took her to see her family, where I always left a rouble; the other, that I had beaten her three or four times, when she wished to keep me from going out. In Russia, the necessity to beat is absolute; words have no strength. A valet, a mistress, a wife, will normally only respond to blows. You'll have the labor for nothing trying to talk reason or morality, and several vigorously applied cracks with a stick or strap are the only means of proving a point. A servant reasons things out after having been beaten, and the reasoning always goes like this: "My master did not dismiss me, he beat me; therefore he likes me; consequently, I ought to be attached to him."

It is the same way with the Russian soldier, naturally, since he comes from the body of the people. Honor means nothing to him, but with blows and brandy, one can obtain from him everything desired.

Mémoires of Jacques Casanova de Seingalt

THE WORM'S-EYE VIEW—VIII

. . . The policy of the Russian Cabinet under the Chancellor Count Vorontzov remained basically what it had been in the ministry of Count Kotchubey, but the only dignity and force it acquired was in form.

This is what happened with regard to Sweden. The two governments were disagreed as to the sovereignty of a miserable little islet in a river which then separated Finland proper from the province of that name belonging to Russia. It was a matter of determining whether the bridge which was to be the frontier was on one branch of the river or the other. The Russian government pretended to prepare for war. Generals drove back and forth along the frontier; the Tsar went there in person.

On his side, the King of Sweden became very obstinate about not giving in to a demand made in so imperious a tone. In the end he had to give in, though the conditions imposed were of no importance and no one in Sweden could have had the absurd thought of making them a cause of war. The Chancellor was very proud of his "victory," which he could have obtained easily and without humiliating Sweden, which would have been the preferable policy to my mind. But Chancellor Vorontzov knew his nation, or at least those who spoke in its name. He was aware that any demonstration of power, just or unjust, pleases the Russians; that to snatch away, to command, to overthrow, is necessary to their national pride. Unable to gain anything from the strong, the Chancellor attacked the weak, and thus sustained the government of the young Emperor in the eyes of his people.

Mémoires of Prince Adam Czartoryski

THE WORM'S-EYE VIEW—IX

. . . I have heard an History, which by a Novel Writer might be worked up into a very pretty Novel. The other night at the little Barbarian's a man mentioned the arrival at Petersburgh of a Girl of 18 from Siberia, to which place her Father had been exiled. He was, in his banishment, obliged to support himself by his own labour, and the Daughter has for some years contributed by her labour to the support of her Father. She found however, that she could do but little to assist him, and she took the resolution of setting off to St. Petersburgh on foot without a farthing in her Pocket in order to petition the Emperor to pardon her Father. She has been above six months upon the Road, and has subsisted all the way upon the bounty of the Peasantry, to whom she told her Story, and it is really to the Credit of the Character of the common people of this Country that she scarcely ever was refused lodging and nourishment. The Barbarian contrived that an Aide de Camp of the Emperor should talk to him of her interesting manner and history. He has alleviated the situation of her Father and given her 2000 Roubles (about £ 250).

Correspondence of Lord Granville Leveson-Gower

16

EVENT, BE BORN!

THE situation had now become impossible, and it was clear that Sieyès had been correct. There is a fourth authority in every state, the governing—a strong but fainéant power, which assures all concerned that no matter what happens to any individual, the state with its guarantees will stand substantially unaltered. The successive conspiracies taught a single lesson: that France lacked a governing authority. From the little plot of Chevalier, the lonely anarchist, to the elaborate structure involving Georges, Pichegru, Francis Drake, and the royal princes, they shared the characteristic of being directed not against General Bonaparte as a person, but against his office—or better, against him in office, as the sole element which could assure the fixity of the Revolutionary solution to the problems raised in 1789.

Even Moreau, that spotless republican, though backed by the intellectual liberals and a good part of the Army, could have given France nothing but another revolution. Anyone in Paris could see that whether he had actually dabbled in treason or not (giving him the benefit of the doubt, few believed that he had)—whether or not he had committed overt treasonable acts, a new revolution that began with

Moreau must end with Louis XVIII. Bonaparte's government of reconciliation had been too successful; had attracted unto itself so much of the energies and intelligence of France that there was not enough left over to make any other government without going back to the Bourbons. At the same time Bonaparte's régime was composed of elements which could be reconciled by him alone, because everyone in it was either identified with some jealous ism or lacked the support of the Army. Put it that there had not yet been time for the reconciliation to take root and achieve a state of affairs in which government could be shifted from one party to another without executions. Bonaparte himself did not execute; at the very moment when he was shooting Enghien and chopping Georges, he reassured all minor Royalists by pardoning everyone in the plot except the top leaders.

All this was aside from the General's personal feelings, which counted for a good deal. When news of the reaction to the Enghien execution came in: "Am I a dog," he cried, "who can be knocked on the head in the street, while my murderers are sacred beings?" Few men are without vainglory, and the First Consul had his share, but it is unnecessary to seek any excess quantity of it in the proceedings of so complete a realist. Certainly he would like to be hereditary ruler; most men would. But there is no evidence that he tried to force the issue. He did not have to; it was required of him only to take no action at all, and he would be pushed into monarchy. Everyone could perceive the only step of any use in putting an end to these plots, plots, plots, which were essentially plots against the Revolution. "To leave things as they are will compromise the safety of that head upon which the safety of all our heads depends," said Rœderer. A man is mortal; nobody could think of anything but a dynasty that would live forever.

Moreover, there was no longer any question of opposition to a Bonaparte dynasty from even the most convinced Jacobin republicans. The event in Vincennes courtyard on the night of 30 ventôse removed the last lingering possibility of any compromise between Bonaparte and the Bourbons. It made him the leading representative of the Revolution, and for that reason it was as much of a success at home as it was a failure among the courts of the Continent.

This was visible in the reaction of the *votants*. Fouché, the child of the Terror, made the arrangements by which the Senate voted, six days after the Enghien execution and to the infinite surprise of presiding officer Cambacérès, to beseech the First Consul "to complete his work by making it, like his glory, immortal"—that same Senate which had debated giving him a monument as its singular pledge of the national gratitude, and had to be prodded into offering a ten-year Consulate instead. The Senate's deputation to ask his acceptance found him at Malmaison, where he had been in seclusion ever since the execution (guilty conscience?), and received a reply somewhat surprisingly temporizing.

The First Consul had not reflected on the subject, needed to deliberate. Probably very few of the bewildered busybodies (who correctly took his acceptance for granted) realized the difficulties. Within the confines Bonaparte now proposed to enter, titles are things. The name of King smells bad in France; "Emperor" would be better, it responds to the national aspiration for glory—with its echo of the days of Charlemagne; and its succession to the Consulate is logical to a generation deeply read in Roman history. Yet for eighteen hundred years the presence of more than one Emperor in Europe has been a cause for civil war, and one Emperor already sits in Vienna with a claim to be the successor not of Charlemagne only, but also of Augustus Caesar. Will he consent to recognize another if the title be specifically "Emperor of the French"?

Allow time for question and answer to run fro and to—question also Prussia, Spain, and the minor states, that they may not feel offended. On 3 floréal, a little less than a month after the Senate's action, the ardently republican tribune Curée proposed a resolution that the imperial dignity should be conferred on Napoléon Bonaparte, and that it should be hereditary in his family. Passed, with only one dissenting voice or vote, that of Carnot. The Tribunate will send orators favorable to the proposition before the Senate.

General Bonaparte to the Senate: "You have judged the heredity of the supreme magistracy necessary to place the French people beyond the reach of the plots of their enemies and the agitations of rival ambitions; our institutions have seemed to you to lack a touch which would assure the triumph of equality and public liberty, thus offering to the nation and the government the double guarantee they need. The more I think on such matters, the more deeply do I feel the need of your wisdom and experience. I invite you to let me know precisely what you think."

On 14 floréal the Senate voted: "Glory, gratitude, devotion, reason, the interests of the state, all unite to proclaim Napoléon Bonaparte hereditary Emperor."

There was only one alteration in the Tribunate's draft, a rather curious one. Fabre de l'Aube drew the proposition, one of the intimate friends of Brother Joseph. When it was passed by the Senate, the words "hereditary in the Bonaparte family" which Fabre had placed in it, were replaced by "hereditary in the descendants of Napoléon Bonaparte." The alteration had been made in the First Consul's cabinet.

Travelers noted that there was some laughter but few cheers in the street when the proclamation was posted; nevertheless another plebiscite confirmed the elevation by three million votes to three thousand.

II

It takes more time and skill to set up an empire than one might imagine. After Toussaint L'Ouverture had been dragged off to France, Dessalines tried it in Haiti, and the institution did not last out his lifetime—that is, he was assassinated. Tropical? Frederick, Wonder of the World, tried in Europe, and the institution did not last out his lifetime either—he was deposed by disappointments. Medieval?

Well then, no one has made a *new* empire or even a kingdom
in the modern world, the days of empire-building are over,
like those of miracles, there is always some dynastic claim,
some wedding with the past, a civil service taken over intact,
an administrative authority (as Sieyès would put it) of land-
holding nobles to support any crown that has proved permanent.

What is necessary to give security to this Empire, which
is at the same time a republic? (Not a contradiction—the
organic *sénatus-consulte* prescribes that the head of the Republic shall be an Emperor, the whole reason for the Empire
is to preserve the gains of the Republic, provide the permanence of a governing authority for a state of social organization in which fathers do not have to sell their daughters and
the Freiherr does not own all the houses of a town and the
labor of all its people.)

What is needed? Great officers, who hold from the Empire so much in power and emolument that nothing else can
offer them as much. Let there be an Archchancellor of the
Empire, the head of all its law; his name shall be Cambacérès. Let there be an Archtreasurer, the head of all finance
—Lebrun. Let there be officers of processional import, whose
dignity reflects the fact that the principle is dynasty, but who
have no executive function—a Grand Elector who has nothing to elect, Brother Joseph; an Archchancellor of State who
has no laws to give, Eugène de Beauharnais; a Constable of
France who commands no forces, Brother Louis; a Grand
Admiral who need not know one end of a ship from another,
General Murat, pretty Caroline's husband. All these are ex-
officio members of the Council of State, which otherwise
passes unchanged from the old constitution to the new, the
most useful instrument of government.

Let there be palace functionaries, whose meaningless titles give them precedence reflecting their nearness to the imperial ear and the fact that they speak with the imperial
voice. A Grand Almoner, who is Cardinal Fesch; a Grand
Marshal of the Palace, Aide-de-camp Duroc; a Grand

Chamberlain, Talleyrand; Grand Master of the Horse, Aide-de-camp Caulaincourt; Grand Huntsman, General Berthier; Grand Master of Ceremonies, Aide-de-camp Ségur. The titles are a sufficiently odd blend of those employed by old Bourbon France and by the Holy Roman Empire, which claims to be the empire of the world. But this is prepense also; here, as elsewhere, remote and recent pasts are fused to provide a broader foundation for the future.

To remark: that though the titles bear the outward glitter of an ancient court, the substance beneath them is altogether new. None is hereditary, they live only with the holder on the one hand and the régime on the other, a nobility strictly of service, bearing to the head the same relation as committee members to the Revolutionary Convention. To remark also: the surprising appearance of Cardinal Fesch among the grand dignitaries, and the surprising omission of Brother Lucien, the earliest and most ardent dynast.

Who was Fesch? Half brother of Napoléon's mother; called "Uncle Fesch" among the salons. He had been brought up to the life of a hedge-priest at Aix Seminary on two meals a day, one of which was "a good piece of bread and a glass of wine," with the other a dinner of soup, four ounces of the meat from which the soup had been made, a fruit, and a gill of the liquid that had cheered the midday meal. Uncle Fesch never forgot this experience and devoted most of his life to making certain that it would not be repeated—at first through local Corsican politics, in which he was unlucky, then by throwing off his frock and following his flaming nephew to the conquest of Italy. Joseph Fesch had no official post, but was vaguely "interested" in furnishing supplies to the armed forces, and "examined" the great Austrian-government-operated pawnshop in Milan; it was at this time he laid the foundation of his fine collection of pictures and gems.

In the early days of the Consulate he did nothing but write poetry so bad that even the family laughed at it, and was much seen at *bals* and gambling houses. One of the annexed features of the Concordat provided for five new French cardinals; Fesch experienced a startling reconversion to the grace of Heaven, just in time to receive one of the red birettas. He was short, fat, and vain; but as soon as he became cardinal, it appeared that his return to Rome was as sincere as it had been opportune, for he began what amounted to a regular campaign for the restoration of the ancient privileges of the clergy, including the re-admission to France of the Jesuits, under the name of "Fathers of the Faith."

Bonaparte was much annoyed, and on the advice of Portalis sent Fesch to Rome to clear up some of the outstanding church questions, and at the same time to persuade Pius VII to come to Paris and officiate at the coronation, a step which would give the new empire a sanction that not even Austria possessed. The negotiation was long, intricate, and difficult. His Holiness was worried about what the other courts would think, and he did not like some of the organic articles by which the Church had been re-established in France, especially that making priests amenable to the civil law. He was particularly anxious that the coronation oath should not contain a phrase about "freedom of religion," which had been in the draft submitted to him. The Consistory said this was a principle Rome could never admit; moreover, His Holiness was as nervous as Consalvi had been about what might happen to his person in that barbarous land beyond the Alps.

Uncle Fesch arranged everything. There would be a declaration that "freedom of religion" referred only to material tolerance. The new Emperor would meet all the expenses of the trip; he would receive the crown only from the Pope's own hands, in an act of high symbolic significance; he would require the bishops from the Constitutional Church to make a more complete submission to papal authority. It is even possible that the good Uncle Fesch arranged things a little too well, with certain assurances about the return of

Italian states to the Church, and about the position of the French clergy; but for the present, nothing about this. Pius sighingly set out for France, leaving behind him an act of abdication, to be produced in case the Sansculottes threw him into prison; and Uncle Fesch became Grand Almoner.

As for Brother Lucien, that bundle of unrestricted impulse had finally ejected himself from the family orbit through the irregular regularity of his private life. When he returned from Spain, Lucien had converted his diamonds into cash and set up a magnificent palace in the rue St. Dominique, where every evening Chateaubriand, Fontanes of the *Parallel Pamphlet,* and a dozen outriders of literature gathered to eat a free meal, make conversation about books, and despise their host. This by no means used up all the energy of a mind as active as Napoléon's own, and neither did the time Lucien spent in the Senate. The remainder was employed at a country establishment as elaborate as his town house.

The original chatelaine of the place was a lady Lucien had picked up in Spain, whom he introduced as the Marquise de Santa Cruz. She was really a German adventuress and did not last long, being succeeded at both town and country establishments by a pretty, vivacious woman whose special skill was that of delicately indicating the presents she would most like to receive. The new incumbent's name was Jouberthou; her husband was a broker who had followed the expedition to Saint-Domingue with the idea of making a fortune in supply contracts. When word came that he had died of the fevers, La Jouberthou intimated to Lucien that her greatest desire was for a wedding-ring, and she backed it up by becoming pregnant. It is fair to say that among Lucien's impulses was one toward generosity. He married her the day after the birth of her son, acknowledging paternity, which made the child legitimate under the new Code. The ceremony was secret, of course, since in Corsican families a wedding is a matter for a family council to decide, and Lucien knew exactly how much chance he would stand of having such a union approved by a group of which his enemy Joséphine was a member.

As a marriage it was a great success. The only trouble was that two days after it took place, Don Luis, the undeveloped adolescent king of Etruria, died. The First Consul summoned his ablest brother and exposed a plan. Lucien should go to Florence as French resident minister, with a kind of general managership over the Italian kingdom. If the task were at all well performed, he could easily marry himself into a crown within a year. Lucien declined, with a cloud of reasons, none of which was that he already had a wife and son, now heir-apparent to the Bonaparte heritage by virtue of his own seniority to Brother Louis.

Self-abnegation on Lucien's part was so abnormal that the First Consul might have become suspicious, had not the Louisiana matter and the row over the Consular succession afforded other reasons for pique just at that time. The great man of the family remained in ignorance till frimaire of An XII, some six months after the Etrurian proposition. By that time the hypochondriac Louis had eliminated himself; Mme. Jouberthou-Bonaparte remained as attractive and persuasive as ever. (In fact, Lucien seems only to have needed the right woman to furnish him with a balance wheel.) He announced the marriage publicly.

There was an explosion. It was not only that Brother Lucien had run wild past the plan of the imperious First Consul. Dynasty was in the air by this time and Napoléon Bonaparte had grasped the fact that one of the surest means by which his new house, with his system of government and all it entailed, could be cemented into the structure of Europe was through a series of marriage alliances with governments already established. Now there were very few Bonaparte hands left to give in marriage for French stability. Himself, Brother Joseph, Brother Louis, Sister Caroline, had all married within France. Sister Eliza had married a soulful-eyed Italiote named Bacciochi, of whom Napoléon tried to make a soldier, and then an administrator, but who obstinately remained a ladies' lapdog and an amateur performer on the violin. On returning widowed from Saint-Domingue, beautiful Pauline had begun to take lovers in so scandalous a fashion that the brothers hastily married her off to a graceful, bookish, impoverished, and impotent Italian prince named Borghese and shipped her to Rome, where she would be beyond range of the paragraphers. There remained only young Brother Jérôme, just emerging from adolescence, and Lucien. By his marriage the latter had dissipated a considerable portion of the family capital, of the capital with which the stability of family, France, and the Revolution could be bought. It was a kind of treason. The First Consul refused to receive Mme. Lucien; and M. Lucien, after a few vain tentatives at arranging matters through intermediaries, wrote to Brother Joseph: "Do not do anything to make peace for me with the First Consul. I am going to Italy with hatred in my heart"—and stepped out of history.

III

What is needed for an empire? Swords around the throne; only glory can give security, the world is still the enemy of the Revolution, the army is the only Revolutionary institution that has survived virtually unchanged. Below the grand dignitaries, above the palace functionaries, are ranked the Marshals of the Empire. Sixteen are permitted on the active list by the new constitution, with as many more inactive or "senatorial" marshals as the Emperor may care to create. The Emperor chose to fill fourteen of the active places and to put four names on the senatorial list. It is important to examine those eighteen marshals; they are the new France, the France of the Empire; they are the challenge from the Revolution to the kings, to whom Danton once threw the head of a king:

   1. Joachim Murat, husband of pretty Caroline, the cavalry commander. A Gascon, big, handsome, black-eyed, and flashing, thirty-seven and the son of an inn-keeper, him-

self once a stable boy, who had founded his fortune by cheating an old man out of a hundred francs so he could enter the army; addicted to boasting, loud talk, and gaudy uniforms, which he invented for himself. He had "Honor and the ladies" engraved on his saber when he followed Bonaparte to Italy in the An IV. His cavalry was everywhere in that campaign, and later at Aboukir in Egypt he broke the Turkish center with a whirlwind mounted charge and captured the Captain Pasha with his own hand after a sensational sword-and-pistol duel. He knew everything about mounted men, almost nothing about anything else but the art of seduction, had never learned to dance, and always finished the most elaborate dinner in his new palace by bringing out a jar of preserved fruit made by his old mother in the south country.

2. Alexandre Berthier, fifty-one and one of the ugliest men extant, son of a surveyor, from whom he had inherited a passion for measurement and accuracy. So perfect a staff officer that Napoléon never had a staff, which later military critics counted as the greatest deficiency of his armies. The master would unroll a map on the floor and fling himself along it, in his hand a pair of dividers set at eight-hours'-crowflight distance, which is ten hours, or one day of marching time. "Lannes' corps at Ivrea on the 2nd," he would say. "Ivrea on the 2nd," Berthier would repeat, making a note. Before the dawn Lannes would receive his orders, with routes and halts specified; there would be other orders for cavalry to scout his wings, for commissary wagons to bring him biscuit, brandy, and extra supplies of shoes. Through all those wars the proud sons of Gaul found everything arranged, where Bonaparte had given only the most outline instructions. Berthier could be waked at any hour to name the commander of any unit, its precise strength, and its exact position. He once worked for thirteen days on end without sleep, the orders at the close of that period emerging as clear and as aptly phrased as those at the beginning; he chewed his nails down to the quick and stuttered horribly, did not go out in society because he made such blunders of speech that

he insulted every lady he tried to compliment, and had conceived a passion for a certain Mme. Visconti so violent that he used to say prayers to her picture every night.

3. André Masséna; old smuggler of the southern mountains, forty-eight and the son of a soapmaker, whom we have

He used to say prayers to her picture

already met at the siege of Genoa, the second general of France, now that Moreau was in exile. A thin, silent man with black eyes and a nose which had so sharp a hook that he was accused (falsely) of Jewish blood. As a hunter of women he was second only to Murat; as a hunter of money, honestly and dishonestly, he was unparalleled. In social intercourse he was awkward and sluggish, taking a long time to make up his mind about trifles; on the battlefield his eye flashed, he talked in epigrams, his judgment was unfailing, and he had saved France in the An VII by beating Suvorov and the tough Russians among the mountains of Switzerland, the only man who ever won a victory from that general. When he was congratulated on his marshal's baton: "Ah, oui, one of fourteen," said he, with the intimation that he should have been the only one, which was very nearly correct.

4. Pierre-François-Charles Augereau, forty-seven and an adventurer. A Paris street cat, dismissed from two employments for seducing maids, who enlisted in the old Royal Army, became a famous duelist and deserted after running through an officer who dared to strike him; traveled to Russia and fought under Suvorov against the barbarous Turks; worked his way to Prussia and entered Frederick the Great's famous guard; tired of that, and with a band of sixty kindred spirits cut his way across the frontiers, sword in hand; drifted to Greece, where he picked up a lady (she was said to be beautiful) and eloped with her to Lisbon. There he fell into jail, but escaped with the aid of a friendly ship captain and, the wars of the Revolution having begun, returned to his native country, which now had employment for adventurers. He was a huge man and a brutal, with a hawk beak and vast moustachios; one of the best blades in France or Europe, and very brave. His battalion elected him its chief and never regretted it, for he was constantly looking after his men. If there were any supplies in the depot, Augereau's soldiers got them, whether the requisitions were filled out or no. A soldier, a soldier, an iron soldier; his men adored him, he kept strict discipline and was the best technician of the Army, with his troops always deployed on the correct line at the right time with adequate fire support. Nothing but a soldier—the women of Paris hated him for the way he stamped through their salons, pinching their buttocks, for his monumental swearing and coarse jokes. But when they complained to Napoléon about him, the reply was always, "Ah, but remember what he did for us at Castiglione!"—referring to the most desperate of all the battles in Italy, where Bonaparte's own heart wavered and he called a council of war. Only Augereau advised attack, saying, "Besides, if we lose, I'll be dead, so my mistake won't matter." The attack was made; Augereau led it to one of the most incredible of all victories. He was forever grumbling that he was tired of everything and only wanted to retire.

5. Jean Lannes, now thirty-five, of origin so obscure that

no one ever really found out whether his father was a peasant or a mechanic. He had been only a major at Millesimo in the first Italian campaign, when Bonaparte saw him lead a battalion into action, and demanding "Who is that man?" promoted him on the spot. Since then Lannes had been one of the closest companions, which aroused the jealousy of the flamboyant Murat, so the two men were always quarreling. Alone among the marshals he dared talk back to the Emperor; they used to have notable slanging matches, from which spectators fled. Lannes was undersized and had a heart as hard as a bullet; his manners were terrible, he was extravagant and usually in financial difficulties, a great crony of Augereau, whom he much resembled in his ability to lead furiously in battle, and his inability to think of anything else. He had lately been on an embassy to Portugal where, meeting the English Ambassador's coach on the road, he helped his coachman to turn the Briton's vehicle upside-down in a ditch.

6. Jean-Baptiste Bessières, a Gascon near-neighbor of Murat, now thirty-six, with a rather better start in life than the rest, since his father had been a surgeon. He came to Paris to make his fortune in the early days of the Revolution; joined the Queen's Guard there, and, when the Guard was disbanded, a regiment of cavalry ordered to Spain. They were all curious characters in the marshalate, but Bessières was one of the most curious; he was big, shaggy, liquid-eyed, and faithful, like a St. Bernard dog. He vastly admired and tried to be like the extravagant Murat, but never could make it because the great bulk contained the heart of a chicken and the big head held no more brains than a mouse. One exception: when the trumpet blew, all his doubt and timorousness vanished, he could fight like a lion. He commanded the Consular Guard, which was become the Imperial Guard. "I make him a marshal now," said Napoléon, "because he will never earn it later."

These six had come up through the Army of Italy during that first wonderful campaign of the An IV. That so many of the fourteen should have been chosen from this command is a measure of the importance attached to the Italian campaign in the making of modern France. There were only three marshals from the Army of the Rhine:

7. Nicholas-Jean-de-Dieu Soult, thirty-six, who had run away from the house of his lawyer father to enlist at the age of sixteen, and worked up gradually through the fighting in Flanders. A reserved, correct military man, with a large cast-iron frame and face, an immense capacity for minding his own business. About him clustered no anecdotes, he possessed nothing but a military record. He could look across a battlefield and grasp the meaning of all the disconnected movements in the flash of an eye. In command of one of the corps for the English invasion, he marched his men constantly, himself on foot with them. A deputation of sergeants complained to Napoléon that they were being worn out. Soult to the First Consul: "Those who cannot endure what I do myself may stay at home; but those who bear it will be fit to conquer the world." His judgment was sound; he was more often consulted by Napoléon on military matters than any other marshal.

8. Edouard-Adolphe-Casimir-Joseph Mortier, thirty-six and the son of a rich proprietor who had gone liberal at the time of the Revolution, and so had been able to obtain for the younger Mortier a commission in the cavalry. He was unambitious, honest, straightforward, kind-hearted; part English and spoke that language fluently; laughed easily and was not very bright, but was one of those men whom excitement steadies, so that he came up through the ranks by good performance in battle. "Short-range Mortar" they used to call him in the Army, to express their opinion of his brains. His wife was a good deal of a shrew and did most of his thinking for him. Marmont, Bonaparte's oldest friend, who did not get a baton, said that the choice of Bessières justified the promotion of everyone in the Army and that of Mortier the granting of military grades to everyone out of it.

9. Michel Ney was from the Saar, spoke German as his

mother-tongue and French with a determined accent. His father was a barrel-cooper; he had enlisted young, as extra sons of impecunious German families often did, and had come up through from a corporal of hussars, his first battle being Valmy. After this he led a small free troop which had no pay, but plunder rights. He was tall, strong and left-handed; he had red hair and ice-blue eyes. "The bravest man I ever saw," Napoléon called him, who had seen not a few brave men; and in an army that contained Lannes, Augereau, and Murat no one ever questioned the name by which Ney was known then and ever after—"The bravest of the brave." The only thing he thought of was military glory; he turned in a remarkable memorandum to the chief, proposing that after a battle the victorious soldiers should be paraded across the field past the corpses, firing a salute of five rounds, while the massed bands played. But in another part of the memorandum he said: "Our soldiers ought to be instructed about the cause of the war. Only when combat is legitimate can one expect prodigies of valor. An unjust war is repugnant to the French character."

To these Rhine generals should perhaps be added one other, who had served both there and in Italy:

10. Jean-Baptiste-Jules Bernadotte, another Gascon, whom it was impossible to pass over, both because of his family connection and because of his prominence in the army. Some of his colleagues thought him slightly mad; it was because he mingled with impulsive conduct his considerable skill in intrigues which, oddly enough, never seemed to get him anywhere—perhaps because he was detested by all the other marshals except Ney, and by Fouché to boot, the most dangerous enemy in France. He was quite handsome and a notable lady-killer; much beloved by his junior officers, for whom he was always doing favors and obtaining promotions; and by his men, in whose service he was as indefatigable as Augereau. As a leader he was not much better than a good executive; Berthier always had to take particular care

with Bernadotte's orders, because he would make a mistake if he possibly could, then blame it on somebody else.

Two of the new marshals had no particular army identification:

11. Guillaume-Marie-Anne Brune, tall, lank, and thirty-four, who had left his father's legal office to turn Revolutionary pamphleteer and that profession to be a soldier—because an actress laughed at a pamphlet he had written on military affairs. His battalion he really gained in the field; beyond that he climbed the ladder on the basis of civism, being one of the leading command agents of the Terror, both in Paris and against the Vendéans of the West. He thought the last service should have brought him to the Ministry of War, as he had an extremely high opinion of his own merits. The opinion was by no means shared in the Army, to which he had supplied the metaphor "marcher à la Brune" by trying to move three divisions along the same narrow road at the same time. Fortune had arranged it, however, that he held the garrison command in Holland during the An VII, when the English tried to invade. Their commander was the Duke of York, probably the worst general in the world. Brune beat him; and as the only ranking general with a record of victory over the English in the field, he had to be made a marshal. He read a great many books, from which he was fond of quoting, but usually got the quotations jumbled, and spent most of his spare time writing poetry. He was tall; Napoléon considered him handsome.

12. Louis-Nicholas Davout, who came from an old military family of the south and had been a soldier almost from his birth, thirty-four years before. His elevation to a marshalate no one could understand, even though he was head of the military police. He was cold, grumpy, disdainful, especially loathed by the Gascon marshals; used to walk out of the room when Bernadotte began an installment of his serial oration on politics. Bourrienne the secretary hated him, too; in the course of the investigations that wound up

the placard plot, Davout had come across evidence that the secretary was tapping the Consular privy purse to support stock-market speculations. The evidence went to Bonaparte; whereupon Bourrienne became an ex-secretary. In the field Davout had never done anything notable. In fact, when he went with the army to Egypt he was known as a bad character—a seniority promotion, dirty and slovenly, a troublemaker. After that same battle of Aboukir when Murat went blazing through the Turkish line, Davout came to protest to the chief against his division's being held in reserve. Men heard the bitter torrent of words begin, and saw Bonaparte lead Davout to his quarters for a private interview. No one ever knew what was said at it, but when the two men emerged the crooked stick had been made straight. From that time forth no man in the army was more careful of his person or studied harder. Troops under Davout's command always had enough ambulances, enough to eat, wear, and shoot with; his discipline was hard but never capricious; they could count on anything he said. He wrote charming letters to his wife.

These were the fighting marshals, distinguished by the ability to lead rather than the ability to think, with three exceptions—the independent Masséna, the incomprehensible Davout, and Ney, who had the sense to realize he could not think and kept a little Swiss staff officer named Jomini to do his planning for him. There were two main currents uniting this group of turbulent and inapposite personalities: love of renown, and a patriotism mingled with and shading into devotion to the Chief.

Of the remaining six marshals, two—Jourdan and Lefèbvre—were carried on the active list, but they were, like the other four, really senatorials. All six were the old republicans who had stood on the frontiers with the armies of the confederated kings before them in '94, and the terrible clop-clop of the guillotine waiting behind for unsuccessful generals. Moncey and Pérignon had beaten back the Spaniards among the Pyrenees; Sérrurier had fought Austrians and

Sardinians along the Var; Kellermann led a wing at Valmy; Lefèbvre and Jourdan were at Fleurus, the battle that had saved the North. The greatest names from that war of desperation were missing: Hoche, Kléber, Marceau were fallen, Dumouriez and Pichegru were traitors, Houchard had been guillotined on suspicion of treason, Moreau had dabbled in it. Put it thus: only at this late date has the Revolution found a means of holding faithful to their trust the turbulent fighting spirits which every revolution must throw up to defend itself from outside.

IV

Beneath the grand dignitaries, the marshals of the state militant and the palace officials, there are needed bodies that can make laws and fill in the details of broad projects in civil affairs as colonels handle the minor tactics of an army in the field; to maintain efficiency a certain amount of criticism is also desirable.

The new government thus presents the double anomaly of an imperial republic and a constitutional empire—the constitution of Sieyès only slightly edited. The Senate remains, but becomes of life tenure and loses the power of co-option, all Senators henceforth to be appointed by the Emperor. The Legislative remains, but practically decreases in importance, because it is so much easier to get rapid and effective action through the use of *sénatus-consulte*. The Tribunate remains, but becomes an adjunct of the Council of State. To supply its place as a factor for moderation, there are two permanent Senatorial commissions, on individual liberty and on liberty of the press; the first of these really acts, and with vigor.

There is no formal difference in the status of the great Council of State itself; it merely increases its powers by a process of magnetic attraction. Long years after, Napoléon placed the debates on Council next to the Code as the peculiar pride of his reign. During the first year 3,756 questions were debated by the full body, an average of about ten a working day, not including matters taken up in the separate sections of the Council. The men were able, executives mostly, no more interested in theoretical questions than the Emperor himself; the debates were uninhibited, practical, succinct. They provided France with a government that was like a chorus of angels compared with those in the rest of Europe or even in the earlier France.

It is, in fact, necessary to distinguish between the practical operation of these government agencies and their theoretical position. The imperial constitution, constitution of the An XII, was purposefully vague at many points. Theoretically (as Napoléon himself put it) "The first representative of the nation is the Emperor; for all authority is derived from God and the nation. The Senate comes next to the Emperor in representative authority." Practically, the Council of State was far more important than the Senate. It was always heard, and not seldom rode down Imperial desires. The First Consul Bonaparte could always be convinced that a step was untimely, even when he believed in its wisdom; the Emperor Napoléon was for the present the same, and his absolute authority merely titular. That Empire was a living organism which experienced growth and change, the more since it was the descendant of a series of organisms that had grown and changed at a cancerous pace. Or put it that the Empire was one step more in the effort of the Revolution to find a stability that did not involve either a perpetual Revolution or a Bourbon restoration, the eighteenth century or 1793.

V

It was intended to hold the coronation immediately after the invasion of England in the late summer of the An XII. An unfortunate event supervened—the death of France's only fighting admiral, Latouche-Tréville, from a fever contracted in the Indies. The event fell on 2 fructidor, at the worst possible time, just when Latouche had his provisions aboard and was about to hoist sail. The news reached Napoléon by M. Chappe's new telegraph at Boulogne, where he was making anew the discovery of Franklin—that even an Emperor cannot have things well done unless he does them himself. They had built him a barraque on the headland above the harbor, a beautiful piece of work, from timbers ready-cut and numbered, the hall of assembly within lined with silver-gray paper, the ceiling frescoed with an imperial eagle guiding a thunderbolt through golden clouds against England; long windows whence the seaward light came in, a single table and one simple chair.

Very fine, gentlemen, but—how is it that there is no drawbridge through the long quay into the arsenal slip, so that ships for repair must be worked slowly round? Why is it that beds are scattered all through the caserne and there is no check on the issuance of tools or furniture to those who ask for them? The Emperor himself must give orders that these things be changed; the Emperor in person must send a note in haste to Marine Minister Decrès that under no account is Dumanoir de Pelley, Latouche's rear-admiral, to take the Toulon fleet to sea, his mind is sluggish, he is only fit to transmit orders. A new commander must be sought and the grand plan (hitherto a secret among Napoléon, Decrès, and Latouche-Tréville) communicated to him.

The plan itself now requires alteration; it was built round the personality of the dead admiral, and how it shall be altered depends upon who is to take his place. Only three officers possess the requisite combination of leadership and technical skill. Eustace Bruix is a sick man, we cannot risk another delay by death, and the Emperor has found reason to doubt whether he is truly hard enough for a man of war. A trial embarkation in some of the praams and light gunboats at Boulogne had been ordered; Bruix glanced at clouds pregnant with coming wind, hesitated and then refused to pass the order. Napoléon himself ordered the trial, and some people were drowned, which proved Bruix right in a moral sense—but the stern rule of war has it that everything must be tried to the hilt empirically and without regard for the moral value of lives used in the test.

Eh bien, Rosily, then. No, not Rosily; he has had no command at sea these fifteen years, the project is not one to be executed by a rusty man. Therefore, Villeneuve by pure elimination—Pierre-Charles-Jean-Sylvestre Villeneuve, an old friend of Decrès, intelligent, of great personal courage, but a highly mercurial character, impressionable to the last degree. Throughout fructidor, the complementary days, and vendémaire of the new An XIII, the Emperor was making a great swing through Belgium and the northeastern départements, to Aix-la-Chapelle, Cologne, Coblenz, Mayence, sending off, in the intervals of dealing with the new Code and local administration, the parts of the new plan woven around quicksilver Villeneuve.

In this version, as before, the English Admiral Nelson's squadron before Toulon was to be decoyed into Egypt. Villeneuve would run out of the Mediterranean, pick up the one ship at Cadiz, and make for the West Indies. So would Missiessy, with the five ships from Rochefort and the two from L'Orient, which should have no difficulty in evading their blockaders, thanks to the configuration of Biscay. It would be strange indeed if the British did not rush a squadron to protect their valuable islands. But let us not count too much on that; let Villeneuve only rendezvous with Missiessy off Martinique, and hurry back to Spanish Ferrol, with twenty battleships under his flag. Six British were blockading our five under Gourdon there; Villeneuve was to release these five, then with the united twenty-five ships bear up for the west coast of Ireland, while a publicity campaign spoke of a new descent there. Indubitably the English would send a fleet to cover that coast. Far enough north and west to be beyond the reach of the Brest blockaders, Villeneuve to swing back eastward into the Channel and hold it.

Brumaire had come, which was October, before all this was arranged and Admiral Villeneuve had familiarized himself with the men and means of his new command. That would make it a winter campaign, waiting on the winds; but in brumaire a new factor entered—Spain. Part of the treaty that brought Louisiana to France was a conditional alliance. In case of a war involving the imperial republic, Spain was either to join her or to furnish 12,000,000 francs a month subvention. The Emperor, as soon as he became Emperor, insisted on the money and was making the Spaniards pay it; and they did not like it.

Now Spain was certainly not pro-English, and was giving all the help she could to French privateers and to Admiral Gourdon at Ferrol. But cash inconveniently ate up the gold of the Americas, which could be so much better used for court expenses. There is no evidence beyond these facts, but by the strangest of coincidences a British frigate squadron was near Cadiz on October 5, 1804, when the annual treasure fleet came from Montevideo. The British squadron signaled halt, their admiral explaining that there was a suspicion the Iberian ships were carrying contraband destined for France. Would they not accompany him to a British port for examination of their manifests? The Spaniards said no, of course; of course the British opened fire, killed a lot of men, captured the treasure ships, and carried them off to England. Obviously Spain would now have to declare war, end the French subsidies in order to maintain her own war effort, for which taxes would pay, while the royal revenue from the mines of America was laid up in limbo beyond the ocean.

Spain had over forty battleships, a reinforcement that Napoléon could not bring himself to neglect, though Decrès wished him to do so. But it would take time to go through the diplomatic passes antecedent to a declaration of war, more time to work out a co-ordinated strategy, and this would postpone the naval campaign to late winter at earliest. Let us no longer delay; summon Ségur, Grand Master of Ceremonies, and hold the grandest of all ceremonies on 10 frimaire of An XIII, which is December 2, 1804 by that old barbarous calendar which men are beginning to use once more.

VI

The day was clear and cold. The Pope left his apartments at ten in the morning, followed by all the clergy, escorted by bugles and the Imperial Guard. At Notre Dame the archbishop waited; behind him the vast nave was filled with generals, representatives from every city, sixty bishops with their minor clergy, the Senators, Council of State, Legislative, princes from the Rhenane country, ambassadors from all the powers but England and Russia. At every moment the bright winter sun filtered through the windows to catch the glint of a new jewel and fling it back across the aisles in a flash of colored lightning.

(In his prison cell, Gallic to the last as the music went past, said Georges Cadoudal; "We have done better than we thought; we hoped to make a king and we have made an Emperor.")

His Holiness entered; the glittering throng stood erect, five hundred musicians intoned the tremendous *asperges* "Tu es Petrus," as for the first time a Pope walked along the ancient basilica of Saint Louis with the cross borne before him. Above swung velvet hangings, broidered with golden bees; before, at the end of the church opposite the altar, twenty-four steps led to a dais where a magnificent double throne had been erected. At the foot of this stairway to glory stood two simple chairs, which the imperial pair would occupy until they had received the pontifical blessing.

There was a long wait. The Emperor arrived at last through cheering streets, in a coach all covered with mirrors and surrounded by marshals on horseback. His lips were firm to the point of sullenness; on his head, as he entered the cathedral, he bore a laurel wreath of beaten gold, and half a step behind came Joséphine with red eyes—for in the dead of the previous night, in profoundest secrecy, she had at last been married to her man by the rites of the Church, and she had been weeping since. At the door of the cathedral the archbishop presented a tiara crown, modeled on that of Charlemagne; it was borne in by old Marshal Lefèbvre, the staunchest republican of all—Lefèbvre, to symbolize that the Revolution as a revolt against authority was dead, and only the revolution against the eighteenth century remained.

The Emperor knelt, then proceeded to his chair. His Holiness touched him with the sacred fluid, blessed the sword of state and girded it round him; the scepter, and handed it to him; and turned to take the crown. Before the Pope could lift it, Napoléon I took the bauble in his own hands and, lifting it over his head, cried in a voice that filled Notre Dame; "God gives me this crown; *gare à qui la touche!*" and lowered it to his own brow, while all the trumpets blew bubbles of lovely chiffon music.

WRONG END OF THE TELESCOPE—IX

Columbian Centinel:

THE *Senatus Confultum* was completed yefterday. *Napoleon Buonaparte* is nominated Emperor. No coronation is to take place at that time, no fpiritual or religious ceremonies; but there are to be fummoned to affift at it the Public Bodies of the State. The homage is to confift of an oath to be taken by all the principal officers. The Confitable of *France* will put the Imperial mantle on the Emperor's fhoulders, and deliver to him the fword of State. Both mantle and fword will firft be confecrated by the Archbifhop of *Paris,* in the Cathedral of *Notre Dame, as the Emperor profeffes The Roman Catholic Faith.*

Report of the prefecture of police:

Arrest—The agents of the prefecture have arrested one Vatripon, who claims to be skilled in the divinatory art. He was caught at the moment of conjuring. Two candles were lighted, a black cock was burning in a corner of the fireplace; on the table were found a knife with blood on it and a vial which contained water and a laurel-leaf; on another leaf were written in letters of blood these words: *anael, uriel, viriel.* The court clerk of Pantin was present when the agents arrived; the accused had promised to bring to him, by means of his spells, an immense treasure, which should rise from the earth.

Diary of Sir George Jackson:

WE have the announcement of Bonaparte having been proclaimed Emperor of France.

It is remarkable that at the time of the murder of the Duc d'Enghien, the French ministers at foreign courts were instructed to enter into a spontaneous justification of that atrocious act. It is pretended, that the internal tranquility of France called for decisive measures, one of which was, the arrest and execution of the duke. And Bonaparte is represented as astonished at, and complaining of the unfriendly language of Russia and other foreign courts.

The Naval Chronicle:

"A Tar being ask'd by his Poll, t'other day,
Should e'er the French land, could he tell in what Bay?
Jack roll'd round his quid, then assur'd his dear friend,
That if they land here—'twill be at *Gravesend!*"

James Monroe to the Secretary of State:

BORDEAUX

SIR—I arrived here last night in seven days from Paris. It is necessary to write forward two days to Bayonne to make arrangements for the mules which are to take me to Madrid. The intermediate country or the greater part of it is said to be almost a desert. There are but few taverns on the route and those furnish neither beds, provisions or other accommodations than that of shelter; in addition to which there is danger of being attacked by robbers, especially to publick characters who travel slowly without a guard, of which an example lately occurred in the case of the Ambassador of Portugal who was attacked and plundered of everything he had with him.

Republican Watch-Tower:

PARIS

ON the 16th ult. a thief had the audacity to steal at 11 o'clock in the morning, in the Cathedral at Nantes, the Golden Sun, in which the holy sacrament is shut up. Upwards of 200 persons were present, and saw him take it upon the altar, but they believed him to be a servant to the bishop, & therefore did not notice it. In leaving the church he put it under his great coat, which was large enough to conceal it, and he was arrested by some conscripts whom he met, and who observed it.— When asked by the police commissary what he intended to do with it? he answered calmly, that he intended to use it in his private devotions.

17

DISCORDANT

Vienna; The Coasts of the Ocean;
Summer 1804–August 1805

IN THE cafés along the Herrengasse, old men with funny hats leaned their umbrellas against the tables and discussed the matter slowly, sipping coffee. *Oesterreichs Schade.* There would be a word or two of similar purport as guests left the concert, and Ludwig van Beethoven strode homeward, uncouth through the streets, to tear up a title page "a un grand uomo." Grand no more! "Then he is only a common man after all," and the score of the *Eroica* would have followed title page into the wastebasket, had not a friend prevented it—or so said the friend, not noted for his veracity. He may nevertheless have been right this time, since nothing but destruction could conceal that at the moment of Austria's shame, Austria's musician had caught the very spirit of the man who shamed her. . . . Years later, in a far country, a veteran of the wars would leap to his feet, crying *"C'est l'Empereur!"* across a startled concert hall as the gigantic chords of the final movement burst forth, at once thunderous and sparkling.

Tore up the title page, then; but without tearing from the score that triumphant bugle-call of glory round which the *Eroica* is built. Nor could tear from heart or mind the strains that soared into "the noblest work of the human spirit" in response to that other spirit beyond the marches, the soldier of the rights of man, who had fought down the armed tyrannies of earth—only to make his own tyranny now.

Tear up the title page; pronounce a bill of divorcement. It will not be permanent, neither indeed can be, mind has spoken to mind across the infinite gulfs of media and nations. "Un grand uomo"—a new type of mind abroad in the world, whose purpose can be caught only by another of equal size, the mind capable of reconciling all discordant elements into the harmonies that fell so unacceptably on ears accustomed to the polyphonic line. Is it seeking too long an analogy to mark that the massive chords, with all the instruments singing together, are first brought into music to celebrate the victory of the man on whose Council of State sat Royalists and Jacobins, whose infantry moved in dense disorderly columns against the precise lines of the eighteenth century? In all symphonies before the *Eroica*, it is possible to interchange any movement with any other; all have that graceful and formal eighteenth-century minuet, with its sweet return and assurance—"*Plus ça change, plus c'est la même chose.*" No more; after the tumultuous Scherzo nothing is the same. No one has ever used so intricate an architecture on battlefield or podium as these two; and almost everything else is a matter for the program annotators.

He tore up the title page. *Oesterreichs Schade*—and Europe's, insisted a tight-lipped young publicist named Friedrich Gentz, who had come down from Prussia to be an Imperial Councilor, when Frederick William found it intolerable that in the midst of the peace of Lunéville an official of his court should be calling for a new war against the French revolutionary monster—calling in a voice that everyone heard, for Friedrich Gentz had both a literary reputation and the skill to support it. "Expressions like 'The fate of this part of Europe does not concern us' should never pass the lips of a ruler or statesman. No isolation, no neutrality, no exclusion from any important negotiations! The more vigorously and courageously injustice and force are

attacked at their first appearance, the less often will it be
necessary to take the field against them in battle. My hatred
for France, and for this perfidious, vain, bigoted usurper,
forced first by the infamy of his contemporaries into greatness and then into the excess of greatness; this wanton, blas-
pheming villainous bandit, has become an obsession with me;
my only one at present."

Gentz was the intellectual leader of a strange little group
of expatriates who gathered at the house of Count Panin,
whom Alexander of Russia had found it expedient to exile—
not because the old assassin-in-ordinary aroused too poignant
memories of a certain night in the Winter Palace, but because, having given the young Tsar the crown, he behaved as
though he could take it back whenever he chose. There was
a Corsican in that group, Pozzo di Borgo, a pimple-faced
man with long, delicate hands which he liked to wave, who
had been drifting around Europe for years in various free-
lance diplomatic employments; the file in Fouché's office
described him as "crafty, spiteful, and intelligent." The last
characteristic distinguished him from the French émigrés
who made Panin's their headquarters, and who need not concern us. More important was a Swede, General Armfelt,
who had been through more adventures than Münchhausen,
including a last-minute reprieve from a death sentence for
treason; he served his royal master, Gustavus IV, which
personage had come down to Regensburg to persuade the
Diet of the Empire to make a new war on the French Revolution, and had offered the services of the Swedish army for
it.

Being a military man, this Armfelt was a great crony of
General Karl Mack, also much seen at the Panin soirées,
tall and rather horsy of face, almost reverend in his gravity,
and very positive of manner. The General had been a prisoner in Paris for two years and hated everything French
with a surpassing bitterness—hated the Archduke Karl
hardly less, for he had wished to come to a composition with
those enemies of the human race. In his soldierly, direct

fashion Mack would explain how groundless were the Arch-duke's apprehensions about a French war; numbers they might have, but these were less important than a good plan of campaign. He himself had drawn two in the past that would infallibly have produced the happiest results against the French (Mack often sketched on the tablecloth as he explained) had not the execution been in the hands of the stupid English in '94 and with the cowardly Neapolitans in '98. General Mack was wont to moderate his adjectives about the English when another frequent visitor came, Sir Arthur Paget, ambassador from George III, to hand Gentz the subsidies H.M. Government was paying to that publicist, and to have this literary councilor write his dispatches for him, Paget being a young man too new to diplomatic usage to perform this service for himself.

Not that Gentz was bought by English money to the serv-ice of what he called "The Good Cause," though he loved high play, loud music, and loose women, and found them all expensive. He would have been on the same side in any case; a philosopher and an honest man who had studied pure reason from Papa Kant's own lips in Königsberg—honest enough to have discarded all formulas and to be cankered by doubts as to whether the cause were after all good. "The most terrible of all," he wrote, "would be to have such canaille proved right. All other evils can be cured, or they lose themselves in a general downfall, but the idea that the rabble may be right has in it something imperishable. In this notion is to be found the real source of all my antirevolu-tionary tendency."

Discard all formulas; but not the categorical imperative, which brings one inevitably (says Papa Kant) to a definition of democracy as a despotism, whether it comes with a red cap or under a red crown. The master's words rang in his pupil's head: "The 'whole people' so-called, who carry their measures, are really not united at all, but only a majority; so that here the universal will is in contradiction with itself and with the principle of freedom." Herr Kaiserlicherrat

Gentz prepared an elaborate memorandum in which he besought Cobenzl to refuse recognition of the French imperial
title.

II

It could not have come at a worse time, or been more unfortunately expressed. If "Mr. Bonaparte" (as Gentz persuaded Sir Arthur to describe him in dispatches) should
make nonrecognition a cause of war, "I, an unknown, insignificant man, a deeply interested but passive observer of
this sad spectacle of error and folly; I, who watch and con-
demn every single step of your pernicious course and dis-
approve of your whole political system, would choose war."
The trouble with this impassioned apostrophe was in the
introduction; Friedrich Gentz was neither unknown nor
insignificant. Graf Cobenzl had intercepted his mail and
knew that the Imperial Councilor was in close correspondence with his friends Pitt and Grenville in England, begging
those enemies of France to do everything that could be done
by a government with a bottomless purse to produce a change
of administration in Austria. Nor was this all; the publicist
was paying assiduous court to Archduke Johann, trying to
draw him into the Panin circle.

The addition of that young man would make the combination a particularly dangerous one. Kaiser Franz did not
often intervene in politics, but he was absolute and could do
so with crushing effect, and he was not unlikely to exert the
Imperial will if his junior brother made a point of it. Archduke Johann was in a position to make a strong point indeed.
Between Archduke Karl's genuine ill-health and the gelati-
nous but ultimately effective resistance of the Aulic Council
to the prince's army reforms, that officer had been forced to
give up the War Ministry. Johann was officially commanding general of fortifications; this left him as the imperial
family's only representative in the high councils of the service and he threw himself into the work with the fervor of his
twenty-two years and of a desire to make people forget the
name of Hohenlinden.

Graf Ludwig Cobenzl could be pardoned a certain amount of irritation over Gentz' démarches toward the Archduke and the English. If he had no thoughts in common with the modern, Kantian idealists whom the publicists represented, still less was he a realist of the Archduke Karl's stamp. No doubt his first principle was to remain in office, but he had a full charge of that older, that medieval type of Austrian idealism; at the very moment when Gentz, in a memorial to Johann, was flaying the minister alive for a policy that was "robbing Austria of her honor and reducing all Germany to shameful slavery," Cobenzl's ambassador in London was telling Lord Harrowby that the acknowledgment of Mr. Bonaparte's imperial title had cost Austria no more than a sheet of paper. At this price time was cheaply purchased—specifically, the time to learn Russia's intentions. Cobenzl's medieval mind conceived of war in the traditional Austrian terms—a vast combination against a weak, ineffective opponent who could be profitably crushed with few casualties, the war of the League of Cambrai; or a crusade of liberation in lands under so incompetent a rule that they fell of their own weight into the Austrian orbit after the fighting was over, like the wars that had wrung the eastern provinces from Turkey.

This was by no means Gentz' idea of the current war against tyranny or how to make it. He thought the world was falling down. His memoir to the young Archduke was written in that sense, with the same terrible urgency that runs through the Englishman Burke's *Reflexions on the French Revolution*—to which, indeed, the memorial owes a good deal, both in idea and in arrangement. Everything burns, cried Gentz: "The catastrophes that we now witness are but secondary phenomena. We live in one of those ominous periods when the whole established structure breaks down." We must forget old rivalries and interests, standing together "to defend valiantly and keep inviolate the social order in which we were born, its laws, and the religious, political, and civil institutions on which it rests."

Therefore, said Gentz, even if the Archduke's facts are correct, his conclusions do not follow. We must make alliances for war on the French Monster. Of all possible alliances, the most desirable is a close understanding with Prussia and that invincible army left to her by Frederick the Great. The Kaiserlicherrat urged his friend Johannes von Müller, the historian, to place his by no means uninfluential pen at the service of Stein, Queen Luise, and the war party in Berlin; began a correspondence on ways and means with the British ambassador there; persuaded Archduke Johann to begin another with Prince Louis Ferdinand of Prussia, Gentz writing Johann's letters for him; and confected a plan for returning Panin himself to Petersburg, to stir Russia on.

For if Prussia was the most desirable partner against France, Russia was the necessary one; the only power whose bulk and distance made it possible for her to tolerate the presence of a force dominating nearly all the rest of western Europe, which in turn made it possible for her to come to terms with Mr. Bonaparte. In fact, a Russian alliance was the only security if the Prussian policy should fail.

That summer the Prussian policy did fail; nothing could wean Frederick William from his beloved neutrality. The Anglo-Russian policy then failed also; Cobenzl intercepted the copies of Gentz' memoir which he had sent to those courts, and sent instructions that the document should be disregarded. The Kaiserlicherrat was no longer allowed at court; received instructions to withdraw to the mountains for a rest and to avoid wearing in public the Order of the Northern Star that King Gustavus had sent him. It was intimated to Sir Arthur that if he wished to remain an ambassador, he had better stop seeing the Empire's malcontents.

III

On 26 nivôse Admiral Villeneuve sailed. The ships ran down past Fort La Malgue and out to sea on a freshening breeze, with a couple of frigate topsails along the horizon to show they were being properly followed. The course was toward the Italian coast; a sharp turn westward and darkened lights easily shook off the pursuit that night, while a lugger put out with carefully faked correspondence regarding a new expedition to Egypt. Next morning found Villeneuve on an empty sea, but one that unfortunately rose in force as the breeze circled round to the southeast, gradually becoming a gale of genuine fury. By the second night the ships had become much scattered, several had lost spars and were drifting toward a lee shore on a tempest that showed no sign of abatement. The Admiral, feeling that to continue now was to lose all, was constrained to order a general retirement to port, which was accomplished by the 29th.

The same wind that drove Villeneuve home again was fair for the escape of Missiessy from Rochefort, in that region being accompanied by scuds of snow that blinded the blockaders. The French were deep in the Atlantic before their enemies so much as missed them from harbor. This was unfortunate in one sense, since the two admirals would not now be able to keep their rendezvous in the Indies, but in the overall result it encouraged. The blockade of any port could be eluded, and the generally favorable impression produced by the two escapes was increased by news that Nelson had indeed gone barking off to Egypt; and later word ran in from the north that the English had detached a whole division of battleships from their Brest squadron to go hunt Missiessy.

The Emperor accordingly sat down to alter the plan as necessitated by the fact that Villeneuve and Missiessy would not meet, the latter being under orders to return if no contact were made off Martinique at an early date. Ganteaume pleaded to be allowed to break through the fifteen British off Brest by battle and main force, but Napoléon rejected this, on the ground that the objective could be accomplished without sea battles. At the same time Decrès' doubts about bringing the dubious Spaniards into the scheme were overridden; their navy was a mere gargoyle on the architecture

of the grand plan, intended not to bear weight but to impress
the eye of the British beholder.

In the new version, Villeneuve would sally as before,
shunting Nelson off to Egypt; halt at Cartagena to pick up
six Spanish battleships from that harbor, obtain eight more
at Cadiz, then sail for the Indies as before. Ganteaume
would similarly slip the Brest blockade, meet Villeneuve off
Martinique, and the two squadrons together return to the
Channel with the overpowering force of fifty battleships.
They would find it well-nigh empty, for the British squadron
blockading Brest would assuredly pursue Ganteaume, in accordance with the doctrine of making the enemy's force in
arms the main objective, which Napoléon had noted to be
the guiding light of the English at sea, as it was his own in
land warfare.

Of course, both Ganteaume and Villeneuve would be long
since gone from the islands when their enemies arrived.
They could not hope to evade the British fleets forever, but
it was only necessary for our ships to be in the Channel long
enough to cover the crossing. When Marmont's guns were
planted on Richmond Hill those British warships would be
quiet enough.

The new plan even had an annex for the case of Ganteaume's failing to win free, something that seemed not altogether impossible, since the inconstant wind that blew
Villeneuve back to port for weeks of repair had changed the
date of the campaign from winter to spring, and in spring
the winds favorable for Ganteaume's exit are somewhat
rare. In case he failed to find Ganteaume among the islands
then, Villeneuve was to return to Europe, release the ships
blocked in Ferrol (now twelve, including Spaniards) and
sail for the Channel with forty ships, leaving Ganteaume's
Brest squadron and its blockaders to cancel each other out.

But there was no provision for the events that took place
after Villeneuve rode out to sea on another favoring wind
on 8 germinal. The first was that the Spanish group in Cartagena were not ready for sea and did not know when they

would be; Villeneuve had to drive on without them. (Decrès must have permitted himself a secret smile or two, but he never said anything.) The second was that milord Nelson, showing a capacity for self-education beyond what was expected of him, refused to be decoyed to Egypt another time, but shot through past Gibraltar to the Indies in hot pursuit of Villeneuve.

Yet it was a third and very startling event that introduced an unexpected element into the operation of the whole plan. Theoretically the six British blockading Cadiz should have avoided Villeneuve's much more powerful squadron, then followed him to Martinique. They did nothing of the kind; as soon as they were driven from the port, they sailed straight north to join the British Channel squadron. Later, in germinal, when three newly-constructed battleships slipped out of Rochefort amid rumors of a new descent on Ireland, the British Biscay squadron let them run, and also bore up for the Channel. Instead of the doctrine of concentrating against the enemy's main force, they were applying that of concentration at the point where that force must take action.

Naturally, Napoléon did not know all this at the time. Through most of the summer he remained convinced that Nelson was still in the waters of Europe, or out of sight, somewhere in the Mediterranean. From Villeneuve in the Indies came no word at all; from Missiessy, just returned, word that he was sick, the cordage of his ships was deplorably bad and their hulls much in need of repair; from Ganteaume at Brest, word that he was short of trained quartermasters, seamen gunners, cordage and sails. So ran the days down to burning thermidor, while along the Channel the Army of the Coasts of the Ocean drilled, marched and smoked its pipes, sang songs in praise of good wine and in sympathy for the poor conscript.

At last, on 20 thermidor, news: Villeneuve was back from the west with twenty-two ships; had fought a battle at the gate of Ferrol with an English fleet of somewhat greater force, in which two Spaniards were lost, but two of the heavy

English three-deckers so damaged that they had returned to port in very evil case. The French admiral had pushed into the port and made his junction with the twelve allied ships there.

The Emperor instantly left for Boulogne and ordered Marshal Bessières to the same spot with the Imperial Guard.

Fought a battle at the gate of Ferrol

To Villeneuve, orders: without losing an instant, he was to sail for the Channel with all the ships under his command. "All Europe waits in suspense for the great event which you are preparing." From the odd behavior of the British recently it seemed that those off Brest, though outnumbered, might throw themselves onto Villeneuve; he was not positively ordered to fight his way through, but that was the clear meaning of his new instructions. Ganteaume from Brest was to put out to help him, and either cover the army's crossing himself or put it in Villeneuve's way to do so.

This was a complete reversal of all the ideas for no battle upon which the grand plan had been founded, but it had now grown so horribly late that nothing any longer mattered except time.

IV

It was perhaps inevitable that both Alexander of Russia's views on the desirability of freedom for all nations except his own, and his concept of the divinity of established ruling houses, should bring him sooner or later to the conclusions reached by Friedrich Gentz, though he lacked the advantage of direct communication with that stirring personality. (There seems to have been some flow of ideas through Graf Stadion, the Austrian Ambassador at Petersburg and a great friend of the publicist.) That the urge to action should have been a comparatively insignificant event in north Italy is surprising only if one fails to understand the state of emotional vacuum in which the young Tsar found himself at the time. His experiment with the Senate had failed; his mistress, the beautiful Naryshkin, was pregnant and approaching her term; and the exchange of insults with the French Emperor had not turned out at all satisfactorily.

Czartoryski and the other young men about the court had no difficulty in persuading Alexander that the dignity of Russia had suffered in the last affair, and through the refusal of the French to furnish any explanation whatever (as demanded by a Russian note) for the occupation of Hanover or the failure to indemnify the House of Savoy for the loss of its territories in Piedmont. The two latter events were made the keys of a new combination proposed by the young men—a combination which would at once enable Russia to stand forth as the truly liberal champion of the rights of small peoples and more than recover the credit lost toward France, make her the arbiter of Europe, to whose assizes every international question must be led. Russia would, in short, offer to mediate in the current Anglo-French war, which was disturbing all Europe, with the threat of throwing her vast weight against whichever opponent should refuse.

But she would not make the offer in the name of selfish advantage (said a memorial drawn for the Tsar by a certain Italian Abbé Piatoli who, after an adventurous career across most of the continent, had come to rest as a client of Czartoryski). It was necessary to establish a new form of international law and international morality, which would set the world free from the tumults caused by the conquests of the French Revolution and the territorial ambitions of England, Prussia, and Austria. To achieve this new general morality there was necessary a power uninterested in any but moral gains, under whose leadership the small maltreated nations could safely unite to impose their will for tranquility upon the ambitious great powers. This role of moral leadership in a new Pan-European confederation for peace obviously belonged to Russia, who had no Hanovers nor Savoys along her frontiers, marched everywhere with great powers against whom she could not have ambitions. Asking nothing for herself, she could with good grace claim from England the freedom of the seas, the restoration of Malta to the Knights, of their colonies to France and Holland; she could ask from France the evacuation of Hanover, of Holland and, above all, of Piedmont and Lombardy, so that an independent Italy might be formed. Any future issues would be referred to Russia for mediation in view of her disinterested conduct in this case.

Nothing could have been better designed to appeal to Alexander than this combination of political theories from Rousseau with practical personal aggrandizement. But it was necessary to begin the business of setting up this universal alliance of mediation at some point, and since there were no Russian diplomatic relations with France, it was decided to begin with England. The Tsar sent to London one Count Novossiltzoff, another member of what the young men called "The Secret Committee," though what the secrets were and whom they were being kept from, the young men would have been rather hard put to say.

Possibly from the Emperor Napoléon. He can hardly have been ignorant of Novossiltzoff's appearance in London at about the time of the coronation, though he assuredly never imagined why the Russian was there. As it happened, the coincidence of dates became important, since one of the first pieces of public business following the ceremony in Notre Dame was a series of conferences between the Emperor and Signor Melzi, vice-president and administrative head of the Cisalpine Republic.

The affairs of that synthetic nation were in none too good shape (the Italian explained); the people spoke the same physical language, but they had been for so many centuries divided under the rule of Savoy-Sardinia, the minor duchies, and Austria, that their political tongues were a Babel, and even their legal system was incoherent. When a citizen of Milan had a cause against one of Turin, for example, the decision on which set of laws was to apply took as long as the case itself, and the matter usually ended in both parties being forced to accept the quite arbitrary adjudication of some French commissioner. The people had neither aptitude nor liking for republican institutions; what they wanted was a unified monarchial state, with a king in whom they could take pride, administered by Italians—and an end to the system under which Cisalpine money was used to pay foreign troops.

With some asperity the Emperor inquired who Signor Melzi thought was going to defend his country, since the Cisalpine refused to enlist troops of its own; and Melzi, who after the manner of statesmen of small nations had been rather hoping that France would do it free of charge in order to keep Italy out of the hands of the Austrians, was forced to change the subject. On the other matters, reports which Napoléon had received from independent sources were in agreement with the Vice-president.

During the winter, accordingly, while Villeneuve was

making his abortive sortie from Toulon, Napoléon went down to Milan to organize the country. It received a system of prefectures like that in France; the Code was installed as soon as it could be translated and the Italian judges had familiarized themselves with it; taxes, police, local administration were placed on a unified, systematic basis, somewhat different from that of France, as Italian custom demanded. There was even an effort to obtain a special Concordat.

There remained only the question of who should be monarch of the new kingdom. The Italians wanted Brother Joseph, no doubt with some thought of playing themselves into a better position on the money matter, and Napoléon thought it would be an excellent idea to give them Joseph, though for quite different reasons. But at this moment Brother Joseph turned subtle; he absolutely refused to jeopardize his "rights to the succession to the Empire" by becoming an Italian king. The other brothers were not wanted. There was nothing Napoléon could think of but to take the new crown himself, and in floréal he was crowned at Milan with the famous Iron Crown of Lombardy.

Long before this date, of course, the news that he would be Italian king had reached London, where Novossiltzoff was deep in conferences with Mr. Pitt on the alliance of mediation and the new form of international law. The astute English politician realized at once how powerful a weapon had been placed in his hands. He agreed to everything—or almost. Russia at the head of a league of small powers? Delighted to see her there. Mediation of all future issues affecting peace? Certainly. Mediation of the current war? Of course. England to evacuate Malta, return the captured colonies? These were matters that would have to be taken up at a general peace conference when the present war had ceased. A new maritime code for the freedom of the seas? He would consult the other ministers.

Mr. Pitt suggested that the extraordinary new map of Europe, with which Piatoli had accompanied his memoir, would have to be redrawn, to give Prussia some territory on the left bank of the Rhine, both the better to enclose France, by placing a powerful military state on her borders, and to give the Prussians an interest in promoting the alliance for peace. Taking Venice away from Austria at present might produce difficulties; but the principles of the map were perfectly acceptable. The two statesmen almost fell on each other's necks, and in the midst of their feast of love and mutual admiration there arrived the news from Italy. Napoléon, by becoming king there, had extinguished half a dozen small independent states at a blow.

In Petersburg, Novossiltzoff was known as a fluent and fascinating talker, who seldom bothered to think beyond the level of pleasing his immediate auditor—"The man of genius, Mr. Facing-all-ways"—but one thing he possessed even beyond Czartoryski: the ability to interpret into action the cloudy mind of the Tsar. Novossiltzoff no longer hesitated; in April England and Russia signed the alliance of mediation, which was to proceed to active measures against France as soon as the two earliest partners agreed that sufficient signatures from the other powers were in.

The specific plan was for the projection against France of three vast masses of force, one up through the boot of Italy, one through the center of Europe, and one along its northern shores. The Italian forces would consist of 25,000 Neapolitans and 25,000 Sardinians with a stiffening of Russians and some British troops. The center force would contain 250,000 Austrians, a contingent of 25,000 from Bavaria, Württemberg and Baden, and another Russian army. The northern column would have 100,000 Prussians, 16,000 Swedes, 16,000 Saxons, 16,000 from Hesse and Brunswick, 5,000 from Mecklenburg, and still more Russians—or, counting 180,000 Russians altogether, something over 656,-000 fighting men.

Historically, this alliance of peace and mediation was to become known as the Third Coalition.

V

Sweden signed at once, and so did the little Mecklen-
burgers. But at Berlin the emissaries of the new interna-
tionalism encountered a streak of Hohenzollern obstinacy.
The negotiation had hardly begun before Frederick William
discovered they were trying to force him to make a decision,
for France or against her. His whole life was based on never
making a decision about anything—and it may be (since
courts are such whispering galleries) that he had heard some
mention of the fact that Mr. Pitt had suggested, and Novossiltzoff had approved, the idea of sending a powerful Russian
army corps down to the Prussian frontier to convince her of
the wisdom of joining. Frederick William first offered to
mediate between the mediators and France, then on being
refused, drew himself upright, cried, "My principles are unshakable; I fear nobody!" and stamped out of the final conference with his spurs rattling and the medals on his chest
clanking.

The loss of Prussia from the combination of course entailed that of her satellite states, Saxony, Hesse, and Brunswick. At first it seemed the coalitionists might lose Austria,
too, owing principally to that engaging conversationalist,
Novossiltzoff, who let it slip that on the new map of Europe
the whole of old Poland appeared reconstituted and in a
crown union with Russia, as Hungary was with Austria.
Kaiser Franz (whom God sustain) could hardly be expected
to join an alliance that had as one of its objectives a considerable diminution of his own dominions.

For a time there was an effort to form a separate coalition
of middle states, with Prussia and Austria as a nucleus, the
warlike Prince Louis Ferdinand coming down to Vienna to
push it along; but that too aborted on Frederick William.

Austria and Cobenzl thus during the summer hung sus-
pended between rival fears, with Archduke Karl still croak-
ing that it would take six months to mobilize, that not a

single battery of the new artillery had its horses, war was impossible. Then Napoléon finished his organization of north Italy with the coronation at Milan and the annexation of the old semi-independent Republic of Genoa, in the interest of unified administration.

The double event produced the shock that Gentz had tried in vain to administer. In this region titles are things. The new title was Napoléon, "King of Italy," which is one of the subsidiary titles of the Holy Roman Emperor, and the crown was the Iron Crown, Charlemagne's crown. There were now two emperors in the world, the signal for civil war. In July Graf Stadion received instructions to join the Russian alliance of peace and General Mack was appointed quartermaster-general, which in the Austrian army is a rank junior only to the Kaiser or an archduke. Mack imagined a means to get his army mobilized secretly. There was an epidemic of yellow fever in Tuscany, and Kaiser Franz wished to keep it out of his country, so he officially established a *"cordon sanitaire"* of troops along all the Austrian frontiers in east Italy, with no passage allowed.

VI

It was the news of this sanitary cordon that hurried Napoléon into his last, desperate change of orders for the grand plan—Villeneuve instantly to the Channel. Why did the man not come?

From Ferrol the Admiral explained. Many of the ships had over a fifth of their crews ill with scurvy, none was without leaks or some other damage that must be made good, the masts were rickety, the cordage rotten, new stores slow to come by, there was an insufficiency of provision in Ferrol. It was probable that Nelson had returned from the Indies and was now joined to the fleet past which Ferrol had been reached.

In Italy in '96 we marched with rags for shoes and those who lacked weapons took muskets from the dead or the enemy. Why did the man not move? If Nelson had reached the shores of Europe, be sure his sails would be visible off Ferrol; moreover, he had but fourteen ships when last seen, while you, M. l'Amiral, command twenty-nine. Move now; you can with Ganteaume throw fifty battleships onto not over twenty-five British in the Channel. "Lose not a moment. Everything is embarked. Be here but for twenty-four hours; six centuries of shame and insult will be revenged."

On 26 thermidor Villeneuve did sail from Ferrol to points unknown, and a brief aurora of hope flared up the horizon. But on the morning of 5 fructidor Scientist Monge stepped round for the usual *al fresco* breakfast at the Imperial barraque. He found Napoléon already at work when he entered the door and there was no recognition in the eyes which stared six inches past the side of his head from across a litter of papers and chocolate-pots. Monge backed out, and a little later made occasion to speak with the military secretary, Daru.

"Do you know what that animal of a Villeneuve has done? He has gone to shut himself up in Cadiz. The Emperor has ordered the troops to the Rhine."

WRONG END OF THE TELESCOPE—X

The Right Hon. A. Paget to Lord Harrowby:

I WAS upon the point of dispatching Sparrow last night, when I heard that accounts had been received here of the Duke D'Enghien's condemnation.

I was with the Vice Chancellor this morning, who seemed not to be acquainted with the execution of that unfortunate and illustrious person.

From Count Cobentzl's language this morning, I cannot help thinking that he begins to consider a continental war not impossible, perhaps even not improbable.

The Columbian Centinel:

PENNSYLVANIA PHILAD. IT would ſeem that *Buonaparte,* in the tragi-comical farce which he is playing for the entertainment of an aſtoniſhed world, is abſolutely reſolved to out-*Herod Herod.* By the following article, it will be ſeen that he has procured himſelf to be canonized as the founder of the Italian *Republick;* and a day has been conſecrated to SAINT *Napoleon!*—Saint *Napoleon*—Saint *Nero*—Saint *Coligula!* Well, ſince theſe things are ſo, we may yet live to ſee a Saint *Jefferson,* a Saint *Burr,* a Saint *Paine!*

The New York Evening Post:

LONDON IT is said that government yesterday received from the Continent, the very important intelligence that the Austrian Ambassador had made arrangements for his immediate departure from the Court of Petersburgh, the Emperors of France and Austria having agreed on the attack and conquest of Turkey. Private letters add, that the King of Prussia had declared himself hostile to this new plan of agrandizement.

Diary of Sir George Jackson [from Berlin]

NOTWITHSTANDING the sensation created here by what has occurred in Paris, all this great town is now completely taken up with preparations for a grand *fête* at the opera house, to celebrate the queen's birthday on the 12th, and the pretty girls of Berlin have been practising dances and marches these three weeks past. The queen herself is to take the part of Statyra, the daughter of Darius, in the quadrille called "Alexander's return from his Indian Victories."

The Court has determined to exclude the *corps diplomatique* from their quadrille, that there may be no question of precedence to settle. They are all quite content to be excluded, and, in white dominos, be spectators only.

James Monroe to James Madison:

LONDON AFFAIRS here seem to be approaching a crisis. It is said that the combined fleets, having been previously joined by the Rochefort squadron, have entered Ferrol, and that the force now there is thirty-seven sail of the line. Sir Robert Calder has joined Admiral Cornwallis before Brest. The French fleet there consists of about twenty-six sail of the line.

This force, so nearly united, is a very imposing one. The menace of invasion is kept up and increased; everything seems to indicate that an attempt will soon be made.

The Columbian Centinel:

A LETTER from a gentleman in *Lifbon,* dated May 24, to his friend in *Baltimore,* fays—"The Firft Conful is elected *Emperor of the Gauls, King of Italy, and Protector of the American and Batavian Republics.*" The titles to be hereditary in his family.

[☞ *The writer of this article, muft have a ftrong fancy.* BUONAPARTE *has not, probably, marked us as a department in the map of* France; *unlefs this was one of the* fecret *articles of the* Louifiana *treaty.*]

The Columbian Centinel:

BUONAPARTE'S EPITAPH
A PARODY
[On Dryden's poem *Under Mr. Milton's Picture*]
THREE Tyrants in three different ages born,
The Poignard's point and Gallows did adorn.
The firft in wanton cruelty furpaf'd,
The next in bloodfhed; and in both, the laft.
The force of Nature could no further go;
To make a third, fhe joined the former two.

THE WORM'S-EYE VIEW—X

. . . The barracks were dug a meter into the ground, which made them very damp. One slept on a big camp bed covered with straw; atop was a linen coverlet. Everyone stretched out on that coverlet, wrapped in a cloth sleeping-bag with a haversack for a pillow; another linen coverlet went over all. Thus everyone slept together, yet separately. Not infrequently some soldier shortened the long winter nights by telling a story. To be sure that people were listening, he would stop from time to time to say *cric,* those who were not asleep replying *crac;* if everyone was quiet the story-teller himself went to sleep. Campaign rations were the rule, with white bread only with the soup, meat, dried vegetables, brandy and vinegar. At the market they bought only fresh vegetables and potatoes. The mid-day meal consisted of an excellent thick soup with vegetables and a small portion of beef; that at evening of potatoes helped out with butter which was generally bad, with onions and vinegar. The army bread was black; the rye that went into its composition gave it an acid and disagreeable flavor; the brandy was to ameliorate the water, and it was not intended that it should be drunk by itself, a rule which was often broken, as one might expect.

Duc de Fezensac—Souvenirs Militaires

THE ARMY OF THE COASTS
OF THE OCEAN

The English Channel, Bavaria;
Mid-September to October 21, 1805

THE headquarters of the I Corps were in Hanover, Bernadotte in command, 18,000 strong. He was to move east around the Taunus and Spessart ranges, through Würzburg on Regensburg. The corps was somewhat less well-drilled than the rest, since its commander found garrison existence a bore, and spent all the time he possibly could in Paris, usually at the salon of beautiful Juliette Récamier, with whom he had undertaken a flirtation in the eighteenth-century style—wit, sighs, and confidences. One of the confidences was about a long interview he had with the Emperor before taking over his corps; interview of forgiveness and advice, like that with Davout in Egypt. The two men reached a basis of agreement. "I did not promise him affection," the Marshal told Juliette, "but I promised him loyal co-operation and I shall keep my word."

Young Marmont (he was only 31, and this was the real reason he had not received the marshal's baton, so much desired) had 21,000 men of the II Corps at Utrecht—his first major command, a reward for good work done on the artillery during the peace. He abolished the old system under which civilian contractors hauled the guns to the battlefield and then took their horses away, so that if the pieces were to be moved, soldiers must haul them by ropes; concentrated all field guns under divisional command instead of scattering them through the battalions, as was done before. He worked very hard with his corps, training the men in building fortifications, studying their psychology, and organizing concerts for them, but he had more desertions than any other corps commander, because many of his soldiers were Dutchmen who did not think it was their cause or their Emperor. His corps was to follow the Rhine to Mainz, swing east to Würzburg, thence follow Bernadotte to Regensburg, there being an excellent highway down to the old Imperial city.

The III Corps belonged to Davout; was cantoned along the coast from Dunkerque to Flushing, with headquarters back at Bruges, a district in which the former head of the military police was useful, since the invasion coast was full of English spies. Davout had a big corps, 27,000 men; it was to move straight eastward, passing the Rhine at Mannheim, march up the Neckar to Heidelberg, then swing a curve just inside Marmont's, to Nördlingen.

Soult's IV Corps at Boulogne was the largest of all, 41,-000 strong, and, as we have seen, the most carefully conditioned. He was to pass the Rhine at Landau-Speyer, move through Sinsheim and Heilbronn to Halle, then turn south to Aalen. He was as much convinced as Marmont as to the value of concerts for the troops, but rather ruined his popularity by building a huge bronze monument to the Emperor, to pay for which he docked every man a day's pay a month.

Lannes' V Corps was also near Boulogne, 18,000 men. He was feeling on top of the world that summer, having just returned from his Portuguese embassy, where the Regent gave him a pocketful of Brazilian diamonds that for once placed him on his financial feet. And he had lately divorced the wife who bore a son to another man while he was in Egypt, to marry Mlle. Louise Gheneue. Her Dresden-china beauty and charm made friends for him everywhere; she was one of the most successful hostesses of Paris. His line of march was by Strasbourg and Kehl, straight through the

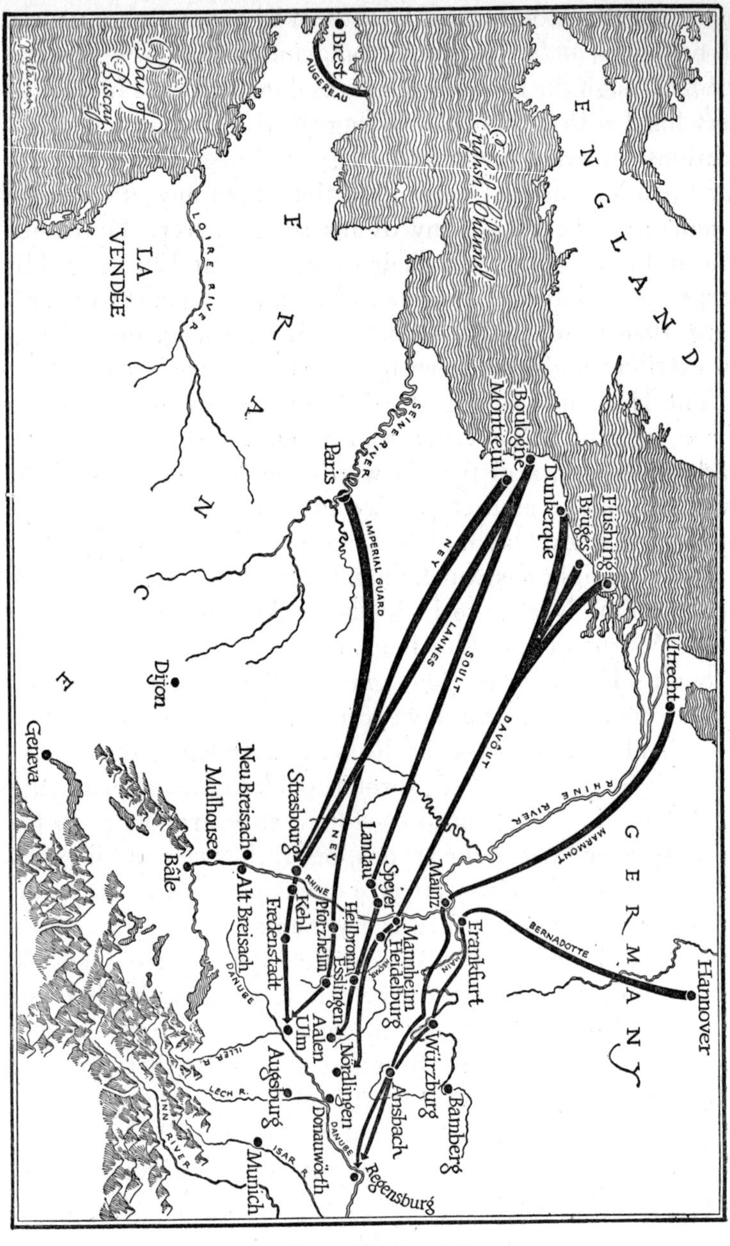
ENGLAND
English Channel
Bay of Biscay
Brest
AUGEREAU
FRANCE
LA VENDÉE
LOIRE RIVER
SEINE RIVER
Boulogne
Montreuil
Dunkerque
Bruges
Flushing
Utrecht
Paris
IMPERIAL GUARD
NEY
LANNES
SOULT
DAVOÛT
MARMONT
BERNADOTTE
RHINE RIVER
GERMANY
Hannover
Dijon
Geneva
Strasbourg
Landau
Speyer
Mainz
Frankfurt
Mannheim
Heidelburg
Neu Breisach
Alt Breisach
Mulhouse
Bâle
Kehl
Fredenstadt
Pforzheim
Heilbronn
Esslingen
Ulm
Aalen
Nördlingen
Würzburg
Bamberg
Ansbach
Augsburg
Donauwörth
Regensburg
Munich
RHINE
DANUBE
MAIN
NECKAR
ILLER R.
LECH R.
ISAR R.
INN RIVER

northern Black Forest to Freudenstadt, then following the main road which skirts the Swabian highland to Ulm.

The VI Corps was Ney's, 24,000 men at Montreuil; it would cross the Rhine at Pforzheim, move through Durlach and Esslingen, also reaching the Danube at Ulm by a route between those of Soult and Lannes. No one in the whole Army of the Coasts of the Ocean had worked harder than Ney after getting his baton, for along with it came a bride selected for him by Joséphine—Mme. Campan, who as a young girl had been a lady-in-waiting to Marie Antoinette; witty, beautiful, and of aristocratic lineage. All day long the Marshal drove his men in musket practice till they became the best shots in the army; half the night he was sitting up with his Swiss, studying infantry tactics, for all his experience had been with cavalry. A swindler got several thousand francs out of him for a balloon that failed to work.

Bessières, with the 6,000 of the Imperial Guard, would march with Napoléon himself. Augereau, who had the VII Corps of 14,000 men, was at Brest, but out of the movement because not fully organized, and also because of the distance, since the V Corps, with the shortest march, was to cross the Rhine on September 29 and be deep on the Danube by October 9—ten days for 160 miles.

Pouring through Strasbourg and the Breisachs, across the upper reaches of the Rhine and through the Black Forest defiles, covering and concealing the heads of all the columns, would move a vast stream of 22,000 horsemen, who served the one command of Murat, all to be across the river by 26 September. This cavalry screen was a new invention, born of the Emperor's meditation on the Marengo campaign, when the enemy had learned all too clearly where his forces were. As for the men, such cavalry had never been seen before, nor ever was again—proud as peacocks, the élite of the army, drunk with the dawn when it was bliss to be alive and the glory of the Imperial name. Élan would describe their state, but not altogether; for this was a new cavalry service, reorganized under the master hand of the Emperor, even more thoroughly than the artillery had been.

In the old wars Austrian or Prussian heavy horse could always stop a French pursuit and usually break a French wing with one of their thundering charges. It did not strike Napoléon that any inescapable law of nature prevented the riders of Gaul from doing as well on the battlefield; they were already all Europe's superiors in screening, scouting, and patrol. He took the small formations of cavalry away from the divisions then, and united them into a corps, as Marmont had taken the guns away from battalion to assemble them under division. The heavy horse he provided with breastplates that would turn a bullet and the great bronze helmet with the horsetail hanging down that one sees in Meissonier's paintings; they became cuirassiers, the envy of the world. All the cavalry were rearmed, the heavy horse with sword and pistol, the light chasseurs who would do outpost duty with carbines, the dragoons who might have to fight on foot, with muskets. The cavalry had its own artillery.

Yet high though the hearts of the horsemen were when they set their backs to the Channel, their faces toward Europe and adventure, they were not higher than those of the rest of the 177,000 men, Army of the Coasts of the Ocean no longer, but now and forever *Grande Armée*. They were young; the old Revolutionary veterans had either moved up to be officers or were back home, repeating over their soup the tales they had told these youngsters before they left to follow the Imperial eagles.* Their officers were young, as among the marshals—only one of the division commanders was over fifty and more than half were under forty. Most, like the marshals, had come up through the ranks, so they drank and joked and shared accommodations with the privates, who learned that an officer was only another of themselves, with a little extra gold braid, and they quite believed

---

* Of the whole army, 50% had never seen a campaign before, and another 25% had seen only Marengo or Hohenlinden. Most of the remaining 25% were either officers or non-coms. In the infantry and light cavalry, where the figures are most significant, the newcomers were 58%.

the Emperor when he said that every man had a baton in his knapsack.

They had all worked together in the camps along the shore, and had learned to know each other's ways. The marches were sixteen miles a day; after each hour there was a halt for a smoke, and there was a long pause at noon. In the evening senior officers bought drinks for the juniors; the day was discussed. The roads had been carefully surveyed, partly by Murat in person, partly by the Emperor's aide Savary; at every crossroad and turning a picket of cavalry waited to guide those who followed. Many times (since the channels through the rough Rhineland country are few) corps and divisions came near each other, but they never intermingled or reached the same town together. The harvest barns were full, but everything taken was paid for in sound ringing metal of the new coinage.

There is also a technical point to remark about the Grande Armée. In all previous Rhine campaigns, in all other services, a corps was a minor army in itself, containing all the arms and services necessary for a campaign. But the six corps that marched across Europe under the eagles were complete in infantry alone. Cavalry, heavy guns, and engineers were in a central reserve under the Emperor's own hand, to be assigned as needed.

II

Glance at the map; see how the steel-tipped fingers reach forth to clutch all along the line of the Danube from Ulm to Regensburg. They were not feeling blind but moving precisely, in response to the war plan of the coalized kings.

After the death of Desaix at Marengo, the Emperor had taken over his leading aide, Colonel Anne-Jean Savary, as a kind of living memorial, and Colonel Savary specialized in intelligence work, since the First Consul was somewhat exercised over the numbers of Austrian spies surrounding his operations. France needed a service as good or better; Savary was directed to find a man who could head it. It would be not long after the proclamation of the Empire that the aide for intelligence brought in a man whom he introduced with, "Here, Sire, is a man all brains and no heart."

Napoléon gazed in frowning astonishment at a white-haired pedagogue, who fumbled with his fingers, ducked his head and said, "Sire, I am Schulmeister." Savary was explaining that the visitor had made himself most useful in the affair of young Enghien by forging a letter from the Duke's mistress, which persuaded him to stay home on the night of the arrest. Some small emergency called the Emperor from the room. He returned to find a youth with flaming red hair, redolent of the gaming-room and *bal:* "Sire, I am still Schulmeister."

Actually, that was not his name, and no one ever found out what the real one was, but as Karl Schulmeister he turned up in Vienna on the heels of the Imperial interview—a young noble of ancient Hungarian lineage, lately exiled from France and well supplied with money from a mysterious estate in Transylvania. Naturally, he gravitated to émigré society, and through it into the Panin circle and the orbit of General Mack. Schulmeister knew so much about the civil and military institutions of the French Empire, was able so clearly to interpret all the dispatches that came in that the Quartermaster-General of the Austrian armies made the young man the head of his personal intelligence staff. By the date of the orders to march up the Danube, two officers of the Reichshofrat, Wendt and Rulski, had been bought out and were furnishing for transmission to Napoléon semi-weekly reports on all Austrian plans and dispositions; and for transmission to Mack whatever it was desirable to have him believe.

What he did believe, and all Austria for that matter, was that Napoléon's attention was fixed at the Channel and the Army of the Coasts of the Ocean would be held there long enough to give Austria the initiative. Even granting to them the extraordinary speed of marching that French soldiers had shown in the Marengo campaign, this army could hardly ascend the Rhine and move through the Black Forest country to attain the upper reaches of the Danube before November 10. The same date was also indicated by logistic calculations (said Mack, who was a logistics expert) ; and if the Emperor of the French did come, he could hardly pass the Rhine with more than 70,000 men. He would have to leave thirty or forty thousand at the coast to demonstrate against the British and prevent a landing by them. Mack's own experience showed there would be another 20,000 in hospitals, and 20,000 more would be needed to keep Paris and the Vendéan West secure against an anti-Bonaparte revolt, which was described as highly probable by advices through the espionage net.

On July 16 General Mack, with Graf Schwartzenburg of the Kriegshofrat, sat down to draw a plan of campaign in which these were the fundamental assumptions, since one must have assumptions of some kind. Russian officers were present. The paper drawn up by the Allies pointed out that the main theater of the struggle must inevitably be the Austro-Italian frontier from Venice to Lake Constance— "on our side because it is only in that direction that we can look for an acquisition of territory and because it is from that the dangers to the Monarchy are nearest and greatest. On the part of the French, since from that region the French armies can most injure our empire, attaining by a single victory across an unfortified frontier, the very heart and capital of our nation; because in such an advance the enemy would have its resources immediately behind its front, whereas by marching on Vienna by Swabia and Bavaria, their armies will have much farther to go before striking a decisive blow. Hence it is on the Adige that we must expect the first and principal operations, and it is there that the Austrian armies should assume the offensive."

The Kriegshofrat quite concurred with these conclusions, and early in August sent Archduke Karl himself down to command the strongest of the Austrian armies, mobilized behind the sanitary cordon in Italy—94,000 men, with a flying wing of 12,000 more around Trent, below the Brenner Pass. The Neapolitan-English-Russian force coming up the peninsula would attack the French southern flank. The remainder of the plan, though outlined by Prince Karl, owed much to Mack's energetic mind. The Archduke had wished Austria to do no more in the north than take up a good defensive position in the Tyrol, to prevent the French from attempting an offensive through the Black Forest and along the Danube. A corps was indeed set up for this purpose, under Archduke Johann, 30,000 men. But in view of the politico-military considerations furnished by the desirability of bringing Bavaria, Baden, and Württemberg into the alliance, and of the certain early arrival of strong Russian forces, Mack's own plan was a good deal more offensive in character.

A strong Austrian force moving on Munich at an early date would bring Bavaria in. South beyond her border a narrow belt of Austrian territories runs right to the Rhine at Freiburg and the Breisachs. Mack wished an army of 84,000 men to operate in this region after having marched through Bavaria and gained her adhesion. It was set up under the style of the Army of Germany, with Ferdinand, youngest of the archdukes, in nominal command and Mack himself as chief of staff.

Mack's main line, until the Russians joined him, would be along the Iller, and his base at Ulm, where Iller falls into Danube. He did not propose to hold the Black Forest region as Kray had tried to do against Moreau, but to strike at the French heads of column as they debouched through the forest into the Swabian lands, where there are wooded sharp hills and little districts of green lawn, country peculiarly adapted to the operations of the fine Austrian light infantry, and to those of the Austrian heavy cavalry. A defeat inflicted on the French there could be followed up either through the Swiss passes into Italy, or directly into the heart of France, with Russian help. Switzerland was neutral, but this hardly bothered the defenders of small nations, since a movement

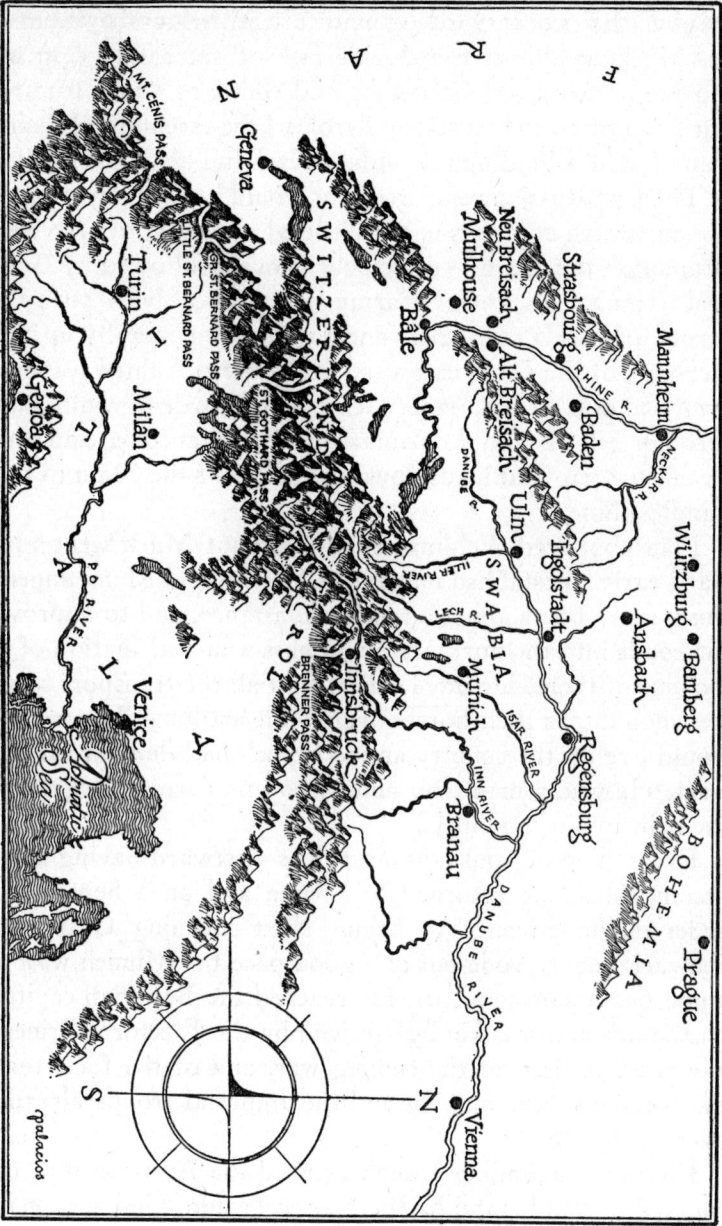

through their country would be for the Schweizers' own benefit. Mack would have a double line of retreat in case of
trouble, either back whence he had come, or south toward
our mountains, the Austrian Tyrol, where Archduke Johann
waited, and behind him Archduke Karl and his big army.

The first Russian reinforcement would be an army of 40,-
000 men with 200 guns under General Kutuzov, to arrive at
Branau on the Inn by 16 October, closely followed by General Bennigsen's reserve army of 30,000, both to pass
through Mack's rear areas and to operate generally up the
left bank of the Danube toward Strasbourg. A third Russian
army, 50,000 strong, under General Buxhövden, would pass
through Silesia and Bohemia to enter Franconia and the
Frankfurt gap that leads down the valley of the Main to the
middle Rhine.

Plan approved. Feldmarschall-Leutnant Mack went forward early to establish magazines at Ulm and Memmingen,
to set more boats afloat on Lake Constance, and to improve
the roads into the northern Swiss passes in anticipation of a
movement there. He gave orders that all the transport services should turn their horses over to the artillery. The troops
would live off the country as the French had done in earlier
wars. He was a man who understood modern strategy and
the principle of mobility.

Everything he could do out to the westward having been
accomplished, he returned to Vienna and on 2 September
ordered the advance to begin. Next morning Graf von
Schwartzenburg rode out at a good pace for Munich with a
numerous honorific escort. He reached the Bavarian capital
on the 6th and was kindly received by the Electoral Prince,
whom he advised of the coming war, and of the facts that
the Russians were moving and the Imperial troops already
over the borders.

Elector Maximilian Joseph assured the Austrian that of
course he would stand by the Kaiser (whom God sustain);
but said that Foreign Minister Graf Montgelas would have
to furnish the details as he never concerned himself with

them. During the two following days Schwartzenburg was in conference with that noble lord, who was inclined to balk at the Austrian idea of breaking up the Bavarian army to distribute it through the regular Austrian formations. Montgelas entertained on the evening of the 8th, the men sitting somewhat late over their bottles. Schwartzenburg woke next morning with a bad head to discover that the Electoral Prince Maximilian Joseph and the whole Bavarian army were already far on the road out northeastward toward Bamberg.

He had been diddled and the Bavarians would fight on the French side, contrary to the interests of small nations. Marshal Mack declined to take a serious view of the occurrence, only detaching a couple of light flying columns on the heels of the Bavarians, who at Bamberg would be easy prey for Buxhövden's army coming through Bohemia, as would the French corps under General Bernadotte, which staff officer Wendt reported a few days later as progressing toward a meeting with the Electoral Prince and his forces. These French were clearly destined for Bohemia and could be neglected by the Army of Germany, since the main road southward from Würzburg and Bamberg ran through the islanded principality of Ansbach. That territory belonged to warlike Prussia, which would surely punish any violation of its neutrality. Marshal Mack also laughed aside a note from Archduke Karl to the effect that neither lentils nor beans were grown in the districts through which the Russians would march; said he had not known that the moujiks were such dainty feeders.

In those fading days of September reports of cavalry combats came in from all through the Black Forest country. From the fact that the French horsemen were frequently supported by artillery it could be deduced that their infantry were behind these screens, but it was difficult to make out their precise strength and line of advance.

Of Mack's staff, no one but Colonel Schulmeister noted that in calculating the date of the Russian arrival the odd error had been made of not allowing for the 12 days' difference between Gregorian and Orthodox calendars; and Colonel Schulmeister sent the report on this occurrence not to Vienna but to Paris.

III

At four o'clock in the morning the Emperor rang for his valet. Méneval the secretary came down a few minutes later, to find him standing in front of the fireplace with a white robe tied round him and a kind of Madras turban on his head, hands behind back. He began dictating at once, and when he had finished, sent for sherbets while a uniform was brought, very plain and without badges. The Archchancellor Cambacérès rode with him in the carriage as far as the Paris barriers, noting that Napoléon seemed a little piqued over the lack of demonstration in the streets; remarked that he would set them cheering again before he returned. It was doubtless accurate enough, but did not particularly lift the spirits of the legist, who was to be interim president of the Council of State. Like everyone else in the government, except perhaps Talleyrand and Fouché, the Archchancellor was oppressed with a feeling of inadequacy—and like all the rest without exception he was thinking of the bullet that had passed between Charles XII's eyes on the ramparts of Fredriksten to bring down the Swedish Empire. The sky was gray and promised rain; the date was September 24, 1805.

Joséphine accompanied her husband to Strasbourg, which was reached on the 26th. That same day the troops began the passage of the Rhine. There was a desperate shortage of horses and one whole brigade of dragoons was going forward dismounted in the hope of obtaining them later. Marmont's corps reported that it was not getting enough biscuit. That day the Emperor wrote that if only a little luck kept Mack three or four days more on the Iller, his army would be so surrounded that only its débris could escape. A day and a night later, night of the 27th, word came from Schulmeister that Mack most decidedly intended to hold the Iller, was fortifying the crossings that lead to the great boulevard through southern Germany to Vienna. Berthier was at once summoned and all the corps orders were changed to produce a far more rapid wheel down to the Danube, on a far narrower front.

Bernadotte's I Corps will now go through Ansbach, whether the Prussians like it or not (Duroc whom Frederick William so much liked was in Berlin; explanations could come later); point through Eichstädt on Ingoldstadt instead of Regensburg, to reach the banks of the Danube by October 8. The Bavarian allies would follow him. Marmont's II Corps to be at Hassenfels, a day's march from the river and west of Bernadotte, on October 7; Soult to prolong beyond Halle and reach Donauwörth on the 8th; Lannes to remain well north of Ulm, attaining Neresheim on the same day that would find Soult at Donauwörth; Ney to arrive at Heidenheim, northwest of Neresheim, still on that same day; Davout to cut across the front of Marmont's march and be on the river at Neuburg, also on the 8th.

On that key date the whole army would be facing south, with Bernadotte on the left wing closest to the river, all ready to make another wheel across it, facing back west to pocket Mack, the pivot point being the corps of Ney, who would be holding behind that affluent of the Danube called Brenz, which is not very considerable but still a military stream. It would give a defense line in case Mack should be visited with the idea of escaping by the north or striking at the French communications. The front would then be some 30 miles from end to end—two days' march, allowing a concentration to either flank in that amount of time, or one to the center in half of it. The Guard, which was following Lannes in, would form a reserve behind the right wing.

The Emperor passed the Rhine on 1 October and that evening was graciously received by the old Elector of Baden and his sons, who consented to place under French orders their diminutive army of 3,000 men and to furnish some horses. It had been intended to push on to Stuttgart the next day, but word came in of trouble encountered by Marshal Ney, whose corps was around the place. Stuttgart is the capital of Württemberg, and the Württembergers said they had orders from their Duke not to open the city gates, nor did they open till Ney had unlimbered his artillery. Napoléon knew all about that Duke—a man so corpulent that he rode especially trained percherons and had to have a semicircle cut out of any table where he sat down to dine, but very active, witty, and ambitious. The Emperor accordingly moved on to Ludwigsburg, where the Duke was in residence, and as he expected, found the fat man amenable to reason. He only wanted to be made a king and to gain some small packages of Austrian territory that abutted on his dominions at the south. The whole business was arranged in half an hour, Württemberg to join the French with a token force of 5,000, furnish some provisions and more horses.

That day there came a letter from Duroc in Berlin, so cautiously worded as to indicate an apprehension that the Prussians were reading his dispatches. There was a good highroad (he said) from Würzburg to Bamberg, and some tracks, even if not very marchable, from there down to the Danube, altogether avoiding Ansbach; would it not be preferable for Bernadotte to take them?

It was already too late to order Bernadotte back, but next day (though Napoléon did not know it) the decision as to whether the grenadiers of Prussia would join the forces against France was doubly taken. Part of it came far on the frontiers of Silesia, where Russian Buxhövden demanded to march through Prussian territory, the more quickly to reach his station, and then marched through it without waiting for permission. The other part was at Ansbach itself, where the Prussian commandant closed the gates and made ready to fight. There was no way round for an army with baggage, but the Gascon marshal's race stood him in good stead. He paraded before the gates 18,000 men, with the buglers blowing tira-lira and after them all, the guns. The Prussian commandant, an old man brought up in the chess-game war tradition of the eighteenth century, surrendered to overwhelming force, and the corps swept through with no blood shed.

Murat had had very bad luck in getting prisoners for information, but Schulmeister passed along word that Mack was withdrawing troops from the upper reaches of the Iller to concentrate around Ulm. There was also a rather mysterious report from a minor spy in Donauwörth that an Austrian brigade was expected at that place, which meant trouble. The Emperor hurried his men forward furiously, now expecting he might have to fight for a passage of the Danube; Soult was urged to outdo schedule by bringing his pontoon trains forward for a crossing on the 7th—"Do not tell me this is impossible, requisition every horse, mount the detachments in carriages, and drive them onward night and day."

He himself had come down to Nördlingen by this time; and Soult's march was possible. He crossed on the 7th, just behind Murat's cavalry vanguard, and was at once shoved south toward Augsburg. That evening the golden autumn, which normally lasts for weeks in Bavaria, broke into sheets of icy rain that were snow among the highlands, and Feldmarschall-Leutnant Mack learned that a French force was crossing the Danube to get across his line of communications.

IV

Even so late Mack does not seem to have been anywhere near imagining the strength of the French forces at hand. He himself was divided into seven corps, all but that of Reisch (30,000 men) much smaller than those of his opponents; the corps of Jellačič (6,500), Schwartzenburg (8,-600), Klenau (5,000), Werneck (6,500), his own, and that of Kienmayer—the last having 3,500 infantry, but mainly composed of 10,000 cavalry, covering the line of communications back to Vienna south of the Danube, with headquarters at Munich.

Except for Kienmayer, they were distributed along the Iller and behind Ulm in a space roughly 100 miles x 60 miles, all able to concentrate, facing westward or northward within 72 hours. Orders had already been issued for Archduke Johann to join with his forces from the Tyrol when the scouting reports as of October 4 indicated that the French had crossed the Rhine at Strasbourg and would work along the north bank of the Danube. Mack began to concentrate— slowly, since his troops and transport were not in good shape after a very rapid and arduous march from the hereditary dominions—up along the Danube from Ulm to Günzburg. Holding all bridges, he could strike into the flanks of their columns in the bottleneck between the river and the territory of Ansbach.

The north bank held only outposts, of which that at Donauwörth was reported driven in on the 6th by heavy forces of infantry. (This would be Division Vandamme of Soult.) Mack himself now rode out to Günzburg; it was toward twilight of the next day, the 7th, before he learned that Bernadotte had marched through Ansbach, and simultaneously that the French were across the Danube in force. At the same time there was an express from Kienmayer: the enemy were coming up both banks of the Lech in great strength, and he himself was pulling back toward Munich in a southeasterly direction—point of contact, Aichach.

There were officers on the staff who advised that the whole army immediately retreat toward the Tyrol, but Mack was made of sterner stuff than to take such counsel of despair, pointing out that the Army of Germany had an extremely strong position on the heights around Ulm, ammunition enough to fight at least three battles, and plenty of provisions for the few days remaining before Kutuzov's powerful Russian forces arrived on the Inn and placed the French between two fires. Moreover, the Austrian troops were still in motion toward the Ulm-Günzburg concentration; it would be two or three days before they emerged into effective tactical control from the country tracks they were following, and our messengers could not locate them where they now were.

As a palliative Mack made up a composite force of 4,500 under General Auffenberg and sent it out to Wertingen to develop the French strength and movements, with instructions to fall back on Zusmarshausen and cover the main Ulm-Augsburg highroad after having obtained the necessary information. Auffenberg reached his post in time to fan out cavalry detachments by nine in the morning. They were immediately set upon by overwhelming numbers of French light horse, since nearly the whole of Murat's cavalry were on this flank, the one toward the Austrian main body. For a time Auffenberg made a stand by forming his infantry around the guns on some hills encircling Wertingen, but now he was attacked by the whole of Lannes' 18,000 men, who had crossed during the night. The French were so numerous that they lapped around both Auffenberg's flanks and their cavalry got into his retreat; the General himself was taken with all his guns and colors, only some 1,300 men reaching the highly temporary security of Zusmarshausen.

That day, October 8, Ney was on the Brenz, Bernadotte began crossing at Ingoldstadt, Marmont was close up to Neuburg, Davout had shot past his head of column and was already across the stream, pointing on Aichach, bound out to be flank guard of the whole operation against any Austrian reinforcements or interruption by the Russians. Both Marmont and Bernadotte were nearer Munich, but the III Corps was better trained, and Napoléon considered its commander more capable of a semi-independent operation, a fact which brought growls from the soldierly Soult, who considered Davout only a provost-marshal. It rained, heavily and cold.

Mack's orders for the next day sent Jellačič's corps back up the Iller to Memmingen, to demonstrate toward Augsburg. The Austrian commander's purpose was now to concentrate north of Ulm, on the left bank of the Danube, but

before he could make it, Ney came down across the Brenz
and stormed the Günzburg bridge in a hot little fight that
cost the Austrians 800 casualties and 1,000 prisoners.

The defeat was minor but it hit Mack hard. He was unable to avoid the evidence that his soldiers were becoming

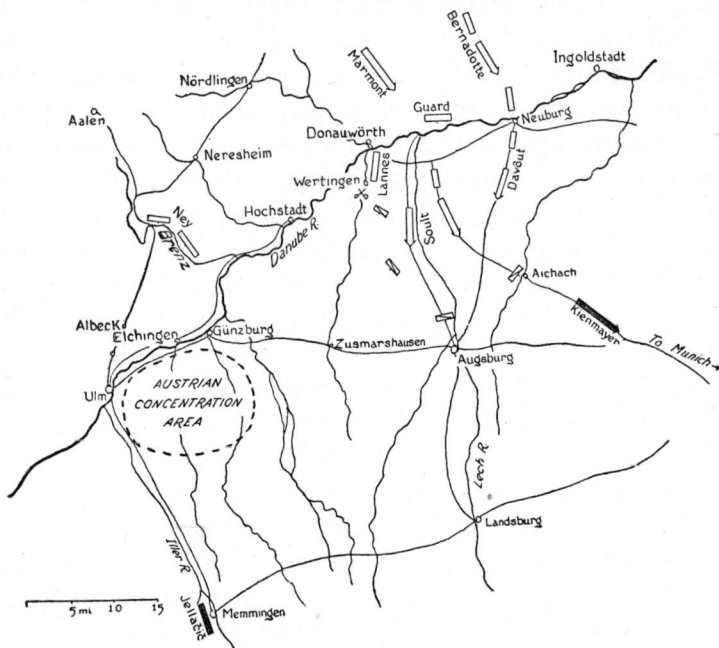

Ulm: October 8 situation

broken, dispirited, much worn with constant marching under
heavy rain; and at this moment of all, young Archduke
Ferdinand chose to assert himself. He had not liked the
Iller-line project from the beginning; now he demanded that
it be abandoned, that the army retreat through Memmingen
into the Tyrol at utmost speed. Mack explained how impossible this was in the physical condition of the troops, the
transport, and the roads. Instead he offered a plan of reorganization, under which all the regiments except those
with Jellacic were distributed among three new, nearly
equal corps.

Now there had been a row a couple of weeks earlier with the Archduke, when he had tried to countermand Mack's strategy, and the General immediately communicated with Vienna. One of the very last messages to come through before the lines to the capital were cut was a letter from Kaiser Franz to the young Archduke:

"I consider that I shall be rendering a true service to you by inviting you to follow the advice of FML Mack, who possesses such wide experience."

Mack quoted the letter. Ferdinand replied formally that, being deprived of all initiative, he refused to take any further responsibility, and all the day of 10 October was taken up with staff quarrels and the efforts of the new corps commanders to sort out their men. Early on the 11th one brigade of Schwartzenburg's corps was left south of the city, while all the rest of the troops were moved across to the amphitheater of hills encircling it on the north bank. A Saxon baron called at headquarters with the news that the English had made a great landing at Boulogne and Paris was in revolt. From the movement of the French, Mack deduced that they were in full retreat, and had the idea of striking at their communications and into their flanks of column on the north bank. The rains poured down unceasingly, now and again changing to snow.

V

Under those lugubrious skies the French spent in marching the 36 hours they had gained through Mack's preoccupation with headquarters detail. They were not without their own difficulties. "The troops are exhausted by fatigue and suffer from a want of food," reported divisional general Vandamme, and in Marmont's corps on the 9th they received only a third of a ration of bread and a few miserable potatoes. Shoes were wearing out, the weather was intolerable; but they marched, by God, they marched.

Davout marched toward Munich, Bernadotte and the Bavarians were switched in the same direction. Soult reached Landsberg, wheeled right and began to make for the Iller at Memmingen. Murat, with Lannes close up and Marmont coming along behind, closed toward Ulm from east and southeast, while Ney pushed westward along the left bank of the river. This wing, two infantry corps and his own of cavalry, had been placed under Murat's general orders, and Schulmeister had been told to report to him, as the man in contact. Napoléon's general instruction was that the infantry corps should "close in together as much as possible, as the Austrians will fight."

Now came a blunder and a check. Schulmeister had believed that Ferdinand would win the headquarters argument about an escape to the Tyrol up the Iller, especially as in his rôle of chief of intelligence he had been urging that course. He had succeeded in convincing both Napoléon and Murat that the Austrians would adopt it, and when Soult's light cavalry scouts discovered Jellačič at Memmingen, Mack's general movement in that direction seemed confirmed. By the time the Austrian decided to go in the opposite direction, to the left bank of the Danube, Murat's horse were so close up to the enemy positions, there was so much fighting going on, that the spy apparently could not get a message through. At all events Murat believed all the enemy army was before him on the south bank and perhaps behind the Iller. He accordingly interpreted Napoléon's order for concentration into one that Ney should bring his entire corps across.

Ney's Swiss Jomini, a good deal bewildered by this performance, persuaded his chief to ask what plans Murat had in mind and received the reply: "I never make plans except on the field of battle." It will be remembered that Ney belonged to the Augereau, or anti-Murat, faction among the marshals. The rudeness was just enough to make him disobey Murat, to the extent of leaving Division Dupont on the north bank, moving toward Ulm down the road from Albeck, supported by a division of dragoons.

Dupont reached Haslich on that road during the afternoon of 11 October, and ran head on into Schwartzenburg's Austrian corps, with Mack himself riding in the advance. As the two forces began shooting into each other through the streaming rain, it became clear that the Austrian numbers were vastly superior (they were in fact 25,000 to 6,000), and they began to work round Dupont's flanks. But every man in that corps had caught something of the spirit of Michel Ney; Dupont dauntlessly ployed into column and charged the enemy center with the bayonet, breaking right through into the village of Jüningen. There the fight swayed back and forth till early dark, the village won and lost half a dozen times. Through the night Dupont retreated behind the Brenz with his division a wreck. He had lost 1,700 men, nearly a third, but he took 3,000 prisoners with him and his retirement was unmolested.

Mack himself had been lightly wounded and was not unreasonably convinced that Dupont would hardly have put on so strong a fight unless there were something very formidable immediately behind him. He changed plans, therefore, to push along the left bank of the Danube to Regensburg, where he would link with the Russians, who must surely be there by time he arrived.

Geology and the Archduke Ferdinand conspired to keep him from executing the movement next day, October 12. All the country south of the Danube is composed of glacial moraines, with a gravelly topsoil and a deep watertable, which becomes sopping wet in such rains as had been falling, but is by no means impassable. North of the stream there runs down to it, and almost to the Brenz, a long spur of the Swabian Alb highland, built of old sea-bottom clay, the finest of powders in dry weather, the most tenacious of muds when wet. Through this ankle-deep mud the Austrian soldiers had been struggling for two days, their feet acting like suction cups, their pace not above a mile an hour under the strongest urging. On the night of the 11th many lay in the mud, under the rain, utterly unable to move more. General Werneck, who had one of the new corps, insisted that they must have a day's rest before any further marching or fighting; the Archduke made it a formal order, no matter what might be said to him. The march for the 13th, then; Werneck's corps, as the freshest, to move by the road to Albeck, where there might be combat. The remainder would push along the Danube bank.

During the 12th Napoléon had become much worried over not receiving contact reports from Ney; while from Lannes, closing in on the south bank, only those showing weak resistance, and from Soult, advices that there were no important enemy forces in Memmingen. The Emperor set out for the front to see for himself, toward twilight catching up with a flowing river of a column moving up, some of Marmont's men, trudging along under a heavy fall of snow. He had them form circle around him and, sitting on his horse in the old scuffed gray greatcoat under the drifting flakes, addressed them: "Soldiers! A month ago you were at the shores of the ocean——" the old ringing tones that had thrilled the Army of Italy once, ending with an explanation of the moves of the campaign and how the Austrians would be beaten. They cheered him wildly—"Our Emperor has found a new way of beating the enemy; he conquers them with our legs." Next day the light infantry, for this was light infantry, had the temerity to attack and to rout a squadron of those heavy Austrian horse before whom all infantry had trembled in the past.

VI

Next day it still rained. Because of the turnaround of Schwartzenburg's corps from the Haslich position, the shift of Werneck to that flank, and the bottomless mud the Austrian columns were hardly eight miles from Ulm, by the night of the 13th, though that represented good marching. By this time Napoléon had solved his problem; the orders were for Ney to take his whole corps back to the north bank by the Elchingen bridge, the nearest, of which the French held the southern end. He would join Dupont at once; Lannes was to follow him hard; Dupont to rally and come back in toward Albeck.

The Austrians had taken up the planks of the Elchingen bridge and had installed some infantry with a couple of guns at their end. Ney put in a battery of 17 cannon which silenced the Austrian pieces, then came up to lead the infantry attack in person, all togged out in his best full-dress uniform, with a star on his chest, as he always was on days when there was going to be a battle. Murat was standing with the Emperor. "Come, watch me make some plans on the field of battle," taunted the redhead, picking at the cavalry leader's arm—then ran forward along the bridge-stringers with his men behind.

The Austrians fled. The planks were replaced, more men and guns began to come over and to spread out into the area beyond. The northern end of the bridge issues into another amphitheater like that opposite Ulm, with hills rising on every side, covered with vines, and to the west the walls of an ancient monastery. Just as Ney and his men reached the pit of this theater the enemy began to come down from the galleries in the usual Austrian route-march formation, that is, in close columns slugging through the mire, with a few flankers out.

Ney charged, and charged again as more of his men and Lannes' poured over the bridge in behind him, a typical Revolutionary attack, working in no formation between the enemy columns, firing from every cover, driving the Austrians back uphill, attacking with the bayonet whenever enough Frenchmen came together. A few horse began to cross; to halt them the Austrians formed square at the break of the heights and were shot to pieces by the French skirmishers. Ney himself led the attack on the monastery as it blazed from every window. The enemy began to go back, the heights were won, and before evening the Army of Germany was locked and double-locked in Ulm.

LE DEPART DU CONSCRIT, avec accomp. de piano par M. H. COLLET, professeur d'harmonie au Conservatoire.

354

For close up on the south Marmont had pushed across the Iller, while farther down, Soult had taken Memmingen, with 5,000 of Jellačič's men, leaving that officer to slip away into the Tyrol with only a remnant. It was full six days more before the presence of French cannon on hills around the town and his growing shortage of victuals convinced Mack that he ought to surrender. He burst into tears as he delivered his sword, saying, "Behold the unfortunate Mack!"—not without accuracy, since as soon as he came under the Austrian flag again they threw him into prison on suspicion of treason.

There were only 27,000 of the Army of Germany left to surrender. Most of Werneck's column had, indeed, shouldered past Dupont on the 14th, but only 1,000 of them with the Archduke Ferdinand really escaped (incidentally through Prussia's Ansbach), since Murat was let loose on their heels with all that cavalry and caught 12,000 of them. 3,000 had been taken in the Elchingen fight and another 1,000 from Kienmayer near Munich to add to the others caught piecemeal, say 70,000 prisoners altogether out of the 84,000 men who had marched west from Vienna.

WRONG END OF THE TELESCOPE—XI

Charles Stuart to his mother:

ST. PETERSBURG
I DO not think it possible that, considering all Paget's late conduct at Vienna and his total ignorance of what has been transacted, literally under his nose, even Court favour can keep him at his Post. To act so totally contrary to his own interests and to the interests of Govt. would, did I not know him to possess at least moderate talents, make me believe him the greatest fool under Heaven, but it shows how idleness and the society of women without character can get the better of a man. There is a story that the Austrian Ambassador in London, Stahremberg, was asked by Cobenzl of Sir Arthur: *"N'est-il pas un peu fou?"* and Paget, speaking to Stahremberg about Cobenzl, asked: *"N'est-il pas trés faux?"* Both were right about each other.

Recollections of the Duc de Fezensac:

THE morning after our arrival at the fort of Leutsch, a woman in mourning whose husband, an Austrian officer, had been killed in the previous day's attack, came to ask permission to find his body. We gladly rendered this sad service for her, and soldiers aided some peasant she had brought. The dead were buried close together and it was a cruel spectacle to see her try to find her husband's body among the rest. When she had recognized him, she embraced the body, spoke to it as though he were still living and fell fainting with the body in her arms. The soldiers stood silent and visibly moved. After a moment, one of them hazarded some pleasantry upon such extraordinary tenderness, and all of them began to laugh, forgetting that an instant before they had been at the edge of tears.

The King of Sweden to the King of Prussia:

IT is with regret that I find myself forced to return to your Majesty's hands his Order of the Black Eagle, which was conferred upon me by the late King Your Father as a precious token of his sentiments for me. Being too well aware of the value of these solemn decorations whose origin is in the most ancient times, and which are founded on the principles and sacred duties of Religion and Chivalry, it is only in spite of myself that I yield to the sad circumstances of the time in which we live, to do something which would be contrary to my manner of thinking and behavior, were it not that too recent events impose this sacrifice upon me as a sad duty. Further explanation would be painful to me; but I find myself obliged to declare as a Knight, that I cannot recognize this respectable title as belonging to Napoleon Bonaparte and His Equals.

THE WORM'S-EYE VIEW—XI

. . . One of our captains, named B——, a fine young fellow, would have been one of the handsomest men in the army if his calves had been in keeping with the rest of his person; but he had legs like stilts, which had a very bad effect with the tight pantaloons worn at that time by the chasseurs. In order to meet this inconvenience, Captain B—— had some good-sized pads made in the shape of calves, which made his handsome figure complete. It was prescribed by the regulations that the officers should have their horses' tails long, like those of the troopers. Our colonel, M. Moreau, was always admirably mounted, but all his horses had their tails docked, and as he feared that General Bourcier, who was very strict in maintaining the regulations, would reprimand him for setting a bad example to his officers, he had caused for the purpose of inspection, false tails to be attached to all his horses. These were so marvellously well fitted that unless you knew you would have thought them natural. We went to the inspection, to which General Bourcier had invited General Suchet, inspector of infantry, as well as General Gudin. They were accompanied by a numerous and brilliant staff; the business took a long time, the movements were nearly all carried out at a gallop, and ended with several charges at full speed. I was commanding a section in the center, forming part of the squadron under M. B——, near whom the colonel had placed himself. They were, therefore, two paces in front of me, when the generals came forward to congratulate M. Moreau on the admirable style in which the maneuvers were carried out. But what did I see? The extreme rapidity of the movements which we had just made had deranged the symmetry of the additions which the captain and the colonel had made to their get-up. The false tail of the colonel's horse had become partly detached; the stump, composed of a plug of tow, was dragging almost on the ground, while the false hair was up in the air, several feet higher, and spread out fan-shaped over the horse's croup, so that he seemed to have an enormous peacock's tail. As for M. B——'s sham calves, under the pressure of the saddle flaps they had slipped forward without his perceiving it, and presented a round lump on his shin bones, which produced a most comical effect; the captain all the while sitting proudly upright on his horse, as who should say, "Look at me! What a handsome man I am!" At twenty years old one has not much gravity; mine was overcome by the grotesque spectacle which I had under my eyes, and, in spite of the imposing presence of three generals, I could not restrain myself from shouting wildly with laughter. I gnawed the sleeve of my jacket: it was no use; I laughed and laughed until my sides ached. Thereupon the inspector-general, not knowing the cause of my merriment, ordered me to fall out of ranks and put myself under arrest. I obeyed, but as I was obliged to pass between the horses of the colonel and of the captain, my eyes fell again on that infernal tail and also on the new-fashioned calves, and there I was again seized with an inextinguishable laugh. The generals must have thought that I was gone mad.

The Memoirs of General Marbot

19

END OF AN ERA

Berlin, The Valley of the Danube: October 21, 1805–
November 13, 1805

ON SEPTEMBER 21, a cold and dark morning, Tsar
Alexander of Russia rolled in his coach out of St.
Petersburg. There had been a solemn service at Our
Lady of Kazan before he mounted. The Tsar was in a
gloomy mood, saying little, for the slow words spoken among
incense and the flutter of violet vestments had served to confirm rather than to efface the melancholy impression of the
previous night, when His Majesty sought to obtain the blessing upon this enterprise of the man whom all Russia regarded as the reincarnated Son of God. Kondrati Selivanov
—"The Eunuch Christ," who preached that only through the
bloody sacrifice of self-mutilation could men attain to God,
denying hell's pleasure of the flesh. The Eunuch Christ had
purified himself with that sacrifice and with many another,
and was swept home from exile in Irkutsk on a wave of
authentic miracles; but in the dark cell whose walls were
never dry, held out little promise of miracle in the war
against "the accursèd Frenchman." "Your time has not yet
come. He will beat you, destroy your army and you will
have to flee in shame"—until the sacrifice of blood was complete.

Some sense of relation between the mystic's doctrine and

his own errand would be upon the young Tsar on that chill September morning, for although he wore a military uniform and was escorted by the Preobrazhenski Guard, it was not as a commander of armies that he went forth. He was bored extravagantly by such military details as march orders, equipment reports, questions of supply and billeting, with regard to which he was supposed to read and initial documents. It was precisely to drive such annoyances beyond the horizon of his mind that he had appointed General Kutuzov commander-in-chief of the army; Kutuzov, the morose old one-eyed, fat-necked leader, who had learned all there was to know about war against the Turks and in Poland, Suvorov's school; Kutuzov, who enjoyed the minutiae.

The want of romance in military detail was also responsible that the Tsar had in some degree withdrawn himself from the young men of the Secret Committee, who were always buzzing around with some complaint that the troops were badly fed, lacked uniforms or muskets. His companion in the traveling coach was a man the Secret Committee hated and were hated by—Prince Peter Dolgoruki, whom the Tsar had discovered for himself; ebullient, of imperious humor, with an ability to get things done, no matter how, that made him peculiarly acceptable as a military aide.

Not that Czartoryski and his friends were altogether shaken off. *Au contraire;* the first destination of the trip was Pulawi on the Vistula, the ancient estate of the Princes Czartoryski where, amid an atmosphere of gaiety and soft shoulders, light laughter and candle-lit fêtes under a silken canopy looking out over the river, it was Alexander's business to demonstrate how thoroughly he had accepted the Piatoli Memorial. There is in every Pole, however frivolous or otherwise occupied, a streak of burning fanatic nationalism; in ministering to this sensation, in sowing among the undertones of the waltz the innuendo that this war could not but end in a restored and greater Poland (undoubtedly in crown union with Russia)—in conveying this, the Tsar recovered his tone. It was the type of seduction he performed exceedingly well, the conveyance of an impression of utter devotion, without backing it up by anything so definite that it could lead to reproaches later.

It was the fear that he might have to perform a similar act of allurement on an individual instead of a mass basis that had left Alexander shaken after his interview with the hermit Selivanov. Queen Luise; her husband had brought her to Memel for the maneuvers three years before, when Alexander came to call on the royal couple. He found that she, who had the ordering of the apartments, had placed him in a bedroom next to her own. Alexander double-locked the doors on that occasion, but there was no way of avoiding her endless letters, or the fact that she was the one channel through whom Frederick William might be brought into the alliance of peace and mediation.

It must have seemed quite probable to the young Tsar that he would have to sell his virtue to this—Armide, as Napoléon called her, after the demon-created beauty in Tasso, whose mission was to tempt Crusaders. The Tsar was too enlightened to be bound by the canons of conventional morality in spite of Selivanov's warning; but his taste simply did not run in the direction of gushing females.

Nevertheless, he buried prejudice and pushed on to Berlin, where a flirtation was duly begun. It had run for only five days when, on October 30, a piece of news shook like an earthquake through the tinsel atmosphere to render the lordly sacrifice unnecessary. Marshal Mack had been shut up in Ulm and forced to surrender by a French army believed to be still on the Rhine. The Army of Germany was destroyed; the enemy were marching on Vienna and there was nothing, absolutely nothing, to stop them.

II

It is possible that the flirtation might have been dispensed with in any case, and that the news from Ulm was in any case superfluous. Frederick William's current Foreign

Minister was Graf von Hardenberg, a German version of the "mere executive" type, who had entered the Prussian service from the Hanoverian and who had been called to Berlin after administering for four years with extraordinary skill the detached territories of Ansbach and Bayreuth. At the capital, like everyone else, he became a great friend of the learned, portly, and amiable Haugwitz, Frederick William's perennial Foreign Minister. The latter was accused by Queen Luise, Stein, and the rest of the war party of having sold out to France, but Hardenberg knew this was so far from the truth that it was Haugwitz more than anyone else who had broken up the French alliance project two years before by attaching impossible conditions.

Frederick William had been no little put out by the failure of that negotiation to be carried farther, since the rôle in which he cast Prussia was that of a neutral benevolent to everyone, bound to obtain Hanover, no matter how the war resulted. Haugwitz had thrown him definitely away from one side. He did not dismiss the man, but sent him on a long vacation, while friend Hardenberg moved in to keep the seat warm.

The arrangement gave council meetings the type of milk-toast result gratifying to His Majesty, since Stein was vigorous on one side and Hardenberg at least pretended to be violently pro-French. The violation of Ansbach, of which news arrived on October 7, was a hideous shock. The Foreign Minister felt for the little principality the affection a father does for his child or a workman for his creation; moreover the act tore to pieces Frederick William's whole policy of maintaining a neutrality so powerfully armed that no one would dare to tamper with it. These French had dared to march through in spite of the Prussian army. When Duroc and Laforêt, the regular ambassador, came round to discuss the matter, Hardenberg sent a message to the door that he had no time, and Frederick William recalled Haugwitz to be dual Foreign Minister beside his successor.

Actually, the Russians were crossing Silesia at the same time, but they had asked permission first, and the news that they had not waited for an assent was so much later in reaching Berlin that an anti-French policy had already been undertaken. Finally, the arrival of the charming Tsar brought a whole new series of personalities into play.

One of them was Clemens Wenzel Lothar, Graf Metternich, the real Austrian ambassador. (The official title was held by an archduke.) Seldom have natural abilities and opportunity so happily met. Metternich was insolent, vain, unscrupulous, clever, handsome, persuasive, gay, patriotic— and he had become a diplomat at twenty by marrying the daughter of that grandfather of Austrian foreign relations, Prince Kaunitz. In Berlin he despised everything he found; the men did not know how to laugh; the women were rigid, cold Protestants, lacking in charm. "This place is like the headquarters of an entrenched camp," he wrote home; there was no pleasure and the only intellectual society centered around Germaine de Staël, who appalled and frightened him. She courted the young ambassador "with assiduity and skill" but "That woman-man kills me," he complained, and welcomed the Tsar's arrival as offering an opportunity to amuse himself usefully.

For even though the once pro-French Hardenberg had come over to the Good Cause, there would be difficulties about Prussia's joining the coalition as long as Frederick William could find anyone to put them into words—and Haugwitz was even more anti-Russian than anti-French. He had learned about the Abbé Piatoli's memorial and the "rational" map of Europe which was the basis of the alliance of mediation. It showed Memel and a good slice of East Prussia under the Russian flag and Poland in crown union under the Tsar. (It was odd how often in that memoir the interests of peace, mediation, and international justice required that territory be transferred to Russia, and how infrequently to any other power.) Protests that similar

Austrian fears had been laid aside in the face of graver dangers from the West were unavailing—or were, down to the arrival of the Tsar's suite in Berlin.

History is made in bed. The young Graf Metternich addressed himself to Princess Dolgoruki, wife of the Tsar's new favorite, opponent of Czartoryski and hence of the Piatoli Memorial. Within three days she was in the Austrian's arms and he had secured from her, who secured from her husband, who secured from Alexander, the requisite assurance that no rectification of the Russian boundaries as against Prussia was contemplated. There three more days—or nights, for they lasted till nearly dawn—of incoherent conversation, with those present always including Frederick William, Queen Luise, Alexander, Dolgoruki and Metternich, and sometimes Haugwitz, Hardenberg, and old Marshal Möllendorf or the Duke of Brunswick.

On November 3 a treaty was signed on terms which the Austrian reduced to writing. Prussia would offer her mediation to settle all outstanding questions if the French would return to the exact line of the Peace of Lunéville; but if this most generous offer were refused, she would join the Allies with 180,000 of the best soldiers of the earth, the grenadiers of Vater Fritz, whom the French had so deadly cause to remember. Alexander would persuade his good friends of England to cede Hanover to Prussia. The ultimatum would not be presented until December (this over Metternich's violent objections to so late a date) ; Brunswick, who was the army commander, said it would take him at least six weeks to mobilize his troops for action.

After the signing, Alexander, Frederick William, and Queen Luise dismissed their suites and slipped through a postern door of the palace, making their way, well cloaked round, along deserted streets to the garrison church. In the crypt beneath lay all that remained of the Great Frederick. A startled guardian produced a single smoky torch. By its light, one hand holding the hand of Armide, the Tsar of Russia approached the sarcophagus to touch it with his lips; then reaching the other hand to grasp that of Frederick William, joined with him in a solemn oath of eternal friendship and mutual assistance.

It is not recorded that the bones turned over; but the vow brought Metternich the order of St. Stefan of Hungary to pin on his coat.

III

Proclamation:

"Soldiers of the Grande Armée, in fifteen days we have made a campaign. That army which, with as much ostentation as impudence, came forward to our frontiers is now struck down. Of 100,000 men who composed it, 60,000 are prisoners; they will replace our conscripts in the labor of the fields. But we will not halt there. That Russian army which has been transported by English gold from the extremity of the universe, we will subject to the same fate. In this combat there is at stake most especially the honor of the infantry; they will demonstrate whether the French infantry is the first or the second in Europe; for there are no generals among the enemy from whom I myself would acquire glory."

In shape the valley of the upper Danube resembles a huge funnel, with the wide Bavarian plain as its bell. The mountains of Bohemia stand so close over the great river on the north that the affluents flowing in from that side are few and of little importance; and neither are there good roads along that bank by which an army may follow the course of the stream. South of Danube the rivers run down from the Tyrol, generally bending in a northeasterly direction to meet the greater water; all are capable of defense.

Kutuzov arrived at Branau on the Inn by 21 October, actually ahead of time, since at the rumor of Napoléon in Germany, he had seized country carts, mounted his soldiers in them, and come along at nearly thirty miles a day. He was to command the Austrian forces in the area as well as his own, and his position was very logical, covering the main highroad to Vienna, forming the right wing of a general Allied line 250 miles long, with Archduke Johann in the Tyrol at its center, Archduke Karl in Italy at its left, and a small flying wing out toward Venice.

An excellent lateral road connected all the parts of this line, following up the Inn to Innsbruck, thence south through the Brenner Pass and Trent to the Adige, where Karl was operating. But there were only 40,000 men in the first Russian wave and Kienmayer, picking up his detachments as he fell back, could bring only 22,000 more. Buxhövden, his line of march changed to join Kutuzov, was still far distant; so was Bennigsen, who was experiencing difficulties in obtaining victual from a country well eaten out by his predecessor.

There was only one Schulmeister, but most of this Napoléon had learned. As early as 12 October, when the successful passage of the Danube made it certain that he would break Mack, he had planned to follow up by pushing on to the Inn and destroying Kutuzov before the other Russians could come. He would then be quite free to deal with the Prussians if they made trouble; for even if Prince Karl slipped away from Masséna, the royal officer would have to make an immensely circuitous march through the Carnic Alps and nearly to Vienna if France once gained the northern outlet of the Brenner. As soon as the surrender formalities were accomplished, then, and a battalion of grenadiers had paraded the streets of Augsburg with every man carrying a captured Austrian standard, orders went out for a concentration along the Isar, its weight toward the left, the north flank, to smash the Russians south into the mountains surrounding the narrowest part of the Danube plain.

Lannes, with a division of heavy cavalry under his command since he was flank man, came down through Nördlingen to Landshut; Davout pushed to Freising; Bernadotte and the Bavarians concentrated at Munich; and Marmont was ordered there by the Augsburg road. Soult's orders car-

ried him from Memmingen to Landsberg, from which place
he could be shifted to either of the wings or pushed along
the axis of the new movement. Murat, with most of the
cavalry, was well forward, headquarters at Hohenlinden,

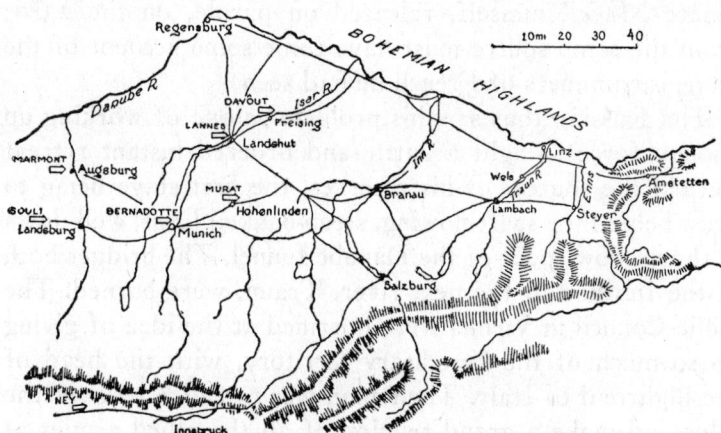

The Danube campaign to Amstetten

his men out in good screening position, and all these arrangements were complete by the night of 24 October. Security
was now furnished by the corps of Augereau, which had already crossed the Rhine and was marching on Kempten, at
the base of the mountains Vorarlberg, to check off Archduke
Johann; and by Ney, whose men were rewarded for having
fought so hard at Elchingen by being allowed a rest in Ulm.
Division Dupont of this corps was, however, detached and
moved close along the Danube to Passau, where Inn makes
its junction. En route this formation was to pick up Division
Dumonceau, detached from Marmont, and two cavalry divisions, to form a flying wing and rearguard of almost corps
strength, which would either support or extend Lannes, de-
pending upon the behavior of those mysterious Muscovites.

   There had been a good deal of talk around Russian headquarters, and still more of it in the entourage of the Tsar,
about getting the useless Austrians out of the way so the
war could be carried on, but Michael Ilarionovitch Kutuzov

took no part in such babble. He wanted every man who could carry a musket, and he came from a military school which believed in exchanging space for time. News of the disaster at Ulm reached him from the lips of "the unfortunate Mack" himself, released on parole, on the 23rd; from the same source must have come some account of the immense numbers of French he had seen.

The Russian thus saw his problem as one of working up enough force to fight a battle and ordered instant retreat toward the sources of his reserves, the first stage being to draw behind the swift-flowing, steep-banked Enns, well down in the narrow spout of the Danube funnel. The bridges both at the Inn and at the next river, Traun, were burned. The Aulic Council in Vienna were horrified at the idea of giving up so much of the hereditary territory, with the head of the highroad to Italy. Their plan was to call Karl over the Alps and make a grand reunion of all the allied armies at the gates of Vienna, a project which Kutuzov denounced as a dream.

In Kaiser Franz' name (he was technically supreme commander) they ordered the Russian to stand on the Inn, but the message only reached him on the 27th, when he was already behind the Traun, Bernadotte across the Inn and Lannes close up to Branau. The last marshal took the town on the 29th, and the Emperor expressed much gratification over the provision found inside, including a park of artillery and 18,000 sacks of flour; but "we march and bivouac in the mud," Napoléon wrote, hoping the Russ would stand at the Traun and he could tempt them into a battle. Ney's corps, minus Dupont, he now ordered down to Innsbruck; if Archduke Karl attempted to force the Brenner, Ney had authority to call in Augereau from Kempten.

The remaining corps pressed on. Bernadotte was at Salzburg on 30 October, Lannes moving on Linz the same day, Soult's big corps well along the road to Wels, Davout pointing toward Lambach, and Marmont, from behind Bernadotte, cutting across between that marshal and Soult, aiming at Steyr to get around the Russian flank if they stood—the strength shifting ever more to the left in the narrowing valley. From Murat in the vanguard came glowing reports of seeing Russian backs, like gray lice crawling down the road ahead; he wanted to follow hard and hit, but the Emperor reined him in. "These Russians are not yet broken; and besides they know how to attack, it would be unpleasant if they broke through you into the spread-out troops behind."

Napoléon had felt out his enemy now and made his estimate; for the first time he was dealing with an opponent who knew how to retreat, and the likelihood of catching him was growing thin, for the French were now traveling through a used country, as testified by burned barns, deserted houses, a shortage of comestibles, and stragglers with sword in hand, desperately hunting food through the rear areas. The difficulty had been foreseen as much as a week earlier, when there were orders to make Augsburg into a depot of the first class, with ovens to make 80,000 rations a day, and a million of them always in store. But the roads were not paved; still in fairly good condition when Kutuzov passed, they were mud-rivers by time the Grande Armée arrived under those rains that did not cease. Only the Guard had regular commissariat wagons, which caused the fantassins of the line to whistle, grumble, and sneer when those dandy troops went past.

IV

Press on.

On 1 November Lannes reached Linz, Soult was at Wels, Davout at Lambach, Bernadotte and Marmont now out on the right wing, the patrols of their light cavalry feeling slantwise down toward the Tyrol for contact with Ney. That day the rains ceased at last; it turned clear and cold. There was something very like a quarrel at Allied headquarters, with the Austrian generals shouting angrily that this barbarous Russki did not seem to care how many of the Kaiser's men or estates he sacrificed. All were agreed that the need was to gain time—time to assemble at some central point the Allied forces which really so much outnumbered the on-rushing French, but which were scattered in a great circle from Silesia to the Po.

The end was no agreement, with each party setting out to gain time in characteristic fashion. Kaiser Franz, as supreme commander, took 12,000 Austrians from Kutuzov's army and, placing them under Graf von Meerfeldt, sent them up the Enns to strike into the right flank of the French head of column. To aid this movement he himself sent forward a proposal for an armistice, all troops to halt in their present position. Kutuzov retreated from the Enns and took up a position at Amstetten, where a range of hills pinches the only road down the Danube into narrow space.

Napoléon had dropped some experienced officers with a brigade of cavalry at Linz to gather a boat flotilla that would give him a means of ferrying troops across the Danube when he chose. He correctly estimated the Amstetten position as a rearguard, but believed that beyond it Kutuzov would be forced to make a stand at St. Pölten, a road junction which was almost the last valid position before Vienna. The enemy would certainly not abandon their capital. Davout was accordingly switched by a circuit through Lilienfeld to flank the St. Pölten position, and Marmont by a still wider circuit over heavy bad mountain roads, through Leoben to fall on the enemy rear. Bernadotte from the upper waters of the Traun to follow Marmont; Lannes behind Murat to push straight in against Amstetten.

The Emperor was becoming much embarrassed by the lack of parallel roads along the right bank, which caused his columns to tail out. In some measure to relieve this a new corps was created under Marshal Mortier, and sent to the left bank by the boat flotilla, the corps consisting of the detached divisions of Dupont and Dumonceau, with Division Gazan, taken away from Lannes, and a strong formation of dragoons. This left Lannes with only one infantry division, but as he was now acting as a storm-formation, he retained command of the cuirassiers that had been given to him previously. The Emperor fretted over not getting scout-

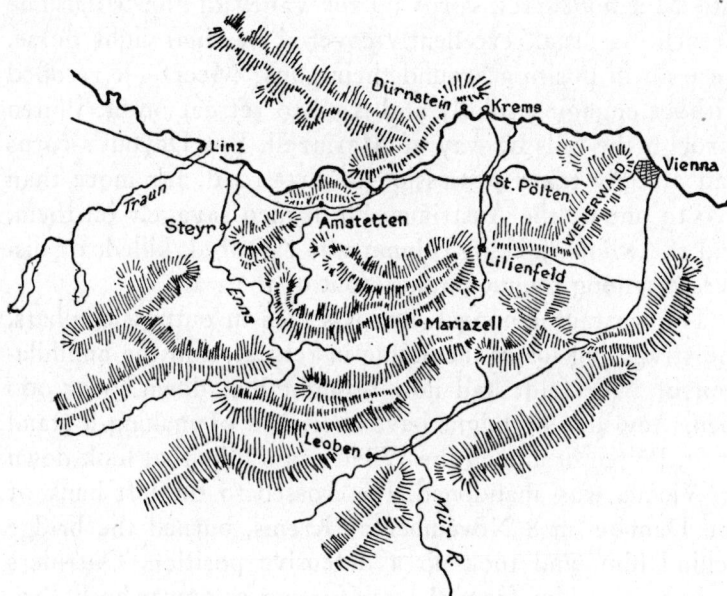

Amstetten to Vienna

ing reports from Murat: "You left me all day yesterday without news. You must write me two or three times a day." The troops were in high spirits, crying heartily *"Vive l'Empereur!"* as he rode past them toward the Amstetten front.

The consequence of the various moves was that Murat and Lannes faced Kutuzov's rearguard at Amstetten on November 4. The Russian commander was a blond Georgian prince named Bagration with much experience in war, and there was nothing wrong with the quality of their infantry, which stood up with wonderful constancy under the attacks of the two marshals and ended by beating them off after both sides had taken heavy losses, getting away to St. Pölten during the night. Word ran through the army that these

Samoyeds were really as tough as reputation pictured them
—"*Formidable! Des vrais sauvages!*"

The slight check was more than paid out two days later,
when Meerfeldt's Austrian flanking column ran head on
into Marmont's full corps up the valley of the Mur. The
French, as usual, excellently covered by their light horse,
were all in position around their guns; Meerfeldt recoiled
without engaging solidly and tried to retreat on St. Pölten
through the hills by way of Mariazell. But Davout's corps
had already taken possession of that road, far more than
two to one of the Austrians. He turned savagely on them,
and the whole flanking column was captured, killed, or dispersed among the mountains—out of the war.

The wastage among Kutuzov's men in outpost combats,
the straggling losses inevitable in retreat, and the annihila-
tion of Meerfeldt had now brought him down to 35,000
men. Any idea he might have cherished of making a stand
at St. Pölten or among the Wienerwald hills that look down
on Vienna was abandoned. He crossed to the left bank of
the Danube on 8 November at Krems, burned the bridge
behind him, and took up a defensive position. Outriders
had reached him from the reinforcing columns; both Buxhövden and Bennigsen were near, the Tsar himself was
coming down from Berlin, it was probable the Prussians
would go to war, and within the mountains of Bohemia the
Russian army would take its stand. Let the French have
Vienna; it would be useless to them; they could not advance
north with Karl coming up from Italy on their rear; they
would hardly dare retreat.

Meanwhile, scouts and country people reported a French
corps on the left bank, threatening the Russian rear, but
lacking connections with its own main army except by boat,
and conducting its movement without good flank guards. On
November 10 its head of column had reached Dürnstein,
where the ruined castle stood that had seen Richard Lion-
Heart's captivity and heard Blondel the minstrel sing to his
master. The building stands in a defile; on the morning of

the 11th Kutuzov sent his General Dokhtorov with a division by mountain tracks to get behind these French, while his General Miloradovitch assailed the pass in front.

The division now at Dürnstein was that of Gazan, with Mortier himself present. He formed line on the approach of Miloradovitch and made a good defense all day long; but when Dokhtorov appeared in his rear toward twilight with 15,000 men, things threatened to go to pieces. Mortier's officers urged him to escape by boat and "not leave a Marshal of France in the hands of the enemy." Instead, he placed himself at the head of his men for a thrust-through in tight column to the support of his other two divisions, reaching them under a romantic moon behind torn clouds.

But Gazan's division was nearly wiped out, and the other two were badly battered next day before they halted the pursuit—a clear victory for Kutuzov. It was partly Mortier's fault for scattering all his cavalry out among the mountain passes and not taking care of his own flanks; but still more the fault of the Emperor, who had moved a valuable piece to the edge of the board and left it there till it was taken. Nothing is ever one's own fault; while the battle was already in progress, before he had heard of its outcome, Napoléon had realized the error and was singeing Murat's hair for making it by pushing past St. Pölten to the Wienerwald:

"My cousin: I cannot approve your manner of movement. Instead of covering Vienna, the Russians have passed the Danube. Without knowing my desires in this new state of affairs, you ordered the leading corps of my army in on Vienna. Your orders were to follow hard on the heels of the Russians. It is a singular manner of pursuing them to move away from them by forced marches."

So here is the campaign in flaw and bad temper. Nevertheless Murat was through the Wienerwald, with Lannes and Soult close behind. Press on: if the great Danube bridge at the city can be won, we shall gain Kutuzov's rear before the other Russians can join him. The army held its course therefore, and on 13 November was tramping through the glum streets of that capital of the world, that virgin fortress, that rampart of the West against Oriental midnights, taken at last from the West. The death agonies would last a hundred years, but the Empire of Charles the Great fell that day; and Herr van Beethoven had begun his Fifth Symphony.

V

The southernmost wing of the vast front stretching across Europe was held by a small corps under General St. Cyr in the kingdom of Naples. There had been a Russian garrison in Corfu since the last war. The Emperor learned early, from one Schulmeister or another, that a force had sailed from England to join these Russians, bring the wobbly Neapolitan kingdom to the Allied cause, march up Italy and fall on Masséna's flank. When he threw up the plan of invading England for that of invading Austria, Decrès was instructed to order the fleet out of Cadiz into the Mediterranean, to base on Taranto and hold these allies at a distance. "If your Villeneuve is not too cowardly to go out"—so many ships should surely dominate the inland sea.

From Strasbourg Napoléon added that old Admiral Rosily was to go down and take command of the fleet if Villeneuve had not already sailed. On October 21, as the troops were turning round from Ulm to flow down the Danube, the imperial mind was changed again; St. Cyr was ordered north up the peninsula to sustain Masséna, to the devil with Naples. The fleet was to be broken up into heavy raiding squadrons to strike out of Cadiz against English commerce.

Too late: as the order was being written Lord Nelson of the Nile lay dying in his flagship's cockpit, with seventy shattered battleships around him, and most of those that had been French or Spanish now bore no flags at all.

Fouché was directed to have the papers say that "some ships have been lost in a gale following an indecisive action." History has taken a somewhat different view, but few people in France, few on the Continent did so at the time, and the Imperial eagles were passing under the gate of the K.K.Hofburg.

WRONG END OF THE TELESCOPE—XII

The Columbian Centinel:

SINCE our laſt, *Handbills* have been received from Newburyport and Portland, announcing the great ſucceſſes of the French; and of another naval victory by LORD NELSON. The following are all the particulars of this laſt reported event:—

Captain Lee, who has arrived at *Portland,* from *France,* ſpoke on the 15th November, the ſhip Neptune, 15 days from *Liverpool* for *New-York,* who informed, that a few hours before he left *Liverpool,* they had advices, that a *Packet* had arrived from the Britiſh fleet off Cadiz, commanded by LORD NELSON, bringing intelligence of his having had an engagement with the combined fleets, and that England had TAKEN SEVENTEEN SAIL OF FRENCH AND SPANISH SHIPS OF THE LINE! Theſe reports ſtill lack confirmation.

William Windham to Lord Grenville:

IN great calamities and dangers, men flock together, even where the distress is such as to leave no hopes of relief from any combination of counsels or exertions. Disastrous as events have certainly been, there will be a hope that all is not yet lost, any that much may possibly gained, if the remains of Mack's army have not actually surrendered, and he himself become a prisoner. It is that last incident of the piece, that finishing stroke, of the general himself being captured—"Romeo banished"—that seems to extinguish all chance of recovery; not, probably, on account of the value of the general himself, but by the evidence which it contains of the state to which things must have been reduced.

The Connecticut Courant:

THE public rejoicings laſt night were partial—Lord Nelſon's death had impreſſed every heart with grief. At the theatre tributes were paid to his memory—there were but few illuminations—tonight, we undeſtand, there will be a general one.

Admiral Collingwood's conduct has obtained the fulleſt approbation; and laſt night diſpatches were ſent off to Plymouth to be forwarded to him by the Acaſta, containing a commiſſion, which appoints him to the commander of the ſhips in the Mediterannean with the ſame power that Lord Nelſon had.

Reeve—Journal of a Residence in Vienna:

WENT to the Wien Theatre to see the new opera 'Fidelio,' the music composed by Beethoven. The story and plan of the piece are a miserable mixture of low manners and romantic situations; the airs, duets, and choruses equal to any praise. The several overtures, for there is an overture to each act, appeared to be too artificially composed to be generally pleasing, especially on being first heard. Intricacy is the character of Beethoven's music, and it required a well-practised ear to understand and distinguish its beauties. This is the first opera he ever composed, and it was very much applauded; a copy of complimentary verses was showered down from the upper gallery at the end of the piece. Beethoven presided at the pianoforte and directed the performance himself. He is a small dark young-looking man, wears spectacles, and is like Mr. Koenig.

The French armies said to have taken Brünn and to be in pursuit of the Russians toward Olmütz. The whole of the Austrian national dominions are overrun, and the government chased and overthrown. The books and state papers are given up and perused by Talleyrand, who is here, living in the empress's apartments and sitting in the emperor's box and the theatre.

20

END OF AN ARMY

North Italy; Moravia:
October 28–December 3, 1805

T HE River Adige slants across the Italian plain to fall
into the Adriatic below Venice. It formed the boundary line between France and Austria; the armies of
both sides were concentrated along it, at the roots of the
mountains and around the Renaissance town of Verona. The
bridges were down; both commanders had established stockades and batteries where the approaches looked across snag-
toothed piles. When deductions were made for guard detachments and line-of-communication troops, Masséna had
some 55,000 in presence, Archduke Karl, 75,000, which
gave the latter the initiative; but the orders of the Aulic
Council were to wait his attack till the Neapolitans had come
up from the south and the Russians in from the east.

Masséna's assignment was to defend the river line, but by
October 17, when he learned that the vast march to Ulm
was in full swing, there had been no sign of movement from
the enemy. He therefore conceived that his defense could
best be managed by giving Austria something to think about.
That night he launched boatloads of light troops across the
Adige and carried the nearest stockades by surprise. All day
there was street-to-street fighting in Verona beyond the
stream; toward evening enough of the bridges had been re-

built for artillery to come over, and the town was won, with the advantage of allowing the French to operate on either bank.

The main highroad out of Verona and through the Julian Alps to Austria follows close along the lower steps of the mountains. After losing the town Prince Karl retreated about eight miles to the village of Caldiero, where a spur comes down close over the route, and dug in. His right rested on the height of Colognola and could not be turned save by a very circuitous march; his center on the stone-built village itself; and his left on the banks of the Adige, here very marshy, the ground much cut up by dikes and canals. The position deprived Masséna of much of his gain. Facing Karl, he could not reach the south bank save by going back through Verona.

Neither army moved till 28 October, when the news of the capitulation of Ulm came in and was received with joyful salvoes of artillery on the French side. It was obvious that Karl must fly back to the defense of the Austrian homeland. Despite the disparity of force, Masséna resolved to attack him, inflict damage, make the retreat as difficult as possible; despite his need for speed, Karl determined to stun his adversary out of any idea of pursuit by a stiff covering attack.

Masséna was in four divisions. That led by General Gabriel-Jean-Joseph Molitor, his best fighting officer, was to storm the height of Colognola. The divisions of Duhesme and Gardanne would make a pinning attack along both sides of the highroad in the center, while Division Verdier, 10,000 strong, should cross to the south bank of the Adige, then cross it again in boats behind the Austrian left wing, the whole operation being a double envelopment.

The Archduke sent his General Hillinger with a division of 5,000 by a circuit through the mountains to fall on Verona in the French rear. Graf Bellegarde on the Austrian right was to make a heavy covering attack from the Colognola hills; and the Archduke himself, with his main body and best troops, would attack straight along the highroad, slanting slightly to the northwest—a plan to break off and destroy the French left wing. Both attacks were set for October 30.

The French moved earlier as was their habit, with Molitor already at break of day driving up the slope against Co-

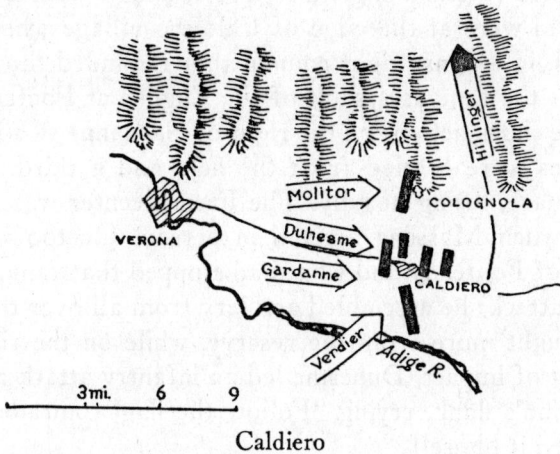

Caldiero

lognola. He captured one redoubt, but before he could make any real progress Bellegarde had his own men in order and his attack under way. Molitor was thrown out of his redoubt and, badly outnumbered, had all he could do to hold a line just outside the Austrian fortifications against attacks which lasted all day. Verdier's double crossing of the Adige came off no better, mainly because the Archduke had prepared for his own attack by anchoring his left along the marshy stream with strong artillery protection. Verdier was late getting started (his lack of energy this day would cost him his command), his barges were seen and taken under fire by the Austrian guns. Nearly half the boats were sunk; the remainder carried only one regiment to the north bank, and that so far to the west that it reached the shore in front of the Austrian lines instead of behind them. The General might still have accomplished something by attacking vigorously through the squash along the left bank, but either his heart or his head misgave him at the sight of all those cannon. He did nothing, his 10,000 were out of the battle.

Thus by not later than ten o'clock, when the morning fog began to lift, Masséna's double attack had failed and the initiative was wholly with Austria. Duhesme and Gardanne had worked forward in good style, sweeping outposts before them, and were at the edge of Caldiero village when Karl attacked, in a dense tight column that reminded those who saw it of the famous assault of the English at Fontenoy. It was pure shock action; on the right of Gardanne two French battalions were carried from the field and a third had to form square, losing heavily. The French center was almost broken when Masséna arrived in person. He too was reminded of Fontenoy and what had stopped that famous column of attack; he assembled artillery from all over the field and brought more from the reserve, while on the right of the point of impact, Duhesme led an infantry attack against the column's flank, crying "Follow the flag, comrades!" as he carried it himself.

Austria was halted and turned back, and Duhesme's swing carried him right in among the houses. Prince Karl brought up reserves and drove him out; Duhesme charged in again, the village began to burn, and all afternoon long the combat swayed back and forth through the littered streets at hand-to-hand, with the Archduke probing and probing for a spot to shoot in the fine Austrian cavalry. Masséna pushed his guns forward in every interval, till they were on the infantry line and the cannoneers swinging rammers to beat off attackers. The guns won in a sense, for the Austrians never did get room to work up the cavalry charge that might have torn everything apart; but when night put an end to the fighting, Caldiero was Karl's, the French butchery-bill was 6,000 killed and wounded, they had lost 2,000 prisoners, and Masséna found it necessary to retire on Verona and reorganize.

Karl himself had lost 5,700 men; what with Masséna's firmness and the news from Ulm, he dared no longer stay, but sent his baggage ahead through the night, dropped a small rearguard in Caldiero, and took to the roads. This ended by making his losses for the brief campaign heavier than those of the French, for the 5,000 on circuit under General Hillinger first got lost among the hill tracks, then were beset by swarms of French light horse, and ended by being surrounded and captured to a man, including their general.

Masséna had made a good battle against a stronger enemy (if one counts out the error of the too-fancy move of Division Verdier), and a fine campaign, but the decision was really made not by him but on the Danube. Archduke Karl retreated, defending every river with persistence and skill against an enemy whose weaker force hardly allowed him to drive in. But now he must take an eccentric route through the Julian Alps by Görtz and Laibach, from whence he climbed over another mountain to reach Marburg on the Drave in the last third of November. Masséna halted his troops at the foot of the Julian Alps, reaching hands and messengers toward Marmont's Corps of the main army, which at that date was on its march to Leoben.

Up in the Vorarlberg meanwhile, Ney's had been the earlier of the two French corps to make contact with the enemy. The Austrian leader was that Jellačič who had escaped the ruins of Ulm with a good part of his troops. He had some 12,000 altogether, part of them from Archduke Johann's Tyrolean command, 2,000 more than Ney. But in accordance with the usual Austrian cordon system, Jellačič had parceled his men out into groups to watch all the deep valleys between ridges, where the rivers that flow into Danube have their rise. Ney came on him through Kempten, rapidly and well concentrated; before Jellačič could pull his scattered men together, his force was split in halves, the larger segment of about 6,500 being thrown off in a northwesterly direction toward the shore of the Bodensee. There it ran into Augereau and, caught between the two marshals, laid down its arms on November 19.

The smaller group, under the French Prince de Rohan, had a strange adventure. Rohan seems to have been a good deal of a soldier; he lost very few men by desertion or any other cause as he led his division through the mountains to the upper valley of the Inn, thence to Innsbruck and the Brenner Pass, making for Venice, where there was a strong Austrian garrison. Now Masséna was far to the east by this time, among the foothills of the Julians, so that Rohan encountered no opposition till he drew close to Venice itself. But there he found St. Cyr with 20,000 men, just arrived from Naples; and St. Cyr, though considerably surprised at finding so many Austrians in Masséna's back areas, was not in the least at a loss what to do about them, especially as he had cavalry and Rohan had none, all the Austrian horses having been lost among the mountains. The French arranged a trap; Rohan walked into it; was shown its dimensions under a flag of truce, and surrendered with all his men.

Archduke Johann had meanwhile received word of the disasters to the north and south of him, and of the presence of two marshals with their corps on his front, with the possibility that he would soon have Bernadotte and Marmont across his line of retreat. He retired so rapidly along the line of the Slavic rivers that a good many men had to be left behind; fell in on Archduke Karl at Marburg on 26 November, and the force under the Kaiserish brothers now totaled 80,000 men.

Thus all the picadors, banderillos, and the men who drag out dead horses were cleared from the arena; the duel of matador and bull was about to begin.

II

The question being which was matador and which bull. From Kutuzov's headquarters it seemed that Napoléon's rush had carried him to a position that would soon become impossible. The French line of communications stretched back 100 miles to the Rhine, and many of their troops were required to maintain it. Archduke Karl was not far from one of their flanks with an army as great as they could bring to the field, and opposite the other French flank, a still greater Austro-Russian force was less than a week from concentration. Hovering over Napoléon's left rear was the mighty army of Prussia, the Sparta of the modern world, ready to strike. The Russian general had spent men and ground to gain time, but time was now nearly run out, the French were penned south of the Danube, Kutuzov had only to wait at Krems for the arrival of his reinforcements.

But on the morning of November 14 he learned that the French were by no means penned south of the Danube and he had better leave Krems in much haste. The day before, riding out of Vienna as rapidly as they had entered it, Murat and Lannes, with a battalion of the latter's grenadiers, came to the great bridge at Spitz, which winds sinuously across the wooded isles separating the subsidiary channels before leaping the main stream of the river. A single hussar was on vedette at the south end; he fired a shot and galloped away across the planks. As the two marshals rounded a clump of trees to gain a view of the main span, they saw guns emplaced at the far end, with some infantry soldiers drawn up around them, and could make out that the whole bridge was mined. Both men had put on their best uniforms for the entry into Vienna—red morocco boots, gold-spangled tunics, ostrich plumes, and blazing stars. They rode unhesitatingly forward onto the bridge, accompanied only by General Bertrand of the staff; informed the cannoneers at the far end (who were too astonished to think of shooting down three men) that an armistice had just been signed and they wished to talk to the commander of the post.

He was a very old and, as luck would have it, very exalted prince named Auersperg, a member of the Aulic Council, who knew all about the plan for gaining time by armistice negotiations while Graf von Meerfeldt made his circling attack of a few days before. It seemed just possible that something had come of that debate; but he argued, and as he argued, the French grenadiers began to advance down the bridge from the other end, followed by a small group of sappers, who pulled the fuses from the mines and threw them in the river. An Austrian sergeant ordered the gunners to fire.

"Is this your famous discipline," inquired Murat down his nose, "where sergeants countermand the orders of generals?" Auersperg placed the sergeant in arrest. Another gunner swung his piece around to point at the marshals themselves; Lannes coolly walked over and sat down on it, and when Auersperg asked why the grenadiers kept coming forward during the parley, replied that they were only marking time to keep their feet warm against the November cold, while Murat and Bertrand wheeled round to shut off His Highness' field of vision. The next moment the grenadiers had arrived, seized guns and gunners, pointed the pieces in the other direction, and the passage of the Danube was won.

By evening Murat with most of his cavalry was out on the west-running road to Stockerau, where the track forks, with one branch going to Budweis, the other through Znaim to Iglau. The rest of the horsemen were on the road straight north to Brünn, while Lannes and Division Suchet of Soult had crossed the river. That night the Emperor himself passed rapidly through Vienna, hardly giving the famous city a glance, and rode the picket lines till midnight, so little satisfied with what he found that he issued a general order about it: "One must always assume during the night that the enemy has made arrangements to attack at daybreak."

With the capture of the Spitz bridge it was clear to Napoléon also that Kutuzov must hurriedly quit Krems. Bernadotte received orders to rebuild the bridge at that spot and get over as soon as possible. Mortier's corps (which the Emperor imagined to be still on the left bank) was placed under Bernadotte's local command as a reserve. Ney was to turn any further Tyrolean operations over to the Bavarians and hurry toward the main army; Marmont to burn all the bridges from Graz up through the Wilde-Alpen range and leave posts with a few guns in the defiles to impose delays on Archduke Karl, should that leader take it into his head to march on Vienna by the shortest route. Marmont's main body to be posted at Leoben.

During the next few days the furious marching, which had carried Davout (for instance) 170 miles in 16 days over bad mountain roads in winter, went on without a break. Lannes was pushed out the Budweis road with two of Soult's divisions behind him; Davout sent one division to Pressburg to hold off anything the Austrians might have coming from Hungary, and took two others out the road to Brünn. Bernadotte was slow about the Krems bridge and got a stinging letter from Berthier:

"The Emperor is much annoyed that at a time when Prince Murat, with Marshals Lannes and Soult, is fighting at two days' distance from Vienna, you have not passed a single man across the Danube; he hopes that when my staff officer returns, he will bring the news that all your troops are over and are pursuing the Russians."

If Bernadotte had in fact hurried across, he could have made things extremely uncomfortable for Kutuzov. With relation to the other corps, the Russians had the shorter route, through Ebersbrunn-Meissau-Jetzeldorf; but it was all mountain and—though none of the roads into Bohemia can be described as boulevards—those over which the Russ were marching were really tracks, especially hard on wagons and artillery. Murat, with Lannes, two divisions of Soult, and one of Davout in close support, was harried forward with all speed in an effort to reach Znaim before Kutuzov and block his path—or at least to strike into the enemy's moving columns, break up its trains, and cut off some troops. Kutuzov had foreseen action along this line, and as he marched, threw out Bagration (who had made the stout defense at Amstetten) to Hollabrunn with 8,000 picked men and orders to resist to the last, halt the French rush. He could afford so large a detachment, since the Vienna garrison of 15,000, with some assistance from Hungary, had joined his column; in any case, fewer would not be a detainer.

Murat struck the outposts of this delaying force on the

afternoon of the 15th and, inspired to imagine that he could move it from the path by talk as he had Prince Auersperg's bridge guards, sent forward a messenger to ask about an armistice. But he was now dealing with one of the most cun-

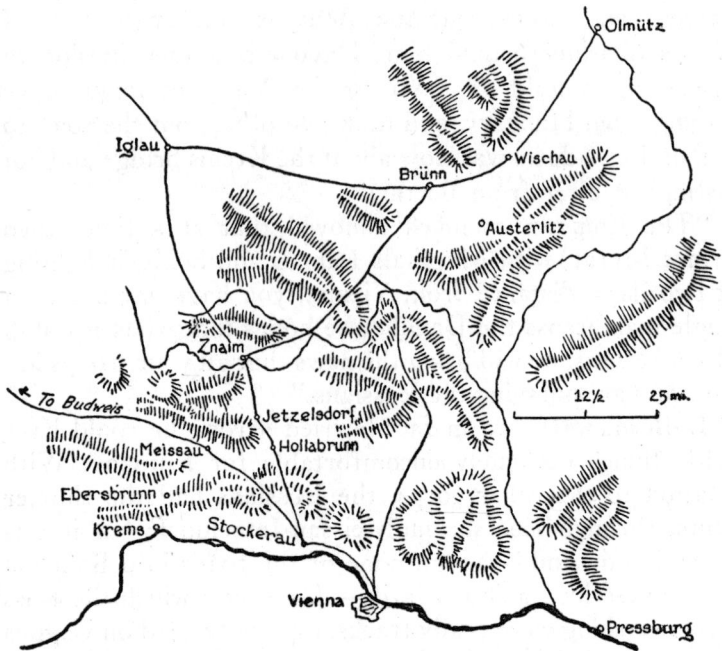

Vienna to Austerlitz

ning men of a court where cunning was a condition of survival. Kutuzov instantly sent back one of the Tsar's aides (there was always a Tsar's aide somewhere around; he had dozens) named Winzigerode, all glittering with medals, who adroitly flattered Murat far into the night, while the Russian main body made a terrific forced march. Toward midnight there was an agreement (which Winzigerode knew would never be ratified) for the Russians to retire from the war, unmolested to their homeland. Murat happily sent off an express to the Emperor in Vienna. By noon the estafette was back with Napoléon's comment:

"It is impossible for me to find words to express my discontent. You are in command only of my vanguard and you have no right whatever to make an armistice without my orders; you are making me lose the fruit of a whole campaign. Break the armistice immediately and march on the enemy. The officer who made it had no more right to do so than you. Officers are nothing when they lack written authority, and this man had nothing of the kind."

Soult's three divisions were now all at the point of contact; the battle began in the afternoon. The ground was open and the only formation possible was that of opposing lines of infantry, which engaged in a furious musketry combat before falling on with the bayonet. The French were so much stronger that as more and more men came in, they lapped round both Russian flanks, and pierced Bagration's center at the coming of twilight in a struggle as hard as any man present had ever seen. The Russian commander, waving a red scroll of honor the Tsar had given him, got what men he could together and cut his way out through the dark, as Mortier had done a week before, leaving behind a smoking village with 3,000 corpses in it. He had gained just enough time for Kutuzov to reach Znaim, where the march was on hard roads at last. It reached Brünn without further molestation, pushing through it to Olmütz, and there on the 19th was joined by Buxhövden's vanguard. Army united.

That same day, Napoléon and his Guard were at Brünn, with Lannes and one division of Davout, temporarily under Lannes' orders. Soult was cantoned out to the right, at the small village of Austerlitz; at Znaim stood Bernadotte, with two French divisions and one Bavarian; two more of Davout's divisions were fairly close to the front (that of Gudin remained at Pressburg, as flank guard on the Danube); most of the cavalry were out in front, or to the flanks. Marmont was still at Leoben, and had just received a rebuke from the Emperor for wandering too far afield; Mortier was in Vienna, but his men were so much worn by battle that Napoléon did not wish to use him, save in an ultimate emergency, and therefore left him in the capital. Not counting Marmont or Mortier then, or Division Gudin, or the cavalry on detached duty, some 70,000 men could be brought together for battle in a few days of marching; and battle was what the Emperor now expected from the sanguine temper of the Russians opposed to him, and the fact that Kutuzov could count his retreat a success.

There was bread and wine in plenitude, now that Vienna had fallen, but the terrible marching had worn out many wheeled vehicles and the men's shoes, so that many were barefoot in the early snow. Orders were issued for the requisitioning of leather; the pace of movement slowed.

III

From Berlin, the Tsar and his suite traveled down rather slowly to Weimar, where Alexander wished to see his sister, who was domiciled in that Athens of Germany, being married to one of the Dukes. The old Grand Duke received his visitors cordially; in spite of his age he was sound as an oak and took long horseback rides every day. The literary men he kept as pets were of course invited to the palace, and Herrn Herder and Wieland made themselves agreeable, discoursing on a variety of subjects with great wit and capacity, to the delight of Alexander and the young men of the Secret Committee. The Duke's peculiar treasure, Herr von Goethe, was somewhat distrait; a ducal aside informed the distinguished guest that the poet had not been the same man since the death of his gifted young friend Schiller during the previous May, and it was unfortunately probable that not much more would come from his pen.

The Tsar and his party received news of the fall of Vienna while they were there, with word that Kaiser Franz, after a short trip into Hungary to rouse the warlike Magyars, would meet them at Olmütz in Bohemia. Little though Alexander liked camp life, it was essential that the invitation be accepted in order to look after the interests of his own people. The majority of the army assembling there would be Russians, but the protocol of the coalition made Kaiser Franz supreme commander under present conditions. The journey was made by easy stages.

It was the first time the two rulers had met; Alexander found his fellow monarch neither intelligent nor witty, but of a genial, philosophical turn of mind, so little discouraged by the earlier defeats that he commented easily on this not being the first time misfortune had befallen him. While they were talking Graf Cobenzl joined them. He had been visited by Gentz, who in a tearful interview (for the intellectual leader of the opposition to France was not oversupplied with physical courage) had borrowed some money from him. In such crucial hours (Cobenzl reported him as saying) it was necessary for sovereigns to place themselves at the head of their armies, as Great Frederick of glorious memory had done.

The advice chimed with Kaiser Franz' ideas, but the young men of the Secret Committee tried to remonstrate with Cobenzl so far as it concerned Alexander. They said they knew old Kutuzov; up to this point he had conducted a very able campaign, but as soon as Alexander began giving orders, he would stop doing so, since in Russia only His Majesty was allowed to have ideas on any subject that fell upon his notice, in opposition to the Austrian system where underlings submitted plans for the Imperial approval. Better the two monarchs should retire.

Cobenzl was adamant—because he was an imprudent and ill-guided man, Czartoryski remarked to his diary, a comment which ignored any real reason behind the needle which the Austrian had just applied to Alexander. There was such a reason, however, and it had nothing to do with the quasi-religious violence against revolution in any form, which Cobenzl had picked up from Gentz as the attitude most proper to such a case. The question of strategy had been discussed at Olmütz castle, and Cobenzl knew as well as the young men of the Secret Committee what Kutuzov had in mind. He

wished to retreat still farther, into Poland, adding Bennigsen's oncoming army to his forces—and this was a plan
which not only Cobenzl, but the entire Kriegshofrat, regarded with exceeding disfavor. Not only would Kaiser
Franz be practically an exile, who would have to bear the
accusation of having abandoned his people—not only would
the general direction of operations be turned over to the
Russians—but further retreat was so unnecessary in a military sense that the suspicion arose that Kutuzov was advo-
cating it for other than military reasons.

The Kaiser's personal chief of staff said as much, plainly
—Colonel Weyrother, a man of great learning and personal
charm, whose erudition did not prevent him from being an
extraordinarily fine performer in a ballroom, or from having
earned a high reputation for courage in battle. He had been
Archduke Johann's staff planner during the Hohenlinden
campaign, but the misfortunes of that operation were held
due to the bad weather and the obstinacy of the Archduke,
so that Weyrother was not blamed. In October he had
traveled to Pulawi to meet the Tsar, and had completely
conquered him—was probably the one strategist in whom
both monarchs had complete confidence.

Weyrother accompanied the two emperors from Olmütz
up to the front on 28 November, when headquarters were at
Prossnitz, with the outposts of both sides in contact between
that place and Brünn. Bagration with the cavalry had pushed
forward to Wischau the day before and captured the town
with some French prisoners after a brief fight. Everyone was
cheerful and full of energy, the French had in various other
contacts shown a disposition to give back, their horsemen
were not out so widely as before, and that night there came
through the lines the usurper's aide, Colonel Savary, with
a somewhat meaningless message complimenting the Tsar on
his arrival in the field and expressing a desire to become his
friend.

At the same time there was a note from Haugwitz, who
was coming down in person with the Prussian ultimatum to

Napoléon. He had halted in Prague with an attack of dysentery, but would present himself before the French Emperor at least by December 1. The Allied monarchs were agreed that Napoléon, no little appalled by the strength of the forces assembling against him, was disposed to treat. Soon after Colonel Savary had left, they sent forward an officer to discover what terms the man would offer for peace, one of the emissary's staff returning on the evening of November 30, technically to bear a message, actually to report that the French were in general retreat, everywhere flowing back in the direction of Brünn. The outposts confirmed this; so did Prince Dolgoruki, who had ridden up to the lines to meet Napoléon, and who had noted that the French engineers were hastily throwing up fortifications.

There was a council of war late that night, with Colonel Weyrother doing most of the talking. The question, he said, was whether to operate by the right, in order to link up with the oncoming Prussians, or to move by the left toward a union with Archduke Karl. He favored the latter; it would at the same time cut Napoléon's communications with Vienna and throw him back against the mountains of western Bohemia. If the French made a rapid retreat to avoid this stroke, the Allied army could the more quickly unite with that of Karl and obtain a crushing superiority. If the enemy did not retreat at once, they could certainly be broken in a battle by an attack on that left wing of theirs, which was a prolongation of the line of communications. The best advices were that Napoléon did not have over 40,000 men under his immediate command (he had scattered his troops recklessly), while Austria and Russia together had 85,000, well concentrated.

Alexander and Kaiser Franz approved all this after some discussion, instructed the colonel to draw a battle plan, and bade the advance go on. The plan was not complete till the next night, December 1, when all the high commanding generals were assembled. Weyrother was a close student of the campaigns of Frederick the Great, and had detected a remarkable resemblance between the positions of the armies here and those at the Prussian king's famous victory of Rossbach. This battle had been arranged on that perfect model, an attack in the oblique order, which would throw the majority of the Austro-Russian forces onto a single flank of the French, and that the sensitive flank, the one of their line of communication.

The Allied moves in feeling for that line of communication had brought the gross of both armies a little south of the main Brünn-Olmütz highway, with the French occupying some hills of fairly steep ascent, but with flat tops, behind the brook Goldbach, which flows south across the highway. This brook breaks out into a series of ponds, which echelon to the southwest, and thus forced the French right to occupy low ground, or else to angle back along the heights behind. It was across the low ground north of the ponds, through the villages of Tellnitz and Sokolnitz, that Colonel Weyrother would deliver his oblique attack, both the ponds and the marshy ground around them being frozen hard enough to bear artillery.

East of the Goldbach a very considerable plateau called the Pratzen dominates the whole region before sliding southward to the ponds, westward to the Goldbach. The Allied troops had forced through the village of Austerlitz behind this eminence to drive the French from the crest on the day before and now held it firmly. The height afforded admirable opportunities for observation and control of the battle. It would be occupied by the main body of the Allied army, and from it the move to turn and crush the French right would be launched.

For the attack the Allied army was divided into commands called "Columns," which were really corps, and would be semi-independent on the battlefield, since the movement involved such vast masses of men, and was of so wide a scope, seven miles from flank to flank. Bagration's vanguard column of 13,000 men was placed astride the Brünn-Olmütz highway opposite where the French had their

main strength; it was to attack and pin them there, the key
of the position and Bagration's objective being a little round
hill called the Santon,* just north of the road. It was a hard
task for Bagration, but he was a hard hitter and would be

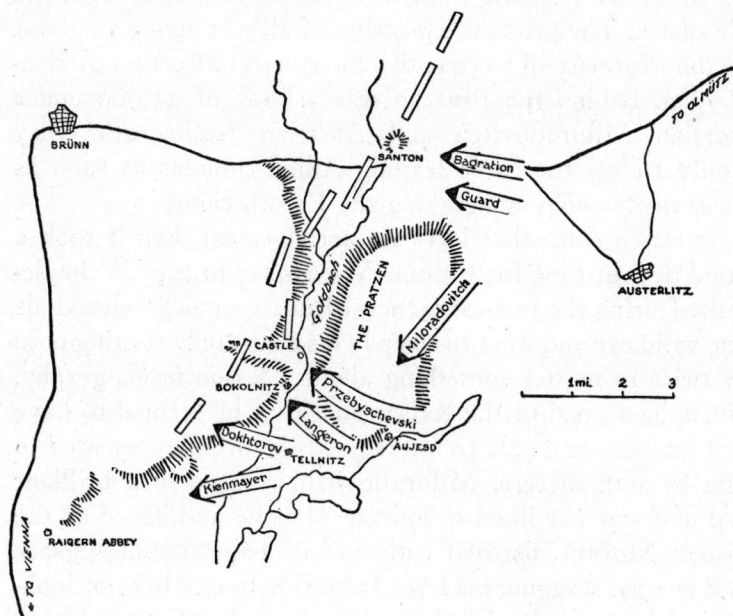

Austerlitz: Weyrother's plan; his picture of the French formation

sustained in his attack by a column of 6,000 cavalry under
Prince Liechtenstein (now out of sight of the enemy behind
the Pratzen); he would have as reserve the Russian Imperial
Guard of 8,500, under Grand Duke Constantine.

Kienmayer, with the Austrian cavalry of the left and some
light Croatian infantry, would lead the attack on that flank,
close along the edge of the ponds, covering the infantry as it
moved in, and sustaining it against any French who debouched from Raigern Abbey, along the Brünn-Vienna road.
General Dokhtorov, with 8,500 of the infantry left, would

* It was so named by French veterans who had been in Egypt and thought
the spire of a little chapel on top resembled the minaret on a hillock named
Santon there; and the name has stuck. No one knows what it was called before.

follow Kienmayer and attack Tellnitz; General Langeron, 12,000, to point on Sokolnitz; General Przebyschevski, 14,-000, to assault in the region of Sokolnitz Castle, a little upstream from the village. All these three columns to turn north and roll up the French line after having crossed the Goldbach. The pre-battle position of all was across the crest of the Pratzen; all were under the general direction of Buxhövden. Behind the Pratzen was a body of 25,000 under Russian Miloradovitch and Austrian Kollowrath; they would follow the three leading Allied columns as soon as these made room by breaking the French right.

It was a somewhat intricate arrangement, and it took a good deal of time for Colonel Weyrother to explain the details. During the process General Kutuzov quietly closed his one valid eye and went to sleep in his chair, only rousing once or twice to mutter something about a lesson in geography. Since the arrival of the Kaiser and Tsar he seemed to have lost interest, and only countersigned the orders presented to him by staff officers. Miloradovitch, dressed in a brilliant red uniform (he liked to imitate what he had heard of the urgent Murat), listened with an expression of intelligence and energy, wagging his head from side to side but not looking at the map. Buxhövden wore a puzzled frown; Dokhtorov bent over the map, noisily sucking his breath between his teeth. Only Langeron, who was a French émigré, expressed any skepticism—"What if the French attack?"—but was patiently argued down by Weyrother, who showed how impossible that would be. As the officers left the room, they passed through a little group of Croatian Grenzers, who were singing the melancholy tunes of their own country around a fire. The attack was set for daybreak.

IV

On the 28th the Emperor had a row to settle. Lannes had been challenging Soult to a duel, the result of an interview the day before, when the former asked Napoléon whether the position beyond Brünn were not untenable? After the marshal had left, the Emperor remarked frowningly that this was the first time he had heard the stormy Lannes advise retreat; and Soult, who happened to be present, agreed that such conduct on the part of a marshal almost defied explanation. Only when the duel question came up did it develop that the idea of retreating had been hatched up by Soult and Murat, who persuaded Lannes to bell the cat because he was the only man of the group who did not fear to say to Napoléon anything that came into his head.

That was behind now; behind was Haugwitz' ultimatum, who had arrived only on 1 December, and readily agreed to go on to Vienna till the pending great battle was over. Behind were two or three days of uncertainty, when the Emperor rode all over the ground from Austerlitz village back to Brünn, climbed the Pratzen and wandered among the pools. The messages and interviews across the lines were over, including the visit of a gilded and insolent Russian prince named Dolgoruki, who said he had come to make an armistice, but when asked on what terms, only answered that his master wished to rid the world of a tyrant and that the small nations of Europe must be free from every influence but that of the liberalizing Russians. Those messengers of freedom were now coming forward so menacingly that on the night of November 30, the Emperor wrote to Talleyrand on a board spread across his knees that there would be a heavy battle here: "In writing to Paris, do not speak of this, for it will disquiet my wife."

The obvious place to accept battle was on the great Pratzen eminence, which offered such good positions for artillery, with concealment for cavalry behind. But as Napoléon rode his rounds, the small explosions of outpost bickering beyond Austerlitz floated through the still air, and the light horse reported that the slow Russians were sliding steadily southward. They were trying to outflank him on that side, cut his communications with Vienna. The attempt could be defeated from the Pratzen readily enough, but gradually there worked through his mind the concept that inflicting such a repulse on the enemy would be "only an ordinary battle"; would have to be followed by moves leading to another combat, in which the enemy might rally on Bennigsen's oncoming command, or the Archduke Karl, or the Prussians.

Why not give the French right a still more impressive appearance of weakness, so that instead of trying to sweep out beyond it, the Austro-Russians would attack there to roll up our line?—invite them to make a close-in attack, instead of a flank march? For such an attempt they must inevitably draw troops from the rest of their line, especially from their center, where they will consider the steep slopes of the Pratzen height a protection. Their front can then be broken through, their army not beaten, but destroyed.

It was only necessary to concentrate toward the left center, then wait till the enemy were committed to their flank attack. The French left was accordingly drawn in from north of the Brünn-Olmütz highway, till Santon Hill, north of the road, formed the outer anchor of the line. The hill itself was fortified and a battery of twelve heavy guns placed on it. Behind it, Marshal Lannes, with his one division of infantry (Oudinot, a grenadier division, big and very good), plus Division Suchet of Soult, and Division Caffarelli of Davout, which had been operating under Lannes for several days.

Bernadotte's march reports were excellent; with divisions Drouet and Rivaud, he would be in during the late afternoon of December 1, and would be placed rightward of Lannes, with the Imperial Guard immediately behind him. Murat, with the cavalry reserve in six divisions, to which were attached for the battle the light cavalry of Lannes and Bernadotte, was drawn up behind the marshals of the left wing. Soult's three remaining divisions (Vandamme, St. Hilaire, Legrand) held the heights down to the villages of Sokolnitz and Tellnitz—Vandamme and St. Hilaire in tight formation, the other division in line. It was not till evening of December 1 that Davout arrived, having marched his men 70 miles in 44 hours. He had with him the infantry division of Friant, Bourcier's and Klein's heavy dragoons; the Emperor placed him near Raigern Abbey and gave him general charge of the right wing. Except for a plug to hold the left (Lannes) and one to hold the right rear (Davout), all the French army was now piled up like a tightly coiled spring, ready to deliver its force against the Pratzen and break the enemy in two as he marched across the front.

A new tactical directive had been issued four days before, a special formation for fighting Russians, heavier than the usual French battle disposition, with the brigade as a unit. The first regiment of each brigade should advance as an extremely dense skirmisher-line; the second regiment in tight column of battalions behind, with light artillery between the columns, ready to fall on with the bayonet as soon as the stubborn enemies were shaken by gunfire and musketry. Cavalry behind each brigade to insure by its menace that the Russians would tighten up to receive the gunfire, to pursue them when broken, and to hold head against the fast-moving Cossacks, who might get around. By night of 1 December the order had filtered down to battalion commanders; everyone understood where he must be. A proclamation had been issued in which the soldiers were told that tomorrow's battle would finish the campaign.

The night was dark and cold. Napoléon stepped from his headquarters behind Soult's men in line, the only building in the whole field large enough to have room for a map table; stepped and looked across to the heights where Austria and Russia were aligned in dark silence. "Before tomorrow night I'll have that army," he said with a gesture, and late though it was, had horses brought and began to ride through the bivouac to make sure everything was in order. From the roughness of the ground, it was necessary for the escort to make torches of pine branches to see their way. The cavalcade had not gone more than 200 yards before Napoléon was recognized; the sleeping soldiers roused, and recalled that tomorrow was the anniversary of the coronation. They seized straw from their beds on the ground and made torches to answer torches, so that the Emperor rode down an endless alley of burning lights and a long roaring surf of *"Vive l'Empereur!"*

Beyond, on the Pratzen, Tsar and Kaiser had long since retired, the earlier to be afoot for the battle. As the twinkling points of fire burst forth on the opposite hills officers were just leaving Colonel Weyrother's conference. They paused to gaze, and Przebyschevski, whom the Russians rather disdainfully called "Prishprish" (he was a Pole), wondered aloud whether the French might be building false campfires to cover a retreat. Comte Langeron, a little sadly, said they did not know his countrymen.

v

At four in the morning Napoléon left his tent and rode with the marshals and their staffs down into the Goldbach valley. There was an overcast above, a heavy fog in all the depressions and over the ponds. Under the first uncertain light the growl of cannon began and the rumor of marching armed men moving from left to right across the front. The Emperor's face suffused with pleasure; he rode back to the eminence from which the whole field could be seen, and, just as he reached it, off to the east beyond Pratzen the sun burst forth gloriously in all their faces—the sun of Austerlitz, showing Pratzen almost empty of troops. "Soldiers, we must finish this campaign in a peal of thunder that will confound the pride of our enemies!" the Emperor shouted to a regiment he passed.

Of the corps leaders only Davout failed to hear him, for Davout already had enough to do, down along the Goldbach beyond the ponds. Kienmayer had struck early at Tellnitz. A regiment of light infantry and some Corsican sharpshooters were under cover in the houses of that hamlet, and the long vineyard-covered slopes behind Goldbach. They emptied a good many of the Austrian saddles, the horsemen could neither co-operate nor work up a rapid swing in that restricted space, and not until Dokhtorov's massive column had taken some losses from the sharpshooters were the Goldbach crossings won at eight o'clock.

Buxhövden was with this column. He was unaware that in their anxiety to keep the commands from mingling, Dokh-

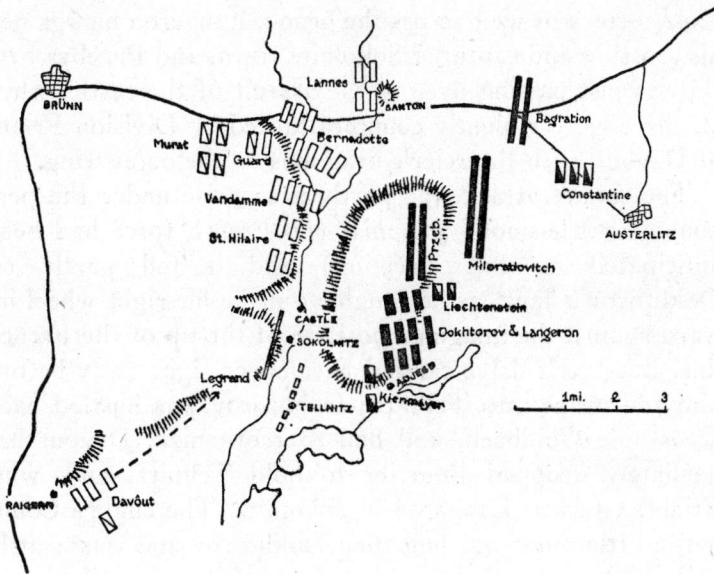

Austerlitz: the dawn position

torov and Langeron had allowed a gap to open between their columns, still further accentuated by the fact that Liechtenstein's Austrian horse, moving to the Allied right, had become entangled with both Langeron and Przebyschevski as it tried to cross them at right angles. In the disentanglement, a second gap opened between Langeron and Przebyschevski; the latter was thus late, and so much crowded in between Langeron's advance and the base of Pratzen height that he could not deploy and must move forward in a dense and narrow mass.

The forces on the French side of the Goldbach, which in

the beginning contained only Division Legrand of Soult, numbered perhaps 6,000 men, against 34,000 Allies, but they were well scattered among accidents in the ground, fighting against opponents who had to climb in masses out of the marshy brook, and for a time they fought against Dokhtorov alone, then against Dokhtorov and Langeron. The Russian soldiers came on valiantly; by eight-thirty Dokhtorov was well across the brook, Langeron had gained his crossing and captured Sokolnitz town, and Przebyschevski was just passing over to the assault of the castle, when all three were violently counterattacked by Division Friant of Davout, with Bourcier's dragoons on the outer wing.

The counterattack was partly a surprise under the pennons of battle-smoke and mist (no French force had been anticipated in that direction) and it fell partly on Dokhtorov's flank, as he sought to make his right wheel inward against the imagined position of the tip of the French line. Bourcier's drive carried Kienmayer right away before him and broke into Tellnitz; Dokhtorov was hustled back across the Goldbach, and had to reorganize. Davout immediately dropped Bourcier to hold Tellnitz, and, with Friant, attacked Langeron in Sokolnitz. The émigré Count had a little more warning than Dokhtorov and was a little better leader. The fighting turned very fierce, the village was taken and retaken half a dozen times with shooting across parapets of dead men, but Legrand was aiding Friant in a front and flank attack against men who could not make their numbers count, and by nine o'clock Davout had gained his point, Langeron was halted.

It must have been nearly an hour before that when Napoléon, seeing the Pratzen clear under the clean sunlight, turned to Soult: "How long do you require to reach those heights?"

"Less than twenty minutes, for my troops are at the bottom of the valley, covered by fog and the smoke of the bivouac; the enemy cannot see them."

"In that case, let us wait a quarter of an hour more."

They had waited. It would be just when the sound of battle rose loudest from the valley where Davout was halting Langeron that the Emperor gave the word, the marshals galloped to their posts, the big divisions of Vandamme and St. Hilaire crossed and began to ascend, with Bernadotte's divisions echeloned behind to their left.

The columns of Miloradovitch and Kollowrath, accompanied by Alexander, Franz, and their staffs, had just begun to slant across the Pratzen toward the sound of guns on their left front, marching in loose route order for speed, since (as they thought) they were well covered by the advance of the columns that had gone before. The Tsar had just administered a memorable rebuke to his General Kutuzov: "Why are the men not moving?"

"We are waiting, Your Majesty," replied the old general, humbly.

"This is not a review on the Empress' birthday."

"It is precisely because this is not a review that I am waiting."

The Tsar said nothing at all, only stared at his general with that bright, fixed, and peculiarly dreadful smile which an autocrat master of life and death can wear. Kutuzov's face became that of a sulky peasant and he ordered the troops to move in the most rapid manner.

Now as the vanguard of these troops reached the crest of the Pratzen, they were astonished and horrified to see huge masses of Frenchmen climbing the opposite slope at a pace no one would have believed possible. Cavalry to stop them? It was all off to the right with Liechtenstein, or to the left with Kienmayer. Artillery? Still on the limbers at the rear of the moving column of foot. There was a wild flurry of shouting, hurry, and nervousness that propagated itself like an electric current through the men who, like all soldiers, were instantly aware of something wrong at the post of command. Aides galloped to recall some of Przebyschevski's men if they could be recalled; to recall part of Liechtenstein's horse, or the Grand Duke Constantine with the

Guard. Miloradovitch in person deployed the first few battalions on a line across a little collection of squalid huts that stands midway the plateau, and then the French were upon them.

There were three or four sharp discharges of musketry before the pieces of the new French brigade formation skirmishers were emptied, and they had to pull aside to reload, while the cannon opened with grape and the battalion columns fell on the riddled Russian line with the bayonet. Miloradovitch's weak and hastily formed defense was smashed and swept away in a minute; Vandamme and St. Hilaire followed so hotly that they caught most of Kollowrath undeployed, crushed his formations under their fire, captured men by hundreds and thousands, and sent the remnants flying in the direction of Olmütz, leaving their cannon stuck in the mud. A brigade sent by Przebyschevski was only in time to be caught front and flank by a whole French division and to be wiped out. It was ten o'clock; Colonel Rapp, covered with blood that was not his own, and carrying a Russian standard that had become his, rode back to tell Napoléon that the battle was won.

Gérard has painted them thus, poised on the peak of victory, the best moment Rapp would know in a long life, but in fact the battle was not completely gained, for it could still go as wrong as murdering Malplaquet unless the French left stood fast, where Lannes was attacked by Bagration, with the Grand Duke Constantine and the Austrian horse of Liechtenstein. Victory on that wing was slow to speak; Bagration had extended rightward to get around the supposed position of the French flank, while Constantine was ahead of time and Liechtenstein was late after his tangle with the center columns. Thus as part of Bagration struck Lannes head-on around Santon Hill, the Grand Duke drove at his inward wing and became involved with Division Rivaud, of Bernadotte's left flank.

Liechtenstein had to pass the Grand Duke's rear and, much crowded between him and Bagration, ran into Murat's leading squadrons. In smoke, mist and tumult, the Russian lancers broke through the first line of French cavalry and followed down between the infantry divisions of Rivaud and Caffarelli. These faced inward and cut the lancers to pieces with musketry, then turned and pressed forward again.

The infantry of the Russian Guard was now at hand, and lost frightfully trying to hold the French divisions, for its formation was ill adapted to meet Napoléon's new tactic and it was outnumbered. Constantine put in his heavy horse to sustain the effort, but it did no more than force the French foot to form square, and Napoléon himself, now on the Pratzen, threw forward Bessières and the cuirassiers of the French Imperial Guard to put an end to matters. As always when he could abandon thought, big Bessières was magnificent; Russia reeled and broke under a shock that caught it just at the end of its own momentum.

Division Caffarelli, Division Suchet, advanced invincibly against Bagration and broke his line. Liechtenstein's heavy horse, the Chevalier Guard of Austria, which boasted it had never known defeat, arrived too late to do anything but try to cover a reflux; and into it rode not only Bessières, but also Murat, with the cuirassier divisions of D'Hautpoul and Nansouty.

By eleven o'clock the whole Allied right wing was going back broken, the General trying to gather men for a rear guard, as refugees from the frightfully beaten center flowed into them, crying defeat and fear. Napoléon had waited only for the result of Bessières' charge before riding to the southern limit of the Pratzen plateau, ordering Soult to wheel his men in that direction and Murat to follow, while Bernadotte took up the pursuit of the beaten Allied right and center. Soult had needed no orders; his Division Vandamme had already captured the village of Aujesd in the rear of the Allied left. Now St. Hilaire hurried his men down the Pratzen along the track Langeron and Przeby-

schevski had taken earlier, and Buxhövden's wing was practically surrounded by two o'clock.

Przebyschevski's column, still crowded together, was so
laced by artillery and now by musketry from opposite directions that even the tough Russians could not stand it; the
command surrendered entire. Half of Langeron's column
did likewise; the rest, pushing to their own left away from
that region of fire, fell in on Dokhtorov, whom Buxhövden
was now leading to a retreat in the only direction possible,
between the ponds and out by a circuit.

Kienmayer's cavalry covered this retreat well, but the
process was neither easy nor inexpensive, with Davout's men
hammering at the Allied rear in a Gallic exaltation over
victory that made them utterly transcend the fact that they
had marched half the night and fought all day. Nor did
Buxhövden even so get his column clear; as it passed Aujesd,
Vandamme struck it sharply in the middle and cut it in two.
The forward half, by sacrificing all its guns, managed to
reach Austerlitz village, where Czartoryski saw Buxhövden,
"without a hat and his clothes in extreme disarray," who
cried wildly, "They have abandoned me! They have sacrificed me!"

The rear and larger part of Buxhövden's column was
folded in upon the ponds and began to stream across their
frozen surfaces. Napoléon mercilessly ordered artillery
turned on the ice through the rapidly fading light. The
cannon-balls crashed through, so did the Russians, who were
drowned by hundreds before the survivors surrendered.

Let no one think they had not fought well; of 70,000
French on the field, 10,000 were dead or wounded, nearly
three times as many as admitted by Napoléon, who had a
curious Latin penchant for making his most splendid achievements more splendid still. Out of the 85,000 Allies, nearly
30,000 were gone, over 12,000 of them prisoners; they
had lost all their baggage, including food and ammunition
wagons; had lost nearly all their cannon; were in a state of
disorganization that prohibited any rally short of a return

to base and complete re-equipment. Napoléon's army was in shape to pursue them to destruction, or he could draw in Ney, Mortier, Augereau, and Masséna and crush the Archduke Karl.

VI

A lively sense of this state of affairs had reached Kaiser Franz' mind as early as the hour when he was being swept through Austerlitz village on the wave of broken-hearted panic. His great and good friend the Tsar could not be found anywhere; was at the moment, in fact, stumbling along a back road on a worn-out horse, attended only by Czartoryski and three Cossacks. Every time they had to stop for anything, Alexander burst into tears. He had a high fever and violent intestinal cramps; they had to lift him from his saddle and carry him to a bed of straw in a peasant's hut, still shaking with sobs and babbling something quite incoherent about the Eunuch Christ. Kaiser Franz would have to solve his problem alone; and he solved it by sending an officer to ask an immediate personal interview with Napoléon, looking toward an armistice. The symbolism of history directed that the French Emperor should be found in the Schloss Austerlitz, occupying the very room where Graf Metternich had taken his bride on the night they were married.

The armistice was made, naturally, on Napoléon's terms. They included the retreat from Austrian territory of all Russian troops, since Alexander, bitter with shame, would have no peace. He hoped the Prussians would still come into action—a hope that proved vain when Napoléon rode down to Vienna to see Haugwitz and tell him that Austria was out of the war. The Prussian minister was a man who liked to agree with the enemy while he was still in the way with him; that was one of the reasons he had been made minister to a king whose personal policy was one of never fighting about anything. When the embassy had left Berlin, old Brunswick had said that it would take Prussia four weeks to mobilize; Haugwitz could not fail to see, nor did Napoléon hesitate to point out, that from its present position the French army could be through the Bohemian passes and into the midst of such a mobilization long before it was complete.

Moreover, the victor of Austerlitz was both logical and generous. He pointed out that with the Austrian surrender there were no issues left for Prussia to mediate. The outstanding questions had been decided on the field of battle, the Treaty of Lunéville had become a dead letter, and Prussia would be laughed at round the zones if she made war to sustain such an absurdity. Instead, an honorable and gainful peace was offered. Prussia should have delicious, desirable Hanover—not in free gift, as before (that offer had been made when France needed an ally), but in exchange for a permanent alliance and the cession of the troublesome enclave of Ansbach, with the little county of Clèves near the Belgian border and the little county of Neufchâtel next to Switzerland; three poor and tiny principalities remote from central Prussia, for one of the largest and richest provinces of Europe. Haugwitz signed, and was allowed to review the grenadiers of the Imperial Guard, who had wept tears of rage and disappointment at not getting into the action at Austerlitz, and needed some mark of favor to quiet their grumbling.

WRONG END OF THE TELESCOPE—XIII

The Columbian Centinel:

THE *London "Courier"* of December 19, 1805, confirms in the moſt poſitive terms, and on the beſt authority, the defeat of **BONAPARTE** on the 5th *December*—the deadly carnage which took place;—the retreat of the French to the river *Swartza;* and the advance of the allies to Auſterlitz, in front of Wiſchau, the ſcene of battle.

The Hon. Charles Grey to Mr. Creevey:

ON the delay of fresh intelligence I think nothing. I remember the same thing happened after the battle of Ulm, when the same inferences were drawn from it, and the opportunity taken to circulate the same reports of the defeat of the French. It seems Robert Ward sent to all the newspapers the paragraphs which you wd. see, asserting the Russian capitulation and Count Palfy's letters to be forgeries. All this, I agree with you, is as much calculated to hurt Pitt, when it is completely exposed, as the disasters themselves, and the folly of doing it is inconceivable. If the defeat of the 2nd was as calamitous as I believe it to have been, it is nonsense to talk any more of Continental confederations. The game is too desperate even for Pitt himself, desperate as he is.

The Farington Diary:

DECEMBER 19.—Mr. A. Phipps I dined at, Captn. Moorshum was in the engagement *off Trafalgar* (on October 21), & commanded the *Revenge*.—Mr. Phipps read some verses written by Lord Mulgrave on the Battle of Trafalgar. —He also read a copy of a Bulletin this day circulated from the Secretary of State's office giving an account of the Battles of Wischew between *the Russians & the French* which commenced on the 2nd of Decr. and were continued on the 3rd & 4th. The Russians on the 2nd were worsted and lost their artillery, but on the 3rd and 4th had the advantage fighting with *Swords & Bayonets* only and recovered their artillery.

Charles Stuart to his mother:

I AVAILED myself of the opportunity to send my servant into Vienna to get letters of credit from my banker. He found 30,-000 French in the town, committing every sort of excess. Marshal Soult lodged at Sir Arthur Paget's house and has a table for forty people at the expense of the house. He had forced open the drawers and made free with all His Ex.'s gold snuff boxes and against their departure was packing up looking-glasses, furniture, and whatever he could lay hands upon to send to France. Several of the French General Officers thought it necessary to do the honours of the Empress and Prince John Liechtenstein's beds in the society of Mesdames Félix and others, whose names I believe you were once well acquainted with!

Reeve's Journal of a Residence in Vienna:

A DEFICIENCY of provisions begins to be felt; the Archduke Charles will not allow any oxen or articles to pass from Hungary to this place. The butchers shut up their shops and only give out small portions of meat to families; many can get none. Famine begins to stare us in the face. Everything is put in requisition; the whole country is quite devastated; all the cows and sheep killed, all the horses put in requisition to transport the cannon and baggage. This is the third time of this place being obliged to furnish provisions for so many troops. The Russians burnt, and ate, and destroyed everything they could lay hands on, to prevent, as they said, anything being left for the French.

The New York Post:

IMPORTANT

BY the brig William from Liverpool, a paper containing dates to the 14th of December . . . the news of the French success and the disaster of the allies given in Thursday's paper is so far from being true—the reverse would be nearer so.

The archduke Charles has gained a victory over Massena in Italy, 10,000 left dead on the field.

Great complaints are made of the exaggeration and falsity of French Bulletins. The victories there so pompously detailed are said never to have existed to such extent but on paper.

Talleyrand is at Vienna.

21

THE GOLD OF
THE AMERICAS

Paris: Summer An XIII–January 27, 1806

IT IS doubtful whether anyone really understood what
happened on the Pratzen plateau but Napoléon himself
and that singular Swiss of Ney's staff, Albert-Henri
Jomini. Mr. Pitt, the minister of England, understood it in
one dimension, to be sure. Half-raising a frame exhausted
by overwork and port wine from a bed at Bath, he de-
claimed: "Roll up that map; it will not be wanted these ten
years"—a curiously accurate estimate. The "Austerlitz
look" came on his face; his friends hardly recognized the
wonder-youth who had discussed Cock Robin in Commons
and assured the empire of Britain. "He took no nourishment
but occasionally a small cup of broth which seldom remained
on his stomach"—and toward the end of January, after
crying according to one account "My country! How I love
my country!" or according to another that he would try one
of Mr. Bellamy's pork pies, there was no longer enough life
left in him to carry on the struggle against the Revolution's
dominion of the world.

On Mr. Pitt's part this was to understand the effect of
the shattering event in Bohemia without understanding what
had produced it. But one would hardly have expected Mr.
Pitt's eighteenth-century mind to inquire into the causes of
the Allied débâcle and the French victory. He was never

tortured by Friedrich Gentz' doubts whether these French fiends in human form might be right. Of course they were wrong. Mr. Pitt was solely concerned with the thought that the Allies had been what Lord Sidmouth called his own government—"both precipitate and remiss" (a pair of almost-antonyms of which the one or the other can be persuaded to cover almost any failure) within the normal terms of reference.

Alexander of Russia had a truer sense of the change from the eighteenth century, though without understanding the focus of the alteration. "How did it happen?" he asked Colonel Savary, when the latter reached Allied headquarters to obtain his assurance that the Russians would march out of Austria. "How did it happen that I was superior to you, yet you were stronger than I at every point of attack?"

Savary murmured something about the art of war and his Emperor's having fought forty battles, which was much the same thing as saying that because Papa Haydn wrote more than a hundred symphonies, one of them must turn out to be the *Eroica*. Actually experience had nothing to do with *Eroica* or Austerlitz. Into the structure of the battle were introduced elements as violently discordant as the diminished sevenths at the close of the first statement of theme in the symphony—which is to say that, on another level, Beethoven was the third man who understood what had happened at Austerlitz (while Haydn would never understand anything but the eighteenth century), and made of his C Minor a gigantic triumphal march for the entry of the Eagles into Vienna. (One of the inevitable consequences of Austerlitz was the C Minor.)

The point missed by Pitt and Alexander and every other eighteenth-century mind was that battle and symphony were total structures, that the diminished sevenths enabled the nearby harmonies to produce a total dramatic effect as overpowering as the advance of Soult against the Pratzen after Division Legrand's 6,000 had been deliberately exposed to the attack of six times their number of Russians.

This is not to make the invidious statement that the Napoleonic battle was "better" than anything previously conceived; it merely rendered more restricted systems of tactics well-nigh impossible. Once the attacking columns had been launched, once the divisions had been given their instructions and their objectives, they could no longer be controlled by the high command, as the movements of a Beethoven symphony could not be reversed.

Moreover, the Napoleonic battle imposed the same restrictions on both sides. Buxhövden could not return to the Pratzen; if anything had gone wrong with Lannes, he could have received no help from Bernadotte, next in line. On the merely tactical level, this was little more than an extension of the terrific Battle of Rivoli, which the Emperor had fought eight years before, when the French wings were beaten, but the center broke through to inflict on the House of Austria one of the worst defeats it ever received. But tactics was not the only issue and Rivoli was in some part an accidental, like the wonderful structure of Beethoven's Third Concerto. Austerlitz and the C Minor Symphony were planned from the beginning to result as they did. The synthesis of melody and discord was deliberate, and in Napoléon's case was another facet of the same synthesis which gave him a Council of State where Royalists rubbed elbows with anarchists.

In the cabinet and on the field of battle this implied an unprecedented confidence in subordinates. Frederick the Great, the best general anyone had heard of up to this time, had designed battles that were models for all ages after him. But they possessed this feature—that the King of Prussia was always in control, he was never forced fully to trust any subordinate; any division leader short of an absolute traitor would have done as well as any other. The same was true of another great military commander, George Washington, whose plans were occasionally ruined because he had absolute traitors on his hands, at Monmouth for instance.

In the Napoleonic system there were far smaller tolerances. It is true that the Emperor planned for movements all across the face of Europe and exercised supervisory control over them, so that there was no such thing as a truly independent command, such as Frederick had given to the Duke of Brunswick or Washington to Nathanael Greene. But the corps commanders under Napoléon's immediate control had far greater liberty of action than those of Frederick, Washington, or any previous commander. Even the misfortunes of the system showed it, such as Murat rushing toward Vienna instead of forcing the passage of the Danube on Kutuzov's heels at Krems, and Mortier's defeat at Dürnstein because he failed to keep cavalry cover on his flank. Neither marshal had been ordered to take the steps he missed, as he would have been ordered by Frederick, Washington, or Gustavus Adolphus. The Napoleonic system assumed that a man equal to handling a corps would think of these things and take the appropriate action by himself, in the light of local conditions which the chief did not know.

The idea and ideal here have more than military importance, for they underlie the whole Imperial structure; but Napoléon was a military man, and it was in war that he made himself most clear. Fundamentally the system stems from the Revolution, and it was a rejection of the absolutist concept that had ruled Europe since the God-Emperors of Rome: the concept of perfection flowing from the head of the state, because he has been called to rule by a power more than mortal, an idea sometimes expressed as "the divine right of kings"—usually by people who do not understand what it really meant or how any intelligent person could believe in it. The English had come to grips with this theory earlier, but their solution had been a typically English compromise which destroyed the practical application of divine right, while leaving the theory unimpaired. They were still ruled by a monarch who could personally do no wrong, and to them "democracy" was still a term of horror and reproach. The American colonists came to grips with it in the

Declaration of Independence, but hardly anyone in Europe had ever heard of that document.

The only trouble with the French Revolution's solution of the absolutist problem, more radical than either of the Anglo-Saxon efforts, was that it failed to find any workable system to take the place of the vanished monarchy; and the achievement of the early Empire, the Empire of 1805, which was the Consulate except for titles, lay in producing the method of specialists working together under a co-ordinating head.

II

When the Emperor returned to Paris the first thing he learned was that such a system was no stronger than the method of choosing the specialists. The great naval building program, the formation of the Army of the Coasts of the Ocean, had been accompanied by a growing embarrassment of the Treasury for funds. This was partly the effect of the conditions under which war had succeeded to the illusion of Amiens. On the signature of that document, every Frenchman who had the means rushed out to buy the Colonial products of which all France had been deprived for a decade —coffee, sugar, spices, cotton—and paid for them in the hard cash of the new coinage.

(That coinage was one of the Consulate's more remarkable minor achievements. Under Revolution and Directory the coinage had been debased in character, disorganized in quantity, and tasteless in design, the pieces crowded with symbolic cocks, liberty bonnets, serpents, suns, and lengthy mottoes. Under Barbé-Marbois, the Treasurer, work on new issues began at once. By the An X and Amiens, the mint was already pouring forth quantities of silver one- and two-franc pieces by Andrieu and Tiollier, of a calm, neoclassical design, better than anything seen in France for a century, and well worth their face value. A whole series of silver five-franc pieces was already in process by this date; the peace brought the emission of beautiful 40s in gold.)

The money that thus rushed across the national borders was better than that of most of Europe, and had not begun to drain back and reappear in the form of tax payments when war was declared. The Treasury was forced to depend upon its own new issues, which was reasonably satisfactory until the American metal from Spain (which furnished the normal cash background for most of Europe) first fell into arrears of payment and then ceased altogether to come, just as military expenses reached their peak. Now the usual resource of a warring nation under such circumstances is debasement, either directly or through the dilution of hard money with paper. But Napoléon had not been Emperor for twenty-four hours before he announced that "while I live there will be no emission of paper."* M. François Barbé-Marbois, Treasurer of France, thus began to feel a need of ready cash before the army left Boulogne. Presenting his troubles to the Emperor would have been the same thing as offering his resignation, for under the system it was his especial duty to find money for disbursement; he was the specialist.

The American ambassadors found this Barbé-Marbois a charming man, and the British (when there was a British Ambassador) had found him honest. In fact, it was specifically because of his record of probity as intendant of Saint-Domingue—honesty in a colonial administration was about as frequent as a blue giraffe—that he had been made Treasurer. The characteristic is certainly a desirable one for a man handling public funds, but it carries no implications of ingenuity. Barbé-Marbois confessed himself at his wits' end to Banker Ouvrard, when the latter called on an afternoon in germinal of An XII, just after the Enghien execution.

This Ouvrard was the same acquaintance of Brother Joseph who had lent the Consular government money to meet its running expenses on the day after its formation. He

---

* A promise which was sternly kept. Nothing is more astonishing than that the close of the reign found France, after all those wars and turbulences, in far sounder financial condition than on the day the Directory was ejected.

had again helped with a loan when there was a flash shortage of wheat in the capital during the An XI; was much
seen in society, a notable sustainer of salons, particularly that
of a certain Mme. de Montesson, which was useful in bringing nobles of the *ancien régime* to the support of the new
court. His friends considered Ouvrard as much a genius in
finance as Napoléon was in war; he was the author of a very
able paper demonstrating that France needed a large public
debt, like England.

When Napoléon rejected the plan Ouvrard took his own
way of providing the country with this indispensable support
for a sound financial system. He did not press for repayment
of the Consular and wheat loans till he was sure there was
not enough cash in the Treasury to meet them. A huge contract had been let for masts, cordage, guns, and internal
furniture for all the ships of the new navy to a man named
Frenais, whose bonds were signed by Ouvrard, and whom
no one had ever seen, though his address (oddly enough)
was that of Ouvrard's country house. Cash settlement on
this account was due at about the time of the banker's visit
to Barbé-Marbois, and formed one of the subjects of their
talk. (Admiral Bruix was a great personal friend of the
financier; Forfait, the marine engineer and at that time
Minister, often went to de Montesson's salon.)

The sum of the engagements to Ouvrard and Frenais,
Barbé-Marbois calculated, had run to 67,800,000 francs at
the time of the banker's visit—an appalling amount. It could
have been with no easy mind that he greeted the financier,
whose credit in real values was considerably larger than
when the debts were contracted, thanks to the steady improvement of the coinage and the consequent general fall in
prices. The two men knew each other only slightly, but M.
Ouvrard placed things on an easy basis by making it clear
that although he wanted his money, his mood was less that
of the importunate creditor than that of the patriotic citizen
offering his financial knowledge in aiding the government to
meet its obligations. He understood that the Treasury had

found itself in default to the naval contracting firm of Frenais.

M. Barbé-Marbois admitted that this was the case; M. Ouvrard exposed his plan.

The Treasury possessed a great resource (he said) in the rolls of the tax-collectors, against which under the Gaudin plan* drafts were made monthly for amounts currently due. He, Ouvrard the banker, would be willing to discount these rolls in advance; would offer 50,000,000 francs, cash paid down, with which the debt to Frenais would be immediately discharged, together with sundry other debts. In view of the gilt-edged character of the tax-collector paper (which rested on the taxes against real property and was certain to be discharged in hard money), he was willing to advance this vast sum at only three-quarters of one per cent a month.

M. Barbé-Marbois could hardly find words to express his gratitude. He was simply stupefied by such generosity on the part of a creditor who, instead of making trouble, opened up illimitable new alleys of resource. The papers were drawn at once; he signed them before his visitor left. As his probity prevented him from frequenting the salons where financiers gathered, he was ignorant that Ouvrard and Frenais were one, and that the operation was a transfer of funds between pockets, which left the banker in possession of the tax-collectors' obligations to the government; and as the Treasurer worked entirely from reports made in his bureaux, he was ignorant that the moment Ouvrard obtained the tax-collector paper at a discount of 9% a year, he would take it to the Bank of France and turn it into cash at a discount of 6% a year.

The operation made Ouvrard realize he had a very good thing in Barbé-Marbois. He sang the Treasurer's praises in influential ears and waited for another emergency to be produced by the military expenses, now that the government's tax income for the year was hypothecated. In fact,

---

* See page 18.

it was hardly two months before Barbé-Marbois was again applying to his benefactor. The Empire had been proclaimed and now the Treasury needed 150,000,000 francs, a sum so enormous that M. Ouvrard doubted whether he could swing the loan without help. He would, however, find someone who could; and he presented M. Armand Seguin.

If Barbé-Marbois had not been an innocent who had spent most of his life in the colonies, he might have been better informed about this Seguin, who used to ride through Paris in an open coach, clad in a flowered bathrobe, with a towel for a turban, and who combined the professions of inventor and financier. In the former capacity he had appeared before the great Convention during the days when all Europe was at war with the Revolution, with a new process for tanning leather for army shoes. Instead of the eighteen months required by ordinary methods, the Seguin system rendered leather tender enough to be worked into shoes within a single week. A commission of scientists examined the process; they said it was perfectly true. In a burst of enthusiasm the Convention voted Seguin a pair of magnificent estates and directed that all the leather in France be requisitioned and turned over to him, as sole contractor for military footgear, a business which he sold out at a fine profit before it was discovered that while the new process did cause leather to soften at the end of one week, the material rotted at the end of four.

M. Seguin had been out of public business for several years, and employed his leisure in thinking deeply on financial problems. He formed a partnership for large financial operations in support of the government—the Compagnie des Négociants Réunis (United Brokers' Company)—which included Michel Brothers (army contractors), Vanlerberghe the banker (army food contractor) and Ouvrard himself, as general manager. The difficulty of France, Seguin pointed out, was the growing shortage of precious metal. The United Brokers' Company would gladly advance the 150,-000,000 francs necessary to meet the bills of Frenais, the

navy contractor, and of the Michels for army supplies—
against tax-collector paper, naturally. (This was done, and
it ate up all future tax receipts for over two years to come,
or until the end of 1806.) But this was a palliative; the
essential was to find a permanent solution, and what better
could there be than to tap, through Spain, the boundless
wealth of the Americas?

Spain owed the money. The alliance treaty required her to
furnish 6,000,000 francs a month and she was now six
months in arrears. The Négociants Réunis felt they could
best render a patriotic service by taking over, on the one
hand, the obligations of the Treasury to the contractors,
and on the other, the obligations of Spain to the Treasury.
They were in a position to solve the difficulties presented by
the British blockade, which prevented Spain from importing
American metal. Ouvrard was in close relations with the
Amsterdam and Hamburg branches of Hope and Baring,
the great London banking houses. As neutrals with London
connections, these firms would experience no trouble in obtaining licenses from H.M. Navy to import gold. Once this
gold was in Europe, the bulk of it would be turned over by
Hope and Baring to the Négociants Réunis in exchange for
the paper of that company. The company would pass the
money to Spain and immediately receive it from Spain again
in a book transaction, satisfying that country's debt; turn
it over to the French Treasury and receive it from that
agency in another book transaction, and so pay it to the contractors to whom the Treasury owed money.

Of course, Spain herself was in bad economic condition,
unable to maintain her normal existence without some inflow
of money, and an arrangement of sorts would have to be
made there. MM. Seguin and Ouvrard thought it could be
done by permitting the Négociants Réunis to issue paper
against the anticipated inflow of cash reserves, as well as
those on hand. A hard-money reserve of 30% was sufficient
for all practical purposes; the experience of those master-
bankers, the English, demonstrated it. In the meantime, as a

purely temporary measure, it would be necessary to find for the Spaniards enough hard money to re-establish their credit.

III

Barbé-Marbois was charmed. The inverted pyramid rested neatly on its point without a sign of overbalance in any direction. The Emperor's consent was necessary for the transfer of tax-collector futures to the United Brokers' Company, but Napoléon was especially busy with the preparations for invading England, and his signature was easily obtained by telling him that the transfer was a purely temporary measure in which the state was guaranteed against loss by the enormous personal fortunes of the members of the firm.

On the other hand, it was considered unnecessary to take up with the Emperor the detail of making to the Company a hard-money Treasury loan for setting the Spanish affair in train, and Barbé did not mention it, merely signed a paper allowing Ouvrard to borrow at will whatever of cash the Treasury contained. Ouvrard went to Madrid, not only as general manager of the brokerage firm, but also as special representative of the French Treasury; Vanlerberghe went to Amsterdam to see the Hopes.

The projects which Ouvrard laid before the court of Spain were by no means identical with those put forward in Paris. It was necessary to conciliate that proud nation before proceeding to business; this Ouvrard accomplished by securing a license to relieve a current corn famine by exporting thither the surplus of an exceptionally fine harvest in Provence. By a curious coincidence the firm of Ouvrard had bought up this surplus grain some weeks before, and was able to sell it in Spain at a price which netted a profit of some eight millions.

Now the financier began to talk about a new company to build a canal bringing fresh water from the Guadarrama Mountains to Madrid, and another canal to connect that

inland capital with the Guadalquivir and turn it into a sea-
port. Minister Godoy spread his hands and said that the
Spanish Treasury was so empty that Their Majesties must
even forgo the customary holiday at Aranjuez; Ouvrard
obligingly presented 500,000 francs for the purpose, and
was permitted to have the ineffable pleasure of waiting on
the Minister while he was having breakfast in bed with the
Queen. Papers were drawn for the canal company.

For the more permanent cure of Spanish finance, the
Négociants Réunis reorganized the Spanish National Chest
Bank, which had no cash reserve at all and was issuing
paper that circulated only by government edict. Under the
new arrangement, the National Chest supported its paper
with bank notes of the Bank of France and hard money
borrowed from the French Treasury, instantly loaning again
to the Négociants Réunis to support the canal enterprise.
The subvention to France? Spain need not worry about that
at all; the Négociants Réunis would take care of it in exchange for a license to import into Europe the gold of the
American mines.

The Minister of Spain expressed some doubt with regard
to the British blockade; Ouvrard triumphantly produced a
letter from his coadjutor Vanlerberghe. Hope of Amsterdam was more than glad to take part in the operation. In
fact, its London branch had been approached by Mr. Pitt
himself, who was finding his own treasury much embarrassed
by the prospect of heavy subsidies to Austria and Russia.
(The Third Coalition was only in the desire stage at this
date.) The English Premier had besought the Hopes to find
some way of bringing American gold to Europe so that he
could purchase it through neutrals. Godoy's last doubts
vanished; he produced a document that gave Ouvrard the
sole privilege of importing colonial gold for so long as the
war lasted, only specifying that the actual handling was to
be done by a new subsidiary of the Négociants Réunis, in
which the King of Spain was a sleeping partner.

Ouvrard went trotting back to Paris, sending on ahead

the joyful news that the big deal had gone through. One can imagine some self-congratulatory meetings of the members of the United Brokers. They immediately began to prepare for profit-taking by selling calls on gold at six months' date, and as they were the only people who knew that American gold would be in Europe by that time, they sold these papers at an extremely good price.

Now it was the late spring of 1805; Novossiltzoff had arrived in London with his proposal for the alliance of peace, and Mr. Pitt perceived that it would not after all be necessary to haul Austria and Russia into the war by golden chains of such weight as to embarrass his treasury. He experienced a change of heart with regard to the Spanish money; explained to a melancholy representative of the Hopes that he had really never meant anything so absurd as allowing Spain, which was at war with England, to import cash. What he had meant was that the House of Hope should buy up stocks of metal already on the Continent. The gold on which Ouvrard's whole structure rested thus did not exist; for even should a sudden peace open the seas to money shipments, the same event would destroy the Ouvrard firm's import license, good only for the duration.

IV

It is worth asking what Napoléon was doing all this time and what he thought of this business. One answer is that the Emperor did not know all the details; the financial Napoléon had arranged things so that no one knew them but himself. When news arrived that Ouvrard had secured his gold-importing license from the Spaniards, the Emperor wrote to Barbé-Marbois that now the temporary emergency was over, he must see to it that the Négociants Réunis at once returned the tax-collector paper to the Treasury. That is, he did not know that this paper had been turned over in permanence. Nor did he know that Desprez, Regent of the Bank of France and himself a member of the Négociants Réunis, had practically emptied the coffers of that institution in return for cash drafts on Caracas, Vera Cruz, and Montevideo, payable as soon as the money could be touched, and issued by the Spanish National Chest to the Négociants Réunis.

On the other hand, the Emperor did know that Ouvrard and his crew were up to some kind of trick. He was realist enough to be aware that the business of supplying armies in the field has an irresistible attraction for vultures. The buyers in that market must have the goods at whatever price, and those goods themselves are rapidly dissipated at points so distant from origin that no machinery of complaint is effective. It was part of the Emperor's policy to use whatever instruments were available without inquiring why they were not better. As long as contractors and financiers stayed within the bounds of reason, the more profit they made, the more they would support the régime, and their undoubted skill in arrangements could be used in accomplishing important tasks. When he became aware of Ouvrard's deal in wheat for Spain, Napoléon merely ordered that half the 8,000,000-franc profit be turned over to the government, which the financier had made his collaborator by using an official position to conclude the sale. The Emperor seems to have believed that the Négociants Réunis were engaged in a speculation, a gigantic bet, on the success of his Austrian campaign.

Perhaps he should have known that bankers never take chances on anything so uncertain as a battle. The army was deep into Bavaria before it became evident that something much more important than a reasonable profit or a gamble on who would win a war was involved. By that date the whole financial structure of France was submerged in a snowstorm of such paper as had not been seen since Joseph financed the seven lean years of Egypt. The Bourse was groaning under the weight of Spanish canal bonds and obligations to pay gold, with some of the latter falling due. 92,000,000 francs in sight drafts against the Bank of France were outstanding, and the bank had only 1,500,000 francs in cash. All the rest of its reserve consisted of uncollectable drafts on the Mexican mines, paper of the Spanish National Chest (this paper itself supported by money borrowed from the Bank of France), and such items as stock in the firm of Grammont of Bordeaux, deposited with the Bank by the United Brokers, when they discovered that Grammont had a credit of only 200,000 francs to support a capitalization of 14,000,000. The Treasury contained nothing but more Spanish paper, and would receive nothing for a year and a half to come, since all the future tax receipts had been made payable to the Négociants Réunis. In fact, practically all the cash in France had reached the strongboxes of the members of that firm. Worst of all, a groundswell of rumor about the stability of the Bank and the condition of the Treasury began to run through the city. Men who had obligations to meet were cashing checks—demanding hard money, not bank notes.

Napoléon was under the walls of Ulm when the rumors reached his ears. Then an overt act; in its lack of ready money the Bank had been meeting obligations with sight drafts collectable at some physical distance. It drew on the military paymaster at Arras—the Bank, which was supposed to hold funds to pay the troops, drawing on the troops to meet the demands of the stock market. The Emperor wrote to Barbé-Marbois: it was not enough for the Treasurer of France to see that the Bank's books were in balance, he must examine the nature of the assets——

"You are to blame. Bank notes and drafts which have no real credit to back them are nothing but fiat money. By behaving in this manner the Bank is, I say it frankly, counterfeiting. I would stop my soldiers' pay to sustain the Bank. I am afflicted by a manner of life which drags me away from the first object of my cares, the first of my heart: a good, solid organization of everything connected with banks, manufactures, commerce."

Now the Bank promulgated a rule that no more than a single 1,000-franc note would be cashed for a holder, and long queues began to form. In November, on the news from Trafalgar, the failures began, the great house of Récamier one of the first to go down, and pretty Juliette must sell her furniture. Police and troops had to disperse money-hungry crowds in the streets. The Négociants Réunis met with Barbé-Marbois and told him the situation was serious; the Vanlerberghe Company was threatened, one of the most important elements in the combine, it would have to be paid at once some of the monies due to it from the Treasury.

—How much is needed? inquired Barbé-Marbois.

—One hundred million francs, he was told. They thought the unfortunate Treasurer would faint or fall into an apoplexy, and his woe became despair when someone pointed out that Vanlerberghe had a monopoly of army provision contracts. Surely a great and victorious nation could not let its soldiers starve through failure to pay the man who fed them.

However (said Ouvrard) there was no need to abandon hope. It was still possible to sustain everything with the Spanish gold. Desprez of the Bank added that it was only a question of gaining a little time, restoring the public confidence, and there were means for that. In the tax collectors' offices were certain sums already collected, waiting for the monthly payment date; the customs offices held more money, so did those of the collectors of special taxes and the receivers on sales of timber from the national forests. Let a Treasury order be issued that these sums should be paid to Vanlerberghe in exchange for his receipts; bookkeeping details could be handled after the emergency was met.

Barbé-Marbois signed the order.

V

The result was the situation the Emperor found when he returned to Paris on January 26 of the new year. Too late to prevent the Treasurer's final order, he had learned of Vanlerberghe's difficulties and wrote from Vienna that the government owed the man nothing; if he were in trouble, let him stew in his own juice. This and other intimations of gathering fury brought Barbé-Marbois to wait on his master an hour after the arrival with:

"Sire, I bring you my head."

"What use is it to me, you stupid ox?" said Napoléon, and convoked a meeting for eight the following morning with the members of the Négociants Réunis, Gaudin, Barbé, Mollien of the sinking fund, and a few minor functionaries. The meeting opened with a report from the Treasurer and lasted nine hours; Barbé had not gone much beyond the first page of forty when the Emperor said:

"Never mind any more; I see. The Négociants Réunis have used the funds of the Treasury and those of the Bank to conduct the business of France and Spain; and as Spain has nothing to give but promises, French money has been supporting both countries. Now you, Desprez, Vanlerberghe, and Ouvrard, are going to turn over everything you own to the government and Spain is going to pay, or you gentlemen will see the inside of Vincennes prison and I will send an army to Madrid."

Practical details were hammered out in the course of the day. Barbé-Marbois turned the Treasury portfolio over to Mollien and went to hide his head in a corner. The Négociants Réunis must bring back all real values from Spain at once. The members would continue to execute their war contracts (after all, they were the only people with the staffs and goods; striking them down would have made a panic to shake the country), but in future they would be paid only one quarter of the invoice value on each contract executed. Austria had paid a war indemnity of 80,000,000 francs; this would go at once into the Bank of France and anyone who asked should receive hard money in exchange for notes.

The assembled financiers heard the news with dolorous faces onto which big wet tears squeezed out—with one exception, the Napoléon of finance, G.-J. Ouvrard. Throughout the nine hours of recrimination and decision he remained on his feet, face as passionless as Mont Blanc. He had placed himself beyond reach; as early as the first bank runs, brothers, cousins, brothers-in-law, uncles, and aunts of the Ouvrard family had begun to experience a remarkable pros-

The assembled financiers heard the news

perity, and at the time of the nine-hour interview the financier was personally a pauper. To the remarks about prison he was perfectly indifferent. He had breakfasted with the Queen of Spain and with Robespierre, and was indifferent to these honors also. He was indifferent to reputation and to what country he lived in. The vital thing in life was the maneuvering that passed papers through a dozen hands and resulted in bank messengers' arriving at his office with little canvas bags of new-minted pieces; and this Corsican squirt was telling him to stop it.

The view was one that Hope and Baring shared; and after all, it turned out that the Spanish treasure plan was not wholly chimerical, for Mr. Pitt was succeeded as minister of England by Mr. Fox, not anywhere near so good a financial manager, who was finally forced to let one treasure ship come through to neutral Hamburg. Most of the 24,000,000 of gold she carried ultimately found its way into the French Treasury.

THE WORM'S-EYE VIEW—XII

. . . We went into the Cour des Fers, where the house surgeon came to examine if we were in a state to bear the fatigues of the journey. We were all pronounced adequate, although some were in the most woeful plight. Each prisoner then put off the prison livery and assumed his own clothes; those who had none were given a frock and trousers of packing-cloth, insufficient to protect them from the cold and damp. Hats and clothes belonging to the prisoners are torn in a particular way to prevent escape; they take for instance the border off the hat and the collar from the coat. No prisoner is allowed to retain more than six francs. This precaution is easily eluded by placing louis inside large sous, hollowed out.

These preliminaries adjusted, we went into the great court, where were the guards of the chain, better known as Argousins,

mostly men of Auvergne. In the midst of them was a large wooden chest containing the fetters. We were made to approach two and two, taking care to match us in height, and attached by means of a chain six feet in length, united to the cordon of twenty-six prisoners, who could thus only move in a body. Each was confined to the chain by a sort of iron triangle called the cravat, which, opening on one side by a turning screw, is closed on the other by being riveted. This is the most perilous part of the operation; the most turbulent then keep quiet; for, at the least movement, instead of falling on the anvil, the blows would break their skulls, which every stroke of the hammer grazes.

We passed the night on the stones in a church. The Argousins made regular rounds to assure themselves that no one was engaged in fiddling (sawing their fetters). At daybreak we were all on foot; at six o'clock we were placed in long cars, back to back, the legs hanging down outside, covered with hoar frost and motionless from cold. On reaching St. Cyr, we were entirely stripped, to undergo a scrutiny which extended to our stockings, shoes, shirt, mouth, ears, nostrils, etc., etc. It was not only files which they sought, but also for watch springs, which enable a prisoner to cut his fetters in less than three hours.

Supper consisted of a pretended bean soup, and a few morsels of half-mouldy bread. The distribution was made from large wooden troughs, containing thirty rations; and the cook, armed with a large pot ladle, did not fail to repeat to each prisoner as he served him, "One, two, three, four, hold out your porringer, you thief." The wine was put into the same trough, and then an Argousin, taking a whistle hanging to his buttonhole, blew it thrice, saying, "Attention, robbers, and only answer yes or no. Have you had bread?"—"Yes."   "Soup?"— "Yes."   "Meat?"—"Yes." "Wine?"—"Yes." Then go to sleep."

Memoirs of Vidocq

22

CHARLEMAGNE

Western Europe; Summer, 1806

THE story of the speculating bankers had a happy ending in the sense that all the 141,000,000 francs that were estimated to have been raided from the public purse came back to it in one form or another without the tearing scandals and the destruction of public confidence which usually follow the discovery that rogues have run wild. Too many people knew the story for it to be kept quiet forever, but the leakage was slow and, when it occurred, tended to increase rather than to diminish the Emperor's credit, since he had brought such characters to heel without recourse to the police. Yet the affair had intricate and not altogether happy sequels, chiefly as the result of forcing Napoléon to take into his own hands functions he desired to deputize, particularly in that field where the general financial reorganization touched on the political reorganization of western Europe.

The latter step had become necessary when Austria was pushed back behind the Inn by the treaty signed at Pressburg, soon after Austerlitz; and the two readjustments were so interlocked that it is almost impossible to deal with them except as parts of a single operation. The use Napoléon made of the military chest may be seen as the point of departure for the dual process. After Austerlitz that chest contained some 50,000,000 francs in gold, the product of contributions levied on enemy cities and captures made in enemy camps, and it was credited with vast assets in military and quasi-military goods taken from the Allies, as guns, wagons, clothing. An appropriation of 20,000,000 francs was due for soldiers' pay.

Now one of the reasons the Treasury had sunk so deep in the Ouvrard mire was its inability to find an emergency lender on terms less than usurious. The military chest was assigned this function in permanence; given a central point of deposit, and a directive to discount tax-collector paper whenever the commercial rate on such discounts should rise above 6%, as well as to buy in sufficient of the nationalized real properties to support the market whenever the rate on these should fall to a low level. It was doubtless merely a bookkeeping arrangement in government finance; but it produced the desired result, and it never had to be altered.

But at the very beginning it was necessary that the military chest be able to beat off the bankers' boycott of the government implied by Ouvrard's attitude toward the punishment of the United Brokers. This need reacted into the region where there was being drawn the new map of what had been the heart of the medieval Holy Roman Empire— a wide stretch running from the North Sea to the Mediterranean, from the French boundary on the west to a line roughly connecting Hamburg and Venice in the east, and including all Italy.

The new map, as such, was a mere surveyor's job. As a reward for joining France instead of the anti-French coalition, Bavaria received Ansbach, the Tyrol, and some minor enclaves; Württemberg and Baden similarly received the crazy-quilt bits within the general outline of their territories, so that all three principalities presented solid blocks of land, in which it was no longer possible to pass three boundary lines (and customs houses) in a couple of hours' riding.

But the reorganization of western Germany was more than a map matter. It included the filling of the power vacuum created when Austria was pushed back behind the Inn, and by the disappearance of the Holy Roman Empire, to which Kaiser Franz abdicated his title, becoming merely Kaiser of Austria. The authority of that Empire had hardly been strong since the days of Frederick Barbarossa, but it was an authority; it offered a systematic body of law, and an agency to which questions could be referred for judicial decision, and it possessed a not inconsiderable quantity of moral force.

When the Holy Roman Empire fell, all that west German territory, with the exception of the well-integrated central part of Bavaria, was left in a state of indescribable political and legal confusion. There were everywhere small principalities ranging from those held by a Freiherr to those held by a Duke. The tenures were feudal; that is, these princelings were absolute rulers with the rights of taxation, coinage, the administration of justice, conscription, and forced labor subject only to, and restrained only by, the Holy Roman Empire. The Empire had now disappeared; there was no restraining power and no power to enforce decisions among the small magnates, who were (as might be expected) extremely litigious.

The situation was not improved by the fact that part of Napoléon's reward to Bavaria, Württemberg, and Baden was securing Austrian consent to the elevation of the two former into kingdoms and the third to a grand duchy. This change of title had a legal meaning; it meant that in these territories feudal tenures could be abolished at the will of the king, who was absolute. Their Majesties willed it right heartily, since the small nobility possessed estates and buildings hardly less valuable than the Church properties whose secularization at Lunéville had provided so delicious a *bonne bouche*. In theory the kings were basing their rule directly on the people, like the Emperor of the French; in practice, the dispossessions were carried out with a rapacity indistinguishable from downright pillage, and which engulfed peasants as well as petty nobles.

No court could be appealed to, no power could give re-dress—except the French army. Napoléon originally in-tended to make the return of the army a leisurely and com-fortable business, with marches of four miles a day. He established Marshal Berthier at Branau on the Inn, as a kind of overseer to the process and gave him authority of first resort in deciding tenure questions on a living basis until they could be settled legally; M. Otto of the diplomatic serv-ice was his assistant.

When this arrangement went into effect Soult's corps was quartered along the Inn and Ney's in the Salzburg district. Bernadotte's men were slowly taking the northerly route through Ansbach down which they had wheeled to Ulm, with Davout and Lannes moving on an inner circuit through the minor lordships that would pass to Württemberg. Augereau had moved up to Frankfurt and the cavalry was spread wide—all this when Badenese, Bavarians, and Württembergers (the last were the worst of the lot) began their program of confiscation and organized disorder.

Nothing could have been more shocking to the neat mind of Alexandre Berthier, and very few things to the Emperor, so anxious to bring regularity out of anarchies everywhere and to prove that the Revolution conferred benefit. The orders were for the troops to stand fast, both as an enforc-ing force for Berthier's emergency courts and as a restrain-ing influence on the south German kings. The latter service the French performed well enough to earn a nascent popu-larity, particularly among the small gentry who bore the heaviest load of dispossessions—Johann Wolfgang von Goethe, for instance.

That this popularity remained undeveloped and confined to the small gentry may be charged to Napoléon's invincible penchant for making every act serve more than a single purpose—the characteristic that makes it so difficult to as-sign a precise motive to anything he did. The matter of establishing the military chest as a discounting agency had just come up. There was still a shortage of hard money in

France, and it would continue until more had been extracted from the cashboxes of the indelicate financiers. The Emperor was extremely loath to see the national resources in the new good coin go to Germany, where he knew they would disappear in response to Gresham's law, since the south German issues were pretty bad. Prussia had begun to act suspiciously, and finally, Austria was so slow about executing the provisions of the peace with regard to Dalmatia that Berthier at Branau could hardly be left without bayonets.

Napoléon issued an order that soldiers on duty beyond the Rhine should receive only one-half their pay in cash, the remainder being placed to their credit in the military chest for issuance when they returned to France. The missing half of their pay would for the present be represented by their food, requisitioned from the districts in which they were cantoned. It seems to have been the clear intention to make payment to the countryside in some form for this food; in fact, there is of record an Imperial order of May 1806 for the shipment from Strasbourg to Bavaria of 30,000 quintals* of wheat from the French surplus, and for another 10,000 quintals to be dispatched from Italy. In the meanwhile, what had been French popularity descended to the level of the lesser of two evils; and there was revealed a necessity for a class of administrators, who should be French (since France had taken the old Empire's place as sustaining and adjudicating power), yet linked to the smaller states around France's frontiers.

II

It is possible that the solution eventually adopted had been gestating in the Emperor's mind for some time, perhaps since the date when he wished to send Lucien to Etruria. In the grand scheme for the invasion of England, we have seen how his plans could grow and change in detail till they

* A quintal is a French hundredweight.

bore little resemblance to the original. Tracing the steps in this case is a job for writers of monographs; but the proximate background of the Napoleonic device for settling the affairs of the old Rhineland Empire lay in the course of events in Italy.

One of the prospective members of Tsar Alexander's alliance of peace and mediation had actually signed and mobilized troops—the Bourbon kingdom of Naples and Sicily, over which the Russians claimed a protectorate. The king was named Ferdinand—probably the most worthless member of a worthless line—used to dress up as one of the Lazzaroni and garrote passers-by in alleys by night for amusement, which naturally made his people love him dearly. His wife was an Austrian princess, quite his equal in both morals and popularity. This was the fourth time they had made war on France in twelve years and Napoléon decided it was time to put an end to them, particularly since the Russian protectorate could so easily have become something more, a Russian troop formation having come over from Corfu to stiffen the Neapolitan army.

The Allies were so slow about getting their war under way that Austerlitz had been fought before they began to march. Napoléon ordered Marshal Masséna in against them with 40,000 men, down the west coast of Italy; St. Cyr followed with another corps, and the Russians with an English contingent took to their ships without firing a gun. King Ferdinand and his Queen fled to Sicily, taking with them the civil functionaries of the realm, its treasury, and the contents of all the pawnshops. (This was the third time they had been driven out and they were becoming expert in the technique of leaving nothing important behind.) The French troops marched in; the French Emperor announced "The House of Bourbon has ceased to reign in Naples," and sent down Brother Joseph as Lieutenant-General of the kingdom.

At the same time Eugène de Beauharnais, Joséphine's son, now reaching the age of discretion, was made an adoptive child of the Empire and Viceroy of a Kingdom of North Italy, immensely extended by the acquisition of Venetia; and the Beauharnais cousin, Stéphanie, was married to one of the sons of the Grand Duke of Baden. This was already so little distant from the rejected draft of the Imperial proclamation—"Hereditary in the Bonaparte Family"—that most people thought Napoléon had capitulated to the idea. When Brother Joseph was proclaimed King of Naples after a brief interval, they became certain of it.

Actually, a far wider and subtler concept than old-fashioned family dynasty was involved. At the level of inception this new concept owed a good deal to Talleyrand, who understood so fully that diplomacy is the art of pleasing. At some date after the fall of Austria he set afloat on a conversation the thought that Napoléon make himself in title what he was in fact—Emperor of the Occident, the arbiter of everything west of the shadow-line from Hamburg to Venice, as Austria, the empire of the east, had been for centuries ruler of everything Oriental to the line of Rhine and Var. The chief brushed the suggestion aside, but there had been one of the eye-flashes, the mobile mouth had indicated that the idea was not unappetizing, so Talleyrand brought the subject up again and again. What his object was we do not know—perhaps no more than to draw what benefit he could from a successful piece of flattery.

The form which the post-Austerlitz reorganization took from here on owed very little to Talleyrand or to anyone else, and was so ill understood that even observers from a distance in time saw in it no more than the substitution of the name Bonaparte for the name Bourbon as that of a family entitled to obeisances. The true key element in the new plan was that King Joseph of Naples did not cease to be Grand Elector of France, nor did Eugène, Viceroy of Italy, lay down the title of Archchancellor of State. This was not absentee ownership; the very reverse. Both rulers went to live in their new dominions, surrounded by cabinets of local men.

It was their vague functions with relation to the French Imperial throne that were exercised from a distance. The system was a method of bringing the acts of the new principates under the review of Paris.

Some such device was necessary if the new administrations were to succeed, in the sense of providing stable and orderly government which included the normal governmental guarantees of security to the individual. Eugène was in his first employment; it included the administration of a territory larger and more populous than Hungary, as well as the systematization of laws, tax structures, and administrative details throughout that territory. Given time, the Italians might have worked these things out for themselves, but time was precisely the thing lacking. It is incumbent upon a government which stems from a revolution and is imposed by a foreign power to produce an amelioration of conditions without the slightest delay. For that matter, it would never have entered the Emperor's head to let the Italians work out their own solution. He had just seen Frenchmen of far greater political aptitude trying to make a new world during the six-year span after the execution of Louis XVI, and in the end they had been forced to turn the whole business over to him. It was far more efficient to take over the Italian settlement from the beginning.

The Neapolitan case was even more acute. If Napoléon had a fairly high opinion of the extent of Brother Joseph's abilities, he was under no illusions as to their character. The man had the capacity of a simple country squire; could administer a going concern with sense and heart. At Naples this amiable bourgeois had been pitched into the ruins of the most corrupt and fantastic absolutism in Europe. There was a certain tradition of liberalism among the upper gentry, and a genuine willingness to make terms with any substitute for Ferdinand and Maria Carolina. But there was no reserve of organizing skill. The fact had been demonstrated eight years before, during the period of an evanescent republic which quite literally talked itself to death, till the country had accepted the return of Ferdinand as the alternative to no government at all. Neither was there any money; the kingdom would have to be financed from France until it had set up machinery and begun to operate.

It was thus necessary that Viceroy Eugène and King Joseph be both French princes and foreign potentates. The arrangement may be viewed as a closer and more controlled form of the Austrian Imperial system, with its grandees who were hereditary rulers of half a dozen parcels of land, scattered across the face of Europe. It was assumed on the outside that the other members of the Bonaparte family would be jealous unless they received dignities equal to the first two; therefore principalities were provided for all. Perhaps; but it was less important in the extension of the Napoleonic system than that some plan was needed to prevent private wars and local trade barriers, while preserving a degree of local autonomy—that is, the power vacuum left by the Holy Roman Empire had to be filled.

Certainly there was no jealousy on Brother Louis' part. He did not in the least mind being Constable of the French Empire, but he objected very strenuously when Napoléon ordered him from his diets and his spas to become King of Holland. (It is significant that the Emperor readily conceded the request of the Dutch that there should be no Frenchmen in Louis' administration. In this case, unlike the Italian kingdom, there was already a sturdy civil service and a rule of law.)

Pauline, already a princess by reason of her marriage to Borghese, had developed into one of the loveliest women of Europe and one of the most dissolute. She was so little avid of further titles that when she received the Italian principality of Guastalla in the reorganization, she asked permission to turn it in to the Italian crown for cash.*

Sister Eliza did indeed put in her claim for a coronet and received strategically located Lucca; nor would pretty

---

* Showing excellent judgment, incidentally; it was a miserable little rabbit-run of a state only six miles square, with a population of 3,000, mostly beggars.

Caroline, the cleverest, most pushing and energetic of the sisters, be left out. Napoléon made her Grand Duchess of Berg-and-Clèves, the little patch of land next to the Belgian border, which Prussia had ceded in part payment for Hanover.

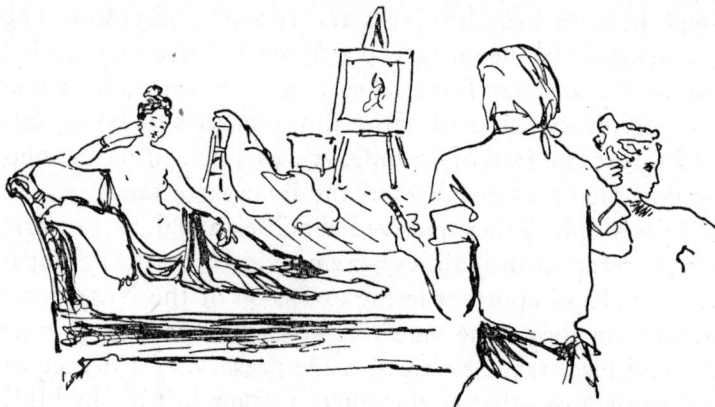

One of the loveliest and one of the most dissolute

III

But the moment pretty Caroline received her duchy everything changed. For Caroline was not only the sister of the Emperor, she was wife to Marshal Prince Murat. When he became a Duke, the seventeen remaining marshals could aspire to do as well, and the principle that hereditary titles belonged to the Emperor alone was abandoned.

In Berthier's case, hope had not long to wait. A day or so after the Murat creation he was made prince of the other Prussian exchange territory of Neufchâtel, on the Swiss border. Everyone recognized this elevation for what it was —a convenience and one of those double compliments the Emperor knew so well how to bestow. Compliment to Berthier, the senior marshal, both in age and in precedence, who worked so hard and never quarreled with anyone; compliment through him to the German princelings with whom he had so many dealings, whose sense of personal dignity was inversely proportioned to their importance, and who found it so much easier to submit their quarrels to the arbitrament of the Prince of German Neufchâtel than to a French general.

There the matter of titles rested until June 5. On that day, without a previous word to anyone, Napoléon suddenly made Talleyrand Prince and Duke of Benevento, and Marshal Bernadotte, Prince of Ponte-Corvo. The principalities were among the richest of south Italian provinces; and the dual nomination produced a magnificent set of pyrotechnics.

One explosion took place in Rome; completely silent, but it blew into atoms the last vestiges of that understanding between Empire and Church which began with the Concordat and reached its most cordial heat at the coronation. Pius VII, that obstinate man, had taken seriously the metaphor which equated Napoléon with Charlemagne. Did not the two control almost exactly the same territory—France, Italy, the Rhineland Empire to the Elbe? Had not the two beaten off all serious enemies so that they were in a position to be generous? The Church had suffered grievous losses during the troubles, not only in France, but also through the secularizations in Germany. She expected to be indemnified in the way the first Charlemagne recompensed Leo III for his coronation, by the extension of the temporal power to a point where its revenues would place the Curia beyond want; and when new provinces were not forthcoming, a little judicious spiritual pressure was applied.

When the Emperor tried to obtain a rationalization of Church affairs in the kingdom of (north) Italy, which was as much a patchwork of ecclesiastical jurisdictions as it was of civil, the answer was a determined No. An effort to reorganize the Church in Bavaria and Württemberg, where the population was overwhelmingly Catholic, but where there had been neither bishops nor chapters since the secularizations, produced an equally negative result. The Curia's position was that when its properties were returned,

it would act; that if it did not act, the faithful would ultimately overthrow the new political settlement and return
to the old days in order to obtain spiritual consolation.

Napoléon regarded these refusals as exhibitions of religious bad temper, "like the blasting of the unfruitful tree,"
and his irritation was unsoothed by the Pope's behavior in
the matter of Brother Jérôme, which arose about the same
time. That last sprig of the Bonaparte tree had come too
late into the world to have known anything but good fortune. As soon as he was old enough to wipe his own nose,
Brother Napoléon put him into the navy as a midshipman,
and sent him to sea. The squadron he sailed with was fortunate enough to capture a British battleship; he boasted
about it as though he had done it with his own hands, and,
being sent out again with the Saint-Domingue expedition,
deserted and went to the United States.

There he had a fine time, borrowing money from the ambassador and all the consuls. (In spite of orders from Paris
they could not bring themselves to be severe with the First
Consul's brother.) In Baltimore he fell in love with some
vapid American girl who had neither position nor money
and went through a ceremony of marriage with her, thus
dissipating the last of the family's matrimonial capital, the
last hand that could be given to link the new France to the
old Europe. She was a Protestant, so the wedding was
clearly void, but only His Holiness could pronounce it so,
and His Holiness refused. Spite work: very well, the Emperor replied by handing over Benevento and Ponte-Corvo
to great officers of the Empire; for these two territories had
been claimed by the Pope during centuries.

Everything must serve two purposes; there were other
reasons than a blow at the Pope for selecting these particular
two. Talleyrand, Prince of Benevento, not only insured that
one of the most avaricious men of France would have an income almost large enough to satisfy him without drawing on
the resources of France itself, but also that until Pius VII
exhibited a spirit of co-operation (when the principate could

be extinguished or exchanged) the foreign policy of France would be firmly anti-Papal.

Bernadotte's elevation to Ponte-Corvo was also a reward and warning. Reward; one thing Bernadotte had handled notably well during the Austrian campaign was the relations of his corps with the territories through which he marched. No confiscations, population respected, two soldiers shot for rape the first time there was a complaint. This was not true of the other marshals, notably Masséna, on whose conduct there were protests from both Eugène and Joseph.

"Tell them all," wrote the Emperor to Viceroy and King, "that I will give them far more than they can take for themselves in this fashion; that their actions cover them with shame, while mine will cover them with glory; that they are making France hated and rousing the peoples against her."

There was an investigation, directed by Fouché; it showed that Masséna had three millions in cash stowed away under different names in vaults at Leghorn, the proceeds of his campaign in the Venetia. One night a messenger beat on the Marshal's door at Naples; Masséna came out in a green dressing-gown to hear that by means of drafts signed with the Emperor's own hand, the Leghorn accounts had been transferred to the Treasury of France. The Marshal's face remained composed: "The Emperor thinks, *alors,* that we are fighting for this puppy of a king," he said, but all the same Bernadotte's purse and not his was enlarged by the Italian campaign.

There was also the point of Bernadotte the Jacobin, de Staël's true hero of the age. How far the "loyal co-operation" he had promised Napoléon would have carried the accomplished intriguer, one does not know. But about the Prince of Ponte-Corvo, one of the richest men in France, there could be no doubt; no one is a republican on a half-million a year from a monarch, even though one adjunct of the gift be the detestation of all the other marshals.

IV

"You are Charlemagne," said Dalberg, electoral archbishop of Mainz, the only one of the old ecclesiastical electors to keep his see. "You are Charlemagne; behave like it.
Regulate Germany for us and save us."

The place was Regensburg, seat of the old Imperial Diet,
which was as near as the Holy Roman Empire came to a
legislative and representative body. The very meeting of
that Diet in 1806 showed how impossible it was to continue.
There was no longer a Holy Roman Emperor to preside.
The secularizations had demolished the College of Bishops;
of the great lay electors, Württemberg and Bavaria had become kings and exempt from Dietary proceedings. The College of Towns had been composed of the old Hanseatic
cities, all of which but Nürnberg and Regensburg itself were
now cut off from south German affairs by Prussia's acquisition of Hanover; they did not even send delegates. The Frei-
herrs and minor gentry formed another College, but those
within the area of the old Rhineland Empire had now been
largely dispossessed, and they represented nothing.

"You are Charlemagne; save us." The Emperor must
have been struck by this singular parallel to the words of
Talleyrand. For a man who had now written almost as many
constitutions as Sieyès, the matter required only a few
strokes of the pen. The new western Germany was merely
the Holy Roman Empire brought into line with modern conditions and renamed Confederation of the Rhine.

It was the Empire as it had stood before Austria was set
out as a guard against the Eastern heathen, before the alien
Czechs had been admitted or the Teutonic Knights gone
crusading against Borussia. The seat of the new Confederation would be at Frankfurt, far nearer the center of gravity
and with better communications than Regensburg in the
south. Dalberg of Mainz would be Archchancellor and
executive in matters that concerned the Confederation as a

unit, and the Emperor Napoléon its protector, under a treaty of alliance. Legislative and judicial services to be rendered through two Colleges instead of the ancient four —one of Princes, including nine minor powers (for it is as sovereign states that all come to the new Diet), and a College of Kings—Bavaria and Württemberg, with the grand dukes of Hesse-Darmstadt, Baden, and Berg-and-Clèves. All the lesser nobility lost their sovereign rights, though not their patrimonies, and became nobles of the states in which they dwelt, instead of being outside states, nobles of the Empire.

It was a neat solution, having this in common with the settlement for Italy, and indeed with the constitution of the French Empire itself—that it set up a quite workable machine for introducing the vast social changes of the Revolution, without doing violence either to the prejudices or practices of the old régime. But mark—how one member of the College of Princes (the Prince of Neufchâtel) and one of the College of Kings (the Grand Duke of Berg-and-Clèves) are French marshals.

V

The sum of the solution in one direction was a silent coup d'état, a dry revolution, more extensive and of greater effect than that which established the Empire. That institution contained no offices or titles but those of actually operative functionaries. Even the Grand Huntsman and the Archchancellor of State appeared on the lists of precedence; were able to preside over deliberative bodies and to sign documents when there was no higher-ranking dignitary available. Except for the Emperor himself, the principle of hereditary governmental function remained as thoroughly abolished as under the Terror.

In the post-Austerlitz settlement that principle was reintroduced. The Grand Duke of Berg-and-Clèves bore that title, not to express the fact that he was a functionary of the French Empire, but to announce that all his descendants forever would be Grand Dukes of Berg-and-Clèves.

This was a revolution, or rather a counterrevolution; yet it was an event which shocked none of the sensibilities roused during the great Revolution, for the hereditary titles and the estates that accompanied them lay outside France. However magnificent these personages might be beyond the borders, for Frenchmen they remain officially merely M. So-and-so, with an added title, indicating the task at which M. So-and-so labored. In this respect the reorganization was an ingenious method of reconciling the egalitarianism of the Revolution with the rest of Europe, which was not ready for revolution and quite agreed with Friedrich Gentz that egalitarianism was an idea that had sprung straight from the doorsills of Hell.

The Emperor had, in fact, found a solution to the problem that had vexed the Revolution from the beginning—how revolutionary France could exist in an absolutist world. His answer was in effect that France would attempt to make no changes beyond her own frontiers, that she did not care what titles Frenchmen bore, as long as they did not bear them in their capacity as French citizens.

Yet in this whole solution, in this whole reorganization, there was something strangely jerry-built and impermanent. Strangely, because everything else Napoléon had constructed up to this time had been built to last, everything he had done had been done in terms of forever. The financial organization was to remain and has remained; the Codes had been written for all time, the prefecture system and Chaptal's agricultural department were permanent. The Consular constitution was set aside solely because events showed that it could be overthrown by a single assassination, and when the Empire was established the word "Immortal" was employed. The new organization obviously contained the seeds of its own dissolution, both in France and among the satellites. It would work only as long as all the present title-holders remained alive.

Suppose the Grand Duke of Berg-and-Clèves or the Prince of Ponte-Corvo to be killed by a cannon-ball. His successor would not be a marshal of the French army, but a thoroughly foreign potentate, French only by ancestry. The delicate system of control arising from the dual capacity was lost. Suppose Napoléon I, Emperor of the French, to be succeeded by the heir apparent, Napoléon-Charles, King Louis' son. The whole system that rested upon the head of the family's being also head of the Empire would collapse.

Napoléon was altogether too astute to have missed this fact and its implications. As to why the plan made no provision, we do not know; all is speculation. Perhaps he had reached the state of believing that the imperial will could make a new world to meet each emergency as it arose. Perhaps he had at last abandoned, half-unwittingly, the search for stability. Perhaps it was that the organization was not complete till late summer of 1806, by which date it was becoming evident that before any permanent settlement in middle Europe could be achieved, there would have to be a balancing of accounts with the terrible army of Frederick the Great.

THE WORM'S-EYE VIEW—XIII

. . . I have arrived at my most painful moment, that when the French escort left and when I perceived on the frontier the Dutch authorities who were waiting for us. To change one's country, be French no more! I experienced a tightening of the heart which prevented me from replying to the harangue addressed to us by the Dutch. My husband took care of it for both of us.

It was very little later when he, who hardly spoke to me at all any more, came in for a long conversation. He preceded it by reading a letter to me in which all our life together was passed in review. His love, his agonies, and my frigidity were explained in detail. Finally he asked me for a reconciliation.

"Stop," I told him, "I cannot consent. You have made me too unhappy with your unjust suspicions and your scandalous efforts to prove me unfaithful. I have pardoned you, but I need time to recover."

He became angry, shed a few tears and told me he did not believe in the virtue of women, that I had been unhappy and must have sought some consolation.

"Yes," I replied, "one you cannot take away from me; that of not having merited the suffering you have inflicted upon me."

He left me on that, and we made our entry into Rotterdam, which was remarkable for the exaltation of the people. But the jealousy of my husband always had the effect of public insult. I was really embarrassed by the nominations he made to my house-hold. My first gentleman, Baron de Rénesse, was a good man, but if he had existed in the time of Cervantes, would have been a model for Don Quixote. The chamberlain, M. Van der Dun, was still more ridiculous in appearance, though a man of sense. As all my attendants were at least sixty I feared riding too fast when I was out. A Frenchman who was only fifty was not allowed to stay long in my service. At the great receptions I began by making a tour of the circle and speaking to each person, but the King told me I was staying too long on my feet, that I should simply salute each person without speaking and take my place by the fireside to wait for him.

Mémoires de la Reine Hortense

23

AT LAST, NOT'UNG!

THE thing the world finds it difficult to credit about these Prussians, with their hatchet or square-cut faces, cold stoicism and not-infrequent brutality, is their sensitiveness. When Haugwitz returned to Berlin with his treaty he stepped into a whirlwind of outraged pride and vanity smarting under contempt. The city was full of the story that the Austrian negotiators at the peace table had warned Napoléon that Prussia would join them if they were pressed too far, and that "Prussia!" the Emperor had cried, "she'll sell to the highest bidder, and I'll offer her more than you."

It was not true, but it represented perfectly the sensation of insult with which Haugwitz' French alliance was received —particularly in the circle where the war party had focused around Prince Louis Ferdinand. He kept open house, a soirée every evening, at which his mistress Pauline Wiesel received, and where her friend, the brilliant Rahel Varnhagen, was always a guest. The de Staël came, Dušek the composer, Johannes von Müller, Humboldt the savant, and a host of army officers, mostly young. There was music; "choice food and good wines, especially champagne, the prince's favorite beverage, satisfied hunger and thirst. The women, stretched out on sofas, jested and were charming.

447

On such evenings the hours flew by unheeded—indeed it sometimes happened that we did not separate until five, six, seven or eight o'clock—" after a night of passionate political discussion, love-making, and faro. It was objected to Seine Königliche Hoheit that not a few of the men he admitted to these occasions were unworthy of the princely confidence and that most of the women could not be received in any other society.

Louis Ferdinand replied that he needed people like that around him to keep his spirits up, just as he needed a fancy dog for a drawing-room ornament, and arranged a performance of Schiller's *Wallenstein,* with tickets supplied to all the young officers, so they might make a demonstration when the patriotic speeches were read. The young officers wanted a war and profoundly despised Austrians—as for that matter, did the older ones, who had fought the whitecoats in the days of the great Frederick, and knew how stupid they were. As for the Russians—"They are all geniuses," said one of the young officers, "only none of them will admit the genius of the rest."

Young and old went daily to the drillyard together; old eyes could see how the young Prussian foot had kept that wonderful precision of movement which Vater Fritz had given to it, how every musket across the long line fired simultaneously and every arm was raised in the motion of reloading as though all were controlled by a single brain. Pfui!— the last time the French warred on us, a mere subsidiary army beat them soundly. "His Majesty's army can produce *several* generals equal to M. de Bonaparte," said General Rüchel, firmly.

All this and much more was reported by Prince Louis to the Queen, who was still the animating spirit for war. She was in a state bordering on hysteria that winter—the failure of her paladin Alexander to deal with the Horror, Frederick William's failure to keep the oath sworn at the tomb, the illness of her little son Ferdinand (he would die when the leaves turned green), the success of Napoléon in Naples—a darkening world. "Beat the Monster, beat him to the ground!" she would cry to her husband, bursting into bitter tears, and for the first time in their marriage so far forgot her own rule for maintaining relations with Hohenzollerns that there were discordant voices in the royal apartments.

Poor Frederick William, doubtless with a sensation of being between millstones, besought Haugwitz to supply him with arguments, but the equally unhappy Foreign Minister could find few of a type likely to appeal to an opposition based on a sense of indignity. What he did offer was the voice of reason: the choice before him at Vienna was simple —Hanover or war. Not war at the end of December, when the Prussian army would be mobilized and might have help from Russia, but on December 5, alone against a veteran and victorious army already at the borders. Surely members of the royal cabinet must see that such a war would end in disaster; the Prussian army by itself was hardly greater than the Austrian and Russian together.

If the honor-worthy members of the cabinet saw anything of the kind, they kept quiet about it. Their answer was to accuse Haugwitz of being an incompetent diplomat; he might have had Hanover without giving up the three provinces, above all Ansbach, that beloved little domain of Great Frederick's beloved sister Wilhelmina. (The union of greed and sentimentality is a peculiarly Prussian characteristic.) No; Haugwitz had dishonored Prussia in the eyes of Europe by turning over part of the German patrimony to a foreigner. It was essential to recover the national reputation by an act which would show that Prussia had not been compelled to take the choice of Hanover or war, but had rather been the dictating party.

Over the anguished protests of Haugwitz (who knew his Napoléon better than they did) the assembled *Rats* advised His Majesty to ratify, but with reservations: the alliance which was part of the treaty should not be an all-out offensive and defensive link, but a conditional one; France should furnish as an annex to the treaty a public "explanation" of what had been done in Italy, what would be done for the Neapolitan Bourbons, who were kings by the grace of God and could not be deposed; Ansbach should remain Prussian; the French Empire must consent to the acquisition by Prussia of the Hanseatic cities along the north German coast.

This satisfied everyone but Prince Louis Ferdinand, who was ordered to join his regiment without even saying farewell to the Queen, the ostensible cause being a memorial he presented, asking for the dismissal of Haugwitz. (It was, of course, written by Gentz.) Haugwitz himself took the reservations to Paris in person, since Antoine Laforêt, the French minister, had accepted them only with the phrase *sub spe rati,* which meant that he hoped they would be accepted by the home government, but thought not.

Haugwitz reached the French capital on February 1, 1806 —that is, at the worst possible date for the success of such a mission, since advices had just come in that England was sick of the war, Fox had succeeded Mr. Pitt with a personal program of making peace. Hanover would be a powerful lever in that direction, considering George III, Defender of the Faith. The Emperor frankly told Haugwitz as much in the course of one of his very best tirades, which he ended by saying that if Prussia placed herself frankly and formally on the French side, neither of them would have any future coalitions to fear, but that such an arrangement demanded the most loyal execution from both parties. There had evidently been no meeting of minds in the present case. The Vienna treaty was unratified; very well, tear it up. It falls to the ground. Let everything be as it was before; Prussia retains Ansbach, Clèves, and Neufchâtel; Hanover returns to France and will be used in negotiation with England.

Graf Haugwitz had dealt with Napoléon enough to know that his was only half rodomontade, but he pointed out that the security offered by a Franco-Prussian alliance rested upon its being written in the hearts of the participants rather than on paper. It was very important (he said) that the anti-French elements in Berlin be overwhelmed by the generosity of France; that the dignity of the King, with which the army so closely identified itself, be restored by some compensation for the violation of Ansbach, which had produced a very evil effect; in fact, that he, Graf Haugwitz, head of the French party in Prussia, return with something to demonstrate that France took care of her friends.

By this time the Emperor had become quite familiar with the character of diplomatic arguments, and he had Talleyrand to coach him, who still wanted a policy oriented toward Austria. He replied rather stiffly that since the Vienna treaty was dead, he would concede to Haugwitz another treaty making Hanover Prussian, but this time it must be surrounded by conditions which left no doubt in anyone's mind about Frederick William's position as the ally of France. Prussia must agree to close the Elbe and Weser to British shipping, which would make a broil with England on the one hand; and must guarantee King Joseph of Naples, which in view of the claimed Russia protectorate in south Italy would make trouble with the Tsar. Haugwitz sighed, signed, and sent the new treaty to Berlin by the hand of Lucchesini, regular Prussian minister at Paris, while he himself stayed on "to study the Emperor."

It was a well-advised step. When the terms of the treaty became known in Berlin, a mob broke all Haugwitz' windows.

II

The Prussians had perhaps deserved no better treatment —whether for their failure to realize that when tempest blows through the halls of the world there are no neutrals, or for their insistence that because they had been so virtuous as not to wage wars of conquest, they should have the conquests without making the wars. But political events seldom take place in an atmosphere of rational ethical criticism; they are decided on a basis of almost pure emotion, and Napoléon had failed to realize that the strongest normal emotion in Prussia is pride. This is perhaps not surprising; the only Prussians the Emperor knew intimately were that long-time minister to Paris, the Italian Lucchesini, whom Talleyrand described with the phrase "too much wit, not enough brains," and Haugwitz, polished within an inch of his life and especially pliable. Lucchesini had no pride to speak of and that of Haugwitz was aberrant—a pride in remaining in office, in knowing all the secrets. He was the kind of man who would submit to being kicked seven times in the posterior if, at the end of the process, one told him the true story of the Queen's Necklace, treated him with consideration in the presence of the Papal Nuncio, and smiled at his epigrams—a typical eighteenth-century mind, which called itself philosophical.

The policy of Prussia, such as it was, the perpetual shifting and eagerness to demand great rewards for merely standing by while the hammers of the gods were forging a new world, made it look to Napoléon as though these two representatives of Prussia were the quintessential Prussians. If he had expressed himself on their nation in words (which he did only to the extent of remarking that the Prussian eagle had a streak of vulture blood), he would have called them bullies who had somehow acquired the techniques of the art of war; like all bullies they would infallibly be found on the winning side.

France was the winning side now, and Prussian interest lay so overwhelmingly in supporting her that Napoléon was not being subtle when he interpreted as an effort to set a higher price on connivance such manifestations as the breaking of Haugwitz' windows, and performances of *Wallenstein* at which young officers rose in the pit to wave swords and sing patriotic songs. The country was an absolutism in fact as well as in theory; Frederick William could put a halt to that kind of demonstration any time he chose, the "mob" that attacked the Foreign Minister's house had worn uniforms and advanced in singularly good order. The Emperor was perfectly aware that Frederick William's device for steering between extremes was to have both points of view

represented at his council table. He had even intimated
that the dismissal of Hardenberg from that table would be
regarded as satisfactory evidence of a determination to make
the French alliance a reality. Undoubtedly he knew that the
Duke of Brunswick was in St. Petersburg, telling the Tsar
that Prussia had accepted Hanover only to keep it out of
French hands.

The Imperial reply to these slippery Prussians, as it had
previously been with slippery Italians, was to give them
less every time they asked for more. It was a thoroughly
logical reply, whose character was at last borne in upon the
court of Berlin; but it was what Sieyès would have described
as the reply of a mere executive, which met the immediate
necessity without settling the fundamental issues, or, indeed,
inquiring whether there were any. The executive type of intelligence always lives from hand to mouth, like an army in
the field—or perhaps it would be more accurate to say that
after Austerlitz, which so thoroughly demonstrated that the
world can be remade as the result of a single battle, Napoléon
realized that he could order the fragments of the world into
any kind of arrangement he desired at the moment. If the
world objected, he would beat it in a battle.

The Emperor was thus only arguing from evidence when
he presented a settlement which took no account of emotion
to these singular Prussians, who rioted in march-step and
wept over their beer in part-songs. He might be wrong—
this was one of the reasons why the Army was retained in
west-central Germany even after the Confederation of the
Rhine had cleared up most of the outstanding issues in that
territory; but the strength of the Grande Armée and his confidence in his own skill were now such that he did not particularly care what happened in Berlin. "Sire," he wrote to
Frederick William, as the strains became more and more
intolerable, "Your Majesty will be beaten. You may treat
now in a manner conformable to your rank; but in a brief
time you will be forced to negotiate on a different basis. Permit me to say that it is no news to Europe that France has

three times the population, as brave and skilled in war, as the states of Your Majesty."

III

This was assuredly the voice of reason, but the Prussians never were a particularly reasonable race, and what little of the quality they possessed altogether melted in the emotional heat of that burning summer. Damaged national pride was not in the least salved by Brunswick's report from Petersburg that Alexander took a very unpleasant view of the way in which Frederick William had carried out his solemn covenant; or that when a Prussian army crossed an angle of Swedish Pomerania to take possession of Hanover, the Swedes resisted to the point of musketry; or that when the invaders reached Hanover, the English resented it to the point of seizing 300 ships, more than half the merchant marine of Prussia. Red fires were burned by night along the streets of Berlin, strangely lighting the undersides of the linden leaves; regiments of cavalry paraded between them, waving sabers and singing the song about Red, White, and Black, the colors of iron and blood. Students heard Professor Fichte declare that "To have character and to be a German undoubtedly mean the same thing," and came out in their caps to shout beneath Haugwitz' windows: and Friedrich Gentz wrote more than five hundred letters.

He was now down at Dresden in Saxony, where he had lately been visited by Johannes von Müller, the historian. The latter was shocked by Austerlitz; had come to doubt the validity of the Good Cause, and needed to be stiffened. Gentz was the man for that task, so charming the historian by appearance and personality that Müller addressed him in the type of love-letters one sends to a sweetheart. Gentz thought him a disgusting old man and said so privately, but made Müller his messenger for the delivery of the five hundred letters—to Louis Ferdinand, the de Staël, Haugwitz, Hardenberg, Queen Luise, anyone who could be of the slightest use in setting the red fires under every rooftop in Berlin, all the missives in the same tone:

"There can and will be no peace as long as crime goes unpunished; I would sooner see the world in flames than see it

Regiments of cavalry paraded

perish in this deadly marasmus." "If Germany should become united, then we can say farewell to Russia, can see England fighting its glorious fight on a sure and grand basis, and can laugh at all the threats of France. To subdue haughty, terrible, mad, impious, detestable, and despicable France—what German can resist so ravishing a prospect?"

The reference to Russia need not surprise; Gentz and his school hated her only less than France, and the five hundred letters are filled with remarks about "the ridiculous puppet Emperor." Russia no longer mattered; nor among the red fires, bands, and shouting horsemen, did it matter that Prussia was officially at war with England and Sweden. Yet it was from Petersburg that the spark was finally set to the fuse. On the morrow of Austerlitz, Tsar Alexander dismissed Czartoryski and the young men of the Secret Committee (to such a pass have they brought us with their plan for making Russia the arbiter of Europe), and installed as grand vizier a doddering old general named Budberg, a great friend of the dowager Empress, who believed strongly in the actual as well as the legal infallibility of Tsars.

As nearly as General Budberg could make out, Alexander was bored with the war, and—as a change of administration implied a new policy in any case—an ambassador was sent to Paris. Oubril (that was his name) found Napoléon and Talleyrand in a conciliatory mood, hopeful that the product of Austerlitz and Trafalgar would be a general pacification, as the end product of Marengo and Copenhagen had been the agreement of Amiens four years previously—a more solid structure this time, since the later pair of battles had so wide an effect.

As soon as the negotiators began to talk Talleyrand perceived that material questions were far less important to the Muscovite than those of influence, of Russia's credit as a peace-making judge, the protector of small nations. France would therefore be glad to accept Russia's mediation of the English war, he said; and the two nations, France and Russia together, would mediate between Prussia and Sweden, to prove that a new international law had come into the world. As for Alexander's protectorate of the Two Sicilies, Napoléon was adamant about putting an end to the Bourbon rule there, but he would recognize Alexander's principles to the extent of arranging that the royal family should become rulers of the Balearic Islands. A beautiful plan; the document was signed and on its way to Petersburg within a week.

This was in July; by time the news reached London the peace-making Fox was on his deathbed, and Lord Grenville had become head of the administration, a much stiffer man. There had been an ambassador in Paris for several months, trying to make peace on the basis of *uti possedetis,* or hold what you now have, with Hanover an exception, according

to the best traditions of British diplomacy, which is always
willing to accept a reasonable general plan provided there
are a few exceptions in favor of England. Now this ambassador received a colleague named Lauderdale, whose recom-
mendation for the post was apparently his bad temper. His
instructions were that Britain would sign no peace which
took Sicily away from the Bourbons, since that island offered the only *point d'appui* a naval power could use against
the Empire in south Europe. At the same time an express
asked Alexander whether he meant to keep his engagement
to make no separate peace, and to remind him that the
money on which he was living came from England. Also,
somebody leaked—that is, Berlin learned that a tentative
treaty had been drafted in which Hanover was returned to
the rule of George III.

The fuse was now sputtering. Marshal Augereau got
drunk in Frankfurt and lifted a glass to the coming war with
Prussia. Murat, Grand Duke of Berg-and-Clèves, shouldered
his way into the small district of Essen to settle with the
strong arm an ancient minor territorial dispute. The Duke
of Hesse (this is Hesse-Cassel, the electoral house, not
Hesse-Darmstadt) came trotting to Berlin with a story that
he had been offered all sorts of inducements to join the Confederation of the Rhine and so extend it to the Weser. The
last tale was untrue, but that made little difference, since it
dropped into an atmosphere where Frederick William was
now trying to promote a new Confederation of the North,
with himself as Emperor, and Hesse's story made it look as
though the French were undercutting him.

The summer deepened and the heat deepened into
August; news ran through Berlin like brandy through the
blood that the Tsar had refused to ratify the French treaty.
The red fires burned and troops marched through the roaring streets, chins high and every step precisely aligned, our
honest German *Bubchen,* so strong and brave, the bands
booming Mozart's *Hymne an Deutschland.* They were
marching to their camps, *vorwärts, vorwärts,* and on 30

September a messenger with a coach pulled Friedrich Gentz from bed and told him he must come at once to Naumburg, the King wanted him, it was definite war against the Monster.

IV

A record of the meetings to which this invitation led survives, in Gentz' own hand. It is written in English, as though he were ashamed or afraid to use his own language, and to anyone sensitive to style it has the quality of a nightmare narrative, like something out of E.T.A. Hoffmann. Naumburg turned out to be army headquarters, where Gentz met General Graf Kalkreuth, who commanded a division. The General kept him for five hours, talking all the time. There was no lunch, and Gentz, who had spent the night with a cocotte, had a frightful headache that may account for the dreamlike quality of the narrative, but he faithfully recorded the General's bitter sarcasms. The publicist was not a little taken aback to hear him denounce in no measured terms the Duke of Brunswick, army commander and Frederick the Great's golden lad, whom the illustrious king had described as "uniting to youth, judgment, and to both, firmness, the perfect soldier."

Kalkreuth described the old man as vacillating, petty, jealous even of his aides. In the campaign of '93 he had found a battalion of the rearguard not marching in order and sent it back to make the march over again, all night long. (This was not really true, but Gentz did not know it at the time.) General Kalkreuth quoted the King himself: "I do not understand the Duke of Brunswick; he is always in want of five hundred men. If he had two hundred thousand he would still want five hundred reinforcements." The General finished by blowing an imperfectly perfumed breath into Gentz' face as he ejaculated over a wagging finger:

"Now remember—if there is not a complete change in our organization within the next eight days this campaign

will end in the same way as that of 1792, if not in a catastrophe that will overshadow the battle of Austerlitz."

The publicist set down an extremely unfavorable impression, without being sure at the time whether the fault lay
with Kalkreuth or with Brunswick, and pushed on to Weimar, where he found everything in confusion and Herr von
Goethe not receiving. Next day he was in Erfurt, being
greeted with a warm handclasp and an invitation to dinner
by Haugwitz, whom he had called a "pacifistic reptile" in
the public prints only a couple of weeks before, with the
amiable suggestion that the Minister be broken on the
wheel. "It was more than good of you to come," said Haugwitz. "What we want is only to hear your impressions of our
undertaking."

He launched into a long explanation of the Cabinet's
course, which had given Prussia an undeserved reputation
for duplicity, whereas her conduct had been in fact irreproachable. The King could not bear the thought of war;
had deceived himself from year to year with the hope that
Napoléon's rickety empire would collapse under its own
internal stresses. "Secondly, would it not be desirable amid
such threatening conditions that at least one state in Europe
remain intact and prepared for a serious emergency?"

While he was talking, another pacifistic reptile came in,
Kabinettsrat von Beyme, whose influence was so much beyond his official position that Gentz had devoted a special
memorial to the project of having him hanged, or at least
banished. He too was gracious, and the disciple of Kant to
him. Haugwitz went on with his explanation; he had been so
opposed to the document signed at Vienna during the previous December that when he presented it, he implored
Frederick William not to ratify it and to dismiss him; he
could prove the fact by witnesses. Beyme nodded and named
himself one of the witnesses. Did not the Chevalier Gentz
agree that their policy had been wise, meant for the best,
that they had nothing to retract?

The Chevalier (who knew both men were lying) by no

means admitted their wisdom; leaving aside minor issues, what he chiefly could not countenance was signing an alliance with the Demoniac. "However, I shall give you this one piece of advice. Let bygones be bygones. The present is bad enough. Let your conduct be unequivocal and firm now; the world will side with you."

Both the Prussians appeared to be much pleased, and Gentz, who thought very highly of his own importance, began to form the opinion that they had invited him chiefly for the impression his presence at Prussian headquarters would make on the world. It developed that there was more to the matter when, after some indifferent remarks, they asked him what he knew of the disposition at Vienna, whether he could present the Prussian position to that court in a just light, aid them with his pen, perhaps assist in smoothing over the trouble with England?

The atmosphere of dream deepened upon Gentz' mind as he replied that his position was rather delicate, a councilor of the Kaiser of Austria who was visiting a foreign military headquarters without the permission of his sovereign. He was out of the government now and therefore out of touch; he was sure that the responsible men of Prussia would never have undertaken so serious an enterprise as war against Napoléon without liaison to Vienna and London.

The pacifistic reptiles did not answer directly and the evening came to an end, but they invited Gentz to dine the next night with Kabinettsrat Lombard, who wished to bespeak his help in drafting the Prussian war manifesto.

Lombard was another of the group described by Gentz as vomit-worthy scoundrels, but he kept the appointment, finding the old councilor so dreadfully stricken with gout that he could hardly bear to be carried from one chair to another; very depressed. "I—I have nothing to look forward to but the grave—" and he handed over a draft manifesto which cited the execution of the Duc d'Enghien, two years before, as the main reason for war, a document that would have to be entirely rewritten.

Army headquarters, which Gentz now visited, were hardly less trancelike, but in an entirely different way, everyone dashing through a St. Vitus' dance with bright, burning eyes, almost shouting any desired information to all comers. Secrets? Did not matter; these French were the men of Rossbach, when they fled before our attack, though nearly three to one; amateur soldiers, weaklings, no character, not like us Prussians, to whom war is the highest joy.

Gentz waited on the Duke of Brunswick; the old philosopher-prince, whom the French had once discussed taking as their king, was heartily glad to see him, but could not be prevented from embarking on a chain of complimentary remarks which ran all up and down the details of his visitor's career. Gentz fidgeted, but it must have been nearly an hour before the Duke took cognizance of his unease, had a map spread out, and began to explain the plan of campaign.

v

The French were well scattered across Franconia, south beyond the great Thüringerwald, which stretches unbroken from a point north of Fulda to where the Erzgebirge forms the northern shield of Bohemia, a wooded mountain country, full of dwarfs and legend, only to be crossed by many marches and with much difficulty. At its eastern end, just before meeting the Bohemian border, the Thüringerwald becomes the Frankenwald, somewhat less tough and savage, which can be crossed in two or three hard marches, since there are at least three roads that will bear artillery.

We have a Principal Army, six divisions strong, around Erfurt (the Duke explained), with a Silesian-Saxon Army under Prince Hohenlohe just south of Leipzig, five divisions; Rüchel's independent corps of three divisions at Mühlhausen, and Blücher's independent cavalry division behind that. These 150,000 men could be projected through the Frankenwald by way of Hof on Bamberg where, provided that no one makes some grave mistake, they would find

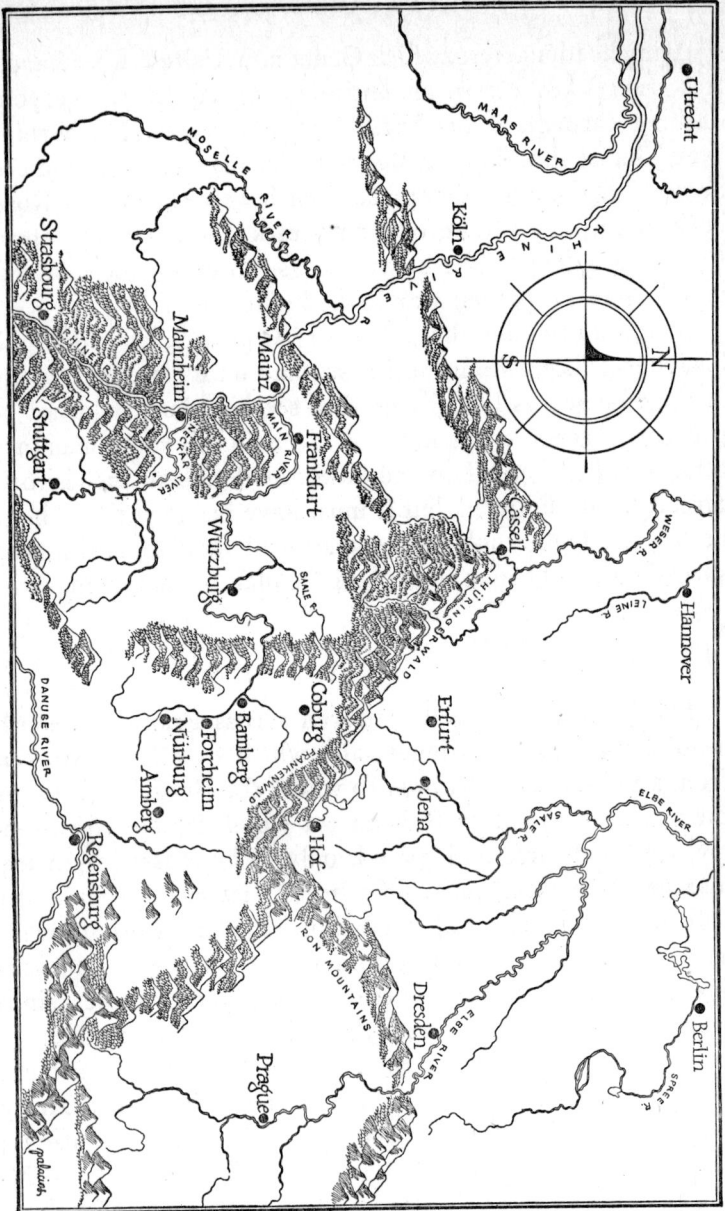

themselves in the midst of the widespread French corps and could beat them in detail.

Gentz inquired if this plan had been adopted. The Duke's lips writhed in what was evidently intended for a smile, and he replied that it has been discussed at the Ober Kriegs Collegium, at which all the leading generals and their staffs presented minutes on each proposal offered. It was also possible (he continued) to leave the Thüringerwald on the left and take the main highway to Frankfurt where, provided no grave mistakes were made, a part of the French army would be destroyed and their main body to the east cut from its connection with France. The objection to this was that the latest advices showed only the corps of Augereau lying in the region of Frankfurt, and even this one might evade us to join their main army in Franconia. It had ever been one of the principles of the Great Frederick to strike at and destroy an important fraction of the enemy forces, lest the blow itself give them time to concentrate the remainder and so to achieve numerical superiority.

A third possibility was to strike through the Thüringerwald toward Würzburg, the geographical difficulties would yield to the surprising effect achieved, provided that no grave errors were made. It was something like this plan that he himself had offered to the Ober Kriegs Collegium (the Duke continued), on the advice of his Chief of Staff and Quartermaster-General, Colonel von Scharnhorst; except that once through the forest, he did not propose to strike rightward toward Würzburg, but straight south. He had suggested a movement of ten divisions in six columns, by Meiningen and Hildburghausen, while Rüchel's Corps thrust at Augereau in the direction of Frankfurt.

—This was the plan, then? inquired the publicist, squirming.

There was still a fourth possible method of attack (the Duke went on, without appearing to hear him) : to separate and move in two or three columns, the more rapidly to overcome the geographical problems—turn the Thüringerwald on both flanks at once to gain speed, at the same time sending a force through it to confuse the enemy. This was essentially the proposal of Prince Hohenlohe and his Chief of Staff, Colonel Massenbach. The Prince wished to have the Saxon-Silesian Army (which was in fact less than half Saxon) reinforced up to six divisions, and with it to hold the outlets of the Frankenwald, while the Principal Army moved along the great highroad via Eisenach toward Frankfurt, General Rüchel covering its right flank from the area of Hesse. He himself, the Duke, considered that such a movement violated the principle of concentration.

—But could it be done? asked Gentz. Brunswick remarked that the publicist was rather like Colonel von Scharnhorst, who at the conference that very day had grown so impatient as to burst out, "In war it is not so much what one does that matters, but that whatever action is agreed upon should be carried out with unity and energy." Himself could not quite agree, although it was possible that even so mad a plan might succeed, provided no one made any grave mistakes——

Said Gentz, who was becoming more than a little tired of this exculpatory phrase; "Sir, surely it is to be hoped that under your leadership none will be made."

Again the rictus around the mouth: "Alas, I can hardly answer for myself, and now I am required to be responsible for others." The philosophical Duke went on to explain that Hohenlohe really knew the French intimately, had been all summer the guest of one of their divisional commanders, and was a very able officer, but easily influenced by violent arguments, not liking to debate. In Colonel Massenbach there had been visited upon him the prince of arguers, a true *génie diabolique.* The pair had nearly gone beside themselves when they heard his (Brunswick's) plan. Old Marshal Möllendorf, now on the shady side of eighty, who could be considered as representing the word of Frederick the Great himself in the Ober Kriegs Collegium, had said the fatigues of modern campaigning were too much for him, he could not decide among the rival plans.

There were arguments in which the Duke found himself isolated, since the others rejected Scharnhorst as a Hanoverian who had no touch with the Frederician tradition. Would you believe it? Hohenlohe had even issued an order forbidding in words that his staff "should make fun of the commander-in-chief's imbecilities." Rüchel, the Duke considered, was a good man, but all too devoted to the King; could not forget that as a young officer he had been singled out by that great and earlier King as possessing the divine spark, believed that no Hohenzollern could make a mistake. Oh, Brunswick was quite prepared to admit that General Rüchel was the best drillmaster in the army, his corps approached most nearly the Frederician ideal of precision; but he always waited for the King to speak, and His Majesty considered himself too young and inexperienced to speak without advice. "I am left alone," said Brunswick unhappily.

But what was the plan of campaign, then?

It was not fully determined. There was a shortage of clerks to write out the necessary orders from the high command to the regiments. Since the conferences in Charlottenburg, which had occupied the whole month of September, so many things had changed. The River Saale, deep and with steep banks, afforded admirable cover for the flank of an army passing through the Thüringerwald, or even for one which the French might attack by reversing that route, but Prince Hohenlohe and Colonel Massenbach were very insistent that our forces cross the river to seal the outlets of the Frankenwald. Bonaparte had been reported at Aschaffenburg in person, and it might be he would attack. However, there would be another council of war in the morning.

The date was now 4 October. Gentz left the interview deeply melancholy and ordered his coach for Weimar. The roads were choked with artillery, his coachman had to turn out into the ditch several times, and he got little sleep that night. The final ultimatum would expire that night, and the manifesto he had written for Lombard would be issued.

WRONG END OF THE TELESCOPE—XIV

George Jackson to his brother from Berlin:

WE are having a revival of balls and fetes, which, while war was impending, had gone out of fashion. They are even now considered by many persons rather *hors de saison*. The Grand Duke Constantine has been here for the last ten days, with his suite, and as he is as fond of dancing as the queen herself, several balls have been given by the Court, and many other gaieties are preparing. *We,* however, do not profit much by it; for the Court, not choosing to see M. Laforet or any of his party, has hit upon the expedient of excluding the *corps diplomatique in toto*. For my part, I do not quarrel with this arrangement; but many of the young men, and especially those of the Russian mission, which has seven *attaches,* think it very hard, and wish politics, war, and Bonaparte at the deuce, for preventing them from leading a dance.

Anon.—Present State of France:

THERE are not ten houfes now building in Paris and its fuburbs, and fome lately finifhed, in the beft part of the town near the *Fauxbourg* (fuburb) of St. Honoré, on the fite of the Convent of the Jacobins, are without occupiers. Great part of Paris exhibits nothing but raggednefs and dirt. The inhabitants, however, contend that it is cleaner fince the revolution than before.

. . . . .

The French are beginning to make fmall advances in the cotton manufactory, and they are endeavouring to improve the woollen. Their boafted porcelain has nothing to recommend it but the dearnefs of the paintings. The famous tapeftry-manufacture at the Gobelins is continued, and furnifhes exquifite fpecimens to adorn the Imperial palaces, and for prefents to foreign powers. They improve in the conftruction of carriages, which however are intolerably heavy in their parts, and which are bought at extravagant prices. They are generally well painted, and much gilding is beftowed on them, but the iron work is very bad. The wages of the workmen are greatly inferior to thofe paid in England; but then they do not do half the quantity of work.

Diary of Lord Fitzmaurice:

OF the Duke of Brunswick's four sons, the eldest was well-nigh imbecile; the second was an idiot; the third was blind; the fourth was the son who fell. "Only private persons," the Duke once told Massenbach, "are happy in the married state."

"As he spoke," says Massenbach, "There was a look of despair on his face, and I mentally compared his eldest son and heir with Forstenburg, his natural son."

Varnhagen von Ense—Sketches of German Life:

DURING the whole summer we had heard of warlike movements interrupted by hopes of peace; but after Napoleon had obtained a firm footing in Germany by means of the Rhenish Confederation, all idea of peace was at an end, and everyone in Prussia who had a voice called loudly for war. I distinctly remember meeting an officer who asserted that the war was as good as ended,—that nothing could now save Bonaparte from certain destruction. When I attempted to talk of French generals, he interrupted me by saying, "Generals! whence should they spring? We Prussians, if you like it, have generals who understand the art of war; who have served from their youth up: such men will drive the tinkers and tailors, who date only from the Revolution, before them like sheep. For God's sake, do not talk to me any more of French generals!" In Treuenbriezen I saw old Field Marshal von Müllendorf on his way to join the army, with a smiling countenance making the most confident promises of victory out of his carriage window to the surrounding crowd; he then drove off amid the loud huzzas of the assembled multitude. The soldiers were singing jovial songs, and rejoicing that at last they were to be led against the enemy.

Reeve—Journal of a Residence in Vienna and Berlin:

AT twelve o'clock we went to hear Professor Fichte deliver a lecture upon the new transcendental philosophy. The professor is a disciple of Kant, but he has pushed his speculations much farther than his master, and is considered the profoundest philosopher and the greatest genius that ever lived. About 120 persons were present, to hear what?—to hear a little costive fellow expound and pronounce words without meaning and old truisms, with all the pomp and solemnity of a new discovery. As far as we could understand anything of this discourse (and three of us puzzled our brains to make out anything like sense), it was to show the nature and essence of our absolute existence, and to prove that God was love. The nonsense was incomprehensible, and it was a matter almost incredible how such a man should have so many hearers.

24

PRUSSIA: MIDNIGHT

Saxony: October 3–14, 1806

ON THE morning after Austerlitz, the 30th and long-
est Bulletin of the Grande Armée was issued. The
Emperor himself wrote it; of the action on the left
wing it said only that Lannes' Corps had advanced as though
on parade and withstood four fine charges of cavalry. In
view of the compliments paid in the same document to his
enemy Murat and to the unspeakable Bernadotte, this was
just a little more than Maréchal Jean Lannes could stand;
he quitted the army at night without saying a word to anyone and rode like the wind for Paris. Not even Murat could
catch him when Napoléon became aware of what had happened, and sent the cavalryman in pursuit a couple of days
later.

By easier stages, the disgusted marshal rode on to his
old home in Gascony, where he spent the winter and most of
the summer entertaining with Lucullan opulence the neighbors who had known him as a poor gamin, and making their
eyes pop out with his prodigious tales of the wars. The Emperor never addressed him a word of reproach—or any
other communication for that matter—but the sound of the
trumpet was borne to his retreat, and on 5 October he reported at headquarters in Würzburg, cheerfully ready to
take over his corps again, as though nothing had happened.

He found things a good deal changed in the army since the morrow of Austerlitz. Old Marshal Lefèbvre had been in command of his corps, the V, now in a concentration area some seventy miles northeast of Würzburg, up under the shadow of the Thüringerwald. The older man was at once transferred to the infantry of the Guard, which had been brought up to 9,000 men, rather more than Bessières could handle in addition to the Guard cavalry. Lefèbvre was quite happy over his new appointment and never exhibited a trace of jealousy about being displaced. All the corps had been reinforced up to book strength, and though there were only six of them present (Marmont with the II was down in Dalmatia, trying to clear some Russians out of the Bocche di Cattaro, which had been imprudently surrendered to them by an Austrian officer; Mortier was on the middle Rhine with the VIII), the total of the army was over 180,000 men, much larger than in the Austrian campaign.

The plan under which the corps had different sizes, more or less accidental in the beginning, had been formalized. Lannes himself, Ney and Augereau, the attack commanders, had only two divisions apiece, with the usual complement of light cavalry. Soult, Davout, and Bernadotte, the maneuvering commanders, had three divisions each, or about 10,000 more men than in an attack corps.

There was a new strategic concept or order of march which (it was explained to the marshal) Napoléon called the *bataillon carré*. Under it the ideal arrangement was to make an approach to the enemy by three parallel roads, with the cavalry screen all across the front. One of the large corps would be on the center road in advance. In the present case this would be Bernadotte with the I Corps from Kranach, for the Emperor had decided to turn the Prussian position by a swift march through the Frankenwald. A little less than a day's march behind, on each of the roads to right and left, would be another corps—Lannes himself on the left in this case, Soult from Amberg on the right flank. A half-day's march behind them, a full day behind the leading

corps on the center road, would come another big corps—
here it was Davout with the III, marching from his present
position at Bamberg. The whole made a lozenge formation;
no matter from what direction an opponent approached, the

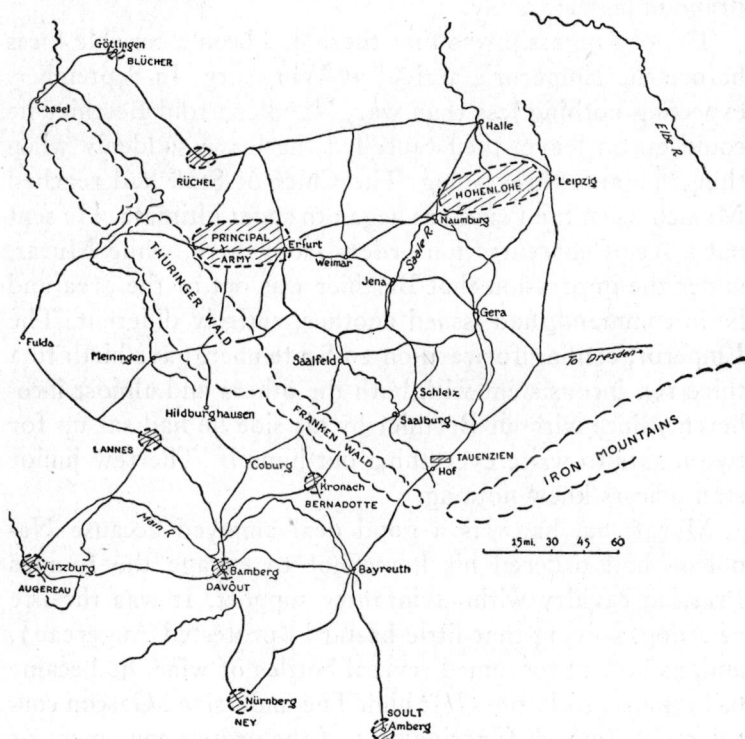

Prussian campaign: the concentration areas, October 3–6

army had only to face him and it would be already provided
with a right, a left, and a center, with a reserve behind the
center. In this case the extra corps were added to the wings,
Augereau with the VII Corps sustaining Lannes on the left;
Ney to follow Soult, coming up from Nürnberg.

Lannes had only a few moments with his old friend Augereau before hurrying off to take over his corps; the big
marshal said that the little bastard was becoming so arbitrary in his manners and leaving his commanders so little

initiative that he himself intended to give all up and retire
to enjoy his rest—as soon as these Prussians were trounced.
He demanded the pleasure of beating them in order to pay
them out for the barbarities he had suffered while a simple
dragoon in their army.

The other gossip was that there had been a terrible mess
before the Emperor's arrival at Würzburg. In September,
expecting nothing less than war, Napoléon told Berthier he
could go on leave, then cancelled the leave suddenly when
things became threatening. The Chief of Staff had reached
Munich when the Prussians began to spout ultimata. He sent
out a set of concentration orders from there, while Murat,
under the impression that Berthier was out of the area and
he in command, had issued another, entirely different. The
Emperor, coming forward on 29 September, gave birth to a
third set, inconsistent with both the others and almost incoherent, since without Berthier by his side he had sat up for
two nights to write everything out himself. The few junior
staff officers knew nothing.

Murat, ha, ha, was a good deal annoyed because Napoléon had ordered his horse not to engage the famous
Prussian cavalry without infantry support. It was the life
of a dog, serving that little bastard (protested Augereau),
and, as he had consumed several bottles of wine, he became
lachrymose, so Lannes left him. The undersized Gascon considered a stomach for wine part of the proper equipment of
a gentleman and a soldier, but lacked the physical capacity
himself, and was not a little envious of his friend's ability to
wake in happy thunder on the morning after a debauch.

II

"I never had a plan of campaign," said Napoléon long
later, an understatement in the technical sense, since he had
a clearly defined plan for swinging his *bataillon carré*
through the Frankenwald into the triangle between Saale
and Elbe, and there provoke a battle by reason of the fact

that he would be nearer to both Dresden and Berlin than the Saxons and Prussians whose capitals they were. This involved marching fast enough to outpace the Prussians, who were celebrated marchers, but the Emperor did not see the achievement as at all impossible. The men who had tramped to Ulm had legs as good as any, and now they would be moving in accordance with a system which applied to an entire campaign the unified architectural structure that had first appeared on the battlefield of Austerlitz.

Napoléon was thoroughly informed as to the constitution and methods of the Prussian army, a subject which Frederick William had enjoyed discussing with the friendly Duroc. In that army the divisions and even the brigades were administrative, not tactical, commands, except on the field itself. The basic method was that by which Frederick of Prussia had carried to the limits of its possibilities the absolutism of the eighteenth century. No confidence was placed in any subordinate except on the field. When a move was contemplated, aides summoned the divisional commanders to the King's headquarters. There they received their orders orally and discussed them with the high command to make certain all was understood, and to offer comments.

Clerks at headquarters then prepared written orders and schedules for each formation down to the regiment, the divisional commanders rode back to their stations, and the march began. The method had been both rapid and precise in Frederick the Great's army, which had gone to Rossbach with 21,000 men, and to its greatest victory at Leuthen with 33,000, rather fewer than Soult had in his single corps. But when it came to handling a force of 150,000, distributed across a front of 120 miles, the time spent in the comings and goings of unit commanders tended to outrun that employed by the soldiers in marching.

In the Grande Armée, on the other hand, the admirable Berthier prepared orders for a corps to be at a given place by a given hour; they were carried off by an aide at the gallop, and the corps commanders broke these generalized in-

structions down into details for brigades and regiments—
while in motion. If Napoléon felt the need of closer super-
vision for any corps he went to the front himself instead of
sending for the marshal affected.

There was also another difference between the two
armies which helped the Emperor's confidence that even
with equal speed afoot he could outmarch Prussia. Nothing
was too good for a soldier in that armed state; even a lieutenant of infantry had one horse to ride and another to
carry his baggage, and there were tents for all the men. The
army supplied itself from magazines by vast caravans of
wagons—another case of something that worked very well
for Frederick and 21,000 men, but which encountered difficulties when the figure was multiplied by seven under Frederick William III. The road-net that enabled the smaller
force to live in luxury from its carts and yet to move rapidly
could not support the bigger army at all. One of two things
could happen: either part of the army would pile up behind
the trains of the advance divisions, or all of it would run
short of food, shelter, ammunition. In practice the Prussian
army was influenced in both directions; it moved slowly and
its men were often cold and hungry, while the fantassins of
Gaul ate well off the country and slept warm in the great-
cloaks which Prussians did not have.

Napoléon thus had good ground for believing that he
could circle round the flank of the enemy before they could
counter effectively, his own left meanwhile protected by the
Thüringerwald and still more by the *bataillon carré* which,
as he was operating on a 38-mile front, would enable him to
bring three-quarters of his force into action in 24 hours and
all of it in 48. Nevertheless the reputation of these Spartans
of the north stood so high that the most elaborate precau-
tions were taken in case the information or the deductions
from it proved inaccurate.

"We shall have more to do than with the Austrians," remarked the Emperor. "We'll really have ground to move
this time." The line of operations and supply would not be.

up the Main, as one might expect; that would be open to a fast-moving counterattack. Rather the communications would run back through Würzburg to Forchheim, Mannheim at the Neckar junction with the Rhine, and Strasbourg. A second line, in case of defeat, was established with depots along the upper valley of the Danube, to the Breisach crossings of the Rhine.

There were some 80,000 recruits in the depots of France; as fast as these were trained, they were being forwarded to Mortier's new VIII Corps at Mainz, where he was expected to have 20,000 men by 12 October to hold against any attempt of the enemy to strike north round the Thüringerwald toward France. Old Marshal Kellermann was in charge of the training area along the Moselle; if anything came in his direction, he was authorized to make use of the central reserve of 8,000 in Paris, could call in Mortier from one wing and King Louis of Holland from the other, who was ordered to concentrate his own army of 15,000 at Wesel, now strongly fortified. The English might try a diversionary landing in Hanover, in which case Kellermann and Mortier would concentrate on King Louis. Napoléon did not think these enemies could come with more than 25,000 men.

III

Having been unable to decide on anything, the Prussian council of war on October 6 decided to do nothing; that is, to watch all the passes and wait for developments. Rüchel, with Blücher's cavalry in support, was pushed out to Eisenach on the northwestern limit of the Thüringerwald, with detachments as far forward as Fulda. Brunswick's Principal Army was in the region of Erfurt, with one division under Duke Karl August of Saxe-Weimar pushing through the great forest to Meiningen in the preliminary move of the Duke's own plan, while Hohenlohe, in pursuance of his scheme and Massenbach's, had his Division Tauenzien as far forward as Hof. The rest of the Silesian-Saxon army,

pretty much scattered, stood along the Saale from Jena to
beyond Naumburg, ready to cross. The total front was something over 90 miles.

Saxe-Weimar had a chief of staff named Captain Müffling,
very forwardly and intelligent; he did his own scouting. On
the morning of the 8th, a report ran in from him that the
French were indeed moving up toward the Frankenwald in
the region of Coburg, but in a most unmilitary manner, with
a good deal of straggling and no proper flank or advance
guards. (This happened to be true enough, but it was Lannes
on a concentration march, where he did not think it worth
the trouble to screw discipline down tight.) Müffling suggested that a force of ten or fifteen squadrons of cavalry
could teach these enemies a sharp lesson, either by stabbing
through the forest or by striking them at its outlets.

Brunswick was much taken with this plan, but as he considered that unsupported horse could accomplish little in the
hilly, forested country, he ordered the formation of two
small columns of all arms, one to join Saxe-Weimar, operating out of Meiningen, and the other to cut through
Fulda toward Würzburg. That same day Tauenzien at Hof
was attacked by cavalry with infantry in support. He retreated in the direction of Schleiz, but the enemy pushed in
on him so rapidly that after a rearguard action in which he
lost some 600 men and a gun, he was constrained to stay on
the roads till after midnight before bivouacking, his men
suffering greatly from exhaustion and hunger.

His report and that of Captain Müffling, with Brunswick's
orders for small columns of attack to take advantage of the
slovenly French marching, gave Hohenlohe an idea. He ordered forward Prince Louis Ferdinand with the division of
his advance guard, 8,000 men, to Saalfeld, where there is a
defile at the break of the Frankenwald, through which Saale
flows in a northwesterly direction just before making its
right-angled turn back to run northeast for the junction with
Elbe. The Prince reached position by the afternoon of the
9th. There were a few French skirmishers about, and some

shots being fired. He had assembled the younger, more literary officers the night before, and they signed a paper together:

"We swear to stake our lives without question and not to survive this war, where fame and high honor await us, or political freedom and liberal ideas will be stifled and overthrown if it should turn out disastrously."

The style is somewhat less effective than that of Friedrich Gentz.

IV

The Prussian ultimatum expired on 8 October, by which date it required every Frenchman to be west of the Rhine. That morning Murat's cavalry with four companies of infantry from Bernadotte took Saalburg and a good bridge over the northwest-running part of the Saale. The next morning early there was a fight at Schleiz, which Bernadotte reported as a "battle" against a Prussian corps of 8,000, which he had decisively defeated—an estimate on which the Emperor placed exactly the weight to which it was entitled. That night Lannes' light cavalry were close to Saalfeld; Augereau a day's march behind him; Bernadotte sleeping the night at Schleiz; Davout's Corps a couple of miles short of the Saale on the same road, at Lobenstein; Soult in Hof, Ney half a day behind him.

Napoléon's October 8 estimate of the situation for Soult: "The Prussians intend to attack; their left was to debouch by Jena, Saalfeld, and Coburg; Prince Hohenlohe has his headquarters at Jena and Prince Louis Ferdinand at Saalfeld; the other commands have issued by Meiningen and Fulda. Gera is the point of concentration for the enemy's army; I doubt if they can combine before I arrive there."

It was a misestimate, placing the Prussian strength too far east, but since the bold front shown by Hohenlohe was without Brunswick's orders, a misestimate that worked to the French advantage. That night there was a good deal of animated correspondence between Duke and Prince about a new order by the former that Hohenlohe should concentrate at Jena and south of it.

At seven o'clock the next morning the light cavalry of Treilhard, which was with Lannes, reached Saalfeld, where the Prussians were discovered, drawn up in front of the town, resting their left-center upon it, at the base of an 800-foot wooded height. The marshal himself went forward, and decided the enemy's position was about as bad as it could be, halfway down a steep slope, with adequate cover to protect an attack in front, and an unfordable stream behind.

Lannes threw forward some cavalry on his right, their left, to hold them pinned; sent a couple of batteries and clouds of skirmishers to the front, who at once began to work havoc in the tight Prussian lines. The bulk of the French corps sidled toward their left, the Prussian right, behind the screen of trees. The weight of firing in that direction told Louis Ferdinand that this wing and his line of retreat were menaced. He tried to sustain the flank by pushing forward a battery to one of the hill spurs, but the French sharpshooters got all around it and captured the guns, the mass of their infantry rushed, and his whole right wing fell into confusion. The Prince had only five weak squadrons of horse, but personally mustered them to make a charge uphill at the center for a retrieve at one o'clock.

It was met by a countercharge of the French hussars, too heavy to be borne, with their numbers and the gradient. As Prussia reeled back, a young French sergeant named Guindet called on Louis Ferdinand to surrender. The Prince wheeled his fine English hunter and slashed at Guindet, giving him a deadly wound. The sergeant thrust back, and again —and again—and again; a bullet hit the fine English hunter, down under a hedge tumbled Louis Ferdinand, "the Alcibiades of Prussia," with thirteen wounds, any one of which would have been mortal.

Now the whole line collapsed, 1,500 men surrendered where they stood, above 2,000 were down, 34 guns lost, the

remainder of Louis Ferdinand's division beaten into a mass
of fugitives, and so deep a shadow of doom was cast all the
way back to Erfurt and Weimar that Friedrich Gentz, riding through the night, set down at the end of his curious
journal that the only thing now to be determined was the extent of the disaster.

V

By morning of the 11th, Lannes' account of the action at
Saalfeld and a stream of reports from the cavalry who had
overrun the countryside all the way up to Naumburg without meeting resistance told Napoléon that the enemy were
not going to concentrate on Gera, but behind the Saale, he
now thought at Erfurt. (Actually Brunswick had fixed the
concentration point between Jena and Weimar. Hohenlohe
had received orders on the night of the 9th to draw together
there, but protested stubbornly, had to be told in the King's
name that the order was peremptory, and did not send moving orders to his regiments in time to save Louis Ferdinand.)
All the better; instead of forcing Prussians and Saxons to
fight with their front making a prolongation of their line of
communications to Dresden and Berlin, Napoléon would
now get across that line and make them fight to cut their way
out. He ordered the army into a general left wheel up to the
Saale, calculating on reaching the river on the 12th along a
front from Kahla up to Naumburg, giving the troops one
day's rest, then cross on the 14th, attack on the 16th.

The wheel involved some changes in the relative positions
of the corps, since the center column (Bernadotte and Davout) were so much farther forward to the north. Lannes,
with Augereau close behind, was to strike the river at Kahla,
following it till the enemy were encountered or Jena reached,
probably by the west bank, since the better road is on that
side in this region. The Guard would head direct for Jena;
Bernadotte move up the river for a crossing at Dornburg,
Davout shoot past him to Naumburg, Soult and Ney from

their positions eastward and behind would cut across the paths of the two center corps to follow the Guard in toward Jena. If the enemy should be found out toward Bernadotte and Davout's flank Soult and Ney would be ready to offer

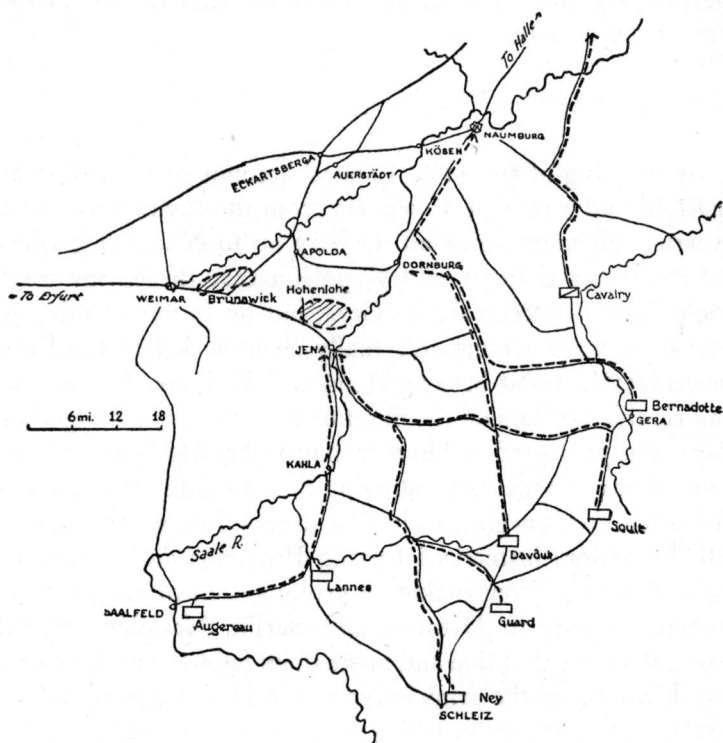

The October 11 situation and Napoleon's left wheel to contact

support to these two marshals. Some of the cavalry went down the Saale toward Halle; there were reports (perfectly well founded) that the Prussians were assembling a strategic reserve of perhaps 12,000 men at Magdeburg, and it would not do to have this force interfering.

Jena town lies at the bottom of a valley, here made quite deep by a tall hill looking down from the northeast, the Landgrafenberg, quite wooded along the slopes. Division Suchet of Lannes reached the town on the morning of the

13th, easily drove out the few Prussian pickets they found in the place, and began to climb, pushing through the trees against weak resistance. Lannes himself arrived and went up to the crest about eleven o'clock, just as the bland October sun cleared the morning mists. The top of the hill was bare, slanting not very steeply upward to the west. All across it was displayed the Prussian army as if for review; over 40,000 men, as the marshal correctly estimated them.

Lannes had only a brigade at the moment, no more than a mouthful for such a host, and he quite expected to be attacked, but it took more than the prospect of desperate battle and sudden death to unsettle Jean Lannes. One aide went to hurry the rest of the corps along, especially the artillery, another to let the Emperor know that the Prussian point of concentration had been mistaken—it was not back at Erfurt, but here on the Landgrafenberg. Now the Marshal put his men in order and waited.

So did the Prussian thousands. A little afternoon bread was passed along the French lines, and cognac; by early afternoon the rest of the corps was at hand, still a force insignificant compared with the enemy opposite. The Emperor arrived at four, looking anxious, and at once confirmed Lannes' estimates that at least 40,000 Prussians were visible; probably the rest were behind. Orders had already gone to all the corps within reach—Augereau, Soult, Ney, the Guard—that the day of rest would be lost, the men who had been marching nearly 20 miles a day for over a week must make one more long hard march and fight a battle at the end of it. Davout was to cross the Saale at Kösen, move forward to Apolda, march on the guns if Lannes were attacked early, or come down on Weimar in the Prussian rear, if the battle were delayed long enough for the main army to reach Jena. Bernadotte was to cross at Dornburg, sustaining Davout or Lannes as occasion should dictate.

In the evening Lefèbvre's Guard infantry began to come and at once went up to the lines where Lannes' men were packed in, genuinely shoulder-to-shoulder, their left on the village of Cospeda, their right on a little wood. Napoléon himself rode forward to reconnoiter. In the dark one of the sentries took him for a Prussian scouting party and fired at him, but missed—which did not give the Emperor half so much concern as the fact that when he reached the lines it was to discover there was no artillery as yet on the heights. Instead of sending to seek the reason, he went himself; and it was well that he did, for down there in the dark, the head of the artillery column, missing its turn, had become involved in a ravine beside the dam for a small paper-mill. It was so narrow that the axle boxes were jammed in the rocks, and the whole column halted; everyone was tired out, cross, and ignorant.

Everyone but Napoléon. He sent a couple of aides to the park for tools, and as soon as they came the Emperor of the French held a lantern aloft himself, directing the work with a few low-voiced orders, a gunner solving a gunner's problem—under the loom of that black height where the army of Prussia waited.

VI

Why did it wait?

It is necessary to go back to the night of the 11th, when some of Hohenlohe's Saxons, retreating from east of the Saale, were in Jena. A single red hussar with a bloody bandage round his head (he would seem to have been one of the floaters from Prince Louis Ferdinand's Saalfeld battle) rode through the gathering twilight, crying wildly, "Get back! Get back! The French are upon us." There was a panic, with artillerymen cutting loose their horses to ride off on them, streets choked with transport, and Hohenlohe himself trying to restore order, till tired men collapsed wherever they were. Colonel Massenbach was occupied all the next day getting them into some semblance of order and into camp. He had chosen a position well back on the Landgrafenberg, facing southeast, where open and rolling ground offered advantage to the orderly Prussian tactics.

In the meanwhile no staff work at all was done, for Scharnhorst, the Hanoverian, "the foreigner," was being sent to Coventry. The earliest conference was at eleven P.M.; by that time an officer had arrived from Naumburg to say that the French were in the place. They were evidently in great strength, and from their position east of the Saale offered a severe menace to the line of communications. It was decided to retreat toward Halle, Magdeburg, and the line of the Elbe, the army picking up 12,000 men of the strategic reserve en route.

Hohenlohe was instructed to cover the retreat from his position on the Landgrafenberg. Brunswick, with the King and the Principal Army, would move by way of Eckartsberga and Auerstädt, detaching one division to hold the Saale crossing at Kösen, the march to begin on the 13th. Rüchel had already been called in and was marching on Erfurt. He and the Duke of Saxe-Weimar's detachment, which was summoned from beyond the Thüringerwald, would fall in on Hohenlohe and join his movement; Blücher's cavalry to proceed with the Principal Army.

It was so late when the conference broke up that march orders could not be prepared till ten in the morning of the 13th, nor the troops begin to move till afternoon. In the meanwhile Hohenlohe found he had something not far from a mutiny on hand when he returned to the Landgrafenberg —a deputation of Saxon officers, headed by their commander, who complained that they had received neither food nor firewood for nearly four days. They were quite ready to withdraw from the alliance unless the Prussian commissariat treated them better.

It was ten-thirty of the 13th before this matter was straightened out, by which time French troops had been discovered at the eastern edge of the Landgrafenberg. To raise the spirit of his troops, Hohenlohe called for forty volunteers from each battalion, with the intention of driving these enemies into the river, since there did not seem to be many of them. The commander's proposal was being received with cheers that promised a happy issue when a messenger came to summon Colonel Massenbach to headquarters for a detailed explanation of how the general plan was being carried out. Both he and the Prince thought it wise to delay the attack until he returned. He did not get back till afternoon, and then after an argument with Brunswick, which resulted in very positive orders that no serious fighting was to be undertaken that day, the object was to disengage, and the Ober Kriegs Collegium was much concerned over getting the detached forces in, the march under way.

The position on the Landgrafenberg was that Tauenzien's division formed the outer wing, generally on a rolling eminence called the Dornberg (this is not the town), which is really an extension of the Landgrafenberg, connecting up with it by a wide saddle, into which from the south slants up a wide depression named Mühlthal. The Prussians were on the right wing, facing generally south, on a line prolonging that of Tauenzien and the Saxons, who were next to that commander. The line ran roughly through the hamlets of Closewitz, Lützeroda, Isserstedt, and Kötschau; the cavalry behind Isserstedt at the center. The French were very active during the night.

VII

The Emperor snatched a little sleep in a straw lean-to built for him by the men of the 40th. He was out by three in the morning, by which time Ney in person had arrived, and there was another ride forward with Lannes and Berthier, for a reconnaissance into a morning fog that had already begun to rise thickly. Division St. Hilaire of Soult had marched through most of the night; was taking a little rest now, and would be put in on the right of Lannes at daybreak, followed by the other two divisions of the same corps when they arrived. Augereau was close up; he would be put in on Lannes' left, and Ney's corps was to fall into reserve originally, then thrust in between Lannes and Soult at the right center as the front widened.

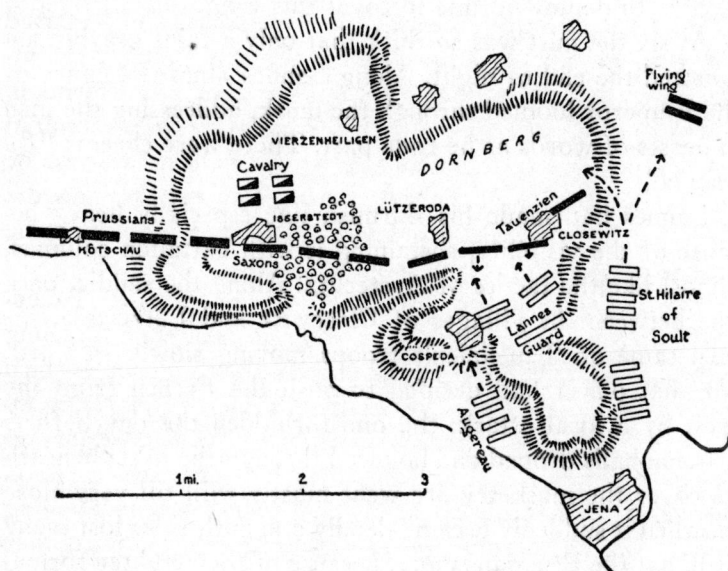

Jena: the morning situation

The difficulty (the Emperor explained) was to find room for maneuver. To obtain it, Lannes must attack from the position where he now stood, his line diagonal across the triangular southeastern peak of the Landgrafenberg, both wings slightly refused. He would drive northwestward, making in effect an oblique attack on the left wing of the enemy (of whose position Napoléon had a good idea), with Soult's big corps swinging round Lannes' right to overpower the Prussian flank and roll up their line, even if they managed to face round in time to hold Lannes. Napoléon did not know that Hohenlohe's orders were defensive; but, even had he known it, would certainly not have changed his concept that Lannes must fight for both time and space. The French were still very inferior on the field, many of the troops could not arrive before eleven A.M.; even those at hand could not deploy till room was gained by an attack, which would surely bring down a counterattack onto our left, where the Prussian weight stood. It was a nice question whether Augereau would be able to deploy in time to cover this wing.

At six the mist was so thick that only a faint graying announced the end of night. Along Lannes' lines the figure of the Emperor loomed through the murk, addressing the men in bursts of words as he rode past. There were cheers: *"En avant!"*

Lannes had made his skirmish line especially heavy because of the visibility, sustaining it with battalion columns, almost like the tactics of Austerlitz. Along the saddle, on a line between the villages of Closewitz and Lützeroda, his men came on Tauenzien's troops moving slowly forward, for that officer had decided to push the French from the crest by a local attack, the one forbidden the day before. Cannon-balls droned and bounced through the mist; beneath its cover the musketry fire went mostly wild till very close in, when it suddenly became deadly and both sides lost many men, but the Prussians more, because of their tighter formation. The guns made muffled red flashing spots in the fog. By seven-thirty both Closewitz and Lützeroda had gone French and the crest between them also; Soult's Division St. Hilaire was swinging into position around Lannes' right rear and Augereau's first arrivals were beginning to mount through Cospeda on his left.

The lay of the ground had caused a big gap to open between Lannes' two divisions, the high Dornberg ground falling just at their joint, with bullets peening across, so the men sought cover on either side. The fault was instantly noted by the Emperor, who was riding back and forth along the front, superintending everything. Into the gap, on the highest ground, he thrust forward a battery of 25 guns. The mist was still thick, but lightening enough to permit some aim; the guns hit Tauenzien's right center very hard, and under their fire Lannes' left division (Gazan) delivered a

bayonet charge that captured 22 pieces of the Prussian artillery, badly wrecked their supporting infantry, and drove
them into the wood of Isserstedt beyond Lützeroda. It was
now eight-thirty.

Hohenlohe had taken the early firing for the usual skir-
misher action when armies are in close contact and quite
refused to believe Tauenzien's first message about being attacked. He even administered a rebuke to divisional General Gräwert, next in line to Tauenzien, who had presumed
to move some of his troops toward the guns without orders.
As the firing grew louder and Tauenzien's messages became
frantic, the Prussian commander realized that the affair was
serious, ordered Tauenzien to fall back into the second line
and Gräwert to cover the retreat with his cavalry. The Prussian infantry was hurried forward into a north-and-south
line on Isserstedt and Vierzenheiligen; the Prince rode forward in person. The French front seemed to be narrow; he
called the Saxons forwards to outflank it on his right along
the edge of the heights. A force of some 5,000 men had
formed a kind of flying wing behind Tauenzien's easternmost
flank, out toward Dornburg, the town. This was similarly
ordered in to attack the rear of the French right as it
wheeled.

This last group of course ran head-on into the heavy columns of St. Hilaire, was utterly smashed and driven from
the field along slopes where the air was now clearing. At the
center Ney was now on the ground, boiling with red-headed
impatience, for he had missed Austerlitz and now here the
lines were everywhere going forward, he would have no
chance to fight; to Lannes all the glory. Riding around in
the mist like a man demented, he finally came on Colbert of
the hussars, leading the light cavalry of his corps, and a
special storm-troop of 4,000 infantry, which Ney himself
had organized. The word was forward, forward, the red
man in his passion for battle not even bothering to look at
his orders, but striking for the nearest part of the line. As it
happened this was past the 25-gun battery, between the two

divisions of Lannes, and not between Lannes and Soult, where Ney belonged.

The mist rose; here within musket-shot stood the long lines of Prussian infantry before Vierzenheiligen. Ney and Colbert looked at each other and the Marshal shrugged. "The wine is drawn and we must drink it," he said, and ordered charge. The handful of hussars, followed by his storm-troop, charged half the Prussian army and broke right into the village. It was the center of gravity of Hohenlohe's entire line. More and more of his men arrived to drive Ney out, but the red Marshal was now thoroughly enjoying himself, some of his remaining troops were coming up, he was getting help from Lannes, and every time the Prussians emerged onto the bare slopes outside the town, their solemn, precise lines lost frightfully to the fire of Frenchmen who did not disdain to lie prone or hide behind a farmer's manure pile.

By one o'clock Vierzenheiligen was won, a good part of the Prussians had been drawn into the contest for it, and were now trying to build a new line in its rear, much shaken by both musketry and artillery fire. On the Prussian right, Augereau the good tactician had found the weak spot at Isserstedt village and had driven through it, isolating the Saxons on another crest to the south. On the French right, St. Hilaire was all in position, out beyond Hohenlohe's extreme left, ready to turn in and sweep down the enemy line. In the rear Soult's other two divisions had come, all of Ney, and Murat with the heavy cavalry. "The battle is ripe," said the Emperor. "Forward, the whole line."

They went forward, the first Prussian break occurring on Augereau's front, between Isserstedt and Vierzenheiligen. Napoléon threw in Murat there with the cuirassiers, who galloped shouting forward as the machine-men of Prussia began to behave just as though they were human, throwing down muskets, abandoning guns, surrendering by battalions, an entire army dissolving into a panic-stricken mob—all but a few brave officers later found dead with colors in their hands. Only where Tauenzien had withdrawn early and somewhat rallied his men was there a semblance of a stand, and these were beginning to go too when, on the downslope from the plateau where the battle had been fought, the

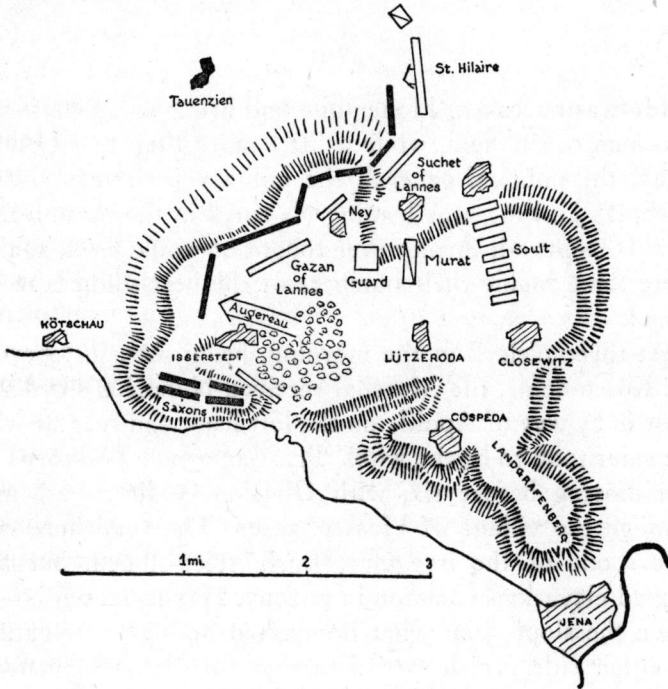

Jena: the battle is ripe

French cavalry encountered fresh and orderly lines of foot. They belonged to Rüchel and his three divisions, arriving late enough to be a little worse than never. He formed line bravely at the foot of the slope, but there could not have been over 13,000 of his men, and down against them over the crest came 90,000 French, mad with victory. Rüchel did not last fifteen minutes under that onslaught before being beaten to bits, his corps a powder of fugitives indistinguishable from those of the larger force. Back on the Landgrafenberg, Murat approached the Emperor to say that the whole of the Saxon body isolated on the enemy's extreme right had surrendered, 6,000 men. Feeling that he had done a good day's work, Napoléon sat down to write a bulletin in which he said that he had destroyed that Prussian army which had been the terror of Europe for a generation and a half.

VIII

He was mistaken. Hohenlohe had brought not quite 50,-000 men to the field, while a little more than twenty miles away, the political general, the military policeman, Louis-Nicholas Davout, was leading his corps in the most terrific battle the Grande Armée ever fought or would fight, against more than double their numbers of the best soldiers in the world.

At three o'clock in the morning, being then just beyond the Kösen defile, the Marshal received Napoléon's order to close in by way of Apolda on the left flank and rear of what the chief took to be the whole Prussian army. The corps began moving before six, with Division Gudin in advance, through the village of Hassenhausen. The road here runs across one of the irregular, fairly steep-sloped, but flat-topped elevations common in Saxony. Hassenhausen is well down the slope, somewhat dominated by higher elevations on either side, which extend farther forward—Sonnenberg on the northwest, the Height of Hassenhausen on the southeast. When there are enemies about it is always well to cover a march by taking possession of any commanding ground. Davout sent some of his light cavalry with a battery and a few battalions to obtain the heights.

At the same hour the Prussian Principal Army, whose vanguard had halted at the village of Auerstädt for the night, took up the road for Freiburg and Halle. The King rode with Division Schmettau, which was leading the infantry column; 2,500 of Blücher's cavalry were out in front, all much hampered by the fog and grumbling, for they had breakfasted on black bread and water only.

The French had only a brigade of light horse in the lead

when they ran into Blücher outside Hassenhausen, but they charged him enthusiastically. Blücher was double their numbers and weight and drove them in with loss, though not until they had taken a few prisoners, given the infantry time to form square and the guns time to unlimber. Blücher was rudely checked by this foot, then driven backward through the town. Much astounded at meeting French artillery and infantry, the Prussian general sent back for more cavalry and some horse batteries. His rallying point was a little north and to the left of the road, somewhat under the Sonnenberg; from this position he prepared to outflank and ride down the French right, while Division Schmettau should deploy enough infantry to pin their line in position.

Davout, who was with the advance, quickly questioned his prisoners and learned that the signs spelled stormy weather. Divisions Friant and Morand were pretty well back; he sent word to hurry them on at double-time, got off an express to Bernadotte, and rushed all the guns available onto the Sonnenberg. Their first discharges galled Blücher's left flank as he waited for reinforcements. The Prussian horse artillery having arrived by this time (a little before eight), he sent them forward to shoot it out with the French pieces. They had the worse of the duel, tried to retire, and were attacked by Davout's infantry skirmishers, now swarming all over the place, who killed all the horses and captured the guns.

Schmettau was now in line, and his reinforcements had reached Blücher, who came thundering down with ten squadrons of the tremendous Prussian cuirassiers. The French chasseurs were swept right away and it seemed that the infantry squares must go under that mailed shock, but Davout in person was with them, who had never let them down; he shouted *"Tenez, les gars!"* over all other battle-sounds and made them hold their fire till the ironclad horsemen were within forty paces. Horse and man went down together under the level sheets of musketry, as the attackers rode round and round, trying to jump the files or shoulder through. Blücher rallied for another try; the Sonnenberg battery hit him again, and he was driven off, badly broken, as the infantry lines locked.

Now Friant had reached the scene, leading his men forward at a trot to the right of Gudin, as Divisions Wartens-

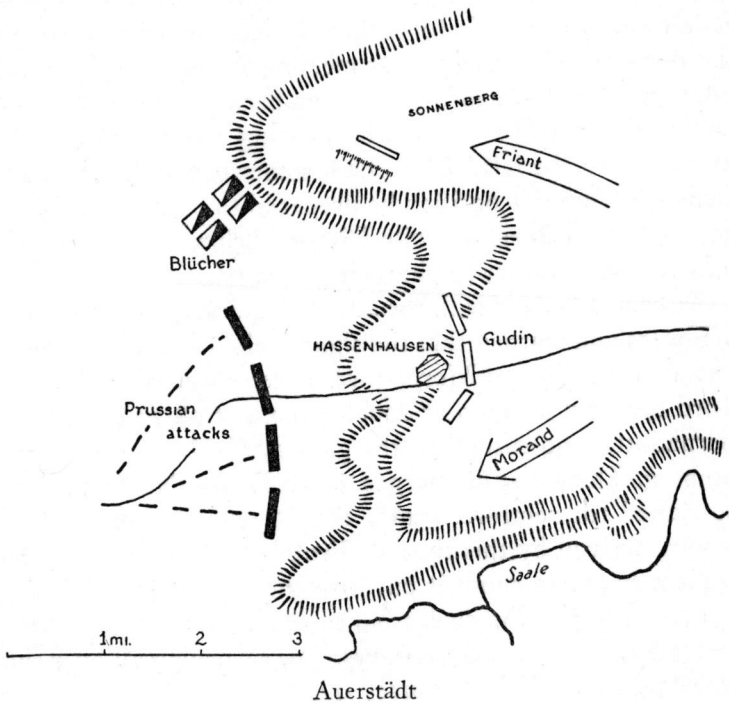

Auerstädt

leben and Orange moved up to help Division Schmettau. Davout was pointing out spots where sharpshooters might hide, leading the men forward—*En avant, En avant*—at every lull, not even thinking of defense, attacking. A bullet carried away his hat; another took off most of what hair he had left, and at the edge of Hassenhausen, Schmettau and Wartensleben were met with Gudin in a dreadful musketry fight.

The French were badly outnumbered and they lost nearly half the division (it is a military axiom that troops who have lost one-fifth of their numbers break and are useless for months). These hung on, yelling as they saw the Prussian officers go down, while Davout and Friant and Gudin rode alone the line; not realizing how many of their own were gone in the smoke with Davout and the "Three Immortals" of the divisions keeping them *en avant.*

Their marksmanship was attest by how high death struck among the Prussians. Nearly half their commanders were shot, the King was hit; Schmettau was killed; old Marshal Möllendorf mortally wounded; the Duke of Brunswick received a bullet through both eyes as he tried to take Hassenhausen with the bayonet, and it would be the death of him; it was ten o'clock in the morning, the mist was clear, and Division Schmettau had had enough.

Blücher, who all through the fight performed prodigies, had rallied some of his own horse and brought up all the remaining cavalry of the Principal Army on Wartensleben's left. Division Orange, Division von Arnim, formed for a new attack under Prince William of Prussia. The infantry went forward with the old precision, firing salvoes as they advanced against Gudin's exhausted and sorely stricken men. Close to the village they opened out and their lines vomited swarms of that cavalry which Napoléon had ordered his own not to engage without infantry support. But Division Morand had now arrived on Gudin's left. Its regiments formed square, Davout galloped from one to another, his uniform covered with powder-burns and blood, a disreputable giant. *"Tenez, les gars!"*

Not only did they hold, piling a rampart of kicking horses all round the battered squares; Morand on the Hassenhausen Height, Friant on the other flank pushed forward, and Davout was in the incredible position of outflanking an enemy double his strength on both wings, so that gunfire and musketry poured along the length of the careful Prussian lines as they wheeled forward. It was the hearts of the iron-souled Prussians that broke; and as they gave back, Gudin, Morand, and Friant counterattacked them with the bayonet. Now Prussia broke indeed, the whole army began to flow and then to run in the direction whence it had come, in prone rout.

Davout's men were too exhausted to follow; he had lost nearly a third of his force, but he had taken 115 cannon and

Its regiments formed square

6,000 prisoners, and had inflicted nearly 15,000 casualties —with 26,000 men against 64,000.

IX

Where was Bernadotte all this time? At Dornburg, within clear sound of the guns. "The miserable Ponte-Corvo" answered Davout's message for help with a disdainful smile and, "Tell your marshal not to worry," to the messenger. He pleaded afterward that he had no orders to support Davout, his orders were for Apolda, and thither he went toward evening, dawdling on the way while battles were being fought to the left and right of him. The lack of positive orders explains his own motions—perhaps; it does not explain why he withheld Sahuc's division of dragoons from Davout, who had no orders for Apolda, and wished to march to the cannon, but Bernadotte's own story was that, his corps being numbered I and Davout's III, he was automatically senior. The Emperor accepted the excuses, since one does not make scandals about a relative, even a relative by marriage.

At least Bernadotte got into the pursuit, which kept the Prussian Principal Army from going back to Weimar, where it expected to be sustained by Rüchel and Hohenlohe, and instead found the disorderly panic from Jena pouring through the streets, beating on doors: "Help, help!"—running all the way back to Erfurt and beyond, the wreck of each force adding to the terror of the other.

THE WORM'S-EYE VIEW—XIV

. . . Already at ½ p. 8 my niece sent for me. Her corner room overlooked on the one side Waldbergen, through which the road from Coburg passes. On the left, shots were falling at intervals, as well as in and around the little village of Gernsdorf, at the foot of the hills, where the Prussian Jägers were posted. Prussian batteries were stationed in the fields near the high road to Rudolstadt, and on the road itself, Fusiliers.

Towards 8 o'clock Prince Louis Ferdinand arrived on the scene, rapidly followed by Horse Artillery and 2 Saxon Infantry Regiments. In the distance their fine band could be heard.

One could see the enemy coming down the hills, and hear the sound of bugles. The fire of the Prussian Battery was incessant, but the French guns seldom came into action. Their Cavalry emerged from the forest and streamed along in a never-ending and terrifying procession. It was a dull, misty morning, but the sun came out later and one could distinguish quite clearly loose horses running about, whose riders were either wounded or dead. For some time I had almost the impression of watching ordinary Manoeuvres, until the sight of a mortally wounded Saxon Hussar being carried past made a cold shiver run down my back each time I heard a shot. The cannon-balls whistled past quite close to the Schloss, and yet no one would come away from the window to which we were as if glued. At every moment fresh French Infantry emerged from the forest, passing through Gernsdorf; the German Batteries thundering away ceaselessly and one could, in between, discern the crackling of the Saxon rifles. A terrible blood-curdling din was kept up by drums and bugles.

Our dinner was brought up to us, but who could eat at such a terrible moment? We could realize only too well the greater strength of our opponents, and petrified with fear, we awaited the end of the tragedy. I cannot describe my feelings when the moment arrived of inevitable surrender. The combatants disappeared behind the hill near Willsdorf and the sounds of fighting died away. I am still almost paralyzed with the horror of seeing the red Hussars rush into the town, shouting and firing, threatening to cut down the Guard at our doors. Infantry now came from Graba, bringing with it all the horrors of an undisciplined rabble.

The courtyard was soon filled with prisoners and wounded. Everything that could be found in the way of kitchen utensils was requisitioned. Nothing was good enough for them and they treated our servants with great roughness and insolence.

In the midst of the turmoil of departing and arriving officers, something drew me to the window. A detachment of Infantry with its eagles, preceded by bearded sappers, marched into the courtyard carrying something on poles. Only when they dropped their burden on the ground, did I recognize the body of Prince Louis Ferdinand. Naked, and only wrapped in a rough cloth, lay this great Prince, his fine head uncovered. No wound had disfigured his face.

Private Diary of Augusta,
Duchess of Saxe-Coburg-Saalfeld

25
REJECTED

Central Europe; Forever

THE pursuit that followed the double battle of Jena-Auerstädt is celebrated, and with justice. It set the standard unto all future ages for dealing with an enemy who has been beaten in the field, but may yet come to it again. Yet that pursuit is perhaps less important in military technique than in politics and philosophy, as a pragmatic criticism of Frederick the Great and the whole age of rationalism, of which Frederick's system was the choicest flower. The last of the kings thought he had built a nation out of what was not much more than a good dukedom; the pursuit after Jena revealed that he had achieved no more than a special form of police state.

His Prussia provided security and order and demanded obedience. The effect of Jena was to reveal that the three taken together are a drug. As soon as the security-giving authority was pulled down, the people under it could think of nothing but to offer their obedience to the nearest promise of security available; and that promise was offered by the French. There was an effort to rouse the countryside to national resistance, and Napoléon certainly gave it every chance to find a focus when, late in the pursuit operation, he proclaimed that Prussia west of the Oder was conquered, and the Black Eagle emblems should everywhere be taken down.

There was no stirring. The loyalty of the Prussian peasant, which was not inconsiderable, had been directed toward the army and not to the nation. The army belonged to the King; and even he commanded the loyalty of the peasant only at the second remove. After the pursuit that little man looked up to see a hussar standing over him, who spoke in a loud voice, and, even though he spoke in a foreign language, the peasant touched his forelock and said, *"Zu Befehl."*

Napoléon had an acute sense of this relation. On the morning after the battle he spoke of his intention to destroy the Prussian army, that corps of Janissaries, that troop of Mahrattas, which had for more than half a century levied blackmail on all central Europe, and indeed all Europe. The fact that the Prussians had taken their payments in territory (inhabited by people) rather than in riotous living; the fact that they were austere Protestants—these concealed the nature of their operation.

But not from Napoléon. His apprehension stands forth in the remark about the Prussian eagle being half vulture. All that the Emperor of the Occident had desired was that this vulture should mind its own business and let him alone to mind his. Up to the last moment he was convinced that there was no essential conflict of interests, and a peace of mutual tolerance could be arranged—as witness the leave granted to Berthier in September 1806. When it became clear that the vulture was insatiable, that its appetite could be assuaged only by knocking the creature on the head, Napoléon determined to do exactly that.

As an executive and above all as a military executive, the Emperor understood precisely how to accomplish this end against a state whose fundamental organization, even its civil administration, was military. A military state rests on success; in the pursuit after Jena, the Emperor set out to demonstrate that the Frederician system produced and was headed by cowards and nincompoops. Some rest for the troops was certainly necessary after the terrible marching that had preceded the battles (as anyone knows who has tried to walk a hundred miles in a week) and the exertions during the fight. Murat, in Weimar that night, had to try three times before he could correctly set down "1806" at the head of a letter, and the Emperor himself went to sleep on the ground across a counterpane of outspread maps. But the pause after Jena had in it also an atmosphere of disdain that was not present in the epilogue of any other conflict. After Austerlitz, even the corps of Lannes and Davout, which had taken such a beating, were on the roads in the morning. After Jena, everybody got a full twenty-four hours, and the difference was so pronounced that the thing was probably prepense.

The pursuit ordered on the 15th, but which did not take up till the next day, took Bernadotte's unengaged corps far out to the left wing to block the roads that might bring the fragments of the beaten army to Berlin by a slant from the southeast. Murat and Ney went to Erfurt to pick up any troops that had not left that place; Soult swung out between Bernadotte and the Murat-Ney combination. At Erfurt the last two corps caught 8,000 wounded with 6,000 sound men. Old Marshal Möllendorf's wounds opened as he tried to withstand a proposal to surrender, they left him lying bleeding in the council hall and capitulated. Murat, with the speed of his horse, hurried north on the track of Hohenlohe's fragment, picking up Soult on the way. Lannes, Davout, Augereau, took the direct road for Berlin, which the Prussian commander must now reach by marching round an arc.

At Merseburg on the 17th Bernadotte struck the Prussian strategic reserve under Duke Eugene of Württemberg (brother of the one Napoléon had made a king), and broke it in halves. The defeated troops retired on Magdeburg, where Hohenlohe arrived on the 21st, his men so beaten up by desperate marching that he had to leave 22,000 in the city, where they were instantly besieged by Soult and Ney. Now came one of the most characteristic episodes of the great pursuit: Napoléon withdrew Soult, and left Ney to continue the siege with only 8,000 men. He had judged correctly; the 22,000 Prussians surrendered to Ney without a fight.

An officer in a blue uniform, accompanied by three chasseurs, captured Berlin, while Hohenlohe was trying to swing past it on the north toward Stettin. The Prussian tried to cover his flank with a defense line along the chain of inland waterways that connects the Oder with the Elbe. His men were without magazines or the tents to which Prussians were accustomed; they raided the fields for food, losing stragglers every day, and the remainder losing heart as they ran. Murat broke through the waterway line and shut them up in Prenzlau, then sent an officer in to tell Hohenlohe he was surrounded. Actually the Marshal had far fewer men than the Prussians and they were all cavalry, but Hohenlohe surrendered without burning a cartridge.

The fortresses, as Spandau and Küstrin, were given up in a similar mood of dismay. At Küstrin indeed, which lies on an island in the Oder, the garrison kindly sent boats to bring their captors in. Only old General Blücher showed any backbone during the pursuit, and he displayed it in a manner still further to discredit the Prussian monarchy. With all the cavalry that could be gathered, he had covered Hohenlohe's rear, lagging far enough behind to pick up the Duke of Weimar's column, which finally fell in on him by a wide circuit round Erfurt. Left behind when Hohenlohe made for Stettin, he tried for the mouths of the Elbe, perhaps hoping for English shipping at Hamburg, but Bernadotte cut him off, he was turned away toward the east front of the Danish peninsula and the mouth of the Trave.

Here stands the old free city of Lübeck, bulwark of the Hansa, carved like a stone jewel, a neutral. Blücher forced his way through the south gate with something like 20,000 men, told the town councilors he must have food and ammunition, and turned the place into a fortress, with artillery in the squares and every house that amounted to anything made into a nest of sharpshooters, inhabitants to the cellars. Soult and some of Murat joined Bernadotte; they stormed Lübeck on November 7, with cavalry charges along the medieval streets and houses battered by guns. Quite understandably, if not forgivably, when the last Prussian was beaten down, the soldiers sacked the place. It was generally considered that the real blame for the occurrence rested with the Prussians.

The Bulletin of the Grande Armée dated 16 November, 1806, says that 145,000 men had marched against France, and every one had been killed, wounded or taken prisoner; "The King, the Queen, General Kalkreuth and ten or twelve officers are all that have escaped." Unlike most of the bulletins this contains so little exaggeration that it is, in fact, an understatement. No army had ever been more thoroughly demolished since the days of the Assyrians, that bitter and hasty nation.

II

The pursuit was, then, a completely successful military operation. The use of the combined arms in it, the technique by which the psychological effect of the lost battle was exploited against opponents who still possessed the physical capacity for prolonged resistance, have been the subject of much study. The operation has had a distinct effect on military tactics; ever since that date military commanders have been more inclined to drive their men to the point of exhaustion in exploiting a moral advantage.

But the pursuit had a much wider effect; one which grew out of the fact that it was the Prussian army, which was really the Prussian state, that had been destroyed. In one direction this represented the final triumph of the Revolution, which had now eliminated the most capably managed representative of the only system that could rival it in Continental Europe. The number of systems of life possible is without theoretical limit, but as a practical proposition the men of that generation and training could produce nothing but the eighteenth-century system or that of the Revolution. They did not think in the right terms or with the right apparatus for anything else; it would take time and experiment and patience before a new method of life could be found.

It had involved too deep a sacrifice on the part of Alexander of Russia to permit his Senate to debate even the abstract question of whether an act was "good" or not. During the brief republic at Naples, the representatives had so long tried to work out a government that no executive acts were performed; and the Cisalpine Republic promptly turned into a monarchy even while retaining its republican form, back in the days of the Directory.

The fact that the Revolutionary system was itself a political failure, which had been forced to sell out to Caesarism, was concealed by its glamorous success in the sphere of power politics—a success the Revolution had early obtained by offering every man a stake in the future. But that success, the fact that the horrid day foreseen by Gentz had arrived when the canaille were proved right, carried with it impossible difficulties in the very field where the Revolution had best justified itself.

When the Prussian army was destroyed there was created in north Germany a power vacuum deeper and wider than the one that developed in south Germany and the old Rhineland Empire when Austria was driven beyond the Inn. To an earlier age this might not have been important—say the seventeenth century, or the sixteenth. In that earlier period it was an insignificant minor prince, Maurice of Saxony, who as head of a league of little princes had called "Halt!" to the greatest empire Europe had seen since Charlemagne, and forced its Emperor, Charles V, to write *"Plus citra"* on the walls of his cage.

No more. With Frederick the Great, and still more with

the coming of the Revolution, the day of the powerful unified state had arrived, against which no coalition of minor powers could stand. In the sixteenth century or the seventeenth the Confederation of the Rhine would have been a quite valid organization. In 1806 its princes had to ask Napoléon, the head of a unified state, to be their protector. They were not bootlicking or acting under pressure when they made the request. They were faced by a choice quite as grim as that of Hanover or war—in fact, they were faced by a choice as deadly as that which faced the prisoner of glory, the Emperor Napoléon I, when he decided to destroy the Prussian army.

III

He did not consider the choice a grim one or a difficult. With his enormous capacity for labor, his immense ability to grasp the fundamentals of a situation (that is, in the practical, operative aspects), he had demonstrated half a dozen times that he could do practically anything better than anyone else—with the help of technical criticism. The constitution of the An VIII, the taxation setup, the prefectural system, the Codes, the Concordat, the reorganization of the army, the Treasury reorganization following Ouvrard's swindle, were examples. If the destruction of Prussia left a power vacuum in the center of Europe, he would fill it himself.

In fact, he did fill it. He filled it far too thoroughly, and he filled it in the terms of the most successful, the most humane, of all the devices by which his government was sustained—the general amnesty, the union of old and new, the Revolution and the pre-Revolutionary world. That is, he placed the upper levels of the post-Revolutionary setup in France atop the familiar Prussian administrative system and brought the two together as closely as possible.

He could not well revolutionize Prussia from the bottom. The Revolution was over. The situation required him to reorganize the Prussian and ex-Prussian territories in a manner that did no essential violence to their way of life. Nobody else could do it, there was no other authority. The Prussian army had been the only authority, and it was wiped out. Even had the Emperor been capable (and he was not) of evacuating the Prussian territories altogether, the result would have been to leave a vacuum into which would flow the armies of England and Russia, with which he was still at war.

As a purely temporary and executive measure, then, Prussia was part of the French Empire. As a temporary, executive measure, precedent to one of those settlements Napoléon knew so well how to make, the signature of Frederick William III on official documents was replaced with that of Napoléon I. The arrangement was doubtless meant to endure only until the Russians and English should become reasonable. When the former refused peace, he ordered the Army to the Vistula; when the English refused, he uttered the famous Berlin Decree—that no one on the European continent should trade with England or purchase English goods.

If enforced it would doubtless have been a long-term benefit to the Continent. After all, Napoléon had found enough English cloth in Leipzig alone to make a new uniform for every man of the Grande Armée, and most of it had been paid for out of resources which the Emperor not unreasonably felt would be adequate to build the new world he proposed to erect upon the ruins of the eighteenth-century states. England had taken a certain amount of goods in exchange, but the bulk of her receipts from the Continent were in cash.

In relation to Germany the Berlin Decree was not much different from many that Frederick William had pronounced. But in relation to France, in relation to the Empire, the decree is one more of those silent coups d'état that followed the establishment of the Empire itself. The Frederician system had now been blended with that of the Revolution;

the will of the Emperor was now supreme; the last fusion had taken place; and that day was visible when Alexander of Russia would ask, "What is Europe but you and me?" and Napoléon would agree.

The *Eroica* now stood rejected as Beethoven had foreseen it would be; he went to the woods to write the Sixth Symphony, *Pastoral.*

Brief Timetable of Events Previous to the Rising of the Curtain

1788. Louis XVI summons the States General, or parliament of France, for the first time in nearly two centuries, owing to the complete breakdown of government through financial difficulties.

1789. The States General meet, and the Third Estate (the commons) runs away with control of the government. The Bastille is taken by a Paris mob and demolished.

1791. A new Constitution, written largely by Abbé Sieyès, is placed in effect, with the King having full veto power. Louis XVI vetoes practically all legislation; is held prisoner. Austria demands release of the King; war on Austria declared.

1792. National Convention called to produce a new constitution without a king. Beginning of the Terror. Austrian and Prussian armies beaten at Valmy. Trial of Louis XVI on charge of high treason voted by the Convention.

1793. Execution of Louis XVI and Marie Antoinette. Committee of Public Safety in charge of the government. The Girondins, or bourgeois moderates, lose to the Jacobin left of Robespierre and Danton and are mostly executed. Toulon revolts against the Convention, receives an English fleet, and is besieged in an operation where Captain Bonaparte of the artillery greatly distinguishes himself.

1794. The High Terror. Jacobins quarrel among themselves. Danton executed. Reaction against Robespierre; he is executed. Surviving Girondins recalled to the Convention.

1795. "The White Terror." Execution of many old Jacobins. New constitution placed in effect, with a Directory of five as the executive, and a bicameral legislature. Revolt of Paris against the "Decree of Two-Thirds" which requires that two-thirds of the legislative shall be members of the Convention. Revolt quelled by General Bonaparte in "the Day of Vendémaire." Victories in Belgium and Holland.

1796. In the first Italian campaign, General Bonaparte conquers all north Italy. French army badly beaten by Archduke Karl in Germany but saved from destruction by General Moreau.

1797. Battle of Rivoli; Austrian army in Italy destroyed; General Bonaparte marches on Vienna and compels a peace. End of the First Coalition. Anti-Conventional rightists carry the election. Legislative and Directory purged by military force under orders of the Conventionals.

1798. Bonaparte's expedition to Egypt. Battle of the Nile destroys the French Mediterranean fleet and isolates him there.

1799. Austria, with Russia as an ally, again makes war. French armies badly beaten in Italy by Suvorov. Directory paralyzed by Anti-Conventional deputies; second purge of the executive departments. Abbé Sieyès arranges a coup d'état to overthrow the Directory, with General Moreau leading the troops, but Moreau refuses. General Bonaparte arrives in southern France, having slipped through the blockade; goes to Paris, and at once falls in with the plans of Sieyès and Fouché, the Minister of Police. Stormy session of the Legislative, ending with the deputies' being driven out by bayonets and the Directors' "resigning."

INDEX

Aalen, 331; maps, 332, 348
Aboukir Bay (Battle of the Nile, 1798), 62, 105, 255, 298
Abrantès, Duchesse d', 38
Acqui, 56, 88, 93
Adda R., 79, 81; map, 73
Addington, Henry, 162, 170, 174, 234, 240, 243, 257, 258, 259, 262, 410
Adige R., 131, 132, 337, 366, 377-79; map, 379
Administration, Ministry of, 31
Aichach, 346; map, 348
Albane, 39
Albeck, 350, 352, 353; map, 348
Alessandria, 61, 77, 81, 82, 84, 85, 86, 90, 95, 232; maps, 53, 73, 89
Alexander I, Tsar, 172, 215, 237, 272, 273-76, 310, 319, 320, 323, 359-61, 363, 364-65, 372, 388-89, 390, 394, 398, 401, 405, 410, 448, 451-57, 502
alimony, 196
Allemand, Zacharie-Jacques, 255
alliance of Austria, Russia, and Prussia, 364-65
alliances, defensive, 170
Alquier, Charles-Jean, 6, 222
Alsace, 13
Amberg, 471; maps, 462, 471
American colonists, 412-13
American Revolution, 256, 411
Americas, money from the, 418-27
Amiens—see Treaty of Amiens

amnesty—for émigrés, 206; for Prussians, 503
Ampfing, 133, 135; map, 134
Amstetten, 370, 385; maps, 367, 371
"anarchist," 150
anarchists, 153-54, 411
D'Andigné, General Louis-Marie, 21, 27, 28, 43
Andrieu, 413
Andrieux, François-Guillaume, 44, 45, 181, 194
Anglican Church, 187
Ansbach, 341, 343, 344-45, 346, 355, 362, 406, 430, 432, 449, 450; maps, 332, 339
Antraigues, d', 260
Antwerp, 173 n.
Aosta, 61, 69, 70; map, 53
Apolda, 481, 490, 494, 495; map, 480
"apotheosis of Romulus," 204-205
Arbuthnot, Secretary, 266
Aréna, 153
Arkwright spinning-jenny, 247
Armand, Joseph-Marie, 22
Armfelt, General Gustav Mauritz, 310
armies of the Allies—see Austrian, Prussian, Russian, and Saxon armies
armistice between France and Austria after Lombardy campaign, 95, 106-109, 125; after Hohenlinden, 125-26, 168 (see

509

Treaty of Lunéville); before Austerlitz, 386-87; after Austerlitz, 405-406

Army of the Coasts of the Ocean, 317, 330, 336, 413 (*see also* Grande Armée)

Army of Egypt, 48, 105-106

Army, French Revolutionary, 9, 124, 205; its songs, 70

Army, French Royal, 231, 293

Army of Germany, 338, 341, 345-55, 361

Army of Italy, 19, 48-49, 54-55, 68, 72-75, 129, 131, 139, 185, 294, 352

Army of the Reserve, 52-61, 72, 75, 77, 80, 87, 128, 151, 225

Army of the Rhine, 49, 52, 59, 60, 67, 113-26, 295

Army of the West, 204

Arnim, General von, 493

Artois, Comte d'—*see* Charles X

Aschaffenburg, 465

Asti, 81; map, 73

Auersperg, Prince, 383, 384, 386

Auerstädt, 483, 490, 497; maps, 480, 492

Auffenberg, General, 347

Augereau, Marshal Pierre-François-Charles, 3, 132, 193, 195, 225, 230, 293, 294, 296, 333, 350; in Danube campaign, 367, 368, 381, 405; 432, 457, 463, 470-72; at Jena, 477-81, 485-88

Augsburg, 123, 124, 345, 347, 366, 369; maps, 111, 117, 134, 332, 348, 367

Augusta, Duchess of Saxe-Coburg-Saalfeld, 495-96

Aujesd, 403, 404; maps, 393, 399

Aulic Council—*see* Austrian Reichshofrat

Austerlitz (battle, 1805), 387-88, 394-406, 410, 453, 456, 473, 499; maps, 386, 393, 399

Austria, 47, 54, 56, 58, 107, 109, 163-69, 171, 192, 257, 272-73, 308-14, 321, 323, 324-25, 336, 389-92, 405, 429, 430-31, 442, 451; character as an empire, 154-65, 167, 273; method of war, 110, 115

Austrian armies, 3, 12, 49, 56-95, 108, 110-27, 132-41, 233, 337-42, 345-55, 369-70, 372, 377-406

—— Chevalier Guard, 403

—— Foreign Office, 166-68

—— Imperial Diet, 442-43

—— Kriegshofrat, 337, 390

—— Reichshofrat, 54, 56, 58, 80, 87, 112, 113, 123, 132, 272, 273, 309, 312, 336, 377

—— relations with Great Britain, 107, 112, 165, 168, 257, 272-73

—— spies, 52, 58, 115, 335-36

Auvergne, 184

Bacciochi, 289-90

Bacciochi, Mme. (Eliza Bonaparte), 289, 437

Baden, 323, 338, 343-44, 430, 431, 432; map, 432

Baden, Grand Duke of, 435, 443

Bagration, Prince Peter Ivanovitch, 372, 385, 387, 390, 392-93, 402, 403

Bâle, 59, 60, 61, 112, 113, 114, 116, 233; maps, 53, 111, 117, 332, 339

Balearic Islands, 456

Bamberg, 341, 344, 461, 471; maps, 322, 339, 462, 471

Bank of France, 416, 423-24, 425

Barante, 24

Barbé-Marbois, François de, 226, 238, 239, 242, 413-17, 419, 421-25

Bard, Fort of, 76; battle (1800), 70-72, 76, 86; map, 53

Baring Brothers' bank, 418, 427

Barras, Paul-François-Jean de, 6, 10, 13, 47

Barrère, Jean-Pierre, 23, 100, 228

bataillon carré, 470, 474

Batavian Republic, 234

Bavaria, 132, 323, 338, 340-41, 345, 365, 430, 431, 432, 439, 442, 443, 449

Bavarian army, 341, 366, 384, 387, 432

Bavarian campaign (summer and fall 1800), 110-26; (winter 1800), 131-39, 186; maps, 111, 117, 119

Bayreuth, 362; map, 471

Beauharnais, Eugène de, 64, 285, 434-35, 436, 441

Beauharnais, Hortense de—*see* Bonaparte, Mme. Louis

Beauharnais, Joséphine de—*see* Bonaparte, Mme. Joséphine

Beauharnais, Stéphanie, 435

Beethoven, Ludwig van, 54, 59, 308

  Eroica Symphony, 308-309, 410, 505

  Fifth Symphony, 374, 410, 411

  Pastoral Symphony, 505

  Fidelio, 376

  Third Piano Concerto, 411

Belgium, 173

Bellegarde, Graf, 378, 379

Benevento, 439, 440

Benevento, Prince of—*see* Talley-rand

Bennigsen, Count Levin August, 274, 340, 366, 372, 396

Berg-and-Clèves, Grand Duke of —*see* Murat, Marshal

Berlier, Théophile, 40

Berlin, 324, 344, 388, 405, 447-50, 473, 500; map, 462

Berlin Decree, 504

Bern, 60, 232; maps, 53, 111

Bernadotte, Marshal Jean-Baptiste-Jules, 2, 5, 23, 28, 193, 204-206, 218-19, 296-97, 330, 331, 341; at Ulm, 343-39, 366-70; 382-87; at Austerlitz, 396, 401, 402, 403; 432, 439, 440, 441, 445, 469, 470; at Jena, 477, 479-81, 491, 494-95, 499, 500, 501

Bernadotte, Mme., 2, 3

Berry, Miss, 201, 240

Berthier, Marshal Louis-Alexandre, 5, 19, 21, 48, 52, 54, 60-61, 67, 68, 71, 77, 96, 97, 157, 206, 222, 286, 291-92, 296, 343, 385, 432, 433, 438-39, 443, 472, 498

Bertrand, General, 383, 384

Besançon, 114, 263, 269

Bessborough, Countess of, 200, 241

Bessières, Marshal Jean-Baptiste, 294, 318, 333, 403, 470

Beugnot of Bar, 43

Beyme, Kabinettsrat von, 459-60

Biberach, 112, 121-22, 123; maps, 111, 117

Bigot de Préameneau, Alexandre-Etienne, 179, 196, 197

bishops, 184-85, 187, 191, 288

Black Forest, 59, 60, 112, 113, 116, 333, 337, 341; map, 117

Blücher, General Gebhart von, 461, 475, 483, 490-93, 500

"blunder worse than a crime," 268, 269

Bodensee, 64, 112, 113, 116, 381; maps, 53, 111, 117

Bohemia, 125, 132, 133, 341, 372; maps, 339, 367

Bois-Préau, M. de, 38

Bonaparte, Caroline—*see* Murat, Mme. Joachim

Bonaparte, Charles - Napoléon, 217, 445

Bonaparte dynasty, 212-14, 282, 289, 435, 445

Bonaparte, Eliza—*see* Bacciochi, Mme.

Bonaparte family, 63-64, 103, 131, 166-67, 205, 213-17, 437

Bonaparte, Jérôme, 290, 440

Bonaparte, Joseph, 2, 4, 63, 127, 163-64, 166, 171, 204-205, 207, 210, 212-14, 216, 218, 219, 238-39, 284, 285, 289, 290, 322, 414, 434, 435, 436, 441, 451

Bonaparte, Mme. Joseph, 2

Bonaparte, Mme. Joséphine, 1, 38, 39, 62-64, 101, 130, 131, 152, 155, 156, 157, 193, 213-17, 242, 262, 264, 289, 304, 333, 342, 434

Bonaparte, Mme. Letitzia, 213, 286

Bonaparte, Louis, 63, 215-17, 285, 289, 437, 475

Bonaparte, Mme. Louis (Hortense de Beauharnais), 64, 130, 214-17, 445-46

Bonaparte, Lucien, 23-24, 44, 63, 64, 101, 103, 104, 148, 150, 152, 154-56, 159, 176, 212-14, 216, 219, 226, 238-39, 245, 286, 288-90, 433

Bonaparte, Mme. Lucien, 288, 289, 290

Bonaparte, Napoléon:
as Consul, 1-8, 19-20, 27, 28-29; proposed as "Great Elector," 32-33; as First Consul, 34, 39, 41, 42, 44, 46-47; offers peace to Allies, 47-48; war plans, 50; orders Bavarian campaign, 59, 61; Italian, 52, 61, 64; on Italian campaign, 65-66, 69-72, 78, 79, 80, 81, 82, 85-86, 91, 93, 95

return to Paris, 99-101, 103; appoints Code committee, 104; talks peace terms, 104-109; institutes censorship, 128-30; orders Bavarian winter campaign, 131

royalist plot against him, 150-51; Opéra plot, 152-54, 155, 281; *Parallel Pamphlet* attack, 154-56; opposes Fouché in royalist threat, 156-57, 158; rue St. Niçaise plot, 157-61; effort to proscribe Jacobins, 160

policy after Lunéville, 169-72; acts on British blockade, 169-70; projects for European system, 170-76; negotiates Concordat, 185-91, 192, 195; works on Code, 195-200; at special Notre Dame service, 195, 204-205; his official status discussed, 207-12 (*see also* succession question); gets "signal pledge," 210-11; made Consul for life, 212; "generals' conspiracy," 218-19

acquires Louisiana, 222; commercial and colonial aims, 222-24, 226-27; sends expedition to Saint-Domingue (*q.v.*), 224; to New Orleans, 225

deals with Swiss counter-revolution, 233-34; reaction to

British claim on Malta, 236-37; sells La. to U.S., 238-40; develops French industries and agriculture, 244-47; strengthens navy, 248; takes action against British navy, 251-52; plans Channel attack, 252-54; orders to Toulon fleet, 256; royalist plot against him, 257-65; has Enghien shot, 264-65, 268; alliance with Prussia, 269-72

proclaimed Emperor, 283-84; crowned, 287, 300, 303-305; recognition refused, 311-12, 313; to Boulogne to direct naval campaign, 318; makes Cisalpine Republic a kingdom, 321; crowned at Milan, 322, 323

decides to invade Austria, 325-26; initiates intelligence service, 335-36; to Strasbourg, 342; to Baden, 343; to Württemberg, 344; crosses Danube, 345; directs battle of Ulm, 350, 352; proclamation to army, 365; directs march to Vienna, 370-71, 373; issues fresh orders to navy, 374; before Austerlitz, 385, 387, 394-95, 397-98; learns of victory, 402; armistice terms, 405-406

opposes paper money, 414; and large public debt, 415; action on Ouvrard swindle, 421-22; on Bank of France, 423; final action on financial situation, 424-26

policy on tenures in W. Germany, 431-32; on army pay in occupied countries, 433; on status of Rhineland and Italy, 433-41; elevates marshals, 438-39; anti-Papal policy, 439-41; relation to Confed. of the Rhine, 442-43; policy on reorganized Europe, 444; dealings with Prussia, 450-53

plans for Jena, 472-75; during battle, 479, 482, 484-86, 489, 490, 495; destroys Prussian army, 498-500; policy toward Prussia, 503-505

methods, military and political, 85, 105, 167, 228, 410-13, 422, 432, 433-34, 470, 472-74, 501

traits of mind and character, 205-206, 228, 282; ideas on his own power and status, 206, 282-83, 284, 429; on the plots, 230-31; on the British, 169; on French finances, 64-65; on friendship, 219; relations with liberals, 127-29, 192; with generals, 193

family relations: on Caroline's marriage, 62-64, 101, 104; Hortense's marriage, 130-31, 215-16; Joséphine's jewels, 152; family honor, 205; assigns thrones to family, 434-38

Bonaparte, Pauline—*see* Leclerc, Mme. *and* Borghese, Princess

Borghese, Princess (Pauline Bonaparte), 290, 437

Bormida R., 56, 57, 86, 87, 91, 95; maps, 73, 89

Bosnia, 171

Bossuet, Jacques-Bénigne, 11

Boudet, General Jean, 78, 79

Boulay-de-la-Meurthe, Antoine-Jacques, 30, 33, 34, 40

Boulevard of Germany, 120, 121, 122, 125, 134, 135, 136

Boulogne, 253, 254, 255, 263, 301, 331, 349; map, 332

Bourbon-Parma branch, 222, 226, 289

Bourbon princes — *see* Louis XVIII *and* Charles X

Bourbons, 150, 153, 156, 157, 173-74, 184, 185, 208, 226, 258, 263, 282, 300, 434, 450, 456 (*see also* Royalists *and* restoration)

Bourcier, General François-Antoine, 357, 397, 400

Bourdin, 5

Bourgoin, Mlle., 248

Bourmont, Comte de, 28, 43, 160, 228

Bourrienne, Louis-Antoine, 1, 61-62, 64, 95, 106, 115, 152, 215, 297-98

Branau, 340, 365, 368, 432, 433; maps, 339, 367

Breisachs (Alt & Neu), 61, 112, 113, 114, 115, 333, 338, 475; maps, 53, 111, 117, 332, 339

Brenner Pass, 338, 366, 368, 382; map, 339

Brenz R., 343, 347, 348, 351; map, 348

Brest, 105, 169, 172, 248, 249, 251, 252, 256, 263, 302, 315-18, 333; map, 332

brigandage, 147

Brillat-Savarin, Anthelme, 25

Britain, 47-48, 50, 105, 106, 107, 108-109, 112, 129, 157, 159, 161, 162, 165, 168, 169-70, 171, 172-73, 188, 192, 223, 230-37, 246, 247, 248-56, 257, 272-73, 365, 409-10, 412, 414, 450, 504; free speech in, 231; concerned in the plots, 151, 159, 230-31, 257-59, 262

British blockade, 169, 251

—— Cabinet, 151, 170, 223, 231, 257

—— colonies, 174, 223

—— commerce, 165, 173, 250-51

—— financiers, 232, 233

—— Foreign Office, 47-48, 258

—— Government, 159, 174, 230-31, 257, 262

—— industries and manufactures, 223, 244, 504

—— press, 231-32

—— relations with Austria, 107, 112, 165, 168, 257, 272-73

—— Royal Marine, 249

—— ships, 48, 56, 74, 82, 87, 105, 109, 169, 172, 173, 231, 234, 235, 236, 249, 250-51, 256, 315-19, 418, 451, 500

—— trade treaty with France, 231

Brodum, Dr. 179

Bruges, 331; map, 332

Bruix, Admiral Eustace, 36, 255, 301, 415

Brune, Marshal Guillaume-Marie-Anne, 40, 54, 131, 132, 193, 297

Brünn, 384-87, 390-96; maps, 380, 393, 399

Brunswick, 323, 324

Brunswick, Duke of—*see* Frederick William, Duke of Brunswick

Budberg, General, 456

Budweis, 384, 385; map, 386

Buffalora, 79; map, 73

Bunzelwitz (battle, 1761), 123

Burke, *Reflexions on the French Revolution,* 313

Buxhövden, General, 340, 341, 344, 366, 372, 387, 394, 399, 404, 411

Cabanis, Pierre-Jean, 217

Cabarrus, Mme., 23

Cacault, François, 188-89

Cadiz, 302, 303, 317, 326, 374

Cadoudal, Georges, 28, 151, 161, 162, 231, 257, 259-65, 272, 281, 282, 304

Caesar, Augustus, 283

Caesar, Julius, 154

Caffarelli, General, 396, 403

Calder, Sir Robert, 328

Caldiero, 378-80; map, 379

calendar, Gregorian and Russian Orthodox, 341-42

calendar, Revolutionary, xv, 67

Calonne, Charles-Alexandre de, 200

Cambacérès, Jean-Joseph-Régis, 5, 25, 29, 34, 38, 41, 42, 44, 99, 100, 103, 104, 160, 194, 196, 208-11, 245, 246, 283, 285, 342

Campan, Mme. Jeanne-Louise— see Ney, Mme. Michel

Campbell, Thomas, 141; *Hohenlinden,* 142-43

Camperdown, battle of (1797), 250

Campo Formio, Peace of, 165

Canning, George, 36

Canova, Antonio, 39

Cape of Good Hope, 174, 226

Carbon, 159, 161

Carlos IV, King of Spain, 169, 174, 214, 220-23, 226, 237, 420

Carnic Alps, 366

Carnot, General Lazare-Nicolas, 13, 14, 52, 67, 69, 100, 102, 104, 115, 122, 130, 131, 153, 176, 212, 284

Casale, 81; map, 73

Casanova, Giovanni Jacopo, 232, 277-79

Cassano (battle, 1799), 55

Casteggio, 82-84; map, 73

Castel Ceriolo, 89-92; maps, 89, 94

Castiglione (battle, 1796), 293

Catherine II, Empress, 274, 275

Cauchy, Augustin-Louis, 22

Caulaincourt, Marquis Armand-Augustin de, 286

cavalry, 333-34

Central Bureau of Police, 146

Ceracchi, sculptor, 152-53

Ceva, 56, 85

Ceylon, 174, 224, 225

Chabran, General Joseph de, 69, 70

Châlons, 59

Chambarlhac, Jacques-Antoine, 67

Champagny, Jean-Baptiste de, 40

Championnet, General Jean-Antoine-Etienne, 48-49

Chappe telegraph system, 84, 301

Chaptal, Jean-Antoine, 41, 245-48, 444

Charlemagne, 217, 283, 305, 325, 374, 439

Charles V, Emperor, 502

Charles X (Comte d'Artois), 28, 151, 231, 257, 258, 263, 281

Charles XII, King of Sweden, 342

Chasteler, General, 113

Chateaubriand, François-Renéde, 29, 178, 288

chemicals, commercial, 246

Chénier, André, 44, 45, 181, 194

Cherubini, Maria Luigi, 26, 54

Chevalier, anarchist, 154, 281

Chouans—see Vendée, La

church v. state, 182-83, 187

church properties — in France, 149, 187; in the Empire, 167, 431, 439

Cisalpine Republic, 152, 212, 232, 233, 234, 321-22, 502

clergy—see bishops *and* priests

Clèves, 406, 438, 450

Closewitz, 484, 486; maps, 485, 589
Coalition, First, 173, 246
Coalition, Third, 323, 420
Cobenzl, Graf Ludwig, 166-68, 171, 312-14, 324, 326, 355, 389-90
Coburg, 476, 477; maps, 462, 471
Code Napoléon, 104, 179-83, 192-200, 205, 210, 211, 213, 217, 288, 299, 322, 444, 503
Coigny, Duc de, 100
Coigny, Chevalier, 151
Col di Tenda, 55, 56, 81, 84; map, 53
Colbert, Jean-Baptiste, 223
Colbert (of the hussars), 487, 488
College of Bishops, 442
College of Conservators, 32, 41
College of Kings, 443
College of Princes, 443
College of Towns, 442
Colloredo, Graf, 168
Colmar, 115; map, 117
Colognola, 378, 379
Commerce, Ministry of, 31
Committee of Public Safety, 210
Compagnie des Négociants Réunis —*see* Négociants Réunis
Companies of Jesus, of the Sun, 29, 184, 258
Concordat, 187-92, 195, 204, 287, 439, 503
Condé branch of the Bourbons, 263
Condillac, Etienne-Bonnet de, 11, 15
Confederation of the North, 457
Confederation of the Rhine, 442-43, 453, 457, 503
Conquered Territories, Ministry of, 32
Consalvi, Cardinal, 188-91, 287

Constant, Benjamin, 44-45, 46, 47, 58, 100, 127, 128, 129, 181, 192, 194, 232
Constantine, Grand Duke, 393, 401, 402, 403, 466
Constitution, American, 198
Constitution, French Consular, 3, 13, 30-34, 99-100, 104, 194, 285, 444, 503
Constitution, French Imperial, 285, 300, 444
Constitutional clergy, 184, 188, 191
Consular Guard, 90-92, 94, 205, 294
Consulate, 32, 34, 101, 103, 184, 258; long-term, 207, 211; life, 212, 283
Continental union against England, 171-72
Copenhagen, battle of (1801), 172, 456
Coppet, 126, 219
Corfu, 374
Cornwallis, Earl of, 202, 242, 328
Corsica, 286
Cospeda, 482, 486; map, 485
Cossacks, 397, 405
Council of State—under the Republic, 31-33, 40-42, 45, 160, 179, 191, 195, 197, 204, 211; under the Empire, 285-86, 299-300, 309, 342, 411
coup d'état of 18 brumaire, An VIII (Nov. 9, 1799), 1-2
Creevey, Thomas, 407
Crema, 79; map, 73
Cremona, 79; map, 73
Cretet, Emmanuel, 40
Crillon, Duc de, 100
criminal code, 198
Croatian troops, 393, 394
Cromwell, Oliver, 154

Curée, Jean-François, 283
Czartoryski, Prince Adam, 274-
75, 279, 319, 323, 360, 364,
389, 404, 405, 456
Czechs, 442

Dalberg, Archbishop, 442
Dalmatia, 433, 470
Danton, Georges-Jacques, 48, 290
Danube R., 60, 112, 118-21, 124,
125, 131, 333, 335, 345, 365,
384; maps, 53, 111, 117, 134,
332, 339, 348, 367, 371, 462
Danube Valley, 365
Daru, secretary, 326
Daunou, Pierre-Claude, 30, 33,
44, 45, 180, 181, 182, 193, 194
David, Jean-Louis, 24, 47, 190,
195
Davout, Marshal Louis-Nicholas,
219, 255, 297-98, 330, 331,
343, 347, 350, 366-72, 385,
387, 396-401, 404, 432, 470,
471, 477-81, 490-95, 499
Decaen, General Charles-Ma-
thieu, 136, 137
Declaration of Independence, 413
Decrès, Denis, 238, 248, 301, 302,
303, 315, 317, 374
Defermon, Joseph-Jacques, 40, 42
Dego (battle, 1796), 65
Deism, 182
Delacroix, Eugène, 43
Delmas, General Antoine-Guil-
laume, 195
Démerville, 153
Denmark, 105, 109, 171, 172
Le Départ du conscrit (song),
354
Desaix, General Louis-Charles,
86, 90-94, 96, 106
Deschapelles, M., 26
Desprez, 421, 424, 425

Dessalines, General Jean-Jacques,
229-30, 284
Dessoles, General Jean-Joseph,
135
D'Hautpoul, General Jean-
Joseph, 403
dictatorship, 148 (*see also* succession question)
Dijon, 52, 58, 61, 67; map, 53
Directory—overthrown, 1-2; 5,
10, 12, 13, 14, 19, 20, 23, 30,
47, 60, 63, 106, 146, 184, 194,
232, 246, 249, 250, 252, 502
divine right of kings, 412
divorce, 197, 205, 213
Dokhtorov, General, 373, 393,
394, 399, 400, 404
Dolgoruki, Prince Peter, 360,
364, 391, 395
Dolgoruki, Princess, 364
Donatist heresy, 188
Donaueschingen, 112; maps, 111,
117
Donauwörth, 125, 343, 345, 346;
maps, 111, 332, 348
Dornberg, the, 484, 486; map,
485
Dornburg, 479, 481, 487, 494;
map, 480
Doubs R., 52; map, 53
Drake, Francis, 258, 261, 262,
263, 269, 281
Drave R., 381
Dresden, 473, 479; map, 462
Dreyfus case, 199
Drouet, General Jean-Baptiste,
137, 396
drugs, 246
Dryden, *Under Mr. Milton's
Picture,* 328
Dubois, Prefect, 219
Duchâtel, Charles-Jacques, 40
Du Fresne, Bertrand, 40

Duhesme, General Guillaume-Philibert, 65, 78, 79, 82, 86, 378, 380

dukedoms given to Marshals, 438-39

Dumanoir de Pelley, Admiral, 301

Dumonceau, General Jean-Baptiste, 367, 370

Dumouriez, General Charles-François, 263, 269, 299

Dunkerque, 331; map, 332

Dupleix, Marquis Joseph-François, 222

Dupont, General Pierre, 350, 351, 353, 355, 367, 368, 370

Durlach, 333

Dürnstein, 372, 373, 412; map, 371

Duroc, General Géraud-Christophe, 50, 71, 108, 139, 214-16, 285, 343, 344, 362, 473

Dušek, Jan Ladislav, 447

Dutheil, 161, 162

Ebersberg forest, 133-36, 163; map, 138

Ebersbrunn, 385; map, 386

Eckartsberga, 483; map, 480

Edgeworth, Maria, 203

Egypt, 48, 105, 106, 108-109, 165, 171, 172, 173, 174, 232, 235, 251, 298, 315

Eichstädt, 343

Eisenach, 464, 475

Elbe R., 271, 472, 476, 483, 500; map, 462

Elchingen (battle, 1806), 353, 355, 367; map, 348

Elgin, Lord, 179

Elizabeth Feodorovna, Tsarina, 274, 276

Elsnitz, General, 56, 69, 76, 77, 81, 84, 85, 88, 89, 94

émigrés, 27, 37, 39, 52, 147-48, 185, 188, 206-207, 208, 258-59, 270, 310, 336

"Emperor," the title, 283

Empire—*see* Austria; Holy Roman Empire; French Empire

Engen, 113, 116, 117, 118; maps, 111, 117

Enghien, Duc d', 263-65, 268-69, 271, 272, 273, 276, 282, 326, 336, 414, 460

England—*see* Britain

English Channel, 250-55, 316, 317, 325-36

Enns R., 368, 370; maps, 367, 371

"enthusiasm," 128 n.

Erfurt, 459, 461, 475, 479, 481, 483, 495, 499, 500; maps, 462, 471, 480

Erzgebirge (Iron Mountains), 461; maps, 462, 471

Essen, 457

Esslingen, 333; map, 332

Esterházy, Prince, 54

Etruria, kingdom of, 174, 185, 186, 187, 191, 289, 433

Eugene, Duke of Württemberg, 344, 499

Eugène, Viceroy of North Italy, 434-35, 436, 437 (*see also* Beauharnais, Eugène de)

Europe, "rational" map of, 363

Europe, reorganization of western, 429-33

Fabre de l'Aube, Jean-Pierre, 284

families, laws relating to, 196-97, 198

Farington Diary, 240, 407

Faypoult, 43

Ferdinand, Archduke, 67, 119, 338, 348-49, 350, 351-52, 355

Ferdinand I, King of Naples, 169, 436-37
Ferdinand of Prussia, Prince, 448
Ferrol, 174, 251, 252, 302, 303, 316, 317, 325
Fesch, Cardinal Joseph, 285, 286-88
Festenburg, Baron, 78, 79
feudal tenures in the Empire, 431
Fezensac, Duc de, 328-29, 356
Fichte, Johann Gottlieb, 454, 467-68
Fielding, Henry, 96-97
Finance, Ministry of, 4-5, 7, 12
Fitzjames, Duchesse de, 23
Fitzmaurice, Lord, 467
Fleurieu, Charles-Pierre de, 40
Fleurus (battle, 1794), 27
Florida, 225, 238
Flushing, 331; map, 332
Foncier, 152
Fontanes, Jean-Pierre, 155, 288
Fontenoy (battle, 1745), 380
Forchheim, 475; map, 462
Foreign Affairs, Ministry of, 5-6, 32
Forfait, Pierre-Alexandre, 5, 248, 252, 415
Fouché, Joseph, 2, 6, 8, 23, 26, 40, 44, 47, 99-102, 104, 129, 145-56, 158-61, 186-87, 191, 201, 212, 204, 213, 214, 217, 219, 226, 261-65, 268, 283, 296, 310, 342, 374, 441
Fourcroy, Antoine-François de, 41
Fox, Charles James, 178, 230, 241, 427, 450, 456
Français de Nantes, Antoine, 43, 228
Franceschi, Captain, 75
Francis II (of the Empire, then Francis I of Austria), 47, 106-108, 132, 139, 140, 143, 164, 233, 272, 312, 324, 325, 327, 340, 349, 368, 379, 388-90, 394, 398, 401, 405, 431, 460
Franconia, 132, 340, 461, 463
Franco-Prussian alliance, 269-72, 447-54
Frankenwald, 461, 464, 465, 470, 472, 476; maps, 462, 471
Frankfurt, 113, 340, 432, 442, 463, 464; maps, 322, 462
Franklin, Benjamin, 245, 301
Franz, Kaiser—*see* Francis II
Frederician system, 497-99, 504
Frederick I, Emperor (Barbarossa), 431
Frederick II, Emperor (Stupor Mundi), 284
Frederick I, King of Württemberg, 443, 499
Frederick VI, Regent of Denmark, 105
Frederick the Great, 49, 115, 123, 163, 271, 293, 364, 389, 391-92, 411, 412, 445, 448, 449, 458, 463, 473, 474, 497, 502
Frederick William of Brandenburg (the Great Elector), 32-33
Frederick William, Duke of Brunswick, 364, 405, 412, 453, 454, 458-65, 467, 475-79, 483, 484, 493
Frederick William III, King of Prussia, 50, 270-71, 309, 314, 324, 327, 343, 356, 361, 363, 364-65, 448-54, 457, 458, 459, 473, 474, 479, 483, 490, 493, 498, 501, 504
Freiburg, 112, 115, 338, 490; maps, 111, 117
Freising, 366; map, 367
"Frenais," 415-16, 417
French agriculture, 223-24, 247, 444

—— armies—pay, 423, 430, 433; shoes, 388, 417; supplies, 19, 69-70, 74, 293, 298, 349, 368, 369, 422, 433

—— bankers, 414-26

—— Bourse, 16, 99, 422

—— censorship, 128-29

—— citizenship, 196

—— coinage, 413, 415, 432-33

—— colonies, 109, 174, 222-24, 226-27, 228, 230

—— commerce, 109, 173, 223, 224, 227, 244-45, 249

—— Consular government—structure, 4-8, 31-34; personnel, 40-44; powers and stability, 205-206, 211

—— Consular Guard, 90-92, 94, 205, 294

—— départements, 18, 31

—— education, 247

—— Empire inaugurated, 284-305

—— finances, 3-5, 7, 16-20, 99, 127, 129-30, 414-27, 430, 432-33

—— government paper, 19-20, 65, 130, 179, 414, 422-23, 430

—— Imperial Guard, 294, 304, 318, 333, 343, 369, 403, 406, 470, 479-81

—— industries and manufactures, 178-79, 223, 244-47, 466

—— judicial system, 104, 198

—— law—*see* Code Napoléon

—— military chest, 230, 429-30, 432

—— privateers and raiders, 250-51, 303

—— Revolution, 41, 42, 60, 115, 149, 164, 168, 170, 176, 184, 185, 187, 195, 208, 210, 224, 228, 232, 246, 255, 270, 271, 283, 293, 299, 305, 409, 412, 413, 443, 444, 501, 502, 503; statutes, 104

—— Royal Marine, 249

—— ships, 227, 248-56, 314-19

—— spies and agents, 107, 159, 160, 219, 261, 263, 335-36

—— trade treaty with Britain, 231

——Treasury, 413-27, 430, 441, 503

Frere, John Hookham, 54

Freudenstadt, 333; map, 332

Friant, General Louis, 397, 400, 491-93

Fulda, 476, 477; map, 471

Fulton, Robert, 179, 203

Gallican Church, 185, 187

gambling, 26

Ganteaume, Honoré, 40, 105, 106, 255, 256, 316, 326

Garat, Joseph-Dominique, 41

Garat, Pierre-Jean, 100

Gardanne, General Gaspard-Amédée, 80, 378, 380

Garafolo, 86, 91

Gassicourt, Chevalier C.-L., 143

Garrick, David, 96

Gaudin, Martin, 4-5, 7-8, 12, 16-20, 31, 42, 65, 100, 129-30, 178, 214, 245, 416, 425

Gazan, General Honoré-Théophile, 57, 370, 373, 486

"generals' conspiracy," 218-19

Geneva, 59, 60, 61, 233; maps, 53, 332

Genoa, siege of, 54, 55, 56-57, 58, 59, 61, 68, 72-75, 77-81, 82, 110, 248; map, 53

Genoa, Republic of, 325

Gentz, Friedrich, 310-14, 319, 325, 389, 410, 444, 450, 454, 455, 458-65, 477, 479, 502; *Journal,* 35

George III, King, 47, 250, 253, 257, 311, 357, 450
Gera, 477, 479; maps, 471, 480
Gérard, François-Pascal, 23, 402
German principalities and princes, 431, 438-39
Germany, reorganization of western, 430-31, 442, 453
Gheneue, Mlle.—*see* Lannes, Mme. Jean
Gibraltar, 226
Girondins, 193
Giulay, General, 119, 120
Godoy, Manuel de, 222, 420
Goethe, Johann Wolfgang von, 271, 388, 432, 459
Gohier, M., 1-2, 10
Goldbach R., 392, 394, 398-400; map, 393
Görtz, 381
Gourdon, Admiral Antoine-Louis, 255, 302, 303
Grammont, firm of, 423
Grand, Mme., 186, 191
Grande Armée, 334-35, 469, 473-74, 490, 501, 504
Gräwert, General, 487
Great Elector—*see* Frederick William of Brandenburg
Greene, General Nathanael, 412
Grénier, General Paul, 124, 125, 135
Greuze, Jean-Baptiste, 24
Grimod de La Reynière, Alexandre, 25
Grenville, Lord, 47-48, 157, 173, 312, 375, 456
Gresham's law, 433
Grey, Hon. Charles, 407
Grouchy, Marshal Emmanuel de, 1, 6-39
Guadalquivir R., 420
Guadarrama Mts., 419

Guard—*see* French Consular *and* French Imperial Guard
Guastalla, 225, 437
Gudin, General César-Charles, 357, 387, 490-93
Guindet, Sgt., 478
gunpowder, 246
Günzburg, 346, 348; map, 348
Gustavus IV, King of Sweden, 310, 314, 356
Gustavus Adolphus, King, 411

Haag, 134, 135; map, 134
Haddick, General, 56, 76, 77, 78, 81, 88, 89
Haiti—*see* Saint-Domingue
Halle, 331, 343, 480, 483, 490; maps, 471, 480
Hamburg, 171, 173 n., 500
Hammond, Mr., 258
Hanover, 171, 173 n., 257, 270, 271, 275, 319, 320, 362, 406, 438, 442, 449-57, 475, 503; maps, 332, 462
Hanseatic cities, 442, 450, 500
Hardenberg, Graf Karl August von, 362, 363, 364, 453, 454
Harrel, Major, 152-53
Harrowby, Lord, 313, 326
Haslich, 351, 352
Hassenfels, 343
Hassenhausen, 490-93; map, 492
Haugwitz, Count Christian von, 362, 363, 364, 390-91, 395, 405, 406, 447, 449-52, 454, 459
Hawkesbury, Lord, 174
Haydn, Franz Josef, 410
    The Creation, 54, 157
    Gott erhalte Franz den Kaiser, 132
Hédouville, General Gabriel-Marie, 27
Heidelberg, 331; map, 332
Heidenheim, 343

Heilbronn, 331; map, 332
Hell Valley, 112, 115, 116; map, 111
Henry VIII, King, 187, 188
Herder, Johann Gottfried von, 388
hereditary principle, 443-44, 445 (*see also* succession question)
Herzegovina, 171
Hesse, 323, 324, 464
Hesse, Duke of, 457
Hesse-Darmstadt, Grand Duke of, 443
Heudorf, 119, 120; map, 119
Hildburghausen, 463; map, 471
Hillinger, General, 381
Hoche, General Louis-Lazare, 249, 299
Höchstädt, 125; maps, 111, 348
Hof, 461, 476, 477; maps, 462, 471
Hoffmann, E.T.A., 458
Hogarth, William, 96-97
Hohenlinden, 367; battle (1800), 133-39, 140-42, 168, 188, 252, 262; maps, 111, 134, 367
Hohenlohe, Prince, 461, 464, 465, 475-79, 482-90, 495, 499, 500
Hohenzollern, Graf, 56, 57
Hollabrunn, 385; map, 386
Holland, 50, 52, 59, 131, 174, 234, 237, 297, 320
Holy Roman Empire, 169, 286, 431, 442; commercial relations, 165 (*see also* Austria)
Hope, House of, 418-21, 427
Hortense, Queen—*see* Bonaparte, Mme. Louis
hospitals, 246
Houchard, General Jean-Nicolas, 299
House of Commons, 235, 257, 409

House of Lords, 199
Hulot, Widow, 131, 193
Humboldt, Baron von, 447
Hungary and the Hungarians, 70, 132, 324, 385, 388
Hyde de Neuville, 21, 27, 151

Iglau, 384; map, 386
Iller R., 122, 124, 338, 342, 343, 346, 350; maps, 111, 332, 348
Imperial Diet, 442-43
Incroyables, 21-22
indemnification, 165-67, 174
India, 171, 172, 226, 234, 250, 251
industrial revolution, 244
"infernal machine" plot—*see* rue St. Niçaise plot
Ingoldstädt, 125, 141, 343, 347; maps, 339, 348
Inn R., 132, 133, 134, 135, 346, 366, 367, 368, 382, 432; maps, 111, 134, 332, 339, 367
Innsbruck, 382; maps, 339, 367
Interior, Ministry of, 5, 101, 148, 154, 245, 246-48
Ireland, 234, 263, 302, 317
Iron Crown of Lombardy, 322, 325
Iron Mountains (Erzgebirge), 461; maps, 462, 471
Isabella, Infanta, 214
Isar R., 132, 133, 135, 366; maps, 111, 134, 339, 367
Isserstedt, 484, 487, 488; maps, 485, 489
Italian campaigns, 3, 12, 19, 69-109, 172, 294-95, 366, 374, 377-82
Italy, Kingdom of, 321-22, 325, 436, 439
Ivrea, 71, 72, 76, 291; maps, 53, 73

Jackson, Sir George, 306, 327, 466

Jacobins and Jacobinism, 3, 6, 7, 10-11, 13, 14, 26, 27, 28, 68, 100, 102, 128, 129, 148, 150, 153, 154, 160-61, 184, 193, 205, 206, 228, 258, 259, 261, 282

Jaffa (battle, 1798), 50

Jefferson, Thomas, 223, 227, 237

Jellačič, General, 345, 347, 348, 350, 355, 381

Jena, battle of, 476-95; maps, 462, 471, 480, 485

Jesuits, 287

Jetzelsdorf, 385; map, 386

Johann, Archduke, 133-39, 140, 141, 312-14, 338, 346, 366, 367, 381, 382, 390

Joigny, 216-17

Jomini, Albert-Henri, 298, 350

Jordan, Camille, 23, 36

Jorry, 28

Joseph, King of Naples—see Bonaparte, Joseph

Joseph of Lorraine, Prince, 116-20

Joubert, General Barthelémy, 114

Joubert, Chevalier, 151

Jouberthou, Mme.—see Bonaparte, Mme. Lucien

Jourdan, Marshal Jean-Baptiste, 3, 27, 28, 112, 193, 298, 299

judicial system, 104, 198

Julian Alps, 378, 381, 382

Jüningen, 351

Junot, Andoche, 47

Justice, Ministry of, 5, 31

Kahla, 479; map, 480

Kaim, General, 56, 69, 72, 76, 77, 81, 88, 89, 91-94

Kalkreuth, General, 458, 501

Kant, Immanuel, 170, 268, 311, 459, 467

Karl August, Duke of Saxe-Weimar, 475, 476, 483

Karl Ludwig, Archduke, 49, 58, 112, 113, 132, 143, 168, 272-73, 310-13, 324, 337-38, 366, 368, 372, 377-81, 382, 384, 391, 396, 405, 408

Kaunitz, Prince Wenzel Anton von, 167, 363

Kehl, 61, 113, 115, 331; maps, 111, 117, 332

Keith, Viscount, 82

Kellermann, Marshal François-Etienne, 90, 91, 93, 94, 299, 475

Kemble, John Philip, 179

Kempten, 367, 368, 381

Kienmayer, General, 113, 115, 120, 123; in Bavaria, 113-23; at Hohenlinden, 133-39; at Ulm, 345-46, 355; 366, 393, 398, 400, 401, 404

kings, 412, 432

Kléber, General Jean-Baptiste, 106, 299

Klein, General, 397

Klenau, General, 133, 134, 345

Klosterwald, 120; map, 119

Knights of Malta, 49, 50, 174, 320

Kollowrath, General, 133, 134, 136, 144, 394, 401, 402

Kösen, 481, 483, 490; map, 480

Kötschau, 484; maps, 485, 489

Kranach, 470; map, 471

Kray von Krajova, Marshal Paul—in Bavarian campaign, 110-26, 132, 139, 140, 143-44, 338

Krems, 372, 383-85, 412; maps, 371, 386

Küstrin, 500

Kutuzov, General Michael Ila-rionovitch, 340, 346, 360, 365-73, 382-87, 389-90, 394, 401, 412

Lacuée, Jean-Gérard, 40
Lafayette, Marquis de, 102
Laforêt, Antoine, 362, 450, 466
Lagrange, Joseph-Louis, 22, 187
La Harpe, Frédéric-César de, 274
La Harpe, Jean-François de, 100-101
Laibach, 381
Lajolais, General Frédéric-Michel, 259-60
Lally, Comte Thomas-Arthur de, 222
La Malgue, Fort, 314
Lambach, 368, 369; map, 367
Lameth, Baron de, 100
Landau, 331; map, 322
Mandgrafenberg, 480-85; map, 489
Landsberg, 350, 367; maps, 348, 367
Landshut, 132, 133, 134, 366; maps, 111, 134, 367
Langeron, General, 393-94, 398-401, 403, 404
Lannes, Marshal Jean, 65, 70-72, 75, 78, 89, 82-84; in Lombard campaign, 70-109; at Marengo, 91-94, 124; 157, 193, 195, 291, 293-94, 296, 331, 333; at Ulm, 343, 347-53, 366-73; 383-85; at Austerlitz, 387, 394-97, 402; 411, 432, 469-72; at Jena, 476-81, 484-88, 499
Lannes, Mme. Jean, 331
Laplace, Pierre-Simon de, 22, 44, 187, 219
La Revellière-Lépeaux, Louis-Marie, 13

La Rochefoucauld, François de, 100
Latouche-Tréville, Admiral Louis-René de, 174, 255-56, 300-301
La Tour du Pin, Mme. de, 37
Lauderdale, Earl of, 457
Laudon, General, 79
Lauer, General, 132
Lavoisier, Antoine-Laurent, 22, 42, 245, 246
Law, John, 223
laws under the Consulate, 104 (see also Code Napoléon)
League of Cambrai, war of, 313
League of the North, 50, 104-105, 106, 165, 170, 173
leather, tanning, 417
Lebrun, Charles-François, 34, 42, 44, 103, 157, 196, 285
Lech R., 59, 124, 126, 133, 346; maps, 111, 134, 332, 339, 348
Leclerc, General Charles-Victor-Emmanuel, 224-30
Leclerc, Mme. (Pauline Bonaparte), 224, 230, 290 (see also Borghese, Princess)
Lecourbe, General Claude-Jacques, 114-26, 135, 136, 143, 193
Lefèbvre, Marshal François-Joseph, 298, 299, 305, 460, 481
Leghorn, 129, 165, 166, 174, 226, 227, 441
Legislative and Legislators, 31, 32, 34, 179-82, 190, 192, 194, 195, 211, 299
Legrand, General Just-Claude, 396, 400, 410
Leibnitz, Gottfried von, 170, 179
Leipzig, 461, 504; map, 471
Leo III, Pope, 439
Leoben, 80, 370, 381, 385, 387; map, 371

Letourneur, Charles, 13, 43
Leuthen (battle, 1757), 473
Leveson-Gower, Lord Granville, 36, 200, 241, 280
liberals—*see* philosophical liberals
Lichnovsky, Prince, 54
Liechtenstein, Prince of, 134, 139, 393, 399, 401, 402, 403, 408
Liguria, 56, 77
Ligurian Alps, 55, 250
Ligurian Sea, 48; map, 53
Lilienfeld, 370; map, 371
Limoëlan, 159, 161
Linz, 368, 369, 370; maps, 367, 371
Livingston, Robert R., 237, 239
Lobenstein, 477
Locke, John, 11, 15
Lodi, 70, 79; battle (1796), 47; map, 73
Loison, General Louis-Henri, 79
Lombard, Kabinettsrat, 460, 465
Lombardy campaign, 69-109, 123, 130; maps, 53, 73
Lorges, General Jean-Thomas, 119, 120
L'Orient, 248, 250, 252, 302
Louis, King of Holland—*see* Bonaparte, Louis
Louis XIV, 6, 151, 223
Louis XVI, 7, 10, 23, 48, 100, 103, 127, 197, 228, 436
Louis XVIII (Comte de Provence), 101, 140, 151, 161, 174, 231, 257, 258, 263, 281, 282
Louis Ferdinand of Prussia, Prince, 314, 324, 447-48, 450, 454, 476-78, 479, 482, 495, 496
Louisiana, 222, 225-30, 235, 237-40, 303
L'Ouverture, Toussaint, 228-30, 284
Lübeck, 500-501

Lucca, 437
Lucchesini, 451, 452
Ludwigsburg, 344
Lugos, retreat to, 55, 87
Luis of Bourbon-Parma, 222, 226, 289
Luise of Prussia, Queen, 270, 271, 273, 314, 361, 362, 448-49, 450, 454, 501
Lunéville—*see* Treaty of Lunéville
Lützeroda, 484, 486, 487; map, 485
Luxembourg, Prince of, 164
Lyon, 59, 75; map, 53
Lyon fusillades, 145, 147, 153

Maas R., 173 n.
Macdonald, General Jacques-Etienne, 132
Mack, General Karl, 310-11, 325, 336-43, 345-55, 361, 366, 368
Madison, James, 327
Magdeburg, 480, 483, 499
Magon de Medine, Admiral, 255
Main R., 114, 132, 475; maps, 462, 471
Mainz, 475; map, 462
Maleville, Jacques, 179, 196-98, 205
Malmaison, 39, 151, 211, 259, 264, 283
Malmesbury, Lord, 177, 234, 269
Malplaquet (battle, 1709), 402
Malta, 41, 49, 50, 105, 108, 174, 235-37, 320, 322
Mannheim, 331, 475; maps, 332, 339, 467
Mantua, 79, 107
Marat, Jean-Paul, 145
Marbot, General Jean-Baptiste, 358
Marburg, 381, 382

Marceau, General François-Séverin, 299

Marengo (battle, 1800), 87-95, 86, 106, 107, 125, 126, 139, 185; maps, 73, 89

Marescot, Armand-Samuel, 64, 71

Maret, secretary, 19

Maria Carolina, Queen of Naples, 436

Maria Louisa, Queen Mother of Austria, 139

Maria Luisa of Parma, Queen of Spain, 220, 222, 426

Maria Luisa, Infanta, 222, 225

Maria Theresa, Empress, 132

Mariazell, 372; map, 371

Marie Antoinette, Queen, 152, 333

Marine and Colonies, Ministry of, 5, 32, 105, 238, 248-49

Markov, Count, 275-76

Marmont, General Auguste-Frédéric de, 40, 65, 71, 72, 93, 295, 316, 330-31, 334; at Ulm, 342, 343, 347, 349, 350, 352, 355, 366-72; 381-87, 470

marriage, 197

Marshals of the Empire, 290-99, 438-39, 445

Martigny, 70, 71; map, 53

Martinique, 174, 227, 302, 315

Masséna, Marshal André—in Italian campaigns, 49, 55, 57, 58, 68, 72, 74-75, 76, 77, 95, 110, 114, 115, 172, 193, 255, 292, 298, 366, 374, 377-82, 405, 408, 441

Massenbach, Colonel, 464, 465, 467, 475, 482, 484

Maurice of Saxony, Prince, 502

Mauritius, 226

Maury, Cardinal Jean-Siffrein, 185

Maximilian Joseph, Elector of Bavaria, 340-41

Mazzeroni, Mlle., 155

Mecklenburg, 323, 324

Mediterranean, 169, 172, 234, 250

Meerfeldt, Graf von, 370, 372, 383

Mehée de La Touche, 258, 259, 262

Meiningen, 464, 475, 476, 477; map, 471

Meissau, 385; map, 386

Meissonier, Jean-Louis, 334

Melas, General Michael Friedrich von, 49, 55-57, 58, 59, 60, 61, 68, 72, 75-86; at Marengo, 87-95, 106; 96, 97, 121, 232

Melzi, Signor, 321

Memel, 361, 363

Memmingen, 122, 123, 340, 347, 348, 350, 352, 355, 367; maps, 111, 117, 348

Méneval, Claude-François, 342

Menou, Abdallah, 106

"Messieurs of the Rhine," 115

Metternich, Graf Clemens Wenzel Lothar, 363, 364-65, 405

Michel Brothers, 22, 417-18

Milan, 69, 80, 81, 183; maps, 53, 73

Millesimo (battle, 1796), 294

Miloradovitch, General, 373, 394, 401, 402

Mincio R., 79, 86, 107

Ministries under the Consulate—*see separate* Ministries

Minorca, 56

Minto, Earl of, 51, 68, 108

Miollis, General Sextius-Alexandre, 55, 72

Miot de Melito, Comte André-François, 24, 47

Mirabeau, Honoré-Gabriel, 128

Missiessy, Admiral, 255, 302, 315
Mobile, 225
Modena, Duke of, 164, 174
Molitor, General Gabriel-Jean-Joseph, 132, 378-79
Möllendorf, Marshal, 364, 464, 467, 493, 499
Mollien, François-Nicolas, 425
Moncey, Marshal Rose-Adrien de, 69, 78, 79, 80, 82, 86, 122, 298
money—*see* French coinage *and* French finances
Monge, Gaspard, 5, 41, 187, 246, 326
Moniteur, Le, 19, 29, 62, 151, 153, 172
Monk, General George, 21, 27, 28, 154
Monmouth (battle, 1778), 411
Monnier, General Jean-Charles, 79, 91, 92
Monroe, James, 238, 239, 306, 327
Mont Albaredo, 71, 76, 77
Mont Cenis pass, 55, 69, 76, 77, 78, 81; maps, 53, 73, 339
Mont Génèvre pass, 232
Montebello, 83, 84, 85, 124; map, 73
Monte Creto, 74
Montenotte (battle, 1796), 58, 70
Monte Ratti (battle), 72
Montesquieu, Charles de Secondat, Baron de, 15, 30, 267
Montesquiou, Abbé, 101
Montesson, Mme. de, 415
Montgelas, Graf Maximilian von, 340-41
Montmorencies, the, 23
Montpellier, University of, 245
Montreuil, 333; map, 332
Montrichard, General, 119

Morand, General Charles-Alexis, 491, 493
Moreau, General Jean-Victor, 23, 49, 52, 59-61, 62-63, 64, 69, 107; in Bavarian campaign, 112-26; marriage, 130-31, 193; at Hohenlinden, 135-38, 163; 140, 141, 144, 193-94, 205, 225, 240, 255, 259-63, 281-82, 299, 338, 357
Mortier, Marshal Edouard-Adolphe-Casimir, 295, 370, 373, 384, 387, 405, 412, 470, 475
Morzin, General, 88, 89
Moselle R., 475; map, 462
Möskirch, 116; battle, 118-20, 121; maps, 111, 117, 119
mosquito, 227, 230
Mozart, *Hymne an Deutschland,* 457
Müffling, Captain, 476
Mühlhausen—*see* Mulhouse
Mühlthal, 484
Mulhouse, 52, 461; maps, 53, 111, 332, 339
Müller, Johannes von, 314, 447, 454
Munich, 122, 134, 340-41, 346, 366; maps, 111, 134, 332, 339, 367
Mur R., 372; map, 371
Murat, Marshal Joachim, 62, 65; in Italy, 72, 78, 79, 80, 82, 86, 169; 176, 185, 285, 290-91, 294, 296, 298, 333, 335, 345; at Ulm, 347, 350, 353, 367-73; 383-86; at Austerlitz, 394, 395, 402, 403; 412, 443-44, 445, 457, 469, 472; at Jena, 477, 488, 489, 499, 500, 501
Murat, Mme. Joachim (Caroline Bonaparte), 62, 64, 101, 113, 213, 285, 289, 291, 438

Nansouty, General Etienne-Antoine, 403

Naples, 169, 185, 374, 377, 434, 435, 441, 450, 502

Narbonne, Comte Louis-Marie, 23

Naryshkin, 319

National Convention, 12, 13, 17, 48, 145, 197, 208, 210, 417

National Guard, 114, 147

Nauendorf, General, 112, 119

Naumburg, 458, 476, 479, 483; maps, 471, 480

Navy, Ministry of the, 5, 32, 238

Neckar R., 331, 475; maps, 339, 462

Necker, Jacques, 64-65, 127, 129, 130, 232

Négociants Réunis, 417-25, 430

Nelson, Admiral Horatio, 253, 256, 302, 315-17, 325-26, 374, 375-76

Neresheim, 125, 343; maps, 111, 348

Neuburg, 125, 343; map, 348

Neufchâtel, 406, 438, 450

Neufchâtel, Prince of—*see* Berthier, Marshal

Newfoundland fisheries, 250

New Orleans, 225, 227, 237, 238 (*see also* Louisiana)

newspapers, 128-29

Newton, Isaac, 170

Ney, Marshal Michel, 115, 117; at Hohenlinden, 135, 138; 295-96, 298, 333; at Ulm, 343, 344, 347-53, 367-69; 381, 384, 405, 432, 470, 471; at Jena, 477, 479-81, 484-88, 499, 500

Ney, Mme. Michel, 333

Nice, 84; map, 53

Nile, battle of the (Aboukir Bay, 1798), 62, 105, 255, 298

Nördlingen, 125, 331, 345, 366; maps, 111, 332, 348

Notre Dame Cathedral, 191, 195, 204, 206, 304-305

Novara, 78, 79; map, 73

Novi (battle, 1799), 86, 91, 92, 114; map, 73

Novossiltzoff, Count, 320-21, 322, 324, 421

Nürnberg, 442, 471; map, 471

Ober Kriegs Collegium, 463, 464, 484

Oder R., 500

offices and honors, nonhereditary, 443-44, 445

Ogogno R., 78; map, 73

Olmütz, 387-92, 402; map, 386

Opéra plot, 152-54, 155, 281

Orange, Prince of, 492, 493

Oratory of St. Philip Neri, 145, 146

O'Reilly, General, 88, 95

Orléans, Duc d', 11, 151

Ott, General, 56, 57, 72, 75, 77, 81, 82, 83, 85, 88-93

Otto, M., 169, 174, 175, 177, 432

Ottoman Empire, 171, 235 (*see also* Turkey)

Oubril, 456

Oudinot, Marshal Nicolas-Charles, 396

Ouvrard, Gabriel-Julien, 22, 35, 130, 183, 414-22, 425, 426, 430, 503

Paget, Sir Arthur, 68, 97, 266, 311, 312, 314, 326, 355, 407

Paine, Thomas, 141

Palais Royal, 202

Panin, Count Nikita Petrovitch, 274, 310, 312, 314, 336

Papal Chancellery, 188, 191

Papal Consistory, 287

Papal States, 174, 185, 288

Parallel Pamphlet, 154-56, 213, 288

Paris Industrial Fair, 178

Parma, 80, 225

Passau, 367

Paul I, Tsar, 49-50, 104, 106, 109, 170, 171, 172, 188, 269, 274, 276

Pavia, 72, 80, 87; map, 53

Peace of Amiens—*see* Treaty of Amiens

Peace of Campo Formio, 165

Peace of Lunéville—*see* Treaty of Lunéville

Peltier, 231

Pensacola, 225

Périer, Archbishop, 148

Pérignon, Marshal Dominique-Cathérine, 298

Permon, Mme., 99

Perregaux, Alphonse-Claude, 41

Peter III, Tsar, 275

Petitval family, 37-38

Pforzheim, 333; map, 332

philosophical liberals, 44-45, 46, 48, 126-29, 182-84, 191, 192, 193-94, 195, 205, 206, 212, 218, 281

Piacenza, 80, 82, 225; map, 73

Piatoli, Abbé, 320

Piatoli memorial, 320, 322, 360, 363, 364

Pichegru, General Jean-Charles, 259-63, 266, 281, 299

Piedmont, 235, 237, 319

Pitt, William, 106, 140, 170, 174, 234, 253, 257, 312, 322, 324, 409-10, 420, 421, 427, 450

Pius VI, Pope, 185, 203

Pius VII, Pope, 39, 185-89, 191, 203, 287-88, 304-305, 439-40

"placard plot," 218-19

Plato, *The Republic,* 180

plebiscite confirming Imperial rank, 284

plots against Bonaparte, 150-61, 204-205, 210, 218-19, 231, 257-65, 281

Plumptre, Anne, 201

Po R., 54, 78, 82, 86, 226; maps, 53, 73

Po Valley campaign, 72-86

Poland, 49, 163, 170, 171, 275, 324, 360, 363, 390

Police, Ministry of, 5-7, 31, 219

police, Paris, 21, 26, 35, 146, 219, 226, 263, 305

Pomerania, 454

Ponte-Corvo, 439, 440

Ponte-Corvo, Prince of—*see* Bernadotte, Marshal

"Porcupine, Peter" (Cobbett), 270

Portalis, Jean-Etienne, 179, 196-98, 205, 287

Porto Fino, 74

Portugal, 169, 174, 331

Pozzo di Borgo, 310

praams, 252-53, 301

Prague, 391; maps, 339, 462

Pratzen, the, 392-403; map, 393

prefectures, 43, 128, 147, 322, 503

Prenzlau, 500

Preobrazhenski Guard, 360

press, liberty and censorship of, 58, 128-29, 231, 299

Pressburg, 385, 387, 429; map, 386

priests, 184-85, 186, 187, 288

prisoners, exchange of, 50

Prossnitz, 390

Provence, Count of—*see* Louis XVIII

Prussia, 49, 50, 105, 171, 235, 257, 269-72, 322-23, 324, 341, 344, 361-62, 363-65, 372, 406,

447-61, 472, 475, 497-98, 501, 504; East, 363

Prussian army, 49, 109, 257, 323, 344, 362, 372, 383, 391, 396, 448, 449, 453, 454, 461, 473, 474, 475-79, 481-94, 498-501, 502

Prussian cabinet, 459, 460

"Prussian eagle half vulture," 498

Prussian Principal Army, 461, 463-64, 475, 483, 493, 495

Prussian Ober Kriegs Collegium, 463, 464, 484

Prusso-French alliance, 271, 447-54

Przebyschevski, General, 394, 398-404

Public Works, Ministry of, 31

Quebec, 223
Quéval, 262
Quiberon, battle of, 174
quintal, 433 n.

Radetzky, Marshal Joseph Wenzel, 56, 74, 78, 81, 85, 87

Raigern Abbey, 393, 397; maps, 393, 399

Rapp, Colonel, 161, 205, 402

Réal, Prefect, 40, 159, 160, 265

Récamier, Jacques, 22, 130, 424

Récamier, Jeanne-Françoise (Juliette), 22-24, 74, 75, 154, 330, 424

Reeve's *Journal,* 408, 467-68

Regensburg, 133, 135, 330, 335, 343, 351, 442; maps, 134, 332, 367, 462

Regnault de St. Jean d'Angély, 41

Régnier, Grand Judge, 264

Reinhart, Secretary, 6

Reisch, General, 345

religion, 27, 35, 97-98, 148-49,

182-91, 287 (*see also* Roman Catholic Church)

restaurants, 25, 243

restoration of the Bourbons, 150, 153, 156, 157, 173, 208, 258, 260, 282, 300 (*see also* Bourbons *and* Royalists)

Reuss, Prince Henry of, 113, 120, 124, 132

revenues—*see* French finances *and* taxation

Rewbell, J. F., 13, 14

Rhine R., 59, 61, 107, 112, 113, 116, 173 n.; maps, 111, 117, 332, 339

Rhineland, 441-42, 502

Richard Cœur-de-Lion, 372

Richepanse, General, 121, 124, 136-39, 163, 193

Riedlingen, 121; maps, 111, 117

Riesch, General, 134, 137

Riouffe, Honoré, 46

Ripario R., 77

Ris, Clément de, 102, 104

Riss R., 121

Rivaud, General, 396, 402, 403

Rivoli (battle, 1797), 55, 411

Robespierre, Maximilien, 7, 13, 24, 40, 145, 157, 182, 184, 255, 426

Rochambeau (of Saint-Domingue), 230

Rochefort, 248-52, 302, 315, 317

Rœderer, Pierre-Louis, 33, 40, 45, 100, 150, 156, 196, 282

Roger-Ducos, Pierre, 3-8, 9, 17, 19, 42, 44

Rohan, Prince de, 381-82

Roman Catholic Church, 14-15, 27, 148-49, 168, 174, 182-91, 195, 208, 439

Romano (battle, 1800), 75, 76, 80; map, 73

Rosenheim, 135

Rosily, Admiral, 255, 302

Rossbach, battle of (1757), 392, 461, 473

Roubaix mills, 179

Rousseau, Jean-Jacques, 179, 180, 182, 268, 274, 320

Royalists and royalism, 11, 20, 21, 26, 41, 65, 103, 104, 128, 129, 147, 148, 150-51, 153, 156, 158-61, 188, 205, 206, 228, 259-65, 268, 282, 411

Rüchel, General, 448, 461-65, 475, 483, 489, 495

rue St. Niçaise plot, 157-61, 230, 258, 265

Rulski, 336

Rumania, 171

Rumbach wood, 118; map, 119

Rumelia, 171

Russia and the Russians, 49-50, 54, 106, 109, 171, 235, 272, 273-76, 314, 319-20, 322-24, 359-61, 363-64, 388-90, 448, 449, 451, 455-56, 504

Russian army, 49-50, 58, 171, 233, 275, 292, 323, 337, 340, 351, 363, 365-72, 382-406, 410, 434, 470, 504

—— Imperial Guard, 393, 402, 403, 406

—— liberals, 274-75

—— Secret Committee, 360, 388, 389, 456

—— Senate, 274-75, 502

Saalburg, 477; map, 471

Saale R., 465, 472, 476-83; maps, 462, 471, 480, 492

Saalfeld, 476-79, 482; maps, 471, 480

Sahuc, General Louis-Michel, 495

Saint-Domingue, 224-30, 236, 251, 256, 288, 290, 414, 440

Saintonge, 184

Salcedo, Juan M. de, Governor of La., 237

Sale, 88, 92; map, 89

Salzburg, 368, 432; map, 367

Sambre-et-Meuse, 114

San Giuliano, 61, 86, 92, 93, 95; maps, 89, 94

Sansculottes, 21-22, 189, 288

Santon, 393, 396, 402; maps, 393, 399

Savary, Colonel Anne-Jean, 265, 335-36, 390, 391, 410

Savona, 57; map, 53

Savoy, House of, 319, 321

Saxe-Weimar, Duke of—*see* Karl August

Saxon army, 461, 464, 473, 475, 479, 482, 484, 487-89

Saxony, 324

Schaffhausen, 59, 60, 116; maps, 53, 111, 117

Scharnhorst, Colonel Johann von, 463, 464, 465, 483

Scheldt, mouths of the, 173

Schiller, Friedrich von, 388; *Wallenstein,* 448, 452

Schleiz, 476, 477; maps, 471, 480

Schmettau, General, 490-93

Schmidt, General, 113

Schulmeister, Karl, 336, 342, 343, 345, 350, 366

Schwäbische Alb, 118, 120, 351; map, 117

Schwartzenburg, Graf von, 337, 340, 341, 345, 349, 351, 352

Scotland, 263

Sebastiani, Colonel Horace-François, 235

secularization of churchly principalities, 167, 168-69

Seguin, Armand, 417, 418

Ségur, Louis-Philippe de, 100

Ségur, Philippe-Paul de, 286, 303

Selivanov, Kondrati, 359, 361

Senate and Senators, 42, 160, 182, 190, 210, 211, 219, 283, 284, 299, 300

sénatus-consulte decrees, 160, 194, 206, 210, 218, 239, 285, 299

Sérrurier, Marshal, 298

Seychelles Islands, 174

Sicily, 434, 456, 457

Sidmouth, Lord—*see* Addington, Henry

Sieyès, Emmanuel-Joseph, 3-8, 9-20, 26, 29-34, 40, 42, 43, 44, 45, 49, 60, 99, 100, 128, 182, 194, 218, 285, 299, 442, 453

Sigmaringen, 120; map, 111

Silesia, 363

Siméon, Tribune, 210-11

Simon, General, 218

Simplon pass, 69, 76, 77, 78, 232, 233; maps, 53, 73

Sinsheim, battle of (1674), 331

Skall, General, 81, 82

Smith, Spencer, 258, 261, 262, 263

Society for the Encouragement of Natl. Industries, 247

Sokolnitz, 392, 394, 396, 400; maps, 393, 399

Sonnenberg, 490, 491; map, 492

Souham, General, 193

Soult, Marshal Nicolas-Jeanne-de-Dieu—in Italy, 55, 57, 58, 72, 74; 295, 331, 333; in Danube campaign, 343-45; at Ulm, 346-52, 366-69; 384-87; at Austerlitz, 394-97, 400, 403; 407, 410, 470, 471; at Jena, 477, 479-81, 484-86, 499, 500, 501

Spain, 169, 174, 214, 220-23, 225-26, 283, 303, 315, 414, 418, 427

Spandau, 500

Spanish canal, 419-20

Spanish Natl. Chest Bank, 420, 422, 423

Spanish ships, 303, 315-17

spectacles and concerts in Paris, 26, 35, 47

Speyer, 331; map, 322

Spina, Monsignor, 186, 187, 188

Spinoza, Baruch, 14

Spitz bridge, 383

Stadion, Graf, 319, 325

Staël, Germaine de, 23, 44, 45, 46, 65, 100, 103, 126-29, 145, 157, 181, 192, 194, 195, 217, 218, 219, 232, 258, 363, 441, 447, 454; *De la Littérature,* 126, 129, 183

Starhemberg, 355

state v. church, 182-83, 187

St. Bernard hospice, 70

St. Bernard passes, 69-70, 76, 79, 81, 85; maps, 53, 73, 339

St. Blassen, 116; maps, 111, 117

St. Cyr, General Gouvion, 114-23, 225, 230, 374

Stein, Baron Heinrich Friedrich Karl vom und zum, 270-71, 362

Stettin, 500

Steyr, 369; maps, 367, 371

St. Gall, 113; maps, 111, 117

St. Gothard pass, 60, 69, 76, 77, 78, 80, 81, 122; maps, 53, 73, 111, 339

St. Hilaire, General, 396, 401, 402, 403, 484-88

St. Jean d'Acre (battle, 1798), 50

St. Julien, Graf, 106-108, 126

St. Malo, 248

Stockerau, 384; map, 386

Stokach, 59, 60, 112, 116, 118; maps, 111, 117, 119

St. Pölten, 370-73; map, 371

Ste. Suzanne, General Gilbert-Joseph, 114-24, 135

Stradella, 82; map, 73

Strasbourg, 59, 61, 67, 113, 263, 268, 331, 333, 342, 346, 475; maps, 53, 111, 117, 332, 339, 462

St. Régeant, 159, 161

Stuart, Charles, 355, 407

Stuttgart, 112, 115, 344; maps, 111, 117, 462

St. Vincent, Earl of, 234

succession question, 100-103, 154-55, 205, 212-14, 216-17, 282, 322, 435, 445

Suchet, General Louis-Gabriel, 52, 55, 69, 72, 77, 84, 88, 357, 384, 396, 403, 480

Suffren, Admiral Pierre-André de, 225

Suvorov, Marshal Alexei Sergei-vitch, 49, 51, 54, 55, 58, 80, 112, 114, 292, 293, 360

Swabia, 59, 107, 333, 338; map, 339

Sweden and the Swedes, 105, 109, 310, 324, 454

Switzerland, 232-34, 237, 338-40; map, 339

Sztarray, General, 113-24

Talleyrand, Charles-Maurice de, 5-8, 14, 25, 28, 33, 97, 99-104, 106-108, 127, 151-56, 158-61, 175-76, 186, 187, 188, 191, 207-208, 210, 236, 237, 239, 242, 263, 264, 268-69, 272, 276, 286, 342, 376, 395, 408, 435, 439, 440, 442, 451, 452, 456

Tallien, Jean-Lambert, 100

Taranto, 169, 275, 374

Tauenzien, General, 475, 476, 484, 486-89

taxes and taxation, 16-18, 178, 416, 418, 419, 430, 503

Tellnitz, 392, 393, 396, 398, 400; maps, 393, 399

territory, acquisition of, 170-71

Terror and Terrorists, 10-11, 13, 41, 145, 158, 161, 185, 297

Teutonic Knights, 442

Texel R., 251

Thibaudeau, A. C., *Mémoires,* 35

Thugut, Baron, 58, 108, 167-68

Thuméry, Marquis de, 269

Thüringerwald, 461, 463, 465, 470, 475, 483; maps, 462, 471

Thurreau, General, 55, 69

Ticino R., 78-79, 81, 86; map, 73

Tiollier, 413

Topino-Lebrun, 152-53

Toulon, 65, 172, 248, 249, 251, 252, 256, 263, 301, 302

Tracy, Antoine-Louis de, 41

Trafalgar, battle of, 374, 375, 407, 424, 456

Traun R., 368, 370; maps, 367, 371

Trautmannsdorf, Graf, 168

Treasury, Ministry of the, 31

Treaty of Amiens, 176, 179, 207, 210, 223, 224, 235, 413, 456

Treaty of Lunéville, 163-66, 171, 173-74, 176, 269, 364, 406

Treaty of Pressburg, 429

Treaty of Vienna, unratified, 450, 459

Trebbia (battle, 1799), 55

Trebbia R., 57; map, 53

Treilhard, General, 478

Tribunes and Tribunate, 31-32, 44-46, 103, 179-82, 190, 191, 192, 194, 195, 197, 211, 217, 284, 299

Trinidad, 174, 175, 222, 224

Tronchet, François-Denis, 179, 196-98, 245

Turbigo, 79; map, 73

Turin, 69, 76, 77, 81, 85; maps, 53, 73, 339

Turkey and the Turks, 55, 235, 275, 327 (*see also* Ottoman Empire)

Tuscany, 222, 225, 325 (*see also* Etruria)

Tuscany, Grand Duke of, 166

Tyrol, 113, 120, 121, 132, 338, 346, 348, 350, 355, 365, 366, 430; maps, 111, 339

Ulm, 67, 112, 122-23, 125, 333, 335, 338, 340, 377, 378, 432; surrender at, 345-50, 368-74, 423; maps, 111, 117, 332, 339

United Brokers' Company—*see* Négociants Réunis

United States, 106, 227, 237-40, 242

United States frigates, 248

Utrecht, 330; maps, 332, 462

Valencia, 87; map, 73

Valmy (battle, 1792), 48, 164, 246, 296

Vandamme, General, 120, 123, 346, 349, 396, 401-404

Vanlerberghe Company, 417, 419, 420, 424, 425

Var R., 52, 55, 56, 57, 68, 72, 75, 77, 84; map, 53

Varnhagen, Rahel, 447

Varnhagen von Ense, Karl August, 467

Vasa, Gustavus, 164

Vendée, La, 11, 27-28, 39, 52, 131, 151, 184, 258, 297, 337; map, 332

Venice, Republic of, 166, 167, 168, 323; map, 339

Verdier, General Jean-Antoine, 378-80, 381

Vergniaud, Pierre-Victurnien, 184

Verona, 131, 377; map, 379

Victor, Marshal Claude, 65, 67, 69, 80, 82, 90-94, 225, 230, 238

Vidocq, François-Eugène, 428

Vienna, 59, 60, 122, 336, 361, 370, 372-74; maps, 339, 371, 386

Vierzenheiligen, 487, 488; map, 485

Villaret-Joyeuse, Admiral Louis-Thomas, 224

Villeneuve, 69

Villeneuve, Admiral Pierre-Charles-Jean-Sylvestre, 255, 302, 314-19, 321, 325-36, 374

Villingen, 112, 116; maps, 111, 117

Vincennes prison, 264-65, 282, 425

Visconti, Mme., 292

Voltaire, 46, 170-71, 180, 182, 187

Vorarlberg Mts., 367, 381

Vorontzov, Count Alexander, 279

votants, 102, 148, 149, 156, 208, 265, 283

Walsingham, Sir Francis, 197

War, Ministry of, 5, 19, 32, 48, 52, 146, 297

warfare, Napoleonic, 410-13

Wartensleben, General, 492, 493

Washington, George, 207, 245, 411, 412

Wasserburg, 135, 141

water-borne trade, 173 n.

Watrin, General, 67, 83

Watt, James, 179

Weimar, 388, 465, 479, 481, 495, 499; maps, 471, 480

Weimar, Grand Duke of, 388, 500

Wels, 368, 369; map, 367
Wendt, 336
Werneck, General, 345, 351-52, 355
Wertingen, 347; map, 348
Wesel, 475
Weyrother, Colonel, 113, 390-92, 394, 398
wheat, 419, 422, 433
Whitworth, Lord, 235-37, 238
Wieland, Christoph Martin, 388
Wienerwald, 372, 373; map, 371
Wiesel, Pauline, 447
Wilde-Alpen range, 384
Wilhelmina of Ansbach, 449
William of Normandy, 252
William of Prussia, Prince, 493
wills, law of, 198
Windham, William, 241, 375
wine-making, 246
Winzigerode, Graf, 386
Wischau, 390; map, 386
woman's position in the Code Napoleón, 199

Wrede, General, 119
Wukassovitch, General, 56, 76, 77, 79-80, 81, 82, 85
Württemberg, 112, 323, 338, 344, 430, 431, 432, 439, 442, 443
Württemberg, Duke of—*see* Eugene, Duke of Württemberg
Württemberg, King of—*see* Frederick II, King
Würzburg, 330, 331, 341, 344, 463, 469, 472, 475, 476; maps, 332, 339, 462, 471

York, Duke of, 297
Young, *Night Thoughts,* 215

Zach, General, 56, 75, 76, 78, 81, 85, 87, 90, 93, 94
Znaim, 384, 387; map, 386
Zubov, 274
Zürich, 59, 60; battle (1799), 49, 55; maps, 53, 111
Zusmarshausen, 347; map, 348